UPSTREAM

BETH ROSE MIDDLETON MANNING

UPSTREAM

TRUST LANDS AND POWER ON THE FEATHER RIVER

THE UNIVERSITY OF
ARIZONA PRESS

The University of Arizona Press
www.uapress.arizona.edu

ISBN-13: 978-0-8165-3514-9 (paper)

Cover design by Leigh McDonald
Cover illustration *Wolólloka* by Danny Manning; photo *Settling Sun Over Fields of Gold* by Kenneth C. Holbrook

All royalties will be donated to three Mountain Maidu organizations: the Maidu Summit Consortium, Maidu Cultural and Development Group, and Maidu We'ye.

Library of Congress Cataloging-in-Publication Data are available at the Library of Congress.

Printed in the United States of America
♾ This paper meets the requirements of ANSI/NISO Z39.48-1992 (Permanence of Paper).

CONTENTS

ILLUSTRATIONS

FIGURES

MAPS

TABLE

PREFACE

I NSPIRED BY the work of the Maidu Culture and Development Group and the Maidu Summit, over the last seventeen years I have been gathering materials on Maidu allotment lands—mostly 160-acre parcels that were set aside for Maidu Indians in the northeastern Sierra, by application and assignment around the turn of the twentieth century. As I expanded the area of focus to Plumas and Lassen Counties, I included materials on Pit River, Paiute, Washoe, and Concow allottees, and found that they were affected by the same processes of state-sanctioned development and conservation.

The allotment lands in this region were part of a national strategy to turn Indians into European-style farmers and open up more of their lands for mining, timber harvest, hydroelectric production, and other development. Maidu and other Indian people, particularly in this part of the Sierra, did not necessarily need or want to farm, nor did they want to give up their land for free for the development of services that would not benefit them. They lived and continue to live in relationship with a large landscape of particular plants and animals, creating what my mentor, Maidu traditionalist Farrell Cunningham [*yatam*] called "the most advanced agricultural system in the world."

When white settlers arrived in this region in the 1830s, they pushed Native people of the northeastern Sierra out of important resource-procurement areas, destroyed plant species with cattle and sheep grazing, spread disease, and waged a direct campaign of violence. Following state-sanctioned destruction and unratified treaties with false promises of land refuges, the federal government offered Maidu 160-acre parcels, or allotments. Many filed for allotments, and the trajectory of trust-land assignment, sale, and cancellation offers a complex historical mosaic reflecting struggles to negotiate an imposed system of laws and rules and to find a way to secure rights within the Maidu homeland. The story of allotment continues to be relevant in the current PG&E land divestiture process, through which Maidu will receive title to approximately 3,000 acres within their homeland.

This book weaves together related struggles for land and human rights in the face of neocolonial conservation and development. It is my hope that, with this material, my son, Wesley, and others in his generation will have more information about the context in which some of their proud and strong ancestors persevered. I write this book also with the prayer that history will not repeat itself with ongoing exclusion and ignorance of non-European ways of relating to the land and that we, as a collective society, will improve our human ability to respect one another, to recognize the impact and importance of history, and to build equitable and inclusive systems of responsible land and water stewardship.

UPSTREAM

INTRODUCTION

With these lands we have an opportunity to begin righting a great wrong. We may be frightened of outcomes we are unsure of but we should be even more frightened of living in a world where the foundation of injustice is honorable and the perpetuation of that injustice acceptable. . . . We cannot change the past but neither can we ignore it. The present and the future are our provenience and yet the present is so fleeting that we must make the future our greatest focus—and we must make it a world in which we can live well. We must make a future of justice. In that way, living in that manner, our past will, inevitably, become good too.

—FARRELL CUNNINGHAM, MAIDU SUMMIT COORDINATOR, "MAIDU SUMMIT CONSORTIUM LAND MANAGEMENT PLAN"

Stealing land, or property, is unacceptable in a liberal democracy, but structuring Native lands as part of the abstract space of the nation eases public outcry.

—MISHUANA GOEMAN, *MARK MY WORDS*

As Great Western Power Company's reservoir filled, fishing areas were destroyed. Basketry material gathering areas were drowned. Food and medicine plants were lost. Cemeteries were inundated. The ancestral villages were buried underwater or washed bare along the water's edge. . . . The private land around the lake is still being sold at high prices, so high that the Maidu people, having disproportionately low incomes in the Almanor and Indian Valley areas, are less and less able to afford to buy access to the water's edge. Reconnecting with Big Meadows through traditional ceremony and land stewardship activities at the shoreline becomes ever more difficult, but from an economic reality rather than a loss of cultural affinity.

—LORENA GORBET, MAIDU CULTURAL AND DEVELOPMENT GROUP VICE CHAIRMAN, LETTER TO THE FEDERAL ENERGY REGULATORY COMMISSION

FROM MANDAN, Hidatsa, and Arikara lands in South Dakota, to Cherokee lands in Tennessee, to Sin-Aikst, Lakes, and Colville lands in Washington, to Chemehuevi lands in Arizona, to Maidu, Pit River, and Wintu lands in Northern California, Native lands and communities have been treated as sacrifice zones for national priorities of irrigation, flood control, and hydroelectric development. Nearly every place in the United States where there is a man-made reservoir, lands and waters were and are being appropriated from Indian people by illegal and quasi-legal means,[1] leaving a painful legacy of displacement and cultural and community disruption. Through cartography, participatory research, archives, and images, this book documents the significance of the Allotment Era in that history of disruption and resistance to both hydropower and conservation in northeastern California. Alongside the work of Maidu and other Native activists in affected communities, this book highlights points of intervention to increase justice for Indigenous peoples in contemporary natural resource policy-making.

THE WATER AND POWER CONTEXT ON INDIAN LANDS

There are 337 reservoirs impounded by 475 dams that are part of the 7.1 million acres under the jurisdiction of the Bureau of Reclamation in 17 western states. State and local water resource agencies and departments manage thousands of acres more of water storage, hydropower, and irrigation projects. In California, the Department of Water Resources manages the State Water Project (SWP), touted as the "nation's largest state-built water and power development and conveyance system" (California Department of Water Resources 2016a). The SWP includes 33 water storage facilities with a total storage capacity of 5.8 million acre-feet. The headwaters of the SWP are the upper Feather River watershed, homeland of the Mountain Maidu people.

An examination of the California Department of Water Resources' (DWR) historic and contemporary promotional and informational materials on the SWP (as housed in the Water Resources Center Archives at the University of California, Riverside, and available from the SWP website) reveals no mention of the contested nature of the primarily Mountain Maidu lands that provide water to 29 water agencies,[2] 25 million Californians, and 750,000 acres of irrigated farmland downstream. This book examines the history of some of these lands and the ways in which Maidu and other tribal members on nearby lands (including Paiute, Pit River, and Washoe) continue to advocate for land restitution, using contemporary conservation processes and mechanisms.

The SWP is also a significant generator of electricity, producing an average output of 6.5 billion kWh annually (California Department of Water Resources, 2016b). The utility Pacific Gas and Electric (PG&E) also generates power on waterways in and above the SWP system. PG&E's "stairway of power" in the North Fork Feather River canyon is intertwined with SWP facilities, which exist downstream (beginning with Lake Oroville) and upstream (including Antelope Lake). PG&E's projects are licensed in 30- to 50-year agreements approved by the Federal Energy Regulatory Commission (FERC). The FERC relicensing process has historically been difficult for affected tribes to participate in, particularly if the federal government does not recognize them as Indian nations.[3]

During the century that PG&E and its predecessor companies (Great Western Power, Oroville Power & Light, and others) have been in existence, they have built up a monopoly on energy production and transmission in Northern California, on lands and waters obtained directly from Indian landowners. The founders of these power companies are part of the community of early timber and railroad barons—the businessmen that developed the United States and whose heirs continue to hold vast tracts of land.[4] Railroads, hydroelectric development, and conservation enclosures went hand in hand to displace Indian landholders, and to attempt to erase any evidence of their histories and rights.

SUBMERGED: FROM FORT BERTHOLD TO COLVILLE

FORT BERTHOLD

In 2010 I showed my undergraduate Introduction to Native American Studies class the film *Waterbuster* (2006) and invited longtime Native American Studies student affairs officer Judy LaDeaux, a citizen of the Three Affiliated Tribes of the Fort Berthold Indian Reservation, to speak about the impact of the Garrison Dam on her life. Paralleling the narrative of the film, she explained the virtual paradise they had lived in before the imposition of the dam. There was plenty of food to be grown on the rich soil, her family had a basement full of preserved fruits and vegetables and maintained a close-knit rural and culturally vibrant community on the plains. When the dam construction began in 1946, LaDeaux's family was forced to surrender their land and move. They watched as the waters of Lake Sacajawea inundated the rich bottomlands that had sustained their people for generations.

With few options for making a living to support his family, LaDeaux's father accepted the terms of the Bureau of Indian Affair's (BIA) Urban Relocation Program and moved to inner-city Los Angeles, a violent landscape for young LaDeaux and her siblings. Without a way to keep his family together and provided for, her father was forced to send his children to an Indian boarding school. There LaDeaux endured nearly a decade of abuse at the hands of Catholic nuns and priests running the school under Carlisle's philosophy of "Kill the Indian, and save the man."

As investigative reporter Paul VanDevelder explains in *Coyote Warrior*, which recounts the fight against the Garrison Dam through the experience of the Cross family,[5] the need for the dam was manufactured, destroyed thousands of years of a settled, self-sufficient lifeway for the tribes, and did not even provide the promised irrigation water for the white farmers that supported it.[6] Even the catastrophic flooding that ushered in support for the dam was later found to be largely manufactured by the Army Corps of Engineers–built levees and dikes that disrupted the natural function of floodplains and wetlands.[7] It was political competition and then compromise between the Corps of Engineers and the Bureau of Reclamation that was responsible for the size and scope of the projects on the Missouri River.[8] According to Roosevelt's secretary of the Interior Harold Ickes, Garrison Dam was larger than what was needed to prevent additional flooding (VanDevelder 2004, 101). The vast majority (approximately 90 percent) of the land flooded was owned by tribes, whose treaty rights and desire to remain in their homeland were violated by the federal decision to pursue the project (102, chapter 5). As Phyllis Old Dog Cross explains: "Suddenly our landmarks, our social and physical landmarks, the framework for everything we were, was gone. Our identity derived from our villages. Those were destroyed. We were born into very dynamic and complex social networks that connected those identities across forty generations. Those went when the villages went." As Phyllis's sister Marilyn added, "We went from being a deeply integrated family and community in July 1954 to being a society of totally isolated individuals who went into social free fall for the next fifty years. This happened to thousands of people simultaneously" (32).

The rank-and-file engineers who worked on the massive project were largely uninformed about the impact on Mandan, Hidatsa, and Arikara peoples—more than two years of working on the site, engineer Byron Sneva did "not remember anyone every discussing how the flood might change the Indians' world" (144). This observation mirrors the lack of mention of the impacts of the SWP on Concow Maidu, Mountain Maidu, and other nations whose ancestral lands and rights were impacted by that massive project. It is those gaps in the archives that this work hopes to help fill.

Dakota/Lakota scholar Vine Deloria Jr. referred to the projects on the Missouri River as a "mentality" enabling the seizure of natural resources and the violation of tribal rights throughout the region. As he wrote in the 2009 foreword to *Dammed Indians Revisited*:

> The Pick-Sloan Plan was, without doubt, the single most destructive act ever perpetrated on any tribe by the United States. If it had simply been one act and had been committed only against the Sioux with the violation of only one treaty, it would be viewed as gross and unfair; but the projects eventually involved almost all tribes living on the Missouri and its major tributaries in the states of South Dakota, North Dakota, Montana, and Wyoming, and the end is still not in sight. Recent discoveries of coal and other minerals make certain that the Pick-Sloan mentality eventually will destroy the high plains of North America for both Indians and non-Indians who live in the region. (Lawson 2009, xv)

This statement strikingly presages the ongoing resistance by water protectors at Standing Rock Sioux Reservation to the Dakota Access Pipeline. The pipeline is designed to carry crude oil from the Bakken formation in northwestern North Dakota 1,172 miles to an oil tank farm at Patoka, Illinois.[9] Water protectors have called for a stop to the Dakota Access Pipeline in particular, as well as construction on all other pipelines, because of the threats continued oil production and transport pose to water, air, and the future of all life. In 2016 the prayerful gathering of water protectors at Standing Rock expanded to include thousands of Indigenous people and allies from throughout the world, who traveled to the site and endured militarized responses from law enforcement. As Standing Rock Sioux tribal chairman Dave Archambault II said in an October 2016 statement:

> Today we have witnessed people praying in peace, yet attacked with pepper spray, rubber bullets, sound and concussion cannons. We urge state and federal government agencies to give this tense situation their immediate and close attention.
>
> We also call on the thousands of water protectors who stand in solidarity with us against DAPL to remain in peace and prayer. Any act of violence hurts our cause and is not welcome here. We invite all supporters to join us in prayer that, ultimately, the right decision—the moral decision—is made to protect our people, our sacred places, our land and our resources. We won't step down from this fight. As peoples of this earth, we all need water. This is about our water, our rights, and our dignity as human beings. (KFYR TV 2016)

This contemporary resistance, like the stand by the members of the Maidu Summit Consortium & Conservancy in northeastern California to receive lands back in the process of power company conservation divestiture, is built on centuries of struggle to be *heard*, to be *respected*, and to be able to continue to care for and protect their homelands without threat of violence or legal action.

THE DAMMED COLUMBIA

In the Pacific Northwest states of Oregon and Washington, the Columbia River system has more than 130 dams, 56 of them exclusively for producing hydropower (Northwest Council 2013). They range as far northeast as the Grand Coulee Dam near Inchelium, Washington, to as far southwest as the Bonneville Dam 40 miles east of Portland, Oregon. The infamous Grand Coulee Dam, which produces the most hydropower electricity in the United States (U.S. DOI n.d.) flooded 21,000 acres of the Colville Indian Reservation, destroyed the tribe's prime salmon spawning habitat, displaced thousands of Sin-Aikst, Colville, Nez Perce, and other peoples, and inundated tribal fishing, hunting, and gathering areas. The pain of the loss of so many traditional places where families had gathered for generations, and of promises broken and disregarded, reverberates into the present generation.[10]

Down on the lower reaches of the Columbia, construction of the Bonneville Dam began in 1933 as part of Roosevelt's public works projects to combat the Depression. The Indians of the Columbia River—Cascades, Wasco, Yakima, Nez Perce, Umatilla, Cayuse, and others—were removed, and their fishing and gathering rights seized. Again, the region's Indian country became the unacknowledged "sacrifice zone" for a national economy based on virtually unrestrained extraction. It was clear that the dam would reduce the fishery and inundate traditional subsistence fishing sites. Some tribal members expressed a sense of hopelessness that, despite the treaties, despite their time-honored lifeways, Congress still had the power to condemn the land.[11]

The Army Corps of Engineers, which oversaw the construction of the Bonneville Dam, was committed to provide fishing sites. In 1937, about six months before the dam gates were scheduled to close, the Corps of Engineers provided a powerboat for a group to tour and document the Indian fishing sites that would be impacted by the dam. Tour attendees included Major Omar L. Babcock, the superintendent of the Umatilla Indian Agency; Indian representatives from the Cascades, Warm Springs, Yakama, and Umatilla; and Kenneth R. L. Simmons, a BIA attorney. The group identified 27 sites over 45 miles between the Dalles and the dam, and later accounts noted that this number was far too low, as the number of fishing sites would increase or decrease depending on the season.[12] All were flooded when the dam was complete. In 1939, two years after the dam was closed, a delegation of Indian people submitted a claim for damages including 23 areas, each with numerous individual fishing sites. The Corps of Engineers promised restitution in the form of six sites totaling 400 acres. As of Ulrich's 2007 account in *Empty Nets: Indians, Dams, and the Columbia River*, this restitution had not been delivered.

The Sin-Aikst and Colville removal behind the Grand Coulee Dam; the Yakima, Wasco, Cascades and others' displacement behind the Bonneville Dam; the Mandan, Hidatsa, Arikara removal behind the Garrison Dam, and the Winnemem Wintu removal behind the Shasta Dam,[13] all exemplify instances of Indigenous displacement and attempted cultural genocide. The social impacts, cultural disruption, and destruction of communities represent incalculable and irredeemable costs, and yet they are dismissed as externalities in a narrative of national progress. In this book I question that "progress" and whose interests it truly serves. In these and other cases, First Peoples lost their homes, their foods, their communities, their places to make a living, their medicines that grew along the shore; it was "worse than terrible."[14]

Listening to experiences of displacement, removal, and abuse in the wake of the Garrison Dam on the Missouri; reading Lawney Reyes's biography of his brother in *Bernie Whitebear: An Urban Indian's Quest for Justice*, which references the impacts of the Grand Coulee Dam on the life of Native Sin-Aikst, Nez

Perce, and others along the Columbia; and hearing a colleague's account of the Eastern Band of Cherokee's fight against the Tellico Dam on the Little Tennessee (Gilmer 2013), placed my ongoing research on Indian allotment appropriation and hydroelectric development in northeastern California in national perspective. The patterns I had been seeing of trespass, extraction, and appropriation of Indian trust lands for the intertwined aims of national development and private enterprise were part of a larger story that is still unfolding on these very same lands, now designated for additional hydropower production, conservation and restoration to mitigate the impacts of historic development and increased water storage.

THE CALIFORNIA CONTEXT

The story of California Indian allotments at the headwaters of what became the State Water Project is a story of rapid cancellation, aggressive timber harvest, and inundation, as federal, state, and local representatives found ways to nullify or purchase allottee's water and land rights in favor of the development of public works projects to convey water and power downstream. These "public works" projects benefited a narrow public—including large landowners, hydroelectric providers, and, later, everyday downstream consumers once their need for electricity was cultivated and established.[15] While the flood control and hydroelectric generation aspects of the projects did enable the urbanization and industrial agricultural development of the Central Valley, the pace and character of that development has led portions of the valley to have some of the most polluted air and watersheds in the state.[16] The valley could have been settled quite differently with attention to the protection of Native lands, cultural values and communities, and environmental sustainability. The fact that these elements were not initially considered has led to ongoing problems that still plague California's water systems today, including a beleaguered delta ecosystem, inefficient water conveyance, declining species due to lack of fish passage on multiple dams, and most importantly for this project, the failure to provide restitution from the cultural, social, and environmental impacts of the dams and other project infrastructure to Native communities.

As the impacts of these public projects on Native communities have become more known and less tolerated, there have been efforts over time to litigate, settle, pay for, and/or restore Native land and water rights. The two California

Indian land claims processes enabled tribes to bring suit against the state (in 1928, with federal authorization) and federal (in 1946) governments for the unratified treaties and for all other lands taken without tribal consent, respectively.[17] However, the limited payoff (not more than $850/person in total from both settlements) could not offset lands and livelihoods taken, and there were virtually no opportunities for actually regaining the land. The payout for the lands was based on their value at the time of taking, rather than the immense value the lands accrued over time and by later development. Water rights and the value of water were not dealt with in these proceedings.[18] Even with the 1908 *Winters* doctrine affirming tribes' senior water rights, quantifying these rights and building the infrastructure to exercise them is expensive and time-consuming. As of 2015, 34 tribal water rights settlements have been completed with 37 tribes, and only three of these settlements were with California tribes.[19]

For more than 40 years (at least since the founding of the International Indian Treaty Council in 1974),[20] tribal participation has increased exponentially in international arenas, as tribal members and leaders have sought international alliances and expanded support for domestic land restitution. Important international legal instruments invoked by U.S. tribes include the American Declaration of the Rights and Duties of Man[21] and the United Nations Declaration on the Rights of Indigenous Peoples (UNDRIP).[22] Led by Indigenous mobilization and advocacy around the globe, international support continues to grow; for example, in September 2016 the International Union for the Conservation of Nature passed a resolution to create a new category of membership for Indigenous peoples' organizations (see Gaworecki 2016). However, decisions in international tribunals are only effective within nation-states at the discretion of that nation-state.[23] As scholar-activist Roxanne Ornelas explains, "It is clear that it is more problematic to achieve in practice what took 30 years to define. In the meantime, the wheels of governmental bureaucracy continue to turn without the UNDRIP and with continuing violations of human rights" (2014, 3). Examples of this include the FERC hydroelectric or other energy project licensing proceedings, in which comments made by Native American tribal governments, Native organizations, and Native individuals alike have been met with "alternatives" that often don't take into account their interests and/or a permitting process that enables consultation but does not mandate incorporating the results of consultation into decision-making. Ornelas offers several recommendations for implementing the UNDRIP, including the development of regulatory mechanisms to enforce the UNDRIP, the creation of a UNDRIP working group and a funded UNDRIP agency, the establishment of regional UNDRIP representatives to focus on human rights issues in particular regions, and prohibiting development in Indigenous homelands without free, prior, and informed consent (12–13).

American public and private conservation decisions follow the contours of the National Environmental Policy Act and state-level statutes such as the California Environmental Quality Act (now amended by AB-52, 2014, to require tribal consultation at tribal request). Although these statutes and accompanying executive orders at both the state[24] and federal[25] levels mandate government-to-government consultation, they do not mandate the incorporation of Indigenous views and/or altering projects to respond to Indigenous concerns. The power of effective eminent domain, to place land within the hydropower reserve or set it aside for conservation without Native participation or consent, works to the detriment of Native land interests. There are notable exceptions in which Indigenous interests prevail (such as the Indian Creek Hydroelectric proposal, which Maidu challenged and were able to prevent),[26] but such exceptions often involve a productive collusion of interests that support tribal concerns.

One effort at restitution, under the Pacific Forest and Watershed Lands Stewardship Council (hereafter Stewardship Council) process, was recently navigated successfully for one coalition of California Indian entities (the Maidu Summit Consortium and Conservancy) and two California Indian Tribes (Pit River Tribe and Potter Valley Tribe). The settlement that created the council did not specifically mention Native communities at all, but focused instead on the conservation of lands impacted by hydroelectric development for the "public." This process impacted numerous California Native Nations, including Maidu and Pit River in the northeastern Sierra, as well as Pomo in the Coast Range, and Mono, Miwuk, Nisenan, and Yokuts in the central and southern Sierra. Despite the scope of the lands and nations involved, it was only through persistent, ongoing Native activism that this restitution process came to directly benefit any Native Americans at all.

In natural resource decision-making in California and beyond, the same interests are persistently at the table—corporate, environmental, and (federal, state, and local) government. These are the interests that have been at the table since Europeans arrived in the Americas, through independence, expansion, and industrialization, and into the contemporary era. Despite the fact that all of California is composed of ancestral tribal lands recently wrested from Indigenous peoples, tribal governments and Native communities are often not at the table in natural resource decision-making. When challenged for their omission of tribes, the proponents of these natural resources bills or proposals defend their initiatives as necessary compromises in order to meet a frenetic timeline of responding to perceived environmental or economic threats.

Water in the west in particular is a fraught arena of jockeying federal, state, private, and tribal interests; limited funds; and a high potential for private profit. My colleagues in Maidu country assert a particular history on and with the land that has not been recognized in deliberations over water and land ownership, access, development, and conservation. The story they tell is one of pain, courage, and persistence, and it demands to be heard before the lands and waters are again reappropriated, this time for conservation that may effectively exclude Indigenous peoples from their own lands in the same ways in which they were excluded by hydroelectric development a century ago.

With historical detail, this text argues why it is so important that tribes and Native organizations always have a seat at the table in natural resource decision-making. Their presence and expertise should be recognized, and affirming and supporting indigeneity should be a priority for state and federal governments. *Upstream* links past to present to underscore persistent patterns of exclusion that undermine justice in resource management and planning, as well as glimmers of hope in successful processes that offer pathways forward. While scholars have exposed different aspects of California Indian land and water history, from violent removal,[27] to buying land back through pooling family and community wages,[28] to acquiring land through conservation agreements (Middleton 2011), there is little comprehensive discussion of how tribes navigate multiple contemporary "public benefit" and environmental regulatory processes to attempt to restore ancestral lands. Indigenous rights have consistently been sacrificed for a "public good," and any "public good" process that does not address this is simply perpetuating neocolonial conservation, development, and industrial interests.

CEREMONY CONTINUES

On a warm, sunny June day in 2006, I was driving with Maidu *yeponim*[29] Farrell Cunningham [*yatam*][30] along dusty, rutted dirt roads, alternately passing through forested stands and dry meadows with *papam*[31] flowers, on our way to a *weda*[32] on the edge of Mountain Meadows. After passing the same few trees for the second time we realized we had lost our way and made a circle on the intersecting maze of unmarked, unpaved logging roads. At a dusty intersection, we ran into Maidu elder Tommy Merino [*yatam*], also looking for the way to the *weda*. We got out and talked; he and Farrell discussed the possible locations of the *weda*, and the geography of the area, and then we continued in a caravan until we saw several cars in a clearing, just off of the meadow. This was the first time in many years a *weda* was being held in this location, hosted by two Maidu members of Susanville Indian Rancheria with ancestors from this area. It was a beautiful Sierra Nevada summer day; the grasses were blowing in the wind, wildflowers nodding, and the pungent scent of wormwood being prepared into sashes and garlands for the dance filled the air. Tables had been set up and were laden with food for the predance feast. We greeted the organizers, and then I went to help with the food and with making wildflower wreaths for the women dancers.

This southwestern area of Mountain Meadows was just high enough to be spared from flooding for a hydroelectric project. The majority of the area now lies underwater and is PG&E's uppermost hydroelectric storage reservoir in the Upper North Fork Feather River operations that form the headwaters of the California SWP. Following the settlement with the California Public Utilities Commission, PG&E made a small portion of Mountain Meadows available

FIGURE 1. Mountain Meadows.

for divestiture, which it later withdrew from the process. As such, the land will have a conservation easement on it held by the Feather River Land Trust, but all of the land and water rights will remain with PG&E.

The meadows surrounding Mountain Meadows Reservoir—Maidu land with a long history of Maidu stewardship, subsistence, and cultural significance—remains largely in PG&E ownership, with other nearby landowners including timber companies and the U.S. Forest Service. There were at least 16 Indian allotments totaling 2,461 acres in Mountain Meadows, and the last transfer of an allotment from a Maidu holder to a corporate entity was in January 1921, when the 160-acre allotment of Ollie Mack (Sus-131) was sold to the Red River Lumber Company.

INSTITUTIONALIZED EXCLUSION FROM ENVIRONMENTAL DECISION-MAKING

While a successful *weda* was held here in 2006, often Indigenous people must petition for their right to *be* on ancestral lands, including their right to carry out their traditional responsibilities to those lands. This requirement of "asking" to be on and care for ancestral lands may exist whether the lands are owned by private industrial or public or private conservation interests. Through the lens of Maidu lands, and Maidu allotments in particular, I argue that the institutionalized lack of attention to history in natural resource policy results in natural resource decision-making that continues to reinforce inequalities and exclude both Indigenous populations and the range of Indigenous ways of being in relationship to the land. This decision-making may be equally related to environmental preservation or environmental destruction; the similarity is disregard for Indigenous land rights and history, sometimes accompanied by an attempt to mitigate the situation, but within a framework of neoliberalism and Eurocentric jurisprudence and values.

As this book shows, public and private processes of both development and conservation (including the establishment of protected areas, the process of restricting use of sites, or the development of conservation-oriented interpretive materials) have worked together to divest and repurpose Indian homelands. While Mark Spence (1999), Karl Jacoby (2003), and others have extensively discussed the negative impacts of conservation, in terms of the development of national parks, the orientation is still to the past; national parks were developed near or before the turn of the twentieth century. It is thought that, with our contemporary enlightened understanding of how not to conserve by moving people off of the land, we should be moving forward in a more productive way, developing conservation projects in cooperation and partnership with Indigenous people, as described by Stan Stevens in his hopeful text *Indigenous Peoples, National Parks and Protected Areas* (2014) and others (see Brosius, Tsing, and Zerner 2005) who chronicle the development and success of community-based natural resource management and comanagement internationally. Indeed, it may be that the Stewardship Council process, as it has progressed, is moving toward building conservation partnerships with the Indigenous peoples that have gained entry into the process, but this is a result of staff and board will, rather than an institutional commitment. Generally, when contemporary conservation initiatives exclude Indigenous perspectives, they are not met with broad public protest; it was only through tribally led outreach and activism that California coastal tribes were able to impact the Marine Life Protection Act process to achieve recognition of and protection for traditional gathering along the coast.[33]

Some tribes and Indigenous organizations are working to bypass public processes by raising funds to buy back land themselves, or working with others to buy either the land or particular rights to it (Middleton 2011). However, if this is infeasible, tribes and Native organizations have to participate in public processes, where the exclusion of Indigenous, site-specific history is rampant and deeply institutionalized. This is an expression of the impulse to relegate Indigenous history to the far past, rather than to see it as irreconcilably intertwined with the present; as Plumas County employees told me when I came to county offices to do research on historical allotment boundaries, "These lands have *always* been owned by PG&E." This lack of information, and associated cognitive dissonance (Bell 1992), is evident in the context of the natural resource decisions made successively and continuously on former Indian allotment lands in the northeastern Sierra Nevada.

The historical amnesia that characterizes contemporary natural resource decision-making is, in part, a factor of institutionalized racism. The lack of attention to the histories of Indigenous peoples and their land rights is the direct result of manifest destiny– or doctrine of discovery–based approaches to European appropriation of Indian land.[34] The lack of engagement with Indigenous rights and worldviews is embedded in the pernicious language of attempted conquest and removal that underlies decision-making in Federal

Indian law and continues to deny Native peoples their land and water rights.[35] It also exemplifies the naturalization of progress and environmental protection as unquestionable public goods. Very little has changed in the arena of public natural resource decision-making since the frontier days of manifest destiny–based claims to land. As Laura Pulido explains, this is no accident, as "the state is deeply invested in *not* solving . . . environmental racism . . . because it would be too costly and disruptive to industry, the larger political system, and the state itself. Instead, the state has developed numerous initiatives in which it goes through the motions, or, 'performs' regulatory activity, especially participation, without producing meaningful change. The problem is not a lack of knowledge or skill, but a lack of political will" (2016). Indeed, to fully address the ways in which the past land theft and persecution results in the current distribution of power and resources, to *decolonize* these headwaters, would require the repatriation of land to Maidu and other upstream Indigenous populations.[36]

THE IMPORTANCE OF CALIFORNIA INDIAN PUBLIC DOMAIN ALLOTMENTS

California Indian public domain allotments are a particularly telling site to expand on our national history of injustice in development and conservation because they represent a significant—albeit often short-lived—recognized Native right to so-called public land that can be followed through successive eras of natural resource development. Under the Land Claims Act (March 1851), all persons who claimed California lands were required to submit their claims for review and approval within two years or they would pass into the public domain. Given the outright violence committed against California Indians during this time, the fact that, at the time, California Indians were not citizens, and the lack of communication to California Indians of this law, no California Indians were able to file their land claims under this statute. Indian Agent Adam Johnston documented his observations when he traveled up the Feather River in 1850, underscoring the impacts of settlers on local Mountain and Concow Maidu:

> The coming in of the whites, Johnston observed, was greatly affecting these natives. Their means of subsisting were being greatly reduced. Miners were destroying their fish dams; strangers overrunning the country were feeding their grass, burn-

ing their timber, and causing great alarm to the natives who had an undefined idea of their right to the soil, the trees and the streams. They were being driven from their finely located villages by reason of the fact that the whites were laying out their towns around them. Johnston found these Indians an inoffensive people, but inhuman massacres sometimes committed upon them for real or supposed injuries caused them to commit acts of revenge. (Ellison 1913, 88)

In 1851 and 1852, agents from the federal government negotiated 18 treaties with approximately 139 groups of California Indians, encompassing about 25,000 people. The treaties reserved 7.5 million square acres, or 7.5 percent of the state, for California Indians. However, intense pressure from private investors, miners, and the leaders of California convinced the Senate not to ratify *any* of the treaties because the lands were considered too valuable and would reduce the state's taxable land area. The treaties were rejected in 1852 and kept under injunction of secrecy until 1905.[37]

As such, the protection of the vast majority of California tribal land was never fulfilled. In the years of genocide that followed, one of the first opportunities for Native Californians to have rights to some of their vast lands recognized was the Indian Allotment Act of 1887. Between about 1887 and 1915 in the northeastern Sierra Nevada (in some cases, all the way up until the Allotment Act was repealed by the Indian Reorganization Act in 1934), Native individuals and heads of household filed for up to 160-acre allotment parcels of land.

Proponents of the Allotment Act considered it a vehicle to "civilize" Indian people by dissolving collective land ownership[38] and encouraging small-scale agricultural self-sufficiency, with the twin benefit of opening up "unused" Indian land for settlement.[39] According to the legal scholar Mark Poindexter, the policy logic of allotment located "tribal strength and identity" in "commonly owned land" and believed that, if land was divided into individually held parcels, it would "undermine" this tribal identity, leaving the individual American Indian "free to assimilate" (1994). However, this assessment failed to account for the strength of American Indian values, including ties to the land and to one another—as Poindexter adds, "The land was not a source of pecuniary power . . . but a source of spiritual nurture to be shared." Ultimately, he concludes, "the internal or policy motivations of the allotment process remained largely unrealized" (71).[40]

While the attempted social reform of allotment was unsuccessful, it was effective in diminishing tribal lands. When the Indian Reorganization Act ended allotment in 1934, then-commissioner of Indian Affairs John Collier reported that Indian people had gone from owning approximately 138 million acres in 1887 to 48 million acres in 1934.[41] The geographer Mark Palmer (Kiowa) documents the loss of trust land that continued even after allotment policy and examines the reasons allottees and their descendants continued to sell their land (2011). While other work examines allotment's legacy of displacement (Kelley and Francis), disruption of tribal governance (e.g., Poindexter 1994), and unwieldy inheritance systems that led to fractionation (e.g., Bobroff 2001, 1559), no authors seem to have examined the significance of public domain allotments in California post-treaty nonratification. For much of California, these allotments actually represented one opportunity to have rights recognized to a small part of one's homeland.

Not long after allotments were established, the Allotment Act was amended to facilitate the use and sale of allotments for development, ostensibly in the national interest. For example, an 1891 amendment (26 Stat. 784, 994-96) enabled leasing of allotment lands if the allottee could not work due to age or disability,[42] and the 1906 Burke Act, or Forced Fee Patenting Act, modified the required 25-year trust period by giving the secretary of the Interior authority to declare individuals "competent" to hold fee title to allotments.[43] According to Bobroff, issuing fee title to allottees during this period "almost invariably (and usually immediately) resulted in the transfer of land from Indians to whites" (2001, 1611). Congress also authorized allottees (in 1907) and heirs (in 1902) to petition for sale of their allotments.[44] Archival records show that agents in Plumas and Lassen Counties often encouraged allottees and heirs to sell their lands, and private investors, including timber barons and natural resource development companies (such as railroad and hydroelectric), were eager purchasers. Maidu allotment lands in particular contained valuable timber and hydropower resources and eventually became the headwaters of the massive California SWP, and other Indian allotments around the state were flooded for other reservoirs and the Federal Water Project, including Wintu lands now under Shasta Lake and Pit River lands now flooded by the system of dams and reservoirs along the Pit River.

My entry point to unravel this history of appropriation and exploitation is the 2003 settlement between PG&E and the California Public Utilities Commission, which forced the private, publicly regulated utility company (PG&E) that generates power from these waters to divest its lands in the northeastern Sierra for conservation and public benefit. Discussed more fully in chapter 5, the wholly ahistorical agreement has far-reaching environmental, financial, social, and cultural consequences. One central missing element of the settlement is the recognition that the lands denoted for conservation ownership in the settlement are not only ancestral Indigenous lands but recently individual Indian allotment lands that were canceled, purchased, or trespassed on to develop the reservoirs and other power company operations that are being mitigated now for their conservation impact, but not their sociocultural impact. While conservation landholdings already dominate the counties of focus (Plumas County is 75 percent national forest) and continue to expand (nonprofit private conservation entities own at least 3,000 acres in the county [GreenInfo Network 2016], and there are conservation easements on another 29,757 acres [GreenInfo Network 2015]), Maidu people still lack both general federal recognition and a land base. And yet, rather than return historic allotments that were taken from Maidu, the Stewardship Council is required by the settlement to transfer these former Indian allotment lands to conservation entities that will manage the land in accordance with six beneficial public values. As such, tribes must frame themselves as primarily conservation entities in order to get this land back that was taken from their ancestors less than a century ago.[45]

As tribes, private conservation groups, and public conservation agencies compete for title to these watershed lands, the terms of the settlement do not call in any way for addressing the history of the lands. This is an example of an ahistorical conservation process, naturalized as a "public good" for an actually quite limited segment of the public. As of 2016, after many years of struggle, the Stewardship Council has voted to transfer 2,966 acres of land to the Maidu. However, 53,185 acres of land in the Feather River Watershed (which includes ten planning units in four counties, largely within the Mountain Maidu and Concow Maidu homeland) will remain out of Maidu ownership, and the Maidu are only one of three California Native entities throughout the state receiving lands, despite similar histories of cancellation of Indian lands up and down the Sierra Nevada and Cascade ranges. The process as a whole remains problematic, and other Indigenous groups continue to struggle to participate.

INTERVENTIONS

The maps associated with this project offer a method for improving natural resource decision-making through incorporating historical, archival, and humanistic data in digital cartography. After drawing the allotments[46] on the map using ArcGIS, I worked with a cartographer to create a private, web-based version of the map that links archival documents to the allotment parcels, so that one can click on a parcel and access original public documents about the allotment application, terms of sale or cancellation, and issues of trespass and restitution. By returning a hidden history to view, the map has the potential to disrupt an ongoing, attempted colonial project that naturalizes these lands as American lands needing "conservation" rather than Maidu lands requiring restitution, protection, and recognition. However, because these lands are still under threat of desecration, the maps created for this project will reside with the Maidu Summit Consortium and Conservancy, the Greenville Rancheria, and Susanville Rancheria, and only limited screenshots of their content and an explanation of the methods applied in their development are included in this text. Additionally, while I am dealing only with publicly accessible information on allotments found in various federal, state, and private archives, out of concern for the privacy of the descendants of allottees, I have endeavored not to include any information in the text or map that heirs might find problematic.[47]

The Stewardship Council process represents an opportunity—made visible in stark relief in this situation of Maidu allotments changing hands with the approval of the state at the turn of the twentieth century, again away from Maidu and in a framework of "public good" in the early twenty-first century—to question the ahistoricism in which natural resource policy operates. It also invokes a responsibility to examine specific histories and apply lessons learned from these contested sites to other Indigenous lands subject to exclusive natural resource policies. The Maidu allotments—lived, held, and memorialized by descendants—are a microcosm of a process of ignoring Indigenous site-specific histories and of relegating a relatively recent event to a perceived far past in order to make mainstream decisions more palatable and naturalize them as inevitable and inherently "good" for the broader public. This book explores this process and lays out a path for identifying the material impacts of historical amnesia in natural resources decision-making in order to contribute to the healing and recognition of communities and landscapes.

That path begins in chapter 1 with an examination of how the massive SWP, managed by the DWR, came to be, and particularly how Maidu lands came to form the basis of the system. Drawing on federal, state, and private archives, I trace the public and private entities involved over time, how the project was paid for, and who benefited from the project, who lost, and in what ways. Ultimately,

I ask how the way the SWP was developed serves to scaffold the present organization of environmental governance, resource distribution, and allocation of costs and benefits.

Chapter 2 begins a series of three chapters focused on upstream public domain allotments as a key point of entry to understand Native histories and futures at the headwaters of the SWP. These chapters contextualize regional Indian land and water rights in historical and contemporary state and national development and conservation. Specifically, chapter 2 focuses on the ways in which Indigenous allottees consistently and persistently advocated for their rights—if not to their specific allotted lands then to nearby or income-generating lands, or to actually receive the profits if they chose to sell their lands. Drawing on correspondence in Bureau of Land Management (BLM) and BIA archives, this chapter traces allottees' work in a range of contexts to maintain rights to and/or receive benefits from their allotments.

Chapter 3 examines archival allotment data and contemporary policy to understand how Indigenous land (particularly the set of contested allotment lands in the northeastern Sierra) was and is valued, and by and for whom. During the allotment period, many allottees were initially allotted forested or rocky lands that they could not farm, only to have those lands either canceled due to their timber or hydroelectric value or undersold based on their determined lack of value. I explore the specific methods (cancellations, condemnations, group sales, and relinquishments) by which "valuable" lands were wrested from allottees, whether these methods were legal in the context of the time period(s), and how allottees continued to resist displacement and disenfranchisement over time.

Chapter 4 explores the role(s) of large natural resource companies (hydroelectric and timber) in the divestiture, development, and conservation of Indian lands at the headwaters of the SWP. I examine the ways in which specific companies worked across time and space, taking advantage of the agency's Indigenous civilizing mission to build monopolies from acquiring Indian land. Drawing principally on archival data, this chapter follows large landowners (specifically, PG&E, Great Western Power, and Red River Lumber) of the former allotment lands and traces how and when most of the land transferred into their hands.

Chapter 5 transitions into a focus on Maidu participation in processes regarding hydropower management and conservation in the upper watershed of the SWP. The Stewardship Council land-divestiture process is discussed in both historical and contemporary contexts, and an update is offered on both the process for and ongoing advocacy to receive restitution and lands. The ongoing FERC relicensing proceedings on the Upper North Fork Feather River Hydroelectric Project are also examined for Indigenous participation and concessions, as well as for institutional barriers to wresting Indigenous benefits from the process. This chapter looks at Indigenous participation in these processes as key sites of intervention in water policy in the face of either agency disregard or limited agency attempts at inclusion without attention to history and its contemporary ramifications. The chapter reaches back to the analysis in chapter 3, examining the structures of value in place today, specifically the ways in which conservation value is assigned to the same lands valued for harvest production and potential 80 years ago. The chapter concludes with reflection on the ways in which Maidu are responding to institutionalized marginalization of their histories in place and asserting their rights to steward their homelands.

The conclusion underscores the role of historic Maidu and other allotment lands as both traditional homelands with thriving Native communities as well as the headwaters of some of the largest, most lucrative water systems in the nation. With attention to methods, I reflect on the central goals of this research: employing multiple methods to natural resource policy-making in historical context; exploring advocacy, valuation, and monopolies on contested Indian lands; enhancing cartographic and other visual presentations of the data; and offering potential applications around the United States in sites of Indigenous advocacy regarding hydropower development, conservation set-asides, and mitigation. I examine the historical and contemporary institutional exclusion of Indigenous histories and the ways in which this exclusion bars decision-makers from being duly informed about the essential nature of Indigenous involvement in determining the future of ancestral Indigenous lands. The chapter concludes with an emerging vision of policy reform that leads to enhanced Indigenous futures on the SWP and on other sites of Indigenous land/water divestiture around the nation.

And so, I return to that day in 2006 in Mountain Meadows, on the edge of a Maidu cultural landscape out of recognized Maidu ownership. That day, traditional *weda* songs mixed with the sound of the wind through the grass, the cries of red-tailed hawks and osprey, and the beat of clapper sticks made from local elderberry. That day, as on many days, the land was Maidu land—not for development, not for water storage, but for understanding, living, and reaffirming Maidu place in creation.

1

UNTOLD STORIES FROM THE HEADWATERS OF CALIFORNIA'S STATE WATER PROJECT

THE PAWNEE legal scholar and attorney Walter Echo-Hawk (2010) terms the laws that enabled and legalized injustice "legal fictions." This chapter navigates the legal and political fictions that enabled vast amounts of California Indian lands to become public (federal and state) water projects, providing benefits to irrigators and urban developers downstream, while leaving environmental destruction and cultural disruption for Maidu, Wintu, Pit River, and other Indigenous nations upstream. The legal and political machinations that enabled these projects, premised on views of manifest destiny, white man's burden, and the "disappearing Indian,"[1] disregarded international human rights as well as both federal and state promises to Indian people in favor of building the infrastructure of California in a way that greatly enriched a small segment of Americans.

This book traces the ways in which these century-old legal and political fictions became so deeply institutionalized that, while Native rights could not be so summarily dismissed today, it remains immensely difficult for Indian people to impact relicensing processes for hydroelectric facilities or to participate in landscape-scale conservation planning within their homelands. This chapter walks through some of the history of the SWP and preceding power developments on the North Fork Feather River, framing this information in the context of contemporary opportunities and barriers to Native intervention.

Placing the histories of Indian land and water rights alongside the development of California water resources reveals the ways in which the dispossession of Indian people enabled the development of the economy of the new state of California. Following statehood in 1850, California passed the Law for the Government and Protection of Indians, which effectively legalized slavery of Indian people by sanctioning indentured servitude and confirming that an Indian person could not represent him or herself in court (see Johnston-Dodds 2002). The first governor of the state of California, Peter Burnett, called on the militia twice in 1850 to "punish" the Indians, and, in his 1851 inaugural address, he predicted that "a war of extermination will continue to be waged between the races, until the Indian race becomes extinct" (20). When citizens were called to file their land claims from 1851 to 1853, Indian people were not able to participate. This left the vast Native homelands of the state open to non-Indians, who were also able to draw on indentured Native labor to settle the ostensibly "free" new state of California.

By 1870 the state was becoming concerned with the haphazard nature of water resource development. In 1873 a President Grant–appointed commission investigated the water resources of the Central Valley and recommended state and federal support for transfer of Sierra Nevada water.[2] This was the first iteration of a State Water Plan that would propose moving water from the wet, sparsely populated Northern California to the dry, heavily agricultural and densely populated regions of Central and Southern California.

FROM INDIAN LANDS TO POWER RESERVES

The 1887 Indian Allotment Act was followed closely by an 1888 congressional appropriation to the Department of the Interior to study the irrigation potential of western lands.[3] The appropriation asserted that all lands deemed potential sites for water projects, and potentially irrigable, be reserved from settlement. This bold caveat was partially repealed by subsequent acts in 1890 and 1891 that reduced the amount of land that could be withdrawn from settlement for irrigation to the minimum necessary for water storage.[4] However, on Indian allotment lands on the "public domain"—that is, under the purview of the General Land Office (GLO) in Northern California—numerous allotments in the region that became the headwaters of the SWP were canceled in the early 1900s. While some were referred to as part of "power site withdrawals,"[5] others were simply condemned without explanation and then flooded. At least 105 allotments (totaling 16,000 acres) of the approximately 665 allotments that I found records for in Plumas and Lassen Counties (totaling 91,919 acres) were canceled, with reasons varying from "land condemned" (Sus-118, Minnie Lincoln, Big Meadows), to "her husband was a white man" (Sus-75, Ora Evans), to no explanation at all (Roy family, Sus-140-144, Chester area). In the Big Meadows / Lake Almanor, Butt Valley, and Mountain Meadows areas, at least 27 allotments, totaling 4,240 acres, were simply canceled. The potential to withdraw lands from settlement for power production was rekindled with a 1910 act that referred specifically to the withdrawal of Indian lands for hydropower development.[6]

While these federal withdrawals conflicted with Indian land rights, settlers' rights, and states' water rights, state agencies like the DWR eventually argued that they ultimately benefited states, as areas reserved from settlement by federal power-site withdrawals were often later developed into state projects or projects serving state interests. In a 1964 presentation to the California Senate Committee on Water, DWR chief deputy director (1961–66) B. Abbott Goldberg pointed to the example of Oroville Dam, the keystone facility of the SWP. Twenty percent of the land inundated by the reservoir is federal, and nearly all of that land is in power-site withdrawals. According to Goldberg (1964), without this federal "protection" over this land, it may have been more difficult to acquire the lands needed to build the project. However, whether the lands were appropriated for federal or state interests, the impact on Indian lands remained, with Indian people often remaining landless after their aboriginal rights and then their allotments were canceled for power-site withdrawals.

In order to construct major water projects in the West, the federal government required a source of revenue. Hearings in 1901 on the proposed Reclamation Act (passed in 1902) clearly contemplate that "receipts from the sales of public lands in the arid and semiarid regions of the US" would be put "to the exclusive purposes of irrigation" (Department of the Interior, General Land Office, 1901). This was formalized into a specific fund in the treasury, the "arid land reclamation fund," for the development of reservoirs and "other hydraulic works" for irrigation and "reclamation of arid lands" (Committee on Irrigation of Arid Lands 1901). As such, the process involved claiming Indian lands[7] as "public" land and then selling those lands to provide revenue to fund large water projects that would in turn support settlement and development of the West by "a most desirable class of people."[8] Thus Indians were displaced by both the annexation of their homelands into the federal land base and the subsequent project development that impacted both their remaining land base and the homelands out of their ownership that they continued to steward.[9]

While federal reservation of land and associated water rights came with nearly all costs for Indian lands, for non-Indians, there were both benefits and costs. On the benefits side, the federal government was taking a broad view of constructing water projects across the West, in order to encourage the settlement and development of the entire region; on the costs side, state and private water and land rights had to yield to federal control. Francis Newlands (D-NV), the U.S. representative and senator for whom the Reclamation Act is named, asserted the federal government's wisdom in designing the legislation "to avert the evils of land monopoly and to promote the division of the public domain into homes for . . . settlers." To this end, he argued for state cooperation with the federal government, "weld[ing] the state and federal officials into one cooperative machine, working for the common good" (Darling 1937, 77). Newlands was committed to promoting the science and practice of irrigation across state boundaries to efficiently develop and "civilize" the West (Rowley 1996, 48–49, 98–99, 147), and he was also an avowed white supremacist.[10] The 1996 biography of Newlands does not mention the Pyramid Lake Paiute people whose homeland, culture, lifeways, and water rights are still being impacted by the infamous Derby Dam of his Newlands Project.[11]

In 1911 the Department of the Interior, Office of Indian Affairs, released the report "Indian Lands for Sale Under Government Supervision," on the department's efforts to sell Indian allotments. The report explained that, since the passage of the Dawes, or Allotment, Act of 1887, the Office had been dividing up Indian reservations and allotting individual Indians up to 80 acres of agricultural land and 160 acres of grazing land, to be held in trust for the individual for 25 years. However, given the concern that allottees who inherited the lands of other allottees became land rich but cash poor, Congress approved that the secretary of the Interior could sell those lands and ostensibly apply the proceeds to the benefit of the heirs. Study of the allotment records, however, reveals how difficult it could be for an Indian heir to access the funds from the sale of his or her own allotment or one that he or she had interest in. The report went on to detail the specific procedure for land sales, based on regulations approved by the Department of the Interior on October 12, 1910, and noting that "all matters concerning the purchase of Indian lands [must be] carried on through this office." Of particular interest to this study is the stipulation that no person "connected with an agency office or the Indian service" be permitted to bid or assist another bidder in the purchase of Indian land.[12] It is this clause that is at issue in the investigation of the timber cruiser Irvine Gardner. As discussed in chapter 4, Gardner appears to have worked simultaneously as an appraiser for the Indian Agency, appraising lands to ready them for sale, as well as for the Red River Lumber Company (hereafter Red River), which purchased many of the allotment properties that Gardner appraised.

DEVELOPING THE FEATHER RIVER'S POWER POTENTIAL

The development of the ten-dam stairway of power in the Feather River Canyon and the storage reservoirs that form the uppermost reaches of California's vast SWP has its roots in the ponderings of a Harvard University geologist and the investments of some of the richest men of the late nineteenth and early twentieth centuries. The rights of Mountain Maidu peoples whose homelands encompass the headwaters of the project and at least half of the region dammed along the north fork of the Feather were not even considered by the academics, engineers, and businessmen who created the project. However, Maidu and others in the region have continued to make their presence known and advocate for their rights, and they today stand to have at least a small portion of this land returned to them via the Stewardship Council process that issued from the 2003 Settlement Agreement between the California Public Utilities Commission and PG&E. This section will trace the interests that assumed the authority to make decisions about the Feather River's water and power from the late nineteenth century through the present day. Readers are invited to join in looking for continuities in the institutions and ideological/ political-economic frameworks that govern natural resource stewardship through time, either in periods of development or conservation, as well as the consistency of Native advocacy.

In the early 1880s, a Harvard geologist sent a party to explore whether ancient channels of gold still flowed under the mountain meadows in the region below Mt. Lassen. One of the individuals in the party, Julius M. Howells, saw Big Meadows and was struck by its hydroelectric potential: "Howells believed that in the Feather River, backed by ample water storage in Big Meadows, he had found one of the finest potential sources of hydroelectric power in all the state" (Coleman 1952, 212). Howells went on to assist with the founding of the San

Joaquin Light and Power Corporation further south in California, but he never forgot about Big Meadows. He returned there nearly 20 years later in 1901 to collect data and reconsider the area's hydroelectric potential. After a trip confirming his interest, Howells met with businessmen brothers Edwin T. and Guy Earl, who embraced the plan. The Earls retained real-estate agent and politician Arthur Breed to obtain options on properties in Big Meadows. Breed secretively obtained rights to purchase 11,481 acres in Big Meadows, with the assistance of Greenville resident Augustus Bidwell. Apparently, Breed had to be secretive or ranchers in Big Meadows would resist plans to buy out their lands for a large reservoir project. Coleman's *PG&E of California: The Centennial Story of Pacific Gas & Electric Company, 1852–1952* describes the way in which the Earl Brothers eventually obtained control of 30,063 acres in Big Meadows and Butt Valley (213). The Earls incorporated the Western Power Company on March 24, 1902.

What is missing from Coleman's account are the 25,200 acres of Indian allotment lands in Big Meadows, Mountain Meadows, Humbug Valley, and Butt Valley that had been conveyed or were being conveyed between 1891 and 1902 to Indian allottees who had always lived in the region but had been displaced from their lands by the incoming ranchers and settlers, beginning in the 1830s.[13] These allotments were quickly canceled, sometimes in county court, or sold with or without allottee approval to make way for the new damsite and reservoir. On August 14, 1918, Bob Shafer made a formal statement to the Greenville superintendent Edgar Miller, explaining how he and his family were divested of 10 allotments totaling 1600 acres in and around Butt Valley:

> About fourteen years ago before they started to build the dam at Big Meadows, Mr. Bidwell now of Greenville, California, who was connected with the Great Western Power Company getting lands under the Great Western Project, came to my place in Butt Valley with another man, I don't remember who the other man was, maybe he was with the Western Power Company, and Mr. Bidwell said to me, "You got to go to Quincy," I said, "what for[?]". He said, "This place they going to make something out of it, you better go get your money." I said, "I don't want to sell this place." He said, "They going to make a tunnel" and I suppose they going to pay me for it. He said, "This your land and if they don't make tunnel here it belongs to you, if they make tunnel you get other land somewhere else." My wife was there, we were working in garden. Two or three days after I went to Quincy, and they took me to a room in a Bank, I don't know whether I signed paper or not, they asked me what kind of money I wanted. Horace McBeth was

Clerk, he paid me about two hundred fifty dollars, Bidwell was at the table, two or three other white men were there, John Jenkins and Thompson Jim were there . . .

I lived on the place about a year after this happened, and I had trouble with sheepman who told me, he rented this place from Power Company and it wasn't my land. I then moved to Prattville.[14]

Following Shafer's statement, and an independent letter of support from the former Indian Agency employee Irvine Gardner,[15] Superintendent Miller wrote to Great Western Power (GWP) to request that the company purchase a homesite for Shafer. In a defensive response, GWP assistant secretary W. H. Spaulding argued that his company correctly followed all procedures:

All this is perfectly clear. Western Power brought several condemnation suits against a large number of the Indians, including a suit against Jennie Meadows, John Jenkins, and Robert Shafer and U.S.A. to condemn the lands of these Indians. . . . This 80 acres [where Bob Shafer lived] was condemned in the suit, which was tried at Quincy in the Superior Court, where Bob Shafer and the U.S. Government were represented by U.S. District attorney. The judgement of the Court in this condemnation suit awarded Bob Shafer $280 and the money was paid by the Company . . . held by the Clerk of Court and paid by the Clerk of Court to the various Indians entitled thereto, so that the matter is one of public record, easily verified.

Following these condemnation suits an Act of Congress was passed, being H.R. 15725 approved May 5, 1908, under which all interests of the United States in the lands described and involved in these various condemnation suits were released, relinquished and confirmed to Western Power Co . . .

It is perfectly clear, therefore, that Bob Shafer's land was duly and regularly condemned by proper proceedings of Court; that the value of the land was fixed by the Court; that the amount of judgement was paid by the Power Co. into the Court and this amount of money paid out by the Clerk of Court to Bob Shafer . . . If these Indians were allowed to continue to reside on these lands, after the decrees of condemnation were entered by the Court and after they had received their money for the lands—then this was merely through the courtesy of the Power Company.[16]

In his response, Miller did not deny GWP's explanation but stated that Shafer felt dispossessed and spoke broadly of being wronged, making both the company and the agency look bad. Allying himself with the company, Miller suggested that, if GWP could find a home for Shafer, "it would redound to your credit and ours, too. This is what we are after." However, he was unequivocal in his frustration with the role of local courts in the cancellation of Shafer's land:

> So far as condemning Indian lands by State courts go all I have to say is I would like to see it tried again in this jurisdiction. I can not see how it was done or how any Superior court of the State could possibly have jurisdiction over lands in which the titles are invested in the Government. Someone surely slept on the job.[17]

In a longer letter to his superior at the Indian Agency, Miller explained that Shafer's allotments 150–59 had been apparently "relinquished" by the allottee in 1901, and allotment 999 was the 80 acres that Spaulding referred to as the subject of the condemnation suit. He framed himself as the only one to investigate these cancellations on behalf of the Indians: "When I came here I soon found out the criticisms about cancellations and have been . . . investigating all of them as I have the time. There was nothing here in the files about any such matters and no one before my time here bothered at all about such matters."[18]

Another instance of unrestored cancellation of several allotments in the same area follows the Meadows family—John (Sus-145 and Sus-1014), Jennie (Sus-149 and Sus-1013), Kate (Sus-147), Lonkeen/Loureen (Sus-148), and Joaquin (Sus-146). Allotments 146–49 were all selected in 1894 and then canceled in 1902, and allotment 145 was canceled in 1901. Jennie and John Meadows were reallotted Sus-1013 and 1014, but both of these second allotments were condemned in 1904 and transferred to GWP.

Jennie Meadows received meager compensation for her land ($420 for 120 acres was equivalent to $3.50/acre), far less than the company stood to generate from the land. However, her husband John Meadows was not even that fortunate. A 1956 BIA note documents a visit to the BIA Sacramento area office by Joseph/Joaquin Meadows inquiring about what happened to his grandfather John Meadows's allotments, Sus-145 and Sus-1014. The note records that Sus-1014 "was relinquished in favor of the Great Western Power Company and there is no record of the allottee having received any compensation for his land."[19] In a 1947 response to an inquiry from Carl Salem regarding payments for the canceled Meadows allotments, California Indian Agency staff explained research they had done into PG&E records:

Allotment 1014, 80 acres,
was condemned by the Superior
Court of Plumas Count in a
decree dated Nov. 22, 1902.
No record has been made of the
compensation to the allottee.

        E.   K..   M.

SEE FILE SUS. 145 AND THE FILE
GREAT WESTERN POWER COMPANY,
RESERVOIR.

Allotment #1013, 120acres,
was condemned in the Superior
Court Plumas County by decree
dated May 9, 1904, and the
allottee, JENNIE MEADOWS,
allowed a compensation of
$420.00, paid direct to her.
Title was given this power
company through special act
of Congress dated May 5, 1908.

          E.   K.   M.
SEE FILE SUS. 145 AND THE FILE
GREAT WESTERN POWER COMPANY,
RESERVOIR.

FIGURE 2. Overview of the history of Jennie and John Meadows' second allotments (Sus-1013 and Sus-1014), located in the area of present-day Butt Valley reservoir, owned by PG&E, which bought GWP in 1930. (Filed in Sus-1013 and Sus-1014, RG75, NARA San Bruno.)

We have . . . found a letter by a lawyer of the Great Western Power Company. . . . "The Power Company deposited in court for the Indian defendants in each case the damages awarded, and did not assume the responsibility itself of making distribution, but left that for the court to do." . . . "The Power Company complied literally with all the requirements of the law relative to the payment of said damages."

The Court referred to was the Superior Court of Plumas County, and it appears that any information concerning the disbursement of these funds would have to come from their records.

It is suggested that you might contact that Court and request them for the information that you desire.[20]

When Rose Salem wrote to inquire about the Meadows allotments in 1951, the director of the BIA Sacramento Area Office was unapologetic in his reply: "As 49 years have past [sic] since action was taken to cancel these allotments, we have no remedy to propose."[21] Despite this stonewalling from the agency and the lack of apparent remedies, not only do the descendants of Maidu allottees continue to live in Big Meadows (Lake Almanor Basin), Butt Valley, and Mountain Meadows, they recall this history, continue to invoke it in consultations on hydroelectric relicensing or conservation planning, and are committed to getting these lands back into Indian ownership.[22]

In 1902, just weeks after the Earls formed the Western Power Company, their colleague Howells posted a notice of appropriation to "100,000 inches of the waters of the north fork of the Feather River for 'milling, mining, manufacturing, irrigation and domestic purposes and for the purpose of water power and the *generation of electric power*'" (Coleman 1952, 215). Not only were the Earls and Howells in competition with Bidwell, they were both in competition with engineer Lloyd Cornell, the son of mining and railroad developer G. P. Cornell of Greenville. The elder Cornell had outlined a very similar plan to construct a large dam at Canyon Dam and generate power at sites in the Feather River Canyon before he passed away in February 1902. Following his passing, his son engaged San Francisco and Richmond investors and promoters in the project. Because Howells had posted about 1,000 feet above, and prior to these two men, he legally had the claim following the doctrine of prior appropriation, or "first in time, first in right," that governs Western water law. What was, again, not considered were the aboriginal Indian land and water rights and the specific Indian land and water rights attached to the Indian allotments, which had been established beginning in 1887. The famous 1908 Supreme Court case *Winters v. U.S.* would later affirm that trust lands carried senior water rights.

Bidwell hurried to Quincy to record the claim, while Howells posted another claim at Butt Valley. Bidwell filed the papers for the Earls and Howells in Plumas County at 8:25 p.m. on April 8, 1902, a full 40 minutes before Cornell's men could reach the county seat and attempt to record. However, Cornell's party then filed for water rights at the Big Bend tunnel and other potential hydroelectric power plant sites in the canyon, incorporating as Golden State Power in October 1902 and effectively forming an obstacle to the Earls' plans to develop the hydropower in the Feather River canyon.

There were other players involved at the coveted Big Bend site as well: situated at a large curve in the North Fork Feather River above Oroville, Big Bend, was already a hydroelectric project to facilitate mining, but the mining had not paid off. The owner of the project, wealthy politician and businessman Dr. Pierce, author of *The People's Common Sense Medical Adviser* (1895) and provider of "Dr. Pierce's Golden Medical Discovery Pills," developed the Eureka Power Company on July 3, 1902, to build a larger power plant. The Earls and their assistants, two San Francisco promoters, purchased the Eureka Power Company soon after, but they still had to address the threat posed by Cornell's Golden State Power Company, which held the waters coming into the Big Bend Tunnel, as well as land (obtained from Central Pacific Railroad) immediately upstream.

The Earls then went about assembling a wealthy and influential group of investors, which involved attempting to educate eastern businessmen about "the wealth of water power hidden in the Feather River Canyon" (Coleman 1952, 218). Members included the presidents of the American Tobacco Company, Standard Oil, Central Trust Company of New York, and Old Colony Trust Company, as well as the head of the Postal Telegraph Company. Consultants were hired: engineers to survey the reservoir site at Big Meadows and possible power sites in the canyon and power company leaders to examine the possible power markets. The surveys were positive, with engineers claiming, "No other water power in California can be so economically developed" (219). Cornell gave up and sold the Golden State Power Company to the Earls in 1906.

Also in 1906, San Francisco was largely destroyed by a massive earthquake and fire. Promoters of the hydroelectric project were able to use this disaster to raise additional backing for the Feather River Project, arguing that new sources of power would be needed to rebuild the West's great city. With increasing financial support, GWP was formed in September 1906, with the majority of shares held by the Western Power Company, a New Jersey holding company run by the group of powerful investors listed above. The Earls received a large amount of stock in the new company, as did other Feather River Project promoters, investors, and advisors. The board of directors was expanded to include Los Angeles, Oakland, and San Francisco businessmen, including railroad-man Henry E. Huntington. The Western Pacific Railroad was central to progress on the project, as the tracks to the station at Las Plumas (located across the Feather River from the Big Bend powerhouse site) were completed as the plant was being built, and facilitated the transport of building materials.

The Big Bend Powerhouse began generating electricity on December 23, 1908, becoming "the largest hydro operation west of the Mississippi" (222). Power traveled on steel lines to Sacramento and on to Oakland, where GWP sold it to the PG&E. PG&E, founded 1904 and incorporated in 1905, was another cabal of wealthy investors, which worked from 1905 to 1911 (weathering the financial catastrophe of the 1906 San Francisco earthquake) to consolidate the California Gas & Electric Corporation and the San Francisco Gas & Electric Corporation in order to develop and reach power markets and distribute electricity efficiently across the region (227–32). In 1912 the Public Utilities Act authorized the State Railroad Commission (which became the California Public Utilities

Commission in 1946) to regulate utilities in all of unincorporated California, and this was extended to all of California in 1915 (249).[23]

Similar to the way in which Alaska Native lands were sold by Russia to the United States and California Indian lands were conveyed from Spain to Mexico to the United States following the Treaty of Guadelupe Hidalgo, many Indigenous people residing in these territories were unaware that their homelands and waterways and, indeed, associated lifeways, had been negotiated away. As discussed further in chapter 2, a survey of Indian allotment records from northeastern California at the turn of the twentieth century reveals tireless efforts by allottees to retain rights to land. However, judges, federal agency employees, and businessmen in San Francisco, New York, and Washington, D.C., turned deaf ears to aboriginal rights. A century later, the Native (and allied) voices demanding justice would begin to receive limited concessions when dam licenses came up for renewal and when conservation land divestitures such as the Stewardship Council process made lands available.

Meanwhile, the PG&E investors' belief in California markets seemed to be paying off, as California's population grew in the first decade of the twentieth century by nearly 1 million people. According to Coleman's laudatory history of PG&E, "In 1911 more than 26,000 new gas, electric, and water customers were added to the P.G. and E. system in addition to 17,000 gained by purchase of other systems" (257). For its part, GWP did not like selling its electricity generated at the Big Bend project on the Feather River to PG&E in order to access the San Francisco Bay Area urban markets. In 1911 it purchased San Francisco's City Electric Company and added more bankers (the Fleishackers, with the Anglo California Trust Company and London Paris National Bank) to its governing body. GWP laid transbay cables to service San Francisco beginning in 1912 and was able to directly reach urban markets. GWP also sold power en route to the Bay to industrial users, agriculturalists, and others. By purchasing smaller electric companies serving cities and unincorporated areas, GWP became a significant competitor to PG&E by 1912 (269). GWP continued to expand its markets, including specific service to agricultural users with their Western Canal Company, formed in 1915. The 40 miles of canals owned by the Western Canal Company sent Feather River water diverted below Oroville to farms in Butte and Glenn counties. As with other GWP holdings, the Western Canal Company came under PG&E ownership in 1930.

From 1919 to 1921, GWP constructed its second power plant on the Feather River, at Caribou. The power from this station was sent to the Golden Gate substation near Richmond[24] and then carried via underwater cable to the city of

San Francisco (274). Caribou is remembered as a popular location for entertaining "bachelor operators of the plant" and "company guests" (274). These activities likely impacted Maidu society, as the Maidu / Pit River historian Beverly Ogle recalls that there was a Maidu settlement at Caribou and a trail that ran from Caribou to Butt Valley (1998, 32, 54). In 1928 GWP completed construction of the Bucks Creek Powerhouse, which conveys water from the higher Bucks Creek watershed 2,561 feet down penstock pipes into the North Fork Feather River.[25]

In order to increase the reliability of power generated downstream, GWP also created the reservoir at Big Meadows, named Lake Almanor after Earl's three daughters. According to Coleman, Julius Howells created the name Almanor by "combining syllables from the names of the three daughters of Vice-President Early—ALice, MArtha, EleaNOR" (269). The project began with clearing the land: "Much of the Big Meadows land was heavily forested, and the Red River Lumber Company, operated by T. B. Walker of Minnesota, was called upon to clear the wide area. A rail line was constructed and a sawmill erected to handle the logging job which produced some 300 million board feet of lumber" (Coleman 1952, 271). As such, Maidu lands in and around Big Meadows were allotted by the BIA, then either canceled by the agency and then transferred to Red River or sold to Red River directly, which harvested the timber and then likely sold the land to GWP.

The first dam at Big Meadows was the Eastwood Dam, constructed from 1911 to 1912 and named for the multiple-arch design of the engineer John H. Eastwood. Due to the geological conditions of the dam site, this dam was abandoned and a 300,000-acre-foot hydraulic fill earthen dam designed by the GWP engineer Julius Howells was completed in June 1914. In response to demand, GWP expanded this dam from 1925 to 1927, increasing the capacity to 1.3 million acre-feet. With a higher level of flooding in the Big Meadows basin, GWP moved roads, facilitated the removal of timber, and relocated a cemetery at Prattville "and three Indian burying grounds" (272). In 1930 GWP reported that the "historical cost" of lands in Big Meadows and Butt Valley was between approximately $31 and $37.50/acre (Rhodin 1930) (although we know from archival information that for some lands the amount paid was from nothing to $3.50/acre), and their current (1930) value was $125/acre (GWP 1930).

Today, the dam now owned and operated by PG&E remains one of the company's largest reservoirs. John Galloway, who was employed as a consulting engineer with GWP, voiced his passion for the Big Meadows Dam in 1923, calling it "the most important structure on the entire system of the power company."[26] Indeed, when the enlarged dam required repairs in 1928, its health was of significant concern to the Federal Power Commission as well as prominent downstream irrigators, all of whom were involved in discussions of how to repair the dam.[27]

The federal regulatory structure of hydropower development instituted with the Federal Power Act of 1920[28] might have easily contained provisions that would have protected Indian lands and waters from inundation by hydropower projects, but it did not. The act applied to facilities proposed on navigable waterways, in/on public lands "and reservations," and for the purpose of harnessing "surplus water or water power" from federal dam projects. Indian reservations were acknowledged specifically as only available for construction of hydropower facilities if the commission found "that the license will not interfere or be inconsistent with the purpose for which such reservation was created or acquired,"[29] but allotments were not mentioned. The purpose of an Indian reservation was generally to provide a home for Indian people safe from the depredations of white settlers—where Indian people might be separated from white society and where they might cultivate a living in the manner of the European yeoman farmer. While public domain Indian allotment lands are similar to reservations in that they are held in trust by the federal government for the benefit of the Indian beneficiary, their status as public domain allotments held in trust for individuals differentiates them from reservations set aside for tribes by treaty or executive order. Allotments can more easily be canceled and/or sold and then inundated than reservation lands, although both happened with frequency and marked inequity. The following example from Southern California illustrates the variation in the rates paid for condemnation of Indian land versus non-Indian owned land.

CAPITAN GRANDE / CITY OF SAN DIEGO

In the same time period in which Maidu public domain Indian allotments were being regularly canceled and sold with or without allottee approval for private hydroelectric development, an extensive legal/political process was underway for a local public project that involved condemnation of Kumeyaay lands in Southern California. While the Kumeyaay affected by the City of San Diego's water project had more of a process protecting their land rights, they still received less restitution for their lands than the surrounding non-Indian landowners. In fact, the geographer Imre Sutton described the Capitan Grande case as "an unconscionable act of land severance on the part of the City of San Diego" (1985, 228).

Between 1890 and 1920 San Diego grew by more than 58,000 people, and city leaders wanted to build a water project to serve this growing populace. The project, as proposed, would flood sections of the Capitan Grande Indian Reservation[30] and allow the development of the first large storage reservoir on the San Diego River (Pyle 1935). Per capita water use had been increasing steadily among San Diego residents—by nearly 55 percent between 1890 and 1922—attributed to "the extensive use made of water for gardens, lawns, parking and horticulture in Southern California." This was noted with pride by water engineers for the city and expected to continue to increase with further development, "as long as there is water to be developed" (1).

A 1922 list details the costs of resettling the Indigenous Capitan Grande residents, including purchasing the Barona Ranch and rebuilding homes, roads, and community facilities (church, school, administrative buildings, water, and other infrastructure). This inventory followed sections 3 and 4 of the Act of February 28, 1919 (40 Stat. L. 1206) that authorized the city to condemn the Capitan Grande lands needed for the water project. The total expenditure to resettle the Capitan Grande Indians at Barona was to be $308,900, accounting for inflation over the project period.[31] The value of the land, improvements, and water rights of the property that the Capitan Grande members would be losing was estimated at $361,428.[32] This was ultimately a small portion of the total cost of the project, which was approximately $5.8 million (Pyle 1935). Funding came at least partially from the federal government, in the form of a 1919 grant.

However, later in 1930, an irrigation district with significant interests in the project area brought a complaint against the City of San Diego.[33] The district alleged that it held water rights and associated water infrastructure to deliver water both on the Capitan Grande Indian Reservation and below it, along the San Diego River. As part of this infrastructure and system of rights, the district held a 13-mile right-of-way, first granted in 1888 to its predecessor the San Diego Flume Company, across a portion of the Capitan Grande Indian Reservation. The complaint offers a history of the ownership of the lands and waters of the San Diego River and argues that the City of San Diego never received a water right to the river (Pyle 1935, 10). In 1931 Mr. Swing introduced a bill in the House of Representatives to amend the 1919 Act of Congress (40 Stat. L. 1206) that granted the City of San Diego specific lands of the Capitan Grade Indian Reservation for damming and inundation to serve the growing city.[34]

In 1932 the San Diego River Project issued a list of costs to buy out the land rights and build the water project facilities. The average price per acre of the rancho (i.e., Rancho El Cajon) and farms (i.e., Riverview and Lakeside Farms) involved was $305.54 (with portions of Riverview Farms valued the highest at $553.50/acre). However, on the Capitan Grande Indian Reservation the value

The

MUNICIPAL EMPLOYEE

SUBSCRIPTION P R I C E
ONE DOLLAR PER YEAR

PUBLISHED IN THE INTERESTS OF CITY EMPLOYEES BY·
THE SAN DIEGO MUNICIPAL EMPLOYEES' ASSOCIATION

Volume III	FEBRUARY, 1935	No. 8

El Capitan
Dam and
Reservoir

By Fred D. Pyle,
Hydraulic Engineer

View of El Capitan Dam and Appurtenances from Upstream Side

HISTORICAL.—About 340 years ago the first white men sailed into the harbor of San Diego to take on fresh water, and since that time water has been a major problem for the inhabitants of this promising locality. In fact, the first irrigation development in San Diego County was constructed about 1800, by the Franciscan Mission Fathers, of which Junipero Serra was the leader. This development consisted of a small diversion dam across the San Diego River, where it enters Mission Gorge fourteen miles above its mouth, and a ditch six miles long, of which three miles were mortar and tile lined, to carry water to the mission lands. Today the City of San Diego, with a population of 170,000, has a water supply system valued at more than $20,000,000, and has just constructed the first large reservoir for storage of water on the San Diego River. The total estimated cost of this reservoir, and a 25-mile reach of conduit to connect with existing University Heights standby reservoir in San Diego, is $5,800,000.

When the Pueblo of San Diego and Mission San Diego del Alcala were established under Spanish grant as the first settlement of Alta California in 1769, all the water of the San Diego river was made the property of the pueblo. For many years this fact was forgotten, but when recalled it led to serious legal complications in water rights. After extended court action the City was decreed to possess in fee simple the prior and paramount right to use all surface and underground waters of the San Diego river from its source to its mouth. The present El Capitan development will provide a net safe duty of 11.6 million gallons of water a day with 10 million gallons a day available for the City's use, or enough water for nearly 100,000 people.

Population and Water Use.—Since establishment of the Pueblo, the average population growth has been 1,000 per year, but more than half of the present population has come in the last twelve years. This has required a great increase in water facilities. The El Capitan development is the first of three reservoirs in the San Diego river drainage basin which will eventually supplement existing sources of supply.

In 1929 the City had a developed supply of about fifteen million gallons of water a day from the Morena, Barrett, Otay and Hodges reservoirs, supplemented by underground development along the San Diego river.

Population growth in the past forty years is indicative of the rapid growth of San Diego:

Year	Population	Gallons per capita per day	Gallons total year
1890	16,159		
1900	17,700	74	478,000,000
1910	40,748	111	1,650,000,000
1920	74,361	136	3,691,000,000
1925	121,000	111	4,902,000,000
1930	147,995	116	6,266,000,000
1935*	170,000	120	7,446,000,000

*Estimated

A general increase in the per capita consumption of water may be noted. Many European cities use only forty to sixty gallons per capita per day. The extensive use made of water for gardens, lawns, parking and horticulture in Southern California, aided by the exceptionally fine climate, is in a large measure responsible for the increase in population. These same factors will result in further growth and development, which will continue as long as there is water to be developed.

Preliminaries—The present development of the El Capitan feature of the San Diego River Project, was made possible by the following:

1. A grant by the United States Government approved February 28, 1919, of 1940

(Continued on Page 4)

FIGURE 3. View of El Capitan Dam and appurtenances from the upstream side.

was much less—as low as $38.66/acre for the vast majority of lands (3,579 acres) involved in the project.[35] Timbered Indian allotments in the Plumas region were valued at a similar price per acre in the same time period. When there was restitution for Indian lands to be inundated for public water projects, the prices that Indian landowners received were generally substantially less than those received by their white counterparts.

CALIFORNIA WATER PROJECTS: BUILDING CALIFORNIA'S WATER INFRASTRUCTURE

Policymakers generally define the problem of California's water situation as both seasonal (wet winters, dry summers) and spatial (more water / less population in the north, less water / more population in the south) (SWRB 1956, 1). Throughout the development of the SWP and the Central Valley Project (CVP), the articulated purpose was to capture the "surplus"[36] waters of the north state's rivers (i.e., the Feather, Sacramento, San Joaquin, Eel) from the Delta and export them to the farms and cities located to the south. Native California nations on both ends of these systems were impacted. The northern tribes lost water and land rights to private and public projects, as well as the associated fisheries and cultural practices tied to the land area, while the southern tribes were displaced from their homelands for development and, if compensated, received far less than non-Native landowners. Tribes on both ends of the system struggled to access any "benefits" of the supposed progress built on their displacement.

Like many large-scale water projects, the plans for Lake Oroville were in the making long before Concow or Mountain Maidu people that stood to be most directly impacted were informed of them. The U.S. Geological Service began gauging flows on the Feather River beginning in 1901 (SWRB 1951, 21, 26), and in 1902 started calculating the impact of the upstream diversions and initial impoundments (23).

In 1919 Colonel Robert B. Marshall, chief geographer of the U.S. Geological Service, proposed moving water south from the Sacramento River through large irrigation canals. Data was collected beginning in the 1920s at the different upstream reservoir sites, including at Prattville and Almanor, to increase the accuracy of data on the "impaired runoff" of the Feather River downstream at Oroville (SWRB 1951, 24, 27). In 1921 the State of California authorized a comprehensive statewide water resources investigation, which contributed to the development of both the CVP and the SWP.

Simultaneously, throughout the early twentieth century, GWP, which became part of PG&E in 1930, was steadily developing the infrastructure that would form the upstream basis of the SWP system. In 1924 the company completed

Table I

ANNUAL FLOWS OF THE FEATHER RIVER AT OROVILLE DAM SITE
Drainage Area 3,610 square miles

All quantities in 1,000 acre-feet

Year	Natural flow	Present impaired flow	Year	Natural flow	Present impaired flow
1902	4,695.5	4,329.0	1926	3,609.8	3,215.8
03	5,419.7	5,016.7	27	5,416.8	4,644.4
04	8,714.1	8,427.6	28	3,867.8	3,436.9
1905	4,025.5	3,745.1	29	2,618.4	2,660.8
			1930	3,237.5	2,934.7
06	7,316.4	6,913.2			
07	9,389.4	9,024.5	31	1,619.8	1,445.5
08	3,369.3	3,137.6	32	3,077.3	2,504.9
09	8,157.2	7,722.9	33	2,042.5	1,771.5
1910	4,066.3	3,830.4	34	2,032.6	1,787.6
			1935	4,179.5	3,759.8
11	6,990.2	6,603.5			
12	2,318.3	2,087.9	1936	4,217.8	3,942.2
13	3,073.7	2,761.2	37	4,489.4	3,984.4
14	7,868.5	7,440.9	38	7,325.6	7,065.0
1915	6,195.8	5,861.7	39	1,747.2	1,550.8
			1940	6,301.3	5,815.2
16	7,080.2	6,708.8			
17	4,820.2	4,493.9	41	6,614.2	6,156.0
18	2,790.2	2,575.5	42	6,282.6	5,943.1
19	3,583.6	3,235.9	43	5,189.6	4,886.8
1920	3,123.4	2,874.8	44	3,063.5	2,762.8
			1945	4,031.7	4,026.8
21	5,136.3	4,756.2			
22	5,245.5	4,880.4	46	3,240.3	3,235.4
23	2,790.3	2,510.4	47	2,193.3	2,208.6
24	1,419.9	1,201.2			
1925	3,106.9	2,687.6			

The mean annual natural and impaired flows for the period 1902–1947 are 4,502,100 acre-feet and 4,186,200 acre-feet, respectively, and the same flows for the period 1921–1947 are 3,855,500 acre-feet and 3,547,200 acre-feet respectively.

FIGURE 4. Table demonstrating annual water flows. (SWRB 1951, 26,)

the dam at Butt Valley just below Big Meadows / Lake Almanor, filled the reservoir at Butt Valley Lake, and issued a plan to fix the tunnel to Caribou with the least loss in hydroelectric generation.[37] In 1926, although GWP considered developing power plants on Silver Creek, a branch of the American River, consulting engineer Galloway advised instead expanding the number of power plants on the North Fork Feather River, because the company already had water rights there and the larger company reservoir at Lake Almanor. He advised that plants could be built on the Feather River and energy delivered more cheaply to Sacramento than from the American River.[38] In 1927 Galloway and another engineer, Euler, assessed the Tunnel No. 1, which conveyed the majority of the water to the Caribou plant, and decided to build a second tunnel to expand capacity, carry flows while the first was being repaired, and improve fall for electric generation.[39]

In 1931 the state engineer Edward Hyatt delivered a "State Water Plan" discussing supply, needs, and engineering to the state legislature and formally recommended the construction of Oroville Dam, initially planned to impound 1.7 million acre-feet of water (Division of Water Resources 1931). In 1937 the federal Natural Resources Committee completed a report on "Drainage Basin Problems and Programs."[40] The "California District" segment of the report advised that the state was in urgent need of redistribution of its water supply. The report recognized the state's own study of its water resources and advocated for correlating federal water planning with the 1931 State Water Plan. Further, the federal report noted that both Los Angeles and San Francisco had expanded their water supplies with projects drawing water from the Colorado River and the Mokelumne and Tuolumne rivers, respectively, but the largest shortages were faced by farmers in the San Joaquin Valley, who had both water quality and quantity issues. To address this, the Bureau of Reclamation was investing in the CVP to "redistribute the waters of the Central Valley" by taking "surpluses from the Sacramento River" to "supplement existing supplies in the San Joaquin Valley" (Natural Resources Committee 1938, 47).

In 1941 the legislature adopted the plan to build the Oroville Dam (SWRB 1951, 3). Two federal agencies (the Department of the Interior and the Army Corps of Engineers) issued recommendations in 1945 to control the Sacramento and San Joaquin rivers via reservoirs on the Middle (Bidwell Bar) and North (Big Bar, Greenville) forks of the Feather River rather than at Oroville, but the state countered that more studies were needed to determine whether those reservoirs would really be more economical than the Oroville site proposed in

Reservoir	Branch of river on which located	Storage capacity
Lake Almanor	North Fork	649,800 acre-feet
Butt Valley	"	50,000 "
Buck's Storage	"	103,000 "
Buck's Diversion	"	5,843 "
Mountain Meadows	"	24,000 "
Three Lakes	"	513 "
Grizzly Forebay	"	1,112
Rock Creek	"	4,660
Cresta	"	4,440
Round Valley	West Branch	1,285 "
Philbrook	"	4,875 "
Lake Wilenor	"	8,600 "
Lost Creek	South Fork	5,200 "

The power and irrigation diversions which do not return to the stream above Oroville are:

Name	Annual Diversion
Palermo Canal	14,500 acre-feet
Forbestown Ditch	15,500 "
Hendricks Canal	41,000 "
Miocene and Wilenor Canals	38,100 "
Total	109,100 acre-feet

In addition to the foregoing developments and diversions, the Oroville-Wyandotte Irrigation District is giving consideration to the development of a power and irrigation project on the South Fork of the Feather River above Oroville. The proposed plan is to store 42,000 acre-feet at the Little Grass Valley reservoir site on the main South Fork and 55,000 acre-feet at the Lost-Sly reser-

FIGURE 5. This table lists the upstream reservoirs that impact the proposed State Water Project system, indicating the way in which PG&E and state projects are intertwined on the Feather River. (SWRB 1951, 2.)

the State Water Plan (3). Subsequent studies by the Bureau of Reclamation found that, indeed, the state's proposal was more economical, because the storage capacity of the Big Bend site on the north fork was much lower than initial studies had predicted (4).

While the early part of the century saw dominance in private, local, and federal projects, the State of California's engagement in water policy, planning, and development of public water works steadily formalized and increased over the twentieth century. The California State Legislature passed the first State Water Resources Act in 1945,[41] which included a detailed State Water Policy and directives and established a seven-member, governor-appointed State Water Resources Board (6). While the focus of water planning continued to emphasize flood control and the storage and conveyance of "surplus" waters north to south, a 1947 amendment to the act added water conservation as a goal. To date, California Native Nations, despite their first-in-time water rights as recognized by the U.S. Supreme Court in the *Winters* (1908) decision, have not had formal roles (aside from the work facilitated by tribal liaisons or tribal working groups) on state water policy and management bodies.

In 1949 the DWR recommended that the Oroville Reservoir be 3.5 million acre-feet in order to effectively capture all of the Feather's flows from a 3,610-square-mile drainage, control its passage into and through the valley, and maximize its irrigation and electricity generation potential (20). The report acknowledged the important effect that the upstream reservoirs (primarily licensed to PG&E) would have on the operation of the reservoir at Oroville (22).

Also in 1949 the involved federal agencies (the Army Corps of Engineers and the Bureau of Reclamation within the Department of the Interior) and state engineers issued a joint statement underscoring the importance of constructing a large-scale multipurpose project on the Feather River and the appropriateness of the Oroville site: "The Feather River above Oroville with a mean annual runoff of 4.5 million acre-feet, represents 1/5 of the runoff of the entire Sacramento River Basin; and a substantial part of the surplus waters that may be developed over and above local needs could be made available for exportation to areas of deficient water supplies. Therefore, these waters should be conserved and utilized to the fullest practicable extent in planning for the development of the waters of the State" (5–6). With the blessing of Elmer Marliave, the supervising engineering geologist for the DWR, who examined the proposed site and reported that a 700-foot-high earthen dam could be built there (43), work on the project moved forward. In order to build the 3.5 million-acre-foot reservoir, a portion of both the mainline of the Southern Pacific Railroad (including 23 miles of track, five tunnels, and three bridges) and State Highway 24 (18 miles) would have to be relocated. In addition, a total of nearly 26,000 acres of land with associated improvements would need to be secured (44–48).

The study estimated the cost for the Oroville Dam project, in 1951 dollars, to be $342.6 million for the dam and an additional $64.5 million for the power plant (50). The associated Oroville afterbay dam, reservoir and power plant would cost another $14.1 million. With the addition of the Delta Cross Channel, the total cost of the Feather River Project was estimated at $444.8 million.

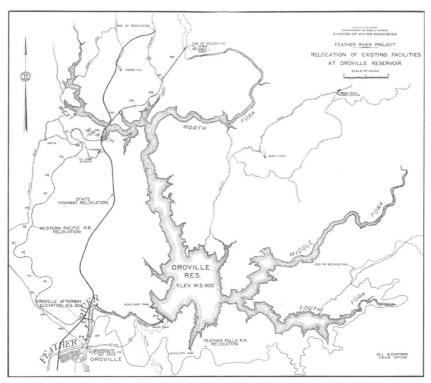

MAP 1. Map representing the changes that would be wrought by the Oroville Dam. From the files of Bernard A. Etcheverry, longtime University of California, Berkeley, civil engineering professor, known as the Father of Irrigation Engineering. Etcheverry served as a consultant to the State Engineer on the State Water Plan. Etcheverry was also appointed to the first State Water Resources Board in 1945, and was serving as its vice chairman at the time of his death in 1954.(Filed in Bernard A. Etcheverry papers, Water Resources Collections and Archives, ETCH Box 1, Folder 1.6, plate 2.)

PG&E data on power system loads and requirements was used during the planning of the Feather River Project to assess the efficiency of the proposed power plant at Oroville Dam. The idea was to generate the maximum amount of power while not compromising the primary goals of the system (flow regulation, irrigation, flood control) and to operate the system with power generated on-site (30). A study conducted from 1921 to 1947 indicated that significant power (1.7 billion kWh of electric energy) and irrigation (500,000 acre-feet/year) could have been generated if facilities had been up and running at Oroville during that time period (32). When data from the Feather River was added to that of other facilities at the Shasta Dam and Folsom Dam, the net water available for irrigation from the delta was 2.8 million acre-feet annually (36). The effect of such studies was to galvanize project supporters to find the funding to institute the project so that they could convey and utilize these services downstream.

The state legislature and the new State Water Resources Board funded the comprehensive development of the State Water Plan. The development of the plan involved three phases: an inventory of California water resources (1951), an examination of current and future water needs (1955), and a planning document for the management and conveyance of California water resources (1957).[42] The phased studies cost more than $8 million (California Department of Water Resources 1959b), and examined population growth, agricultural water needs, and California's untapped hydropower and water storage potential (Division of Water Resources Staff 1955, 10). Regarding irrigation, the study found that the 7 million irrigated acres used 90 percent of California's water, while up to 13 million more acres were irrigable (9, 11–12; SWRB 1951, 7–8). Regarding hydropower, the study found that 2.8 kW were generated in 1953, far below the potential 10.7 kW that could be generated.

While the pending water plan focused on moving waters from north to south to facilitate development and support population growth (Division of Water Resources Staff 1955, 17), the rights of upstream regions were to be protected by "county of origin" requirements that reserved water for local development (Water Code of California, Section 10505). The recommendations to facilitate the conveyance of water from north to south were massive, including construction of dams, storage reservoirs, power plants on "nearly every stream in the state," and an extensive aqueduct system that would move more than 23 million acre-feet of water from "the Oregon line to the Mexican border" (Division of Water Resources Staff 1955, 17). The Feather River was "the most important tributary of the Sacramento River," with a huge drainage area and erratic seasonal flows that could be both tempered for flood control and stored to send "surplus" waters to drier areas (SWRB 1951, 2). The SWP was to kickoff with the Feather River Project, "the first state wide project ever proposed for California," including the dam at Oroville, planned to be the largest in the United States (Division of Water Resources Staff 1955, 23).

The DWR attempted to convince upstream jurisdictions of the necessity and benefits of the project. In a 1957 address to the Northern California Supervisor's Association entitled "Northern California's Stake in the California Water Plan," DWR director Harvey Banks called the plan "one of the greatest forward steps in the history of California," dismissed the "'threats' to the water supplies of northern California" as an ongoing issue not limited to the Feather River, and promised financial and other support for the development of upstream projects to protect upstream interests.[43] He underscored that "there is more than enough water for all if properly controlled, conserved, and distributed," citing the estimate that Californians were only using 23 of the available 70 million acre-feet of water available in the state per year, and letting the other 50 million

COMPARISON OF OROVILLE DAM WITH OTHER
MAJOR DAMS IN UNITED STATES

	:Height, in :feet above :stream bed	: Crest : length,: : in feet:	: Gross : reservoir : storage :capacity, :in acre-feet:	Volume of : concrete, : in cubic yards	: : : :	Volume of earth embankment, in cubic yards
Oroville (earth)	735*	5,760	3,500,000	----		79,814,000
Shasta (concrete)	602	3,460	4,500,000	6,541,000		----
Trinity (earth)	465	2,450	2,500,000	----		33,180,000
Boulder (concrete)	726	1,244	31,140,000	3,764,835		----
Grand Coulee (concrete)	550	4,173	9,517,000	10,585,000		----

* Will be the highest dam in the United States

FIGURE 6. Comparison between the proposed Oroville Dam and other major dams in the United States. (L.A. Public Information Office, with data from the State Dept. of Water Resources, 1959, filed in Cooper 76/10, Box 8, WRCA.)

acre-feet "waste" into the ocean. This view, that all water available could be put to a "productive" use of development and agriculture, controlled by storage to ensure availability throughout the year and to reduce flood risk, completely ignored diverse cultural perspectives and needs of upstream tribes, tribal water rights, and ecological needs such as in-stream flows that support the life cycles of anadromous fish.

In 1959 the Los Angeles Public Information Office drew on data from the DWP to compare the SWP with the Federal CVP. The SWP was to be funded by the California Water Resources Development Bond Act (California Stats 1959, chapter 1762, p. 4234). Funding from the sale of the bonds and the California water fund would be used to build the Oroville Dam and five dams upstream, as well as a water conveyance system to serve the San Francisco Bay area, the San Joaquin Valley, and parts of Southern California.[44] Primary proponents of the Bond Act included Southern California interests, agriculturalists, and urban interests, whereas primary opponents included labor interests. The first phase of the SWP, the Feather River Project, was scheduled to provide 3.8 million acre-feet of water annually from the delta to points south ("Substantiation" 1959).

Governor Edmond Brown posed California's water problems as particularly urgent in a January 1960 address to urge voters to support the California Water Bond in the upcoming election. He argued that Northern California was "wasting huge quantities of water" in floods and by letting water escape to the ocean, "completely unused," while Central and Southern California were regularly facing "critical" water shortages (Brown 1960). The bond would fund the completion of the SWP, already begun with the preparations for construction of the Oroville Dam. From Lake Oroville, water would be released to the delta, and from the delta, it would be sent down the South Bay Aqueduct (to serve Alameda and Santa Clara Counties) and down the North Bay Aqueduct (to serve Marin, Napa, Sonoma, and Solano Counties), south to the San Luis Reservoir (to store water for export to the southern San Joaquin Valley and Southern California, the latter to be pumped over the Tehachapis into the West Branch Aqueduct to serve Los Angeles County and into the East Branch Aqueduct to serve Riverside, San Bernardino, and San Diego Counties). The bond would also fund local water development projects in Northern California—both the Sierras and the Coast Range. The 1.7 billion in bonds that voters would consider in the 1960 election included $130 million for small local projects in the Grunsky-Davis Act (State of California, Department of Water Resources, 1959).

Land acquisitions for the project were underway by 1956, when the legislature authorized $9.3 million for the Feather River and Delta Diversion Projects (SWP, together) for planning, surveying, and acquisition of properties and rights of way. An additional $273,000 was set aside for the acquisition of dam and reservoir sites for the five upstream reservoirs on the Feather River system (Department of Water Resources 1959, 6). Appropriations continued in 1957, 1958, and 1959, at a total cost of $111 million. DWR's efforts to acquire the public

This map shows the main features of the Feather River Project which would transfer Northern California surplus waters to San Joaquin Valley, coastal areas and Southern California. The drainage conduit would be a runoff channel for irrigation water between the Delta Pool and Kings River, 175 miles to the South. Proposition I, if passed Nov. 8 by Californians, would provide most of the funds for building this unprecedented State water project.

MAP 2. 1950s-era map outlining the plan for the proposed Feather River Project / State Water Project. (Filed in Erwin Cooper papers, Water Resources Center Archives, University of California, Riverside.)

and private lands required for the project got a boost in 1959, when the state legislature appropriated $69 million for the acquisition of lands and rights-of-way associated with the Oroville and upstream Feather River Dams, as well as the San Luis Reservoir and project construction (7). By 1962 (for the upstream reservoirs) and 1968 (for the Oroville Dam and Reservoir), initial water deliveries were already being made ("Summary" n.d.).

Despite the wrangling between state and federal interests at the outset of the SWP, some of the funding for the massive SWP came from the federal CVP. The keystone facility of the CVP is Shasta Reservoir (with a capacity 4.5 million acre-feet) on the Sacramento River. The CVP encompasses a 400-mile system for flood management, hydroelectric generation, and water conveyance from Wintu, Hupa, and Karuk homelands in the north (the McCloud, Upper Sacramento, and Trinity Rivers and their tributaries) all the way to Kumeyaay Country (in San Diego County) in the south. The Central Valley Project Act of 1933 (Chapter 1042, California Statutes 1933) that enabled the construction of the project included the establishment of a new state agency, the Water Project Authority, with members including the director of Public Works, director of finance, attorney general, state controller, and state treasurer, which was to issue and sell bonds for $170 million to fund the CVP build-out.

The promoters of the SWP pointed out persistently that, while the reservoir facilitated flood control in the upper Sacramento River, more flood control was needed along the middle and lower Sacramento, as "the entire area between Feather River and Sutter Basin south of Gridley with the exception of the Marysville Buttes was subject to inundation."[45] Of course, this flooding was essential to maintaining the local riparian ecology, which had already been disrupted by agriculture and gold mining by the mid-twentieth century and by "reclamation districts" to control the flooding via levees and other mechanisms beginning in 1873 (SWRB 1951, 53). However, the impact of the floods that occurred in the late nineteenth and early twentieth centuries in and around the Feather River watershed cities of Oroville, Marysville, Yuba City, Gridley, and Colusa was measured in terms of the "value" of the lands impacted, which was measured by agricultural quality and urban and other improvements.[46] In 1950 a study of the value of the properties (including improvements) in the area subject to inundation (the "Feather River floodplain") found a net worth of $340.4 million, vulnerable to inundation by the Feather unless the facility at Oroville was built (72–73). The project supporters argued that substantial flood control could be provided by the SWP and should be supported by federal funds (57, 79).

The 1937 Rivers and Harbors Act (Public No. 392, 75th Congress, 1st Session), in reauthorizing funding for the CVP, emphasized that its core purposes were "improving navigation, regulating the flow of the San Joaquin River and the Sacramento River, controlling floods, providing for storage and for the delivery of the stored waters thereof, for the reclamation of arid and semiarid lands and lands of Indian reservations, and other beneficial uses, and for the generation and sale of electric energy (13–14)." Power generation was explicitly listed last, until "preservation of fish and wildlife" was added to the list (16). Power generation and sale was to be for the purpose of funding the project operation and supporting the other activities of the project. The CVP, as such, did not have electric energy production as its core purpose, while the project that became the SWP was already partially built out at the headwaters as a primarily electricity-producing project, because initial works on the Feather were built by GWP and its predecessor companies to generate and convey power to the emerging Central Valley and San Francisco Bay Area markets. With the CVP, the federal government made it clear that it was in the business of supporting projects that accomplished river regulation, navigation, flood control, and agriculture, with power generation as a decidedly lower priority (14, 16). Work began on the CVP in 1937, water began collecting in the Shasta and Friant Reservoirs in 1943–44, and the first power was generated from the project in 1944 (17).

Despite wrangling between federal and state interests early in the planning of the SWP, the SWP and other water projects under Governor Brown's tenure enjoyed a generally high degree of federal support. In 1966 California was awarded $144.3 million for more than 100 water projects in the public works bill approved by the House Appropriations Committee. Congressman and chair of the House Appropriations Committee Michael Kirwan lauded Brown's leadership, California's investments in state water works, and its cooperation with the federal government: "All of the things they have accomplished in California have been coordinated with the federal programs for the conservation and utilization of our water resources. In building California and the West, we really are building America."[47]

On November 5, 1966, Feather River water got closer to the Los Angeles Basin when construction began on the Angeles Tunnel of the SWP. The tunnel would convey water from the Pyramid Reservoir to the Castaic Reservoir, where it would be stored and generate power at the Castaic Power Plant. In a press release, Governor Brown heralded the 4-mile-long, 30-foot-diameter tunnel as "one of the great water conveyances of the world."[48] Further, in 1967 the California Society of Professional Engineers named the nearly completed Oroville Dam one of the seven wonders of engineering in California. In 2009 in a continued race-blind celebration of colonialism, the U.S. Postal Service included the dam in a series of 40 stamps entitled "Wonders of America: Land of Superlatives," because it remains America's tallest dam (770 feet).

MAP 3. Current SWP facilities. (Courtesy of the DWR.)

PG&E AND THE FEATHER RIVER POWERLAND

The proposed SWP was of great interest to academics, agriculturalists, urban developers, and politicians. In 1957 the University of California hydraulic engineering professor Hans Albert Einstein (son of the physicist) attended a popular 3-day University of California tour of the "Feather River Powerland," which now included six functioning hydroelectric plants on the North Fork Feather River,[49] three additional plants under construction,[50] and one planned.[51] The tour was to travel from the University of California, Berkeley, all the way to Prattville at the edge of Big Meadows, touring the plants along the river, including the proposed Oroville Dam site, and then returning to campus (University of California 1957). PG&E offered the tour with pride, noting that, once their 10-dam stairway of power was complete, "the Feather River will . . . be California's greatest producer of hydroelectric power. This construction will complete Pacific Gas & Electric Company's development of the hydroelectric potential between Lake Almanor, the principal storage reservoir, and the upstream end of a reservoir to be created by the State of California's construction of the Oroville Dam" (PG&E c. 1957).

PG&E's high level of construction on the North Fork Feather River was reflective of its other operations throughout the state. PG&E continued to grow steadily throughout the 1950s. In 1954 the company reported record sales of gas and electricity, the highest gross operating revenues it had ever had ($386.2 million), and the largest number of customers (2.9 million, following the merger of Coast Counties Gas & Electric Company and acquisition of the Pacific Public Service Company) (PG&E 1954b). PG&E also continued developing new plants to enhance power production on rivers like the Feather: work had begun on the Poe Hydro Plant on the Feather River, and the Federal Power Commission authorized licenses for three new hydro plants, Butt Valley, Caribou #2, and Belden (PG&E 1954a, 9). In 1956 the company reported its highest-ever gross operating revenues of $470.7 million, up 6 percent from the previous year, but it noted that these gains would have been even higher were it not for climate variations that reduced demand (PG&E 1956). According to the company, it had increased its electric generating capacity from 1.6 million kW in 1945 to 4.5 million kW in 1957, making its hydroelectric system "the largest investor-owned hydroelectric system in the United States" (PG&E 1957). PG&E was striving to prepare to meet the energy demand of the growing population of California,[52] and by 1956 its customer base was already 3.2 million Northern and Central Californians (a 123,181 increase from the previous year).

P·G and E's
FEATHER RIVER
Powerland

Rock Creek Powerhouse

PACIFIC GAS & ELECTRIC COMPANY

FIGURE 7. Cover for promotional brochure on the "PG&E Powerland," or "Feather River Powerland." This document lauds PG&E's "Stairway of Power" in the Feather River Canyon. (University of California 1957.)

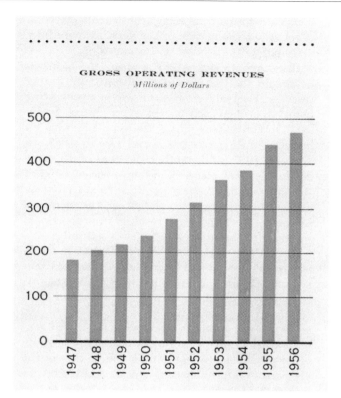

FIGURE 8. PG&E gross operating revenues, 1956. (PG&E 1956.)

Two years later in 1958, PG&E reported a gross operating revenue of $534.7 million, a 6.7 percent increase from 1957, despite the lower-than-anticipated sales of natural gas due to warm weather and increases in electric and gas rates (PG&E 1958, 7). PG&E was also continuing construction and expansion, adding 685,500 kW of electric generating capacity in 1958 alone, for a total of 5.2 million kW in 76 plants around Northern and Central California. The company had grown to 3.5 million customers and 18,000 employees. Concern with government regulation is particularly apparent in the 1958 annual report, in which the chairman of the board and company president noted:

> The Company's well-being as a business enterprise will depend largely upon the wisdom with which governmental policies are formulated and administered. Policies calculated to encourage further encroachment by governmental agencies into the commercial power business, or policies that would result in further inflation

and erosion of the purchasing power of the dollar would be harmful not only to
our investors but to our customers and employees as well . . .

Similarly, the Company's well-being as a public utility will be affected in
large degree by the wisdom with which the regulatory power is exercised at both
the federal and state levels. Properly exercised, regulation provides public utility
enterprises with an element of stability which protects the investor as well as the
consumer. (Chairman of the Board and N. R. Sutherland [president] 1958b)

The company's 1959 Annual Report lauded the previous decade's "exceptional
growth and prosperity," due to population increases, industrial expansion, and agricultural mechanization, all of which increased demand for the company's electricity
and gas. Revenues in 1959 were $583.4 million (approx. two-thirds from electric sales
and one-third from gas sales), a 9.1 percent increase from 1958 (PG&E 1958a, 5).

Based on its $2.4 billion in assets, the company again described itself as "the
Nation's largest gas and electric operating utility" (PG&E 1959b, 3). Indeed, the
company's sales volume of 21.5 billion kWh in 1959 "exceeded that of any other
operating electric utility in the United States" (PG&E 1959a, 13). The company
served 1.9 million electric customers and reported connecting 5,000 new customers each month in 1959 (14). The company also continued to work closely
with the federal government, and the agreement to manage the power (inputs
and outputs) supporting the CVP was extended from the original 1951–59 period
to 1971. However, the company's proposal to jointly develop the Trinity River
water/power with the federal government as an extension of the CVP was
rejected by the House of Representatives.

The relationship between the federal and state governments and the company was a delicate one, as the company relied on a favorable regulatory environment. The president and chairman of the board reiterated the company's
concern with the possibility of public encroachment on their sovereignty, indicating a larger political struggle during this time period: "We would be remiss if
we did not direct the attention of stockholders to some threats to the otherwise
bright future we envision for our Company. One is the continuing efforts of a
small but vocal group which has as its objective government ownership of the
electric power industry. The fundamental issues involved in this struggle are
the preservation of our personal liberties and the private enterprise system. If
our industry falls to the blandishments of the socialists, other industries will
almost certainly be engulfed by the same force" (4). It was PG&E's relationship
with the state and attempted utility deregulation that led to the company's
bankruptcy proceedings in 2000. PG&E then entered into an out-of-court

settlement with the California Public Utilities Commission, approved in 2003, resulting in the plan to divest itself of 68,899 acres of land nonessential to utility operations and have conservation restrictions placed on 140,301 acres. As the process has progressed, PG&E is retaining title to an additional 32,901 acres of its lands (for a total of approximately 101,800 acres retained), bringing the total to be divested down to approximately 38,500 acres (Pacific Stewardship Council 2015). PG&E also continues to hold water rights on all parcels. As illustrated by Maidu engagement with PG&E over time, this text is explicitly interested in the relationship between public regulations and agencies and private corporations, as the two spheres combine to institutionalize Indigenous exclusion from decision-making about traditional lands and waters.

BENEFITS AND LOSSES

After the SWP was approved in 1960, entities who stood to receive water from the system signed contracts for allocations of water. The first contract was signed between the DWR and the Metropolitan Water District of Southern California in 1960. The majority of the 29 other contracts were signed between 1961 and 1965, as the SWP was built out between 1957 and 1973.

Who benefited from the SWP, which stopped the passage of salmon up the Feather River beyond Oroville and completed a series of ongoing impacts on the North Fork Feather River system that had once sustained thousands of Maidu? The promised flood control and increased water for agriculture and urban development could have been provided much differently if the system was designed to always protect and foreground Native American cultural and community survival and the fragile ecologies of California. The destruction of the communities and associated ecosystems are not requirements of development; they are the result of natural resources development policies that frame Indigenous peoples and their land and waterscapes as externalities of development, if they are considered at all. One goal of this book is to think through the logic that created the SWP, which caused so much destruction and trauma for Maidu and others, examine how it is perpetuated today in how the system is accepted and continues to operate while Maidu remain collectively nearly landless at the headwaters, and envision how a more just policy may be developed in current and future land and water management decisions.

The question of benefits received from the SWP may be better posed as "who benefitted most," and the answer may be traced partly to a struggle over the meaning and application of a clause in Section 5 of the 1902 Reclamation Bill known as the excess land law, which states that water furnished from public irrigation projects could not be purchased to irrigate private single-owner parcels over 160 acres. According to Paul S. Taylor, this clause effectively "limited 'the amount of project water available to each individual in order that benefits may be distributed in accordance with the greatest good to the greatest number of individuals.'"[53] President Theodore Roosevelt was an early supporter of the acreage limitation in a 1901 message to Congress: "The Government should make clear . . . its intention to pursue [reclamation] policy on lines of the broadest public interest. No reservoir or canal should ever be built to satisfy selfish personal or local interests."[54] Despite these concerns, the geographer Rodney Steiner's research on large landholdings in California found that the aqueduct in fact increased the concentration of large agricultural landholdings in the southern San Joaquin Valley (1982, 323–24).

Among the complexities of the development of the SWP were the regulations governing the San Luis Reservoir portion of the project, which would be a joint federal/state facility serving both a federal and state service area. On December 30, 1961, the DWR and the U.S. Bureau of Reclamation committed to share costs of land, rights-of-way, and construction of joint-use facilities, including the San Luis Reservoir. It was not clear whether the acreage limitation that applied to federal projects would apply to state projects, particularly because Section 8 of the 1902 Reclamation Act upheld state sovereignty.[55] A group of large landowners in the southern San Joaquin Valley saw the potential benefit of low-cost irrigation water to be delivered via the project. However, this benefit would be lost if regulations regarding excess land holdings were applied to their extensive land ownership. As Senator Douglas voiced his frustration in 1959: "The current effort to escape acreage limitation is 'one of the greatest land steals that has ever been attempted in the history of this nation.'"[56]

Landholding interests in the southern San Joaquin Valley became very concerned about federal regulations associated with federal water projects when it became clear that the San Luis Reservoir portion of the SWP would be a joint federal and state endeavor. Indeed, on May 16, 1960, the Bureau of Reclamation and the DWR agreed to coordinate operations of the SWP and the CVP. According to the DWR's director at the time, Harvey Banks, the agreement provided "for harmonized operation of two of the largest water projects in the world" (Banks 1960, 10). Both federal and state legislation was enacted to authorize collaboration, particularly in the San Luis Unit, which would store and convey water from the southern San Francisco Bay Area to Southern California.[57]

In 1959 the California legislature asked whether the state should "establish a limit on the amount of water which will be available from state projects to irrigate land in order to prevent unjust enrichment" in addition to several other questions addressing water and power pricing and delivery, and possible differential rates for public and private customers.[58] While there was some debate over the validity of the concept of "unjust enrichment,"[59] the DWR defined it as "Project benefits accruing to a small number of individuals or corporations at the expense of the public or other beneficiary." Unjust enrichment was not just about the result of owning large amounts of land that could be irrigated using low-cost federal water, but also about asking higher prices for the lease of that land once the water was available.[60] Following House Resolution No. 293 (June 18, 1959), the state legislature convened an interim committee to examine whether "unjust enrichment" could take place as a result of SWP development and, if so, how it might be addressed.[61]

Special Consultant on the matter of unjust enrichment Leland O. Graham traced the term to a 1957 letter to then–attorney general Edmund Brown from six California congressmen articulating the importance of the federal acreage limitation as "one of the basic tenets of reclamation law":

> The moral basis of the 160-acre limitation is to prevent unjust enrichment resulting from the subsidies to irrigation provided by interest-free Federal money and public power revenues. Congress, in our opinion, will not permit the unearned enrichment of large landowners at the expense of the Federal treasury which can occur without an acreage limitation.[62]

Indeed, Graham's study of Kern County, which stood to benefit from the waters available following the development of the SWP, noted the large private land interests in Kern County in particular, including the Kern County Land Company, which held 223,534 acres, and Tejon Ranch, which held 38,689 acres.[63] According to Graham, the Kern County Land Company's extensive land ownership in the region ran contrary to portions of the California constitution and subsequent case law intimating that lands should be granted by the state to settlers in amounts less than 320 acres, specifically for cultivation and habitation.[64] In a September 1959 hearing of the Assembly Interim Committee on Water, the definition of unjust enrichment regarding the SWP was made even more specific:

> Persons owning or controlling large areas of land receiving water from facilities of the California Water Plan shall be enriched by being allowed to purchase unlimited amounts of water to service their holdings either for agriculture or industry, thus allowing them greatly to increase private agricultural or industrial production with water supplied by public monies. . . . The term . . . shall also apply when such landholders who are receiving unlimited supplies of public waters in such areas shall become enriched from the renting or selling of their lands at prices greatly increased above the value of the land before such unlimited supplies of water were available.[65]

However, alternate views expressed by parties such as the California State University, Sacramento, economics professor Milton Baum found the concept of "unjust enrichment" as little more than a "value judgment." While he noted that "the Governor and many of the votes are concerned with the question of whether large amounts of excess net profits above a normal return for investment and risk are going to accrue to the large landowners as a result of state development of a resource belonging to all the citizens of the State," Baum felt that the cost of water and the taxes on capital gains would be high enough to offset any imbalance.[66] Even those generally in favor of the federal land limitations acknowledged that the application of those limitations presented numerous legal and practical problems, including situations of temporary use of water, joint project administration, land appraisal, types of crops and soils, and enforcement.[67]

Graham considered these positions in his report and ultimately suggested a move away from the term "unjust enrichment" and toward a concept of working toward "equitable distribution," using such mechanisms as differential water rates for landowners seeing differential benefit from project water.[68] Indeed, in the November 1959 "Policy Recommended for Adoption to Implement the State Water Resources Development System" by the director of the Water Resources' Special Study Group, the concern with "unjust enrichment" seems to have dissipated; authors felt that it could be mitigated completely by effective policies on "cost allocation, pricing, and repayment" (Director of Water Resources Special Study Group 1959, 2). By 1960, in the governor's address to encourage support for the SWP, it appeared that the "unjust enrichment" question had been resolved by establishing different prices for large and small landowners, with larger landowners (more than 160 acres) paying for the cost of the water as well as the market value of the power used to pump it, and small landowners paying for the cost of the water but only the actual cost of the power to convey it, minus the benefit from the sale of power (Brown 1969, 5).

The vision for the SWP was to "make water available throughout the State in a manner which will most adequately and equitably meet the economic and social needs of all of the people of California" (Director of Water Resources Special Study Group 1959, 1), by moving water from areas of abundance to areas of deficiency.[69] However, perhaps the state and federal government should have looked less at unjust enrichment of southern San Joaquin Valley landholders and more at unjust disenfranchisement leveled on Indigenous populations at the headwaters of the project. The SWP built on and solidified the importance of the power system developed by PG&E and its predecessors and ensured that anadromous fish would stop their migration lower in elevation, pausing a way of life that had endured for centuries on the Feather River and its tributaries. In my review of the documentation of the legal and political wrangling over the SWP, there appears to be no mention of its impacts on Indigenous populations save the Enterprise Rancheria, which had one parcel that was directly displaced by the Oroville Dam.

PUBLIC/PRIVATE INFRASTRUCTURE

In 1960 the University of California, under the leadership of the project director Joe Bain, undertook a comprehensive study of the "water industry" of the state, which involved interviews with PG&E staff and leadership.[70] On December 20, project staff interviewed John Bonner of the engineering department and, among other questions, asked him about the difference in PG&E and Bureau of Reclamation operations. Bonner noted that PG&E did not get a subsidy for flood control when it built dams. He also noted that the Public Utilities Commission had some role in the favorable pricing of power for farmers, to some chagrin on the part of PG&E because of the high degree of power use in agricultural operations.[71]

On June 11, 1959, PG&E's chief engineer and assistant to the vice president John F. Bonner gave a talk entitled "Teamwork in Water Work" to the Commonwealth Club of California. He noted that "water conservation got its start in the Sierras with the gold rush to the Mother Lode" (1959). Unbeknownst to him, this statement is extraordinarily accurate for the ways in which the seizure and transformation of the state's water resources that began during the gold rush continues in contemporary water infrastructure. The dams, power plants, aqueducts, and reservoirs that compose this infrastructure have become embedded in the socioeconomic, political geography of the state, where it underlies industries from tourism to agriculture to construction. This makes Indigenous decolonization (following the 2012 definition of Eve Tuck and Wayne Yang, which calls for a removal of such infrastructure and the frameworks that support it) more challenging. However, movement toward decolonizing the land and water is not impossible, as shown by the work to remove the four dams on the Klamath River and the recent removal of the Elwha Dam in Washington (see Houston 2017; Howard 2016).

In his 1959 address, Bonner marveled at the agricultural productivity of California and articulated the necessity of electricity to power irrigation water delivery. Electricity, he noted, was also essential to fund California's water storage projects, which protected the state from floods and provided water year-round to downstream urban populations. At the time of his talk, PG&E owned 59 storage reservoirs, impounding 1.7 million acre-feet in California. Although he did not mention Lake Almanor in this particular address, at 1.3 million acre-feet, Almanor remained the largest of PG&E's storage projects.

Bonner also framed PG&E as "financially aiding" public water conservation projects by either purchasing "by-product power" generated by these projects or installing infrastructure to capture the power and then making "falling water payments" (1959, 6). According to Bonner on behalf of his company, both practices were essential to supporting the costly construction and management of public water projects. The company proposed to support the SWP in similar ways to how it supported other public water projects, by selling the project "low-cost off peak power" to operate the pumps conveying water out of the delta and to points as far south as San Diego. More broadly, PG&E's purchase of power on projects statewide would help to fund the construction of the California Water Plan's recommended 376 new reservoirs: "Revenues from the lease of power privileges to agencies which can sell electric power at full market value under state regulation will help make possible this gigantic and vitally needed water conservation development" (12).

However, how PG&E determined the value of the power it purchased from these projects was termed by some to be PG&E's "secret," based on "some calculations . . . of what dependable capacity and energy might be vis-à-vis alternative costs of power, but in proportions undisclosed . . . [and] how they estimate that power will fit into PG&E's system."[72] PG&E generates revenue in several ways, including selling water wholesale from power developments and selling water retail directly to cities and other entities for resale. The University of California researchers documented information about the structure and type of PG&E water sales contracts. When PG&E contracted to provide water to irrigators, industrial customers, and districts/cities/water companies, the Company always included a clause that the contract was an "accommodation" to the purchaser, not a dedication of PG&E "facilities to public service."[73] Records from particular contracts and the research itself indicate that PG&E often found itself in competition with the Bureau of Reclamation, and responded by reducing rates and extending contracts for significant customers, such as the West Stanislaus Irrigation District, in order to retain their business.[74] PG&E also purchased power generated by the Bureau of Reclamation and smaller public agencies, ostensibly to save public money on building transmission lines but also to retain its monopoly on electricity transmission and provision in northern and Central California.[75] PG&E had long attempted to draw attention to the near–tax exemption for government-owned utilities, which enabled the Bureau of Reclamation to offer utilities at lower rates than an investor-owned utility such as PG&E.[76]

The 1960 University of California research into Northern California's water and power industry revealed the complexity of overlapping water rights, claims, and requirements on river systems including the Feather, which is central to PG&E operations. In addition to PG&E's projects, there are minimum flow requirements for fisheries imposed in the hydroelectric facility licenses, as well as overlapping rights of other users, individual and corporate, public and private. The researchers tried through extensive requests for data to PG&E, the California Public Utilities Commission, and the Federal Power Commission, to get information on the scope of potential conflicts and how the different parties resolved them.[77]

ALTERNATIVE APPROACHES

While the problems of water seasonality and distribution relative to urban, industrial, and agricultural demand are well documented in California, there are brief allusions to approaches other than the development of massive dam and conveyance systems. For example, a 1959 statement by the DWR on California water problems and solutions includes a brief discussion of watershed approaches: "The possibilities of increasing the water supply by vegetational management in the watershed is good. Where watersheds are covered with brush growth which has no value and it is possible to supplant this growth with grasses, more water is retained in the soil and the grass has a value as forage" (California Department of Water Resources 1959a, 12). However, the DWR concluded that "more experimental research is required" to evaluate the effectiveness of this approach in comparison to constructing water resources infrastructure.

In their 2005 comments to the FERC on the Environmental Impact Statement regarding the relicensing of PG&E's facilities at Lake Almanor and Butt Lake (Project 2105, the Upper North Fork Feather River Hydroelectric Project), the Maidu Cultural and Development Group (MCDG) requested that the commission "include a license condition requiring PG&E to explore off-site upstream restoration as a way to further enhance and improve the fish habitat in the Upper North Fork Feather River and its watershed."[78] Plumas County also made this recommendation to the State Water Resources Control Board (hereafter Control Board), which is charged with issuing a water quality certification to PG&E before the FERC can relicense the project. In its consideration of alternatives to address how PG&E could manage its facilities to reduce water temperatures in the North Fork Feather River, the Control Board dismissed restoration as a viable alternative, saying that it would result in only a "minor improvement" (SWRCB 2014, sec. 4.3).

Upstream restoration is linked to overall system conservation, which was also not part of the original SWP design. In a 1960 statement, the DWR explained that more water was needed because California residents were using more and more water: "The very instruments of better living for the housewife—her automatic washing machine, her automatic dishwasher and her garbage disposal unit—require huge amounts of water to perform their tasks . . . And people continue to invent new ways to use water" (State of California, Dept. of Water Resources 1960, 1). Keeping up with these new ways would be the only way, according to the department, to maintain the "phenomenal economic growth and prosperity of California." Indeed, "without man-made development of water resources in ample quantities, we would not today be the second most populous state, ranking 6th in manufacturing, 1st in agriculture, 2nd in personal income, and with a true valuation of more than $100 billion" (2). The statement went on to laud the productivity of the state's water and power projects, valued then at more than $6 billion, yet in need of expansion to keep pace with expanding industry and population. Noting that agriculture is California's most important industry and requires substantial water, that flood control is a primary public safety issue, that water quality is an increasingly serious problem, and that recreation is among the top three industries in California, the statement concludes that the engineer's answer to all of these issues is to "construct projects" (5–12). If the bond were to fail, the results on welfare and economy would be "disastrous," and Southern California's "tremendous economic expansion" would "grind to a sickening halt" (12). Thus, the DWR was unbridled in its support for the bond issue and the state project, which, in its view, would provide water to support the state's "welfare and prosperity" (13). The bond passed on November 8, 1960.

CONCLUSION: RECONSIDERING THE PRICE OF CALIFORNIA'S SWP

The federal government (the Department of the Interior and Bureau of Reclamation) and the state government (the DWR) developed an agreement in 1960 for joint operation of the federal and state water projects.[79] In order for both projects to be successful, each had to agree to proportionally less water at times when there was less water in the system. The two systems would be complementary, and the state system would appropriate specific amounts of unappropriated water in rivers with federal project facilities. Indian water rights are not mentioned in this agreement, despite the fact that Indian land and water rights were seized in the creation of both systems, and existing unquantified Indian water rights continue not to be addressed in the operation of both projects.

In 1953 the Department of the Interior responded to the Federal Power Commission and the Water Project Authority of the State of California regarding the Feather River Project (License 2100) near Oroville. The Interior endorsed the project as it had in 1952, and responded to two of the Authority's stipulations; one dealt with leaving enough water for fisheries downstream and the other with compensation for damage to Indian lands. Regarding the latter point, compensation for Indian lands was to be provided for two specific parcels affected by the Oroville Reservoir: one held by Enterprise Rancheria and the other by an individual allottee, John Pinkey. The BIA within the Department of the Interior was surveying and appraising these lands and would then take steps to compensate the owners, with the secretary of the Interior's approval.

Such a narrow notion of affected Indian lands and required compensation meant that changes to land and culture would continue to be wrought by the SWP (including the Oroville Dam and the upstream facilities owned by PG&E, authorized by the Federal Power Commission) without compensation to Indian people suffering the ongoing project impacts.[80] One of the most painful aspects of this realization is that it did not have to be this way: from the earliest development of the power projects on the Upper Feather River, the developers sought to build demand for the electricity they created. GWP encouraged downstream electrification, thereby creating a market for the power the company was capturing from the Feather River. By the 1950s, these and other water and power projects had built burgeoning industrial, agricultural, and domestic demand downstream—so much demand that new projects continue to be required in order to meet the high-energy requirements of current and future users. Now, with higher population, increased drought frequency, and ever-higher energy needs, the focus has shifted to conservation rather than to increasing electric and water consumption needs, yet again without attention to Indian land and water rights.

With a focus on Maidu organizing and advocacy in a context of willful disregard for Indian land and water rights, this text attempts to offer an alternative view of the "nation's largest public water and power conveyance system," California's State Water Project. The subsequent data reveals the incalculably high prices of the project: genocide and removal of both Indigenous peoples and culturally important species. These are not past impacts but present issues that continue to plague us today culturally, spiritually, and ecologically, across a riverine ecosystem plugged by concrete dams. Throughout the last century of state-sanctioned removal, construction, conveyance, enrichment, and denial remains the steadfast continuation of Maidu culture in the face of inexpressible losses and the tenacity of Maidu organizing to acquire restitution and restoration of aboriginal lands and waters. The next three chapters focus on this Maidu activism and resistance to development without their consent, from the turn of the twentieth century to the present.

2

FROM THE BEGINNINGS

Indigenous Advocacy

T HIS CHAPTER begins a series of three chapters tracing themes in upstream Indian allotment ownership, transfer, and sale over time. While I document the rampant attrition of Maidu and other northeastern California Indigenous lands over the nineteenth and twentieth centuries, leading directly to the present configuration of so little Indian landownership in the Sierra, it is important to recognize that the Indigenous allottees and their descendants have always been active participants in working to retain their homelands. From managing ranches and running timber crews, to participating in land conservation and watershed-level planning processes, to intervening in hydroelectric facility relicensing procedures, Indigenous allottees and their descendants have consistently and persistently seized and developed opportunities to maintain and strengthen access to and jurisdiction over their lands and waters. Drawing on correspondence in BLM and BIA archives, this chapter traces allottees' work in a range of contexts to maintain and strengthen rights to, fulfill responsibilities toward, and receive some benefits from their homelands. Included are histories of successful advocacy with the eventual support of agency personnel, as well as instances of struggle and marginalization under corrupt agency employees and policies.

FIGHTING THE LEGAL FICTIONS ENABLING CONDEMNATION OF INDIAN LANDS

The legal history of Federal-Indian relations is one of articulating legal theories to justify colonial actions. The doctrine of discovery, an invention of papal authority, was developed and applied in the Americas to enable European nations to assert authority over American Indian people and lands. The process by which Indian allotment lands were condemned and made available for hydroelectric development follows a similar convoluted logic, invoking "legal fictions" (Echo-Hawk 2010) of government and industrial land and water rights, manifest destiny, and the need for electrification. Given the force of law and policy, these perspectives steadily reduced aboriginal Indian land rights and condemned even recognized Indian lands to flooding for hydroelectric development and storage to benefit downstream urban and agricultural users.

A document promulgated by the Department of the Interior, Office of Indian Affairs, entitled "Indian Lands for Sale Under Government Supervision," explained the policy of the Office of Indian Affairs sale of Indian allotments. The document argued that Indian people were becoming effectively land rich and cash poor with the inheritance of multiple allotments. To remedy this situation for Indian people that the government deemed "noncompetent" to manage their own affairs, the secretary of the Interior assumed the authority to sell Indian allotments. The acts of June 25, 1910, and October 12, 1910, respectively, required the secretary of the Interior to determine the heirs to the lands sold and to advertise the land (including specific details of its description and value) for 60 days (Department of the Interior, Office of Indian Affairs n.d.). A warning was included in bold print at the end of the document that "it is a serious offense under the act of June 25, 1910, to enter into a contract or agreement for the purchase of land held in trust for an Indian without authority of the Department of the Interior. Such contracts or agreements are absolutely void" (2). As such, following *Johnson v. McIntosh* (1823) nearly a century earlier, the federal government reaffirmed its role in overseeing the sale of Indian land. In practice, however, as exemplified by allotments in the Big Meadows region, the local courts were involved, and sometimes companies dealt directly with allottees.

An April 12, 1916 letter from Roseburg Agency superintendent Horace Wilson to Greenville Indian School superintendent Edgar Miller lists ten allotments in Big Meadows that were condemned by GWP. The allotments of Meley Mack (127), Goodseener Jenkins (163), Charlie James (208), Maggie Bacala (179), Charlie Bacala (180), Harper Jenkins (165),[1] Nancy Jenkins (236), Jennie Meadows (1013), Hester/Hosler Jenkins (164), and Minnie Lincoln (118) were all condemned, yet Wilson notes that only riparian rights on allotments 165 and 236 were condemned, and there was some confusion about how much of the acreage in addition to the riparian rights were condemned on allotment 164. Wilson references his own report of October 15, 1912, which details "the condemnation proceedings of Indian allotments by the Great Western Power Company instituted in the Superior Court of Plumas County, California." As affirmed by the Commerce Clause to the Constitution, the Trade and Intercourse Acts, and case law, states and lower courts (i.e., county) were to have no jurisdiction over Indian affairs. Civil proceedings, such as condemnation proceedings of federal land held in trust for Indian individuals, would not be under state, much less local jurisdiction, prior to Public Law 280 (1953). The only lands that might be subject to state jurisdiction would be those covered by PL 109 in 1908, which relinquished 890 acres to GWP, but the majority of allotments affected by that formal relinquishment had already been canceled in 1902 by the GLO (see table 1 below).

TABLE 1. PL 109, "An act to relinquish, release, and confirm the title of certain lands in California to the Western Power Company," canceled 890 acres of state and federal land and transferred it to the power company.

Relevant Areas Canceled by PL 109 (1908)			
	Township	Range	Section
	27N	7E	22
			27
			34
	27N	8E	22
	28N	8E	28

Allotments Affected					
Allot #	Name	Township	Range	Section	Cancellation
145	John Meadow	27N	7E	22	1901
146	Joaquin Meadow	27N	7E	27	1902
149	Jennie Meadow	27N	7E	27	1902
147	Kate Meadow	27N	7E	34	1902
163	Goodseener Jenkins	27N	8E	22	Cancellation order revoked, later sold
1014	John Meadow	27N	7E	27	1902
127	Meley Mack	28N	8E	28	Cancellation order revoked, later sold

The cancellations overlapped with the areas of seven Indian allotments, but five had already been canceled several years earlier and two appeared to be unaffected and were later sold to the Red River Lumber Company.

INDIAN ALLOTMENT APPLICATION FOR LANDS OUTSIDE OF ANY INDIAN RESERVATION.

(Act February 8, 1887, Stat. 24, p. 388, as amended by act February 28, 1891, Stat. 26, p. 794.)

United States Land Office,

Susanville Cal.

March 28. 1894

APPLICATION No. 180

I, *Old Joe Bacala*, being an Indian of the *Big Meadows* tribe, do hereby apply to have allotted *my minor child Charlie Bacala* *8 years of age*, under the provisions of the fourth section of the act of Congress, approved February 8, 1887 (Stat. 24, p. 388), as amended by act of February 28, 1891 (Stat. 26, p. 794), the [2] *S½ of NW¼ Sec 17*

S½ of NE¼

NW¼ of NE¼ of Sec 18 T27 N R 8 E

MDM

the land above described is only valuable for grazing purposes.

containing *160* acres.

Old Joe X Bacala
his mark

Witnesses:
W. B. McCall
T. A. Roseberry.

United States Land Office,

Susanville Cal.

March 28. 1894

I, *T. A. Roseberry*, Register of the Land Office, do hereby certify that the above application is for *Surveyed* lands, and that there is no prior valid adverse right to the same.

T. A. Roseberry
Register.

[1] Insert "to me, as the head of a family," or "to me, as a single person over eighteen years of age," or "to my minor child" (giving the name of the child), as the case may be.
The same blank may be used in making application in the case of an orphan child, the agent's or special agent's name being inserted in place of the parent's, and the phraseology changed to suit the case.
[2] Insert description of the land, if surveyed, by legal subdivisions; if unsurveyed, by metes and bounds, beginning with some object that may be readily identified, or a permanent artificial monument or mound set for the purpose, or in such other manner as to admit of its being readily identified when the official survey comes to be extended.
If the application is for grazing land, it should be stated in the application that the lands are "only valuable for grazing purposes."

FIGURE 9. Allotment application for Old Joe Bacala. Application includes numerous handwritten notations indicating changes to the status of the allotment. (Filed in Sus-163, RG75, National Archives.)

One allotment with a particularly confusing trajectory is Sus-163, for Good-seener Jenkins. The land was held for cancellation in 1902, the cancellation order was revoked in 1903, and, despite the fact that it was wholly included in the area of land relinquished to the Western Power Company in PL 109, the allottee was able to sell at least a portion of the land to Red River in 1921.

A docket of "Decisions Relating to the Public Lands" decided March 17, 1913, discusses the authority for cancellation of Indian lands, whether on Indian reservations or on the public domain (allotments), for hydropower development. According to sections 13 and 14 of the act of June 25, 1910, the secretary of the Interior is empowered to reserve power and reservoir sites within Indian reservations. Section 14 of the act specifically authorizes "the Secretary of the Interior to cancel Indian Trust patents issued on allotments within power or reservoir sites, *within Indian reservations*" (emphasis added). The secretary is empowered to act on lands within tribal boundaries, but authority over public domain allotments is not specified.

Department of the Interior assistant secretary Lewis Laylin acknowledges the papers submitted by the acting commissioner of the Indian Office and the director of the U.S. Geological Survey regarding the "Big Meadows scheme of the Great Western Power Company" (qtd. in Hesselman 1914, 4). GWP is described as a state corporation that has purchased "a considerable area of privately owned lands along the north fork of Feather River, California." Further, Laylin notes that

> through condemnation proceedings instituted and prosecuted in the California courts under the provisions of the act of March 3, 1901 (31 Stat. 1083), it has acquired title to a considerable area of lands allotted to Indians. A confirmatory act passed by Congress May 5, 1908 (35 Stat., 100), quitclaimed, so far as the United States is concerned, the title to certain lands therein described and confirmed same to the Western Power Company . . . [which has,] in accordance with the laws of the State of California, appropriated certain waters for the generation of hydroelectric power and for irrigation and other purposes and have already expended approximately $300,000 in the construction of improvements at a proposed dam site. (5)

Laylin explains further that withdrawals were made November 23, 1911, and February 15, 1912, under the provisions of the act of June 25, 1910 (36 Stat., 847), (power-site reserves numbers 234 and 245). These power-site withdrawals contained "about 2,250 acres of lands covered by Indian allotments, as well as about 1,080 acres in unapproved State and lieu selections, and 80 acres [of] homestead entries" (5). Research by longtime MCDG board member Lorena Gorbet (Maidu, Washoe) indicates, however, that there are parcels for which ownership was never determined, and to which Indian (Maidu) land rights had never been formally canceled.[2] Gorbet created a detailed map of these lands, now located under Lake Almanor, by hand, but the map was destroyed in a 2017 house fire.

According to Laylin, the U.S. Geological Survey made a recommendation on November 1, 1912, that the power company acquire the Indian allotments by condemnation, under the provisions of section 14 of the act of June 25, 1910 (36 Stat. 855-8) or "to create an Indian reservation including the lands" (5). No reservation was ever created. The Indian Office made a report on December 31, 1912, arguing that the Indians were "not concentrated upon a given area of public land" and were "not maintaining tribal relations" (6), and would be better served by the sale of their lands, based on "their value for agriculture, timber, and power purposes" (5). Upon further examination of the June 25, 1910, act, Laylin concluded that trust patents could not be canceled on allotments unless the land was reserved for irrigation purposes authorized by Congress, and, if these conditions were met, the Indian allottee was to be allotted land of equal value. However, given that only 140 acres of the 63-foot dam site (covering 12,500 acres)[3] were vacant public lands under government control, the secretary made the decision that "the Department [of the Interior] does not feel warranted in interposing this as an obstacle to the development of the power company's power and irrigation projects" (6). As such, the way was opened for a private company (GWP) to develop a power project on Indian and private non-Indian (homesteader, rancher) land, with government support, despite the contrary statements in the law that intended to protect the nominal remaining Indian land holdings in this central area of the Mountain Maidu homeland.

The Department of the Interior, under Laylin's leadership, agreed with the determination of the commissioner of Indian Affairs that it would be appropriate to sell the Indian allotments needed by the power company, "upon the express condition that the lands be first appraised on the basis of their value for agriculture, timber, and power-site purposes, and disposed of for not less than that valuation" (6). Laylin then directed the commissioner of the GLO to forward GWP's land requests to the department, which would then recommend the requisite power-site withdrawals to the president of the United States.

GWP acquired 30,000 acres and began its hydroelectric project on the Upper Feather River in about 1902. The company began construction of Canyon Dam to impound Lake Almanor in 1910. From 1913 to 1927, Lake Almanor was known as the world's largest man-made reservoir.[4] The Caribou #1 Powerhouse below the Butt Valley Reservoir is credited with enabling the urban development of

A 7% Investment Combining Soundness, Safety and Attractive Yield

For every man or woman who saves, Great Western Power Company of California 7% Preferred Stock offers an unusual investment combining what every investor should seek,—safety, soundness and high yield. From every point of consideration, this offering should appeal to discriminating investors, large or small, first, by reason of the attractive return, and, second, because of the Company's past record and future outlook.

Safety

GREAT WESTERN POWER'S hydro-electric plants on the Feather River and upper tributaries generate their electric energy from water power derived from the perpetual snows of the Sierra Nevada Mountains. These plants now produce electric energy exceeding 175,000 h. p., but the potential energy from the eight power sites now owned by the Company is over 792,000 h. p., enough to take care of over four times the present volume of business. Hydro-electric energy is not only the most economical but is the only inexhaustible power known.

California's future progress, its industries, streetcar systems, telephones, and the light, heat and power for its many cities and towns are dependent largely on hydro-electric power. The Company now supplies thirty-one communities, including San Francisco, Oakland, Alameda and Berkeley, and the constant demand for electric energy in the territory it serves assures the Company of a ready market for all that can be produced.

The funds derived from the sale of this preferred stock, which is authorized by the California Railroad Commission, are used in constructing hydro-electric plants, steel tower transmission lines, sub-stations, distribution lines and equipment, all tangible assets. Thus every investor is doubly assured of soundness and safety by the Company's property, equipment and its business of supplying what is virtually a necessity to every individual.

High Yield

Great Western Power's 7% Cumulative Preferred Stock has a par value of $100.00 per share and is being sold by the Company direct to the public.

Dividends are exempt from the Normal Federal Income Tax and are tax free in California except as to Inheritance Tax.

Your money invested in this preferred stock will begin immediately to earn 7% per annum for you. It will be invested in a hydro-electric public utility which produces a recognized basic necessity, and this class of security is recognized as having the highest rating. There is a ready market for this stock in case of necessity for liquidating, and it is also acceptable as security for loans at banks.

Rarely is opportunity presented for securing so high a rate of return on investment, coupled with so high a degree of safety.

Partial Payment Plan

So that even the most modest investor may enjoy the opportunity offered by this investment, the Company has developed a special partial payment plan of $5.00 per share down and $5.00 per share per month. Each partial payment earns 7% interest, and when they have been completed the stock then fully paid for earns the regular 7% dividend payable quarterly.

Great Western Power Company of California

530 Bush Street, San Francisco

DISTRICT OFFICES

San Francisco Oakland Sacramento Petaluma Napa Santa Rosa Rio Vista Pittsburg Half Moon Bay

FIGURE 10. A 1924 Great Western Power advertisement. (Filed in Erwin Cooper papers, Box 12, WRCA.)

the greater San Francisco Bay Area when it began sending power downstream in 1924. GWP stocks were advertised as providing a steady, high yield, based on ever-increasing demand for the "necessities" of light, heat, and power, building "California's future" and bringing "direct benefit to every community."[5]

However widely these projects were lauded as development and engineering feats of their time, the costs of this production were not discussed. Specifically, the ongoing impacts of Maidu displacement and the seizure of Maidu cultural, economic, and ecological resources were framed as externalities to the development process, if they were noted at all.

There are records of Maidu allottees reporting land and water seizures by representatives of lumber and power companies to Indian Service employees. A December 9, 1911, letter from Superintendent C. H. Ashbury to Superintendent Horace Wilson in Roseburg, Oregon, outlined the concerns communicated by Isaac Jenkins, son of John Jenkins, who noted that he had paid to have a surveyor show him the location of his land, and that he had received trust patents to the land, but then

> a man named Golden, who, he understood, represented the Walkers,[6] had been after him for his timber for some time . . . took his trust patents for examination, told him that they were not right, that [Golden] was going to Susanville . . . and would have them fixed up right . . . [and] get the land in shape so he could sell it and that his money would be ready for him in a short time; that he does not know what [Golden] did with the trust patents and he is uneasy for fear they may change them in some way and affect the title to his land.
>
> He also reports that Gus Bidwell, representative for power company, (he thinks the Western Power Company) has been surveying on their land, has cut timber, made roads, laid a pipe line, all on what they believe to be their land, and has told Jenkins that he was mistaken as to the location of his land as his land was some distance from that claimed. He tells me that these conditions have been called to the attention of Supt. Mann, also more recently to Supt. Campbell.[7]

Wilson's immediate response assured Ashbury that Isaac Jenkins's and his father John Jenkins's rights to their allotments "would be protected."[8]

In a series of correspondence between the GWP superintendent A. R. Bidwell and the Greenville Indian School superintendent W. S. Campbell (1912–13), it became clear that GWP had leased deceased Harper Jenkins's allotment (Sus-165) for "stone-quarrying and business purposes"[9] and was making payments in-kind by furnishing Harper's father and heir John Jenkins with "supplies . . . winter provisions . . . food and clothing."[10] The second assistant commissioner of the BIA, C. F. Hauke, responded unequivocally to Campbell when he learned of this practice: "The company should be required to pay the rental into your Office, for the use and benefit of the lessors, in accordance with the stipulation in the lease."[11] Upon hearing this rebuke, Bidwell responded defensively to Campbell that the direct payments to furnish supplies had been a "temporary" arrangement, "with the full knowledge of your predecessor and yourself."[12]

The Jenkinses petitioned to sell their group of allotments (Sus-161–163, John, Ellen, and Goodseener Jenkins; inherited allotments Sus-164 and 165, Hosler and Harper Jenkins; and Sus-166, 236, and 237, belonging to Jay Side / Ike, Nancy, and Girl Jenkins, respectively) in 1912.[13] John Jenkins's land was described in cruiser Joseph Murphy's 1912 appraisal as "rough and rocky" and of "not much value after timber is taken off." Of the four segments of the parcel, only one is described as having timber, the rest had already been harvested "years ago" and was only worth $7/acre.[14] The Indian Office evidently wanted to examine this absence of timber on the Jenkins' allotments and wrote to Greenville Indian School superintendent Charles McChesney in 1915 noting that the allotment of Harper Jenkins (Sus-165) had been leased by GWP beginning in 1911, and the company was to pay for any timber removed, in addition to the annual lease fees. Assistant Commissioner E. B. Merritt requested a "detailed report" of the amount of timber cut and the amount paid to the office to benefit the Jenkinses.[15] McChesney replied with information about a 1914 report by Crescent Mills–based timber cruiser George Hall[16] of the timber cut on the allotment by GWP and record of a payment made to the previous superintendent, W. S. Campbell.[17] No further correspondence is available in the file to ascertain whether this report was accurate, if the funds were paid, if any other leases were involved, and if any payments reached the allottees/lessors.

In 1920 eight heirs of John Jenkins (d. 1916) sold his 160-acre allotment to sole bidder GWP for a consideration of $11.75/acre, acknowledging that the land was in the "Powersite of the Great Western Power Co. and will become flooded when completed."[18] Regarding the sole bid, the report on the sale argued that the land was "worth more to the G.W.P. Co. as powersite than to any other bidder. Readvertisement would not benefit the Indian."[19] According to a 1918 appraisement by cruiser-at-large Irvine Gardner, the land "touches 4500' contour line of Great Western Power Company reservoir Big Meadows" and was of very low value—"gravelly and rocky . . . no soil Agricultural NONE, Grazing very poor."[20] As with many of the other allotments condemned and sold during this time period, heirs wrote many years later to inquire what had happened to the funds due to them for the sale of the lands and whether the condemnation of the lands had been legal. In 1954 attorney F. G. Collett wrote on behalf of Mrs. Nellie Peck, heir to the Jenkins estates. He specifically inquired about Sus-163 (Goodseener Jenkins), which was described as "decreed to the Great Western Power Company," asking whether or not that "decree" meant "condemnation," and noting that Mrs. Peck's sister Goodseener had "never received any money whatsoever" for her land.[21] Douglas Clark from the BIA replied that a portion of the allotment had indeed been condemned by GWP (SE/4 of SW/4 of Sec. 15, and E/2 of NW/4 of Sec. 22) and approved by an act of Congress in 1908. Another portion (SW/4 of the SE/4, Sec. 15) of the allotment was sold to Red River, with a fee patent issued in February 1921.[22] These two companies were the principle purchasers of Indian allotments in the lands that became the head-waters of the SWP and PG&E's Feather River "stairway of power"—GWP as predecessor company of PG&E and Red River as one of the largest forest landowners in the state, and often involved in purchasing and clearing timber on parcels later sold and developed for hydropower.

PG&E purchased GWP in 1930 and the North Fork Feather River Project build-out continued through 1969 with the Belden Powerhouse. Today, PG&E owns and operates more than 30,000 acres in their Upper North Fork Feather River Hydroelectric Project, which includes Almanor and Butt Lakes, as well as four other nearby hydroelectric projects within the Mountain Maidu (and, as they extend down the Feather River Canyon, Concow Maidu) homeland: Hamilton Branch, Rock Creek Cresta, Bucks Creek, and Poe (EIR 3-3, Nov 2014). While the significance of particularly the upper part of the canyon is clear in Maidu oral and written history and tribal members' own memories of culturally significant sites throughout the Feather River region,[23] a small fraction of the land remains in Maidu ownership.[24] The majority of the land is currently held by the U.S. Forest Service, private timber companies, and PG&E. There is a sense of deep loss associated with the ways in which the hydroelectric projects have impacted the land- and waterscape. Cultural knowledge, songs, and practices have been submerged as salmon and other species were removed from the upper watershed (Braxton 2014). As Lorena Gorbet told journalist Jane Braxton Little in 2014, "Along with their gathering sites, the Maidu lost salmon and snapping turtles, ceremonies, language, and song—'everything that goes with the land. . . . We have always been looking for compensation for what we lost. Always.'" Struggles continue to protect the cultural sites and to steward culturally/ecologically important areas of the Feather River canyon.

The historic allotments in the canyon region, which I will define here as including both the north fork and middle fork Feather River canyons, are much smaller than the typical 160-acre, or quarter-section, allotments. This can be attributed to topography, as arable land areas are smaller in the canyons, as well as pressure to maintain the land's accessibility for possible hydropower production. One example is a 20-acre allotment that was approved on the middle fork of the Feather River for James Taylor in 1918. A 1915 letter from Special Indian Agent C. H. Ashbury to the commissioner of Indian Affairs in Washington, D.C., recommending approval of the allotment describes it as encompassing 60 acres, but the 1918 final approval lists the land as 20 acres. Ashbury's support for the allotment articulates a specific vision of the allotment process as supportive of Indians without reservations living on what became defined as the "public domain":

> These Indians have lived in the same general locality for generations, so far as we know it was their original native home. They have taken up their homes on the public domain, where they could get a little water to irrigate a garden and orchard and do some agricultural work and these homes have been occupied and improved to some extent by them for many years. This is the case with this particular applicant, Joseph Taylor, and he makes this application in good faith, with the hope of securing title to the land where he is living and has lived. He has never taken up land on the public domain before, nor has he had any reservation rights and he is typical of the class of Indians for whom the various allotment acts were passed and I recommend that a certificate be issued as to his eligibility to take land.[25]

Once allotted, Taylor's land remained in trust status until the 1950s, when it was purchased by another Maidu man in 1952.

Back upstream, in the headwaters region of the north fork of the Feather River, a Maidu man named Ole Salem received an allotment in 1891. However, nearly 30 years later, a 1919 deposition shows that he was still fighting for his land rights. Ole Salem's December 23, 1919, statement was given when he was 48 years old, and he is described as a full-blooded Indian, a member of the Big Meadows band, and born near Taylorsville, California, in the southeast corner of what is now known as Indian Valley. His father was identified as Salem Dokesim of Chester, California, which is on the northwestern edge of Big

Meadows. Dokesim had an allotment, but Ole Salem's mother died when he was a baby, before allotments were made.

Following his allotment application in 1891, Ole Salem was allotted a parcel in the area now known as Fredonyer Pass, between present-day Westwood and Susanville, California.[26] The site of his allotment was northeast of the land his father was allotted and significantly northeast of the site where he was born, in Taylorsville, California. Nevertheless, affidavits from Maidu Captain DeHaven and Salem Dokesim note that Ole had made improvements on the land he applied for, as required by the legislation, and that he was planning to live there with his family.

Following the approval of his allotment, Ole selected allotments for his son, Arthur/Sargent, and his wife, Lou, near Haun's Meadow between Greenville (located at the northwestern end of Indian Valley) and the southeastern end of Lake Almanor / Big Meadows.[27] According to his 1919 deposition, Ole lived on his allotment near Fredonyer Pass for more than a year and improved it with a cabin, garden, fencing, and wagon road starting near where the grade going up to Fredonyer begins. Then he came down to take care of his sick father near Westwood, renting his land to a white man who ran stock. When he tried to rent his land again, he found it had been canceled (the BIA and BLM records note that the land was actually canceled in mid-December of 1901), along with the allotments he had gotten for his wife and his son. Although Lou's and Arthur's allotments were canceled the next year, on April 18, 1902, all three allotments were canceled by Commissioner "G."[28] When Ole inquired about the cancellation, he was told that "when you left land to go help your old father, you relinquished it. . . . You have no land, and your children they have no land, because somebody wanted the timber, and it was too good land for an Indian to have."[29] Ole maintained that he never relinquished the land or otherwise agreed to its cancellation: "My last land was taken from me by stealing. I went to school and signed my name better than I do now, and they tell me my mark was on papers giving up my old land."[30]

Voluminous records show that Mr. Salem was not the only allottee in this position, but he was one of a smaller number of allottees who learned to read and write, and he applied his education to stand up for his land rights. As he stated in the 1919 deposition to Irvine Gardner, cruiser-at-large, U.S. Indian Service: "Not only was I entitled to an allotment, but my relatives all had allotments. My first cousins the Peconom family all getting theirs, as well as my father. I can sign my own name and any relinquishment purporting to be signed by me for my land, for that of my wife, and that of my son, is a forgery." Witnesses including Red River co-owner Fletcher Walker signed this statement. The Walker family, through Red River, purchased 56, or more than one-third, of the roughly 150 allotments in the region of hydroelectric speculation—including Butt Valley, Humbug Valley, Big Meadows, Mountain Meadows, and the area between Big Meadows and Greenville in Indian Valley.

The Greenville Indian School and Gardner sent a letter to the commissioner of Indian Affairs on December 23, 1919 corroborating Ole's statement and lauding his character. Gardner noted that some of Ole's original allotment was now within the Lassen National Forest, although "this Indian's rights so greatly antedate the creation of the forests that there is no question that he can be restored to his rights in this land." He wrote again on December 26, 1919, offering the facts of the case, including the locations of the allotments, when they were approved and canceled, respectively, and their current ownership status. According to Gardner's data, Ole's land was still held by the government, while both Lou's and Arthur's were mostly owned by Red River. Gardner recommended that any land not in private ownership be returned to Ole.

Following Ole's 1919 deposition, the chief clerk of the BIA, Hauke, recommended that Ole, his wife, and son, all file for new applications on their lands. However, both Ole's wife and son had died by this time, and their allotments (totaling 320 acres) were all patented to other parties, save a remaining forty acres, which was inadequate restitution for the land they had lost.

Greenville superintendent Edgar Miller sent a letter, dated January 5, 1920, lauding Ole's character and industriousness and noting that he was now living on a corner of the timbered allotment of his father-in-law, Rob Roy, near Chester, where he had cleared the land and put up a home, "a splendid and neat dairy," and rents pasture for his cows nearby, but this land will "soon not be available owing to the flooding from reservoir waters and he must seek other lands. He evidently lost his land through no good reason or fault of his. He can write well, is very intelligent, and knows absolutely how to take care of his own property."[31] On January 12, 1921, Gardner (ostensibly under direction from Superintendent Miller, whom he reported had "turned the matter over to me to adjust for Ole") wrote to the commissioner of Indian Affairs to request that the commissioner ask the GLO to expedite a survey of the Salems' proposed new allotments. He explained that the land he helped Ole apply for was land "near where Ole was born . . . on East shore of what is now Lake Almanor, but was then a big meadow." Gardner had already "ran out" these allotments, "under office instructions," and Ole had moved on to the new land, made significant improvements, and was raising dairy cattle.[32] A survey of the lands was needed so that Ole could fence it and thereby better maintain his cattle herd.[33] Gardner ended his letter with a nod to Miller's opinion of Ole as "progressive," and requested that the land survey be expedited.

In May 1921, the GLO requested information from the commissioner of Indian Affairs regarding whether Ole Salem, along with his children, was "qualified as an Indian to receive an allotment on the public domain."[34] Later that month, Chief Clerk Hauke transmitted the GLO's request to Miller, asking him to investigate the matter. In June 1921, Hauke wrote to the commissioner of the GLO, William Spry, affirming that George Salem was entitled to receive an allotment, and other affirmations likely were transmitted as well but were not retained in Ole Salem's file at the National Archives in Washington, D.C. In his December 16, 1921, letter to the commissioner of Indian Affairs in Washington, D.C., Ole Salem relayed the way in which his allotment had been taken and asked the commissioner to "hurry up and have my land surveyed and patented so no white people can take it away from me again."[35] Hauke replied and asked him to submit an affidavit, signed by two witnesses, describing the "character and date of settlement, the improvements made, and the nature and length of any use or occupancy" of his former allotment.[36] On February 15, 1923, Ole produced these affidavits and Gardner transmitted them to Miller, noting that they were "requested by the Dept. and [are] a necessary perquisite before he can make application to have the lands patented." Gardner's final line conveyed veiled tension between him and Miller: "Ole surely has made a fine showing and I am glad to help him in any way I can, as I know you are."[37] Ole produced another affidavit in the same time period (mid-February 1923) detailing the locations and character of the newly selected allotments, enumerating his improvements (i.e., the size of the house, garage, and barn he built, and the number of stock animals he owned) on his own newly selected allotment, and testifying that none had mineral value or was part of an existing mining claim. Miller then transmitted the affidavits to the commissioner of Indian Affairs by February 20, 1923.[38] The acting assistant commissioner of the GLO replied on November 15, 1923, citing the affidavit and offering approval of the allotments and the issuance of patents once a land survey was complete.[39]

On November 17, 1923, Hauke sent a letter to the secretary of the Interior recommending the approval of eight Salem allotments (for Ole and his sons Dell, Edward, George, Nelson, Joe, and Roy, and the heirs of his son Ted) near the east shore of Lake Almanor / Big Meadows.[40] Nearly two years later, on August 31, 1925, Hauke wrote to GLO commissioner Spry at the behest of Ole Salem, inquiring as to whether the land survey had taken place and when patents might be expected.[41] On February 21, 1927, the acting assistant commissioner of the GLO directed a reply to the Register in Sacramento, noting that the lands had been surveyed on June 28, 1926, and the plats accepted on November 12, 1926.

As such, in 1927, eight years after his 1919 deposition, Ole Salem's new allotments on the east shore of Lake Almanor were surveyed and allotted to him and to seven of his remaining sons. Ole's struggle to get these allotments approved within his homeland took 35 years. On December 27, 1927, about nine months after the allotments were approved, Ole Salem applied for a fee patent on his new allotment. On the application, Salem is described as 55 years of age and reported that his schooling consisted of attending the "white school at Susanville" for one year, and his occupations besides agriculture on his own land included working as a stockman and road foreman. At the time, he had a working farm, including 40 head of cattle and six head of work horses, and expressed pride in not owing money: when asked question number 14 on the application for a fee patent, "Are you in debt? If so, whom do you owe, how much, and for what, and have you given security for the debts?" he responded, "Not a cent." He did not lease any land, and held significant interest in the allotments of his deceased wife and children. His reason for requesting the fee patent was "so I could tend to my own business and not be hampered in any of my dealings. I have taken quite a few different contracts and would have money to handle some without borrowing."[42] As such, Salem had been successful and wanted to manage his own affairs.

The Report on Application for a Patent in Fee, undated yet signed by Sacramento Indian Agency superintendent L. A. Dorrington, indicates full faith in Salem and corroborates his statements regarding occupation and skills in the Application for the Patent in Fee. When asked why he recommended the issuance of a fee patent to Salem, Dorrington responded, "Because I believe him entirely able to manage his own affairs."[43] On February 27, 1928, the Department of the Interior issued a fee patent for Salem.[44]

Further correspondence between the Salems and the agency is evidenced by letters regarding expenditures of funds, trespasses by Red River, and appraisals of land for sale. A March 6, 1928, recommendation from Dorrington addresses Edward Salem's request to use about half of his funds on file with the U.S. Indian Service to purchase a car. As evidence of the type of "intimate colonialism" so well documented by Cahill (2011), Edward's request was transmitted from the Sacramento Agency (led by superintendent Dorrington) with detailed justification for the purchase ("Edward Salem is one of the best thought of Indian young men of this jurisdiction. . . . His request to purchase a car is reasonable. . . . He is employed by the Red River Lumber Company") and approved by the assistant commissioner of Indian Affairs (E. B. Merritt) and the assistant secretary of Indian Affairs (John Edwards) in Washington, D.C., on March 20, 1928.[45]

Following a successful trade of timber on his land for adjoining agricultural land held by Red River in 1929, Ole Salem oversaw the sale of the timber allotments of six of his sons. Dorrington supported this process, as evidenced by a June 1930 letter to the commissioner of Indian Affairs, in which he supports the approval of these sales, noting that the prices are good given changes in the timber market, the Salems are "leading and progressive," and that they recently lost much of their timber holdings to fire, so their justifications for the sales are valid.[46] Salem and the agency also successfully negotiated with Western Pacific Railroad in 1931, when the railroad requested a nine-acre right-of-way to cross Salem's land. Western Pacific offered to move all of his buildings, rock fencing, and orchard; pipe his water under their railroad; insert a temporary cattle pass; and purchase the timber in exchange for the right-of-way.[47]

The work of Ole Salem over the first half of the twentieth century to obtain allotments for himself and his family and negotiate with surrounding landowners and the agency to grow his agricultural and other enterprises represents a very rare and significant example of successful advocacy in a region that was under intense pressure for timber harvest and hydroelectric production. To show the rarity of this work, I turn now to nearby Butt Valley, where there are several examples of the more common story of persistent advocacy, yet ultimate loss of land, and ongoing struggle to receive adequate restitution.

BUTT VALLEY: A LAND/WATERSCAPE OF DISPLACEMENT

Residents of the valley that is now the reservoir of Butt Valley, just below and southwest of Lake Almanor, were not so fortunate in maintaining and/or restoring their allotments. Butt Valley is one of three reservoirs that compose the Upper North Fork Feather River Hydroelectric Project, owned and operated by PG&E. Compared to Lake Almanor's storage capacity of 1,134,016 acre-feet, Butt Valley has a much smaller storage capacity of 49,900 acre-feet. It relies on the flow of Butt Creek, a tributary of the North Fork Feather River that once flowed through the meadow.

Of 19 allotments totaling 2,960 acres (18 160-acre allotments and one 80-acre allotment) in and around the Butt Valley reservoir, at least 17 were canceled for hydroelectric development. In the case of Robert Shafer, who received 160-acre allotment 150 in Butt Valley on March 27, 1894, his land was canceled in February 1902 and condemned in November 1902. A June 3, 1912, letter from the Greenville Indian School to the superintendent of Indian Affairs asks why Shafer never received a patent, and notes that no information was available in the land records office on the parcel. This indicates that Shafer was never told of the cancellation of his land. Further investigation by the Indian Office following the 1912 letter revealed that Shafer's was one of a number of allotments condemned on November 21, 1902, by the Superior Court of Plumas County in favor of the Western Power Company under the act of March 3, 1901 (31 Stat. 1058-1084), vesting in the company fee simple title to the lands. No patents went to the allottees because of the above decree and a subsequent affirmatory (Department of the Interior) decision of June 29, 1907 (36 L.D., 648), recognizing the court's authority (see L.R. 58490-12 and 65770-12).

In response to a July 21, 1922, investigation of the Greenville Indian Agency, Superintendent Miller wrote that the agency had expended $3,500 on May 2, 1922, to purchase Robert Shafer a home in a nearby town through GWP. As such, Shafer and his family received allotments in Butt Valley and lived through a period of great uncertainty in which they believed their rights to Butt Valley to be affirmed, while those rights were actually legally divested for hydroelectric development. Then, the Shafers were relocated to a house paid for by the power company in partial restitution for the appropriation of their land.

RACE, GENDER, AND LITERACY IN POWER-SITE WITHDRAWALS

On July 9, 1924, Assistant Commissioner E. B. Merritt wrote to the Sacramento agency superintendent L. A. Dorrington regarding the allotment application of Rosie Meadows (previously known as Loukeen Meadows, Sus-148), then-wife of Ole Salem.[48] Salem had been reallotted lands after his initial allotments were illegally canceled. Rosie Meadows wanted to apply for lands that Ole had formerly applied for. These lands were now part of a forest reserve, and because Ole did not file for them before they became part of the reserve (per Section 4 of the General Allotment Act), and because Rosie was not head of household, these lands were no longer available. The commissioners of the GLO and BIA recommended that Rosie Meadows apply for lands located northwest of Dixie Valley and near the Pit River.[49] The GLO agreed to allow her two years to show evidence of use and occupancy of the land, per April 15, 1918, regulations regarding Indian allotments on the public domain.[50] At the end of this period, the allottee would be required to file an affidavit signed by two witnesses, explaining "the character and date of settlement, the improvements made and the nature and length of any use or occupancy of the land. Such occupancy must be shown for a period of two years."[51]

Dorrington was concerned about this requirement, which would require Rosie Meadows to leave her family, including small children, to establish a presence on the distant allotment. Dorrington noted her history—her father, John Meadow, actually applied for the allotment on her behalf in 1894, it was approved in 1897, and then canceled in June 1902. The cancellation was made because her mother, Kate Meadows McKenney, was married to a white man, so Loukeen/Rosie's application for allotment, as well as Kate's, were both determined ineligible and canceled.[52] Rosie was not told of the cancellation, and occupied and improved the land for seven years, building a "nice cabin, and fine garden spot, fine improvement then they canceled it for me."[53] Dorrington argued that Rosie should be given the new allotment without the requirement to live on-site, as credit for the allotment that was previously taken from her without compensation. He also noted that her initial allotment had become valued at $10,000–$12,000, and was part of the "project of the Great Western Power Company." Dorrington concluded his 1925 letter with a statement of concern regarding the practices of the agencies involved: "Now, Mr. Commissioner, it is cases such as these and there are others similar in this jurisdiction, that have caused many of the Indians to lose confidence in the Government officials and to believe and follow persons who are unfriendly to the Indian Service and whose good faith we doubt."[54] GLO acting assistant commissioner Parrott replied in November 1925 with a resounding no: "There is no law under which the Indian can be credited on the land now wanted with the use and occupancy of the land in the canceled allotment. The Indian should comply with the intention expressed in her affidavit that she would begin use and occupancy of the land."[55]

Three years later, Ned Bogunda signed a statement in front of Lassen County notary public Irvine Gardner that he grazed his herd on Rosie Meadows Salem's allotment, which adjoined his lands in Clarks Valley, Little Valley, and Eby Lake lands. The point of his statement was to show "use or occupancy of the above described land of Rosie Meadows Salem."[56] Dorrington again voiced support for Rosie in his June 15, 1928, letter to the commissioner of Indian Affairs, noting that "she has made all the use possible of the land . . . without deliberately leaving her home." He noted further that requiring her to go live on the new allotment "seems a shame . . . after she has shown good faith by using and improving the land covered by her first application for approximately 7 years she should lose it, particularly when the value at the present time would probably be around $15,000."[57]

Despite Rosie's statements, Bogunda's formal letter, and Dorrington's support, the GLO rejected the allotment application on September 17, 1928, finding that Rosie had not "improved or personally used or occupied the land." Leasing the land to Bogunda "did not meet the requirements as to settlement and improvement." The GLO felt that "the requirements of the law and regulations as to settlement and improvement have not been complied with." The case was closed on December 7, 1928.

Although similarly penalized by racialized allotment policy, across Lake Almanor near Chester, allottee William Charley (Sus-312) received some land after having his allotment canceled. Charley's rights to land were supported by his service in the military, which was looked on favorably by the BIA. Kate Charley (Sus-311) received an allotment for her son, Willie Charley, in 1894. However, like Rose Meadow Salem's allotment, the land was canceled in 1902 (the same year that GWP incorporated) ostensibly because Willie's father was white. The allotment was also within a power-site withdrawal, indicating that it had already been designated as a prime parcel for hydroelectric development. Power-site withdrawals for lands valuable for water resources were first enabled by an act of October 2, 1888, just one year after the Indian Allotment Act was passed in 1887.[58] The 1888 act was later repealed by an 1890 act that stated that only reservoir sites would remain in withdrawal status, and this land was to be a reservoir site (F. F. Lawrence, C. E. Nordeen, and H. L. Pumphrey 1963). The secretary of the Interior can approve or revoke these withdrawals. This particular role of the secretary represents a potential conflict of interest, as the Department of the Interior is the primary agency charged with upholding the trust responsibility, as the home of the BIA. Despite this responsibility, the secretary of the Interior did not intervene to stop power-site withdrawals from encompassing Indian allotment lands.

According to the allotment application, Kate had selected the land for her son, and was living on the site. She received a cancellation notice in 1901, but was illiterate, so she saved it and showed it to Gardner in 1918. In 1920 Gardner wrote to the commissioner that the allotment was wrongfully canceled, as he could prove Kate and Willie were both Indians and Willie served in the army during World War I.

In 1922 the Office of Indian Affairs made an effort to amend the original allotment application to cover a portion of the allotment containing 40 acres and to permit Willie Charley to make a new application for an additional allotment of 120 acres, contiguous or noncontiguous to the above, in order to make up the full acreage of 160, to which "he may be entitled."[59] The work of the BIA to get Charley allotment land was complicated by the fact that, in 1903, an O. W. Barnes (half brother to T. B. Walker of Red River) found that the allotment was canceled and applied for a 40-acre portion. Barnes was given title to this acreage in December 1920, and the remainder was in power-site withdrawals. He then mortgaged his interest to Red River, which desired to, according to a February 1922 letter from Gardner to Superintendent Miller, "protect themselves and also the Indian. Mr. Walker will also give the Indians a free use of other 40 acres for grazing. This east 40 has all fences, old building, etc., on it and will make Willie a fine pasture of its own." On June 22, 1922, Red River sold the 40-acre parcel to Willie Charley for $10, and deeded the land to him.

Willie Charley applied for fee or private title in March 1923. Generally, allotments were held in trust for the individual Indian allottee or his or her heirs by the BIA. If the allottee desired fee ownership, which included the ability to sell the parcel at will, he or she had to apply to the agency and prove competency. In support of Charley, the agency called for removal of restrictions on the property "on the ground that there is no man of Indian blood in his jurisdiction more capable of attending to his own affairs. He is both worthy and capable."[60] Today, the site of Charley's old allotment is wholly out of Indian ownership and partially owned by PG&E, the U.S. Forest Service (Lassen National Forest), and the timber company Sierra Pacific Industries. The portion of Charley's allotment that is owned by PG&E and above the 4,500' contour line (below that line is PG&E's essential property for operations) will be retained by PG&E in the Stewardship Council process, with an easement held by the Feather River Land Trust.

Incidentally, Willie Charley's allotment was the only one of the three Charley allotments that remained, for at least some length of time, in the family's ownership. The other two allotments were canceled (as was Willie's), but never returned. One of these, the allotment of Kate Charley (Sus-311), was canceled and then sold to GWP. In response to a 1922 investigation of what happened to so many canceled allotments and their landless allottees, the Greenville Indian Agency reported that it had purchased a ranch in Tehama County for Kate Charley, likely using the revenue from her land sale to GWP to make the purchase. Today, 40 acres of Kate Charley's old allotment belongs to a timber company, and the remainder is within the holdings of PG&E.

Like the Charleys, four of the five allotments belonging to the Bill family (Jennie Bill, Sus-423; Eli Bill, Sus-424; John Bill, Sus-425; and Lucy (Rosa) Bill, Sus-427) were recommended for cancellation by both the GLO[61] and the commissioner of Indian Affairs because "the applicant[s] in question are the children of [a] white man."[62] The remaining allotment, that of Emma Bill, Sus-426, was not canceled. Jennie Bill was apparently notified of the suspension on May 26, 1902, and notified a second time (via letter) on April 6, 1903, allowing her 60 days to show why the four allotment applications for her and her minor children should not be canceled. Jennie did not take action, although it is unclear if she received or was able to read the letter, and Commissioner G canceled the allotments on January 11, 1904.[63]

Eli Bill, who attended Greenville Indian School and graduated from Carlisle Indian School in Pennsylvania, began communicating with the office on or before July 1915 in an effort to acquire his allotment and those of his mother, brother, and sister.[64] Carlisle Indian School administrator General Richard Henry Pratt wrote to the Office of Indian Affairs in support of Eli's request to have his land rights confirmed, noting that previous explanations regarding the status of the land from the office had been "unsatisfactory," especially as pertaining to Eli's race. Pratt noted Eli's strong school record and laudable work ethic following graduation in 1907, concluding that "such . . . independence merits strong encouragement and . . . none of the rights so fully accorded to those less worth [sic] should be denied."[65]

In December 1919, Gardner reopened the Bill files and inquired with Miller about the cancellations, noting that, while they were canceled by Comissioner G on November 18, 1901, "records" from the Susanville Land Office dated May 1902 showed that they should have been "suspended . . . not cancelled." He argued that all of the allotments remained in federal title, that other family members had "received titles to their land, have perfected and sold the same," and "we can obtain these lands for these allottees or their heirs."[66] Miller apparently forwarded Gardner's communication to the Office of Indian Affairs in Washington, D.C., and received a reply in January 1920 upholding the rejection of the allotments and declining to reopen the cases.[67]

In May 1926 E. G. Scammon of Red River inquired with the agency regarding the Indian allotments of the Bill family. Scammon noted that "Ole Salem . . . succeeded in getting appropriations for his heirs where the conditions were about the same," and requested advisement regarding "what can be done with these three cancelled applications." Scammon reminded the agency that the allottees were still living and one "is a well educated Indian [who] graduated from Carlyle [sic] School in Pennsylvania." He noted that two of the allotments were "unsurveyed territory" near Ole Salem's new allotments but may be within the Forest Reserve, and inquired as to whether there was "an opportunity to have them reinstated."[68] Dorrington replied shortly thereafter, noting the history of the allotments and their cancellation, explaining that the 1916 investigation was precipitated by General Pratt's involvement in the matter on Eli Peazzoni's behalf and including a copy of the 1919 letter from the Washington office to Miller upholding the cancellation. While he indicated that there was "no way" that these lands could be reinstated, he responded directly to Scammon's question as to whether the Bills could work out a similar land swap as Ole Salem, noting that this could not be considered unless (1) allottees had lived on the land for at least two years before the National Forest was created, or (2) the Forest Service "clear listed" the lands to open them for entry. Dorrington concluded his informative letter by thanking Scammon for "calling this matter to my attention, and the many other courtesies that you have shown this office,"[69] indicating a friendliness between the agency and the timber company.

The following year, Dorrington wrote to the commissioner of Indian Affairs in Washington, D.C., after having spoken with Eli Peazzoni (Bill) about the canceled allotments. In a nearly apologetic tone, Dorrington explained that he knew that the agency had investigated the matter in 1916 and concluded that the cancellations were justified, but he noted the stature of Eli Bill (Carlisle-educated, now working as a high school teacher in Southern California) and the apparent validity of his questions about why four of the five Bill allotments had been canceled.[70] Chief Clerk Hauke responded soon after, noting that cancellations took place in 1904, because Jennie was married to a white man who was the father of three of her children (Eli, John, and Lucy) and because "the wife took the status of her husband" and "the status of the children was also the same as that of the father," none of them were entitled "as Indians, to file on public land." He explained that Emma's land was not canceled because no evidence was provided to disprove the assertion that her father was Indian. Hauke's tone indicated impatience and frustration, as he concluded the letter: "Eli Peazzoni has been informed of the status of these cases a great many times throughout correspondence, and in person when visiting the Office in 1915."[71] Dorrington forwarded the reply to Peazzoni within the week.[72]

In July 1938 Eli (Bill) Peazzoni went into the Sacramento Indian Agency to inquire about his canceled allotment and those of his mother (Jennie), sister (Lucy), and brother (John). He argued that all of the Bill allotments were heavily timbered except Emma's, which was not canceled, thereby "the reason that they were only of ½ Indian blood was not conclusive in refusing them an allotment." Peazzoni also felt that an error had been made in canceling his mother Jennie's allotment "on the grounds that the applicants were the children of a white man," when Jennie was "full blood Indian." Finally, he explained that "the required notice of cancellation was never sent" to his mother, and he did not hear of it until he came home from Carlisle Indian School in 1905 to be with his mother during her final illness. According to Mae Hooper in her memo to Superintendent Nash following Peazzoni's visit:

> Mr. Piazzoni seems to feel there was something "crooked" in this deal, involving the Red River Lumber Company. Evidently they were frustrated in their attempts to secure the timber when it was taken into the Forest Reserve in 1905. . . . He states that he has written to the Indian Office . . . but he has been unable to secure any definite information as to whether or not any correction of this error is obtainable.[73]

Nash wrote back immediately, responding to each of Peazzoni's points and refuting his assertions. He noted that, at the time of cancellation, allotments were not available to either the children of a white man or the Indian wife of a white man. He also argued that Emma Bill had a different father than the other children, as evidenced by her probate hearing, during which Eli Bill's father, Chris Peazzoni, stated that he was the father of all of the Bill children but Emma, whose father was an Indian. He also referenced the letter from the Indian Office to Greenville superintendent Miller in 1920 declining to reopen the case. In light of all of this evidence, and "the long lapse of time," Nash concluded that the case should not be reopened.[74] Twelve years later, in 1950, Eli's sister Rosie Walker (as Lucy Bill) inquired about her allotment, Sus-427, and Acting Area Director James B. Ring replied with copies of Nash's 1938 letter and the 1920 letter from the chief clerk, again declining to open the case or to reallot Lucy Bill.[75]

RESISTING PATERNALISM

The BIA often made it difficult, if not impossible, for allottees to act on their own behalf. The paternalistic attitude that accompanied the language in the 1887 Allotment Act included the requirement that the land stay in trust for at least 25 years or until the allottee was deemed "competent" to sell. Allottees could apply at any time for a fee patent on their land, thereby releasing the trust patent and acquiring private ownership of the allotment. One allottee, Jack Mullen (Sus-41), applied for a fee patent on his 157-acre allotment in March 1928. Mullen lived on his allotment, had it fenced, and was raising horses and cattle there. He stated his reason for requesting a fee patent as follows: "I want my own way. If anybody comes to me to say anything about the land I want to be able to say."[76] However, when Commissioner of Indian Affairs Chas Burke and Assistant Secretary J. Edwards reviewed his application, they replied that, although he indicated some business acumen, "he is a full blood Indian . . . has never attended school and signs his name by his thumb mark." They expressed concern that he would not be able to decipher a contract if he were to enter into any real estate or other contract on his land. They decided that the current trust title of his land was of greater benefit to Mullen then the perceived independence of the fee patent and denied his request in April 1928.[77] The land remained in trust for another 20 years, until it was included in the "Public Sale of Indian Lands in the State of California by the California Indian Agency" on December 21, 1949, and sold in 1950.

Allottees were also hampered by the agency when they desired to sell their allotments, if such sales were not the agency's priority. In a 1939 petition for the sale of her allotment in Dixie Valley, Mandy Roseberry stated that the land was of little value to her, "It is just a pile of gravel and no land where I could have a garden," and that she needed the money to continue to care for her aged parents on her father's allotment (Sus-8, Billy Roseberry).[78] Other correspondence from the agency indicates that it had been actively leasing out these allotments since at least 1929 and was planning to lease them again in 1939.[79] In 1943 the field nurse Florence S. McClintock wrote on Mandy's behalf, asking if her allotment and her sister's could be sold and naming a buyer.[80] Superintendent John Rockwell's response to McClintock was terse: "For your information, you are advised that until such time as the public domain allotment land study report is completed and sent to the Indian Office for approval as to our recommendation, no allotments will be sold. You can pass this information on to any Indians or white people who inquire regarding the sale or purchase of Indian lands."[81] In 1944 Mandy's aged mother Mary Roseberry wrote to the agency again asking permission to sell, citing Mandy's illness and the family's need for the funds, and naming a possible buyer.[82] Rockwell wrote back that the agency continued to study the Indian allotments and determine whether a sale was justified. He concluded that he did not know when they would get to her particular allotments, but hopefully "some time this year."[83] This series of bureaucratic, paternalistic responses from the agency did not address the evident need expressed by the Roseberrys for funds from the sale. Indeed, Mandy Roseberry died in October 1944, and her heirs petitioned to sell again in 1949. This time, the state director recommended the sale, noting that it was "in full accord with our withdrawal program,"[84] and the land was sold in 1950.[85]

As Mandy Roseberry's case shows, even with allottees' own advocacy, along with support from field staff like McClintock (who, despite her own paternalistic position,[86] was more aware of conditions allottees faced on the ground than employees at the urban agency more than five hours' drive away), sometimes they were not able to impact the agency's plans for their lands. The agency was only willing to sell some of these lands once the termination policy was pending in the early 1950s. The BIA's responsibility to manage land as a trust asset, in the best interest of Indian allottees, lapsed as allottees suffered and died waiting for some small amount of revenue for the sale of lands that they could not directly make a living from. The lack of mention of lease revenue despite the documentation that the land was being leased also raises questions about whether the funding from the lease ever made it into the Roseberrys' hands. Those funds may have become part of the vast amount of mismanaged and misplaced individual Indian monetary accounts that were the subject of the decade-long *Cobell* class-action lawsuit that began in 1996 and settled in 2009.[87]

POWER AND TIMBER ALLOTMENT ACQUISITION WITH BIA BLESSING

Like the Charleys and Bills, many other allottees in and around the reservoirs had their allotments canceled without their knowledge. Many were never real-lotted. Of the roughly 165 allotments in the Big Meadows / Humbug Valley /

Mountain Meadows / Butt Valley areas considered (and mostly developed, with reservoirs in all but Humbug Valley) for hydroelectric development, at least 65 allotments were canceled, mostly by Commissioner G, and were relinquished. Thirty-three of the cancellations were revoked but, of these, 29 were sold to a timber company (26 to Red River), and one was sold to GWP directly. Often the sales were pushed through by the agents and include standard language indicating the need to sell the parcel in order to provide funds for subsistence for the allottee or his or her heirs.

If public domain allotment sales did not directly or indirectly facilitate hydroelectric development, they fed the growing land monopoly of timber companies in the region. Historic petitions to sell allotments contain standard language that indicates a time pressure to sell due to timber companies working nearby and do not indicate directly whether allottees wanted to sell or had viable livelihood alternatives to selling. In Indian Valley, just southwest of Big Meadows / Lake Almanor, William Washoe's allotment (Sus-134) is an example of a parcel that was nearly canceled (a 1902 cancellation order was revoked in 1903) but then sold by heirs to a timber company. It is unclear whether a benefit accrued to Washoe's heir, Mary Washoe Johnson, as the seller. In the early 1920s, heir Mary Washoe Johnson and/or the Greenville Indian Agency empowered by the 1906 Burke Act (34 Stat. 182), or Forced Fee Patenting Act, decided to sell William Washoe's allotment.[88] In Mary Johnson's application for sale of the land, filled out by the Greenville Indian Agency on her behalf, it notes that the Greenville Indian Agency land and lease clerk F. W. Coppersmith didn't know of anyone who

> would be willing to pay $24 per annum for the use of this land, or any adjoining lands, as they are not worth over $.10/acre for grazing purposes. It has always been the practice of this Office to obtain all that we can for the Indians, in the Sale or Leasing of their lands. Lands leased in 1921 for $.20/acre, would probably lease for 10 or 15 cents for the year 1922.

Given this ostensible loss in value, Coppersmith proposed that Johnson's land be sold to one of the lumber companies, the Wolf Creek Timber Company. Johnson is recorded on the application as wanting to sell both the land and the timber because the land "would be of no use to her." Whether or not Johnson actually made this statement, or if she knew that the land would be sold and she would lose her rights and access to it and possibly not receive payment is unclear, since this same language is repeated on nearly all of the applications for sale during the time period. It is unclear whether the allottees agreed to the sales, actually received the amounts paid, and were able to acquire other land or homes. Johnson's allotment was included in the "Public Sale of Indian Lands at Greenville Indian Agency on January 16, 1922," and a fee patent was issued later that year to the Wolf Creek Timber Company.

Allottees also had to fight against the loss of their land by bureaucratic means—including lack of communication by different federal and state agencies with varying established claims on the land that ignored Indian land rights. A Maidu man known as Little Pete Thomas confronted this problematic system in 1915, when he tried to sell an allotment that he thought had been approved for him in 1894. Thomas was living up north in Pit River country with his wife, Martha Thomas, and wanted to sell Sus-183 so that he could use the proceeds of the sale to do further improvements on his wife's land. However, in the process of attempting to get the petition to sell approved, it became clear that the allotment to Thomas had never been finalized. A February 1916 letter from Chief Clerk C. F. Hauke of the Office of Indian Affairs in Washington, D.C., explained that the land was never allotted: "Inquiry at the General Land Office developed the fact that it was selected for him but that the application was returned for amendment December 2, 1898, since which time apparently nothing has been done."[89] Hauke recommended working with the allottee to perfect his application and obtain a trust patent, and then resubmitting the petition to sell. However, a March 1916 letter from Roseburg supervisor Wilson to the Commissioner of Indian Affairs explained that the land was already "covered by State selection as swamp land and was approved in 1875 and 1876. In view of this, assistance will be rendered Little Pete Thomas to make another selection should he so request."[90]

Apparently, Thomas was never apprised of this situation, because in 1920 he wrote to the supervisor of the Greenville Indian School, Edgar Miller, asking about his land: "Mr. Miller, I want to know about my land. Mr. Gardner told me my land had been sold and he asked me if I never [sic] got my money. I told him I did not. Now I want to know why I do not get that money and what is the matter."[91] Miller replied a few days later that the office had no record of any sale of his land or of any land allotted to him. Miller briefly mentioned allotment 183, but offered no solution to its status: "We take it that you are allottee #183 and if so that land is Swamp Land and you have no title to same."[92] In the 1932 examination of Little Pete Thomas's inheritance after his death, it was found that he had applied for two allotments, Sus-183 and Sus-1052 (for his wife, Martha), but "neither application was perfected"—Sus-183 because it had been claimed by the state and he was never offered the opportunity to select other lands, and Sus-1052 because he and his wife did not prove that they lived on the land and improved it within the required time period. In the end, the examiner of inheritance noted that "at the time of his death he was unallotted." He did inherit revenue from the sale of his mother's (Cora Roy) and other relatives' lands at Big Meadows to GWP and Red River, but by 1932, his trust estate consisted of only $3.[93]

Another significant issue for many allottees was that of trespass. While some lived on their allotments and others did not, all possessed a trust title to lands that had value for grazing, timber, water, and other rights. There were many reports of trespass in the Big Meadows, Mountain Meadows, Madeline Plains, and other areas, and the Office of Indian Affairs was supposed to investigate these matters and collect trespass damages on the allottees' behalf. In some instances, once the agency communicated the trespass concern to the perpetrator, that individual or company then consented to purchase the allotment.

Near Madeline in Lassen County, for example, the allotment of Charlie Leef (Sus-409) had been leased by a Pierre Mendibourne, but the lease had expired, and Mendibourne had not complied with the new regulations, which called for seeking the approval of at least a majority of heirs (if not all heirs) before he could renew. Following a series of letters, the state director of the California Indian Agency sent the following missive to Mendibourne in 1948:

> We have received information you have been using the allotments. We have also been informed you have had some of the Indian owners sign the lease forms and that you had told some of them you had sent $200.00 to this office to cover payment for the use of their land. Upon checking our records, we do not find any remittance made by you to cover the leases for the use of the allotments involved.[94]

Shortly thereafter, Mendibourne purchased the 160-acre "undeveloped" allotment, appraised as most adapted for grazing, for $660.[95]

The Macks in Mountain Meadows dealt with trespass issues with Red River. Bob Mack received an allotment on the edge of Mountain Meadows for his daughter Ollie in 1894. The allotment was held for cancellation by Commissioner G in 1902 and then the cancellation order was revoked, also by Commissioner G, in 1903. Ollie died in 1906, leaving her mother, Sally Mack, as heir. Sally Mack petitioned to sell the allotment in 1916, indicating that it was "timber land and could not even be rented," yet she received "no benefit from it" even though she was blind and needed money for her subsistence.[96] Irvine Gardner, who was later found to be working for both the Office of Indian Affairs and Red River simultaneously, appraised the land at valuable only for its timber, worth a total of $4,566.[97]

However, a 1915 or 1916 examination of the land by C. E. Dunston found that Red River had "recently logged off between 10 and 15 acres of the best timber on this allotment in trespass." Dunston also noted that "at the time of examination deep snow on this area made it impracticable to measure this trespass cutting. A trespass examination should be made next spring." In response, the Indian Service sent out two forest assistants to investigate, and they found that Red River had "logged up to the allotment lines but . . . not cut any on the allotment."[98] As such, the allotment was cleared for sale to Red River in 1919 for $4,737. Red River was the only bidder, and this was justified because Red River "is Logging this district now and have tracks laid—they will pay a better price now while in a position to log this land than later."[99] As such, Red River's monopoly on land in the region supported its continuing expansion. Sally Mack agreed to the sale with her thumbprint in October 1920. The November 1920 "Report on Cash Sale of Allotted Indian Land" indicated that the land had been trespassed on before and trespass damages collected. The fee patent was issued to Red River on February 25, 1921, and the sale was complete.

The report of trespass on an allotment had to be accompanied by substantial evidence, including the name of the trespasser, the names of witnesses, and details of the property impacted, yet the penalty was often not significant for the trespasser. In 1913 the clerk wrote to John McClellan regarding McClellan's report of trespass on the allotment of Fred John, agreeing that no one, including a white person, had the right to cut timber on Indian lands without permission from the Indian Office.[100] McClellan must have submitted the required evidence about the trespass, because a subsequent letter was addressed to the trespasser, Mr. Paul States, from the clerk. However, the clerk was very accommodating and lenient with States, offering to "adjust" the cost with him directly rather than involve the federal courts. He also only charged him a reduced rate and allowed him to keep the property taken: "On the assumption that the trespass was not made with malice or intention, the amount of damages assessed . . . is not the maximum amount allowed by law. The payment of this sum will for the same reason allow the timber to be used by the trespasser."[101] The clerk then requested that the amount due be sent to the office or paid to him in person, leaving some question as to whether it ever reached allottee Fred John. The clerk was similarly accommodating to another trespasser, H. or A. J. Doyen, choosing to rely on a state statute, even though this land was held in trust by the federal government, rather than a more stringent federal statute:

> The payment of the sum of six dollars will constitute a satisfactory adjustment of the trespass on the allotment of Fred John. This is in accordance with Section 3346 of the Civil Code of the State of California. Under the Federal law, the amount of damages would be many times in excess of the amount mentioned; but inasmuch as this is the first offense, the case will not be presented to that court.[102]

As such, even when allottees advocated for the agency to respond to calls of trespass and cite trespassers accordingly, local ranchers and timber operators were often dealt with in the most generous of possible terms and allowed to continue to profit from stolen property.

In addition to trespass, allottees and Indian lessees of allotments had to fight neighboring landowners that would appropriate water from their lands. According to a 1943 map, the Orbey Charley allotment had a spring on the south boundary of the allotment with United States Forest Service land and two streams crossing it. Charley had received allotments for himself, his wife, and two children in 1894, with the idea of retaining an older settlement near the springs. Two of the allotments were canceled and Orbey's was reduced by half, and a trust patent on the remaining half was issued in 1920. A July 1941 letter from M. C. Kerr to the Indian Agency argued that the spring was on Orbey's original allotment, before it was reduced.

In August 1941 Indian Agency staff filed an application to appropriate the water on behalf of the allottees with the DWR. The DWR approved the application in October 1941 and advised that they post a notice on the property. Neighboring landowners submitted a protest with DWR, asserting that they had been using the water prior to the establishment of the allotment.[103] In 1942 the Indian Office withdrew the application with concerns that it established the artificially late date of Indian appropriation at 1941.[104] In 1943 the Indian Office told the allotment lessee that he could continue using the water.[105] However, the neighboring landowner prevented the lessee from using the water for allotment irrigation, asserting that the water rights associated with the non-Indian land were superior.[106]

Investigation into the history of the parcels revealed that non-Indian squatters and homesteaders had been using the water since 1862.[107] The question then became, "Who used the water first?" Based on the 1872 water code, in order to establish a right to water, a party had to divert it, and investigators found that both the Indian and non-Indian landowners had diverted the water for irrigation since at least the 1890s. Superintendent O. H. Lipps argued that Charley had a right to the land dating back at least to the approval of his allotment in 1894, and that the land along with the water was held in trust and any dispute needed to go to a federal tribunal. In 1943, drawing on evidence that the Charleys lived on the land prior to white settlement,[108] the attorney argued that the Charleys had the land prior to allotment. In effect, he was trying to prove aboriginal, unceded title.[109] A July 1943 exploration of the site by Indian Service personnel found that the spring would be capable of furnishing water to both the allotment and the non-Indian homestead, and encouraged an agreement between the parties.[110] Despite this, in 1948, when a Maidu lessor diverted some of the water to irrigate the land for agriculture and grazing, his diversion works were removed by the neighbor who asserted rights to all of the water in the stream. As such, even when an allottee had recognized legal and aboriginal rights to water, in practice it was difficult to uphold these rights relative to neighboring, hostile users.

CONCLUSION: AGAINST THE ODDS

Individual Indian allottees and their heirs negotiated state, federal, corporate, and private interests in order to either keep their lands, trade allotted lands for other lands that they could live on and cultivate, and/or gain revenue from selling their allotted lands. Whether they were successful or not, the historical record shows that they labored to be heard and served by an alien system that disregarded their rights and was hostile to them and their interests. Today, that spirit of resistance remains strong, and descendants of those allottees in the Mountain Maidu and Pit River homelands continue to enjoin processes (such as the FERC relicensing and the Stewardship Council land divestiture) and seize opportunities (i.e., to comanage and purchase lands) to access, steward, reclaim, and restore their homelands.

3

VALUING LAND

ARCHIVAL ALLOTMENT data provides a window into understanding how the former Indian allotment lands in the northeastern Sierra were and are valued, and by and for whom. When the BIA and the GLO (now the Bureau of Land Management) approved Indian allotments, the agencies emphasized value for grazing and agriculture to encourage Indigenous assimilation. When lands were surveyed, if they were found more valuable for timber or water resources, they risked cancellation. However, when appraised for sale, their value was often understated in order to facilitate transfer to non-Indian companies and individuals.[1] Finally, none of these agency and corporate valuations spoke to the intrinsic and cultural value of the land to Maidu and other allottees—as Shoemaker explains, "Tribes do not . . . communicate their land ethics or organize social relations through the mess of jurisdictional checkerboards." Indigenous people living through this time may have had to exercise a "double consciousness" related to land—retaining their beliefs about the importance of places alongside negotiating imposed federal, state, and private evaluations of their homeland.[2]

In an example of fluctuating values imposed on her land, Maidu allottee Coreno Washoe was allotted land in present-day Williams Valley, outside of Greenville, in 1894, only to receive a notice of cancellation on April 21, 1902, because a special agent of the GLO had found the tract "chiefly valuable for timber." Washoe was given 60 days to comply with or appeal the decision, and, if she did not take action, "the case" would be "reported for appropriate action"—that is, cancellation without further notice.[3] The land escaped cancellation and heirs petitioned to sell in 1917, with an appraisal by Irvine Gardner that actually found 60 acres of the land valuable for timber and the remaining 100 acres of "no value," with "shallow soil" and "numerous rocky ridges."[4] Whether the land was canceled because it was too valuable for timber or undersold because it wasn't valuable enough had significant consequences for the allottee's ability to make a living and have a home there.

Many allottees were initially allotted forested or rocky lands, only to have those lands canceled due to their timber or hydroelectric value and then purchased or claimed by either agencies or private companies (facilitated by public processes such as condemnation for hydropower reserves) for hydroelectric development or public conservation by the U.S. Forest Service. The Indian Office was also vulnerable to corruption in the case of land appraisals, as it was obliged to rely heavily on the work of independent field staff. According to Sacramento Indian Agency chief clerk Hauke, this was necessary because "allotments on the public domain in California are so widely scattered and in most cases so inaccessible to Superintendents, that the appraisement of lands as well as timber has been left largely to timber cruisers."[5]

In one case, the Greenville Indian Agency land and lease clerk F. W. Coppersmith caught a $20 mistake in appraiser Irvine Gardner's calculations after the purchaser had already agreed to the price. Coppersmith was obliged to write to purchaser J. J. Fleming to request that he pay the $20 difference or the D.C. office would reject the sale on account of the error. The interesting point about this mistake is that Coppersmith framed the request to Fleming as not amounting to much, given the low prices he had paid for other allotments in the group of allotments he was likely to purchase: "The difference is surely offset by the low values of the Harry and Mayfield Lee allotments that you will no doubt purchase at some time."[6]

An offhand comment that is often made about reserved Indian lands is that they were the lowest-value lands—the lands that non-Indian homesteaders did not want or that federal and state governments had found no specific use for. However, if these allotments were so low value, why were they sold and canceled so rapidly? One of the goals of this text is to unpack assumptions about Indian land to reveal who is making such statements, and for what purpose. Indeed, there is a consistent agency emphasis on allotting land to Indian people that is not useful for purposes other than small-scale farming or grazing, per the Allotment Act.[7] Take, for example, the language approving the allotment of minor Danny Jim in 1919: "The land contains no power or reservoir site possibilities, is non-irrigable, non-mineral, and is useful principally for grazing purposes."[8] This was standard language in recommendations to allot Indian people on the public domain. However, in a 1919 statement, Jim's stepfather, Frank Norman, described why he and his family settled the Jim allotment: "We lived here as my own allotment is all rocks and big springs no place for a home."[9] While the agency documentation persistently emphasizes the land's lack of value, and therefore its fit for an allotment, Jim, his stepfather Frank Norman, and other family members recognized significant value in Jim's land, relative to other parcels.

The following pages explore the specific methods (cancellations, condemnations, relinquishments) by which lands deemed more valuable were wrested from allottees, as well as how allottees were able to work to protect their interests within the constraints of the agency's administration. I believe specificity is required in order to articulate what occurred, advocate for restitution, and ensure that future policies to do not reproduce the same injustices. As Mary Nagle explains: "Most Americans today are aware that the vast majority of the lands in the United States were acquired from Native Americans. . . . [But they] have no idea *how* this taking was fully accomplished [or] . . . legally justified. . . . Numerous legal doctrines were created in the nineteenth century to justify taking Indians lands. However, Americans' collective ignorance as to the origins of these constitutionally suspect doctrines has led to the perpetuation of several nineteenth century doctrines that have no place in a post-colonial, democratic, twenty-first century America" (2013, 63). Our knowledge of how these statutes and processes were used to dispossess in the past will help us to safeguard against such use in the future.

This chapter also lays the groundwork for a discussion of value in chapter 5, which focuses on conservation planning via the FERC relicensing and Stewardship Council. The council and partners have examined the value of these lands for public benefits and determined associated criteria that prove capacity to steward the lands. Tracing the manipulations of "value" of Indian lands at the headwaters from the 1890s through the present, I ask how accepted land values regularly exclude (even when they ostensibly claim to include) Indigenous peoples. This chapter examines the institutionalization of attempted exclusion via the supposedly neutral language of "value"—both utilitarian (production) value as well as conservation value—on Indian lands at the headwaters.

SAME LAND, DIFFERENT VALUES

Sometimes land values on a single Indian allotment changed significantly between appraisals, in response to the interests of sellers, changing markets for timber and agriculture, and the goals of the allotment policy of the Office of Indian Affairs. For example, the allotment of Bob Mack, approved in 1892 and posthumously trust patented in 1907, was initially appraised in 1912 by Joseph Murphy for $2,600, principally valuable for timber.[10] However, in 1915 C. E. Dunston appraised the land and found it worth only $1,385, describing it as "absolute forest land with very little value for grazing and, except for about 30 acres, none for agriculture."[11] The land was appraised again in 1918, this time by Gardner, for $2,304, solely for the timber, which was divided into Sugar and Yellow Pine, Jeffrey Pine, and Douglas Fir and White Cedar. Gardner noted that the allotment adjoined landholdings of Red River and was "badly burned in spots," and also had "dense . . . brush,"[12] thereby possibly reducing the value of the land due to the presence of nontimber species and its propensity for fire. When Mack's heirs applied to sell his land in 1919, Red River's operations in the vicinity are listed as a reason for the sale: "This company will pay more money for the land than any other party on account of inaccessibility to other parties."[13] Interestingly, on the superintendent's report, the listed value is that of Gardner's 1918 appraisal, but the land is described using the language from Dunston's 1915 appraisal. Further, despite the value of the land being ostensibly principally in timber, the response to the question "Is there any valuable timber on the land?" is "No timber of value." Bob Mack's heirs accepted the sale of the land to Red River for $2,304 in 1920, Sallie Mack with her thumbprint, as witnessed by Gardner and Edgar Miller, and Burt Bob with his signature, as witnessed by Gardner,[14] and a fee patent was issued to Red River on January 28, 1921.

Another example of varying appraisals, accompanied in this case by agency resistance to the exercise of the privileges of citizenship to maximize benefits to heirs, is evident on the allotment of Hank Wano (Sus-45). Hank Wano died in 1896, leaving Ellen Wano heir to his 80-acre allotment located about three miles from Susanville. When Ellen Wano died, the land was left to her husband, Edward Curtis, an African American and a citizen, and her half sister, Susie Powers. The "Petition for the Sale of Inherited Indian Land" offers the reasons for sale that "Susie Powers needs the money for support[and] . . . Ed Curtis is a full citizen and we have no control over him." When the petition asks if the petitioners need money from the sale of this land, the typed response reads,

"Susie Powers need[s] money for medical attention and support. The land is bringing her nothing. Edward Curtis is a citizen and bothers us considerable over this land. It should be sold and he out of our problems."[15] In 1910 Joseph Murphy appraised the land at $850, worth principally for the timber, as the "land very rough and rocky and steep."[16] However, a 1920 letter references an appraisal of the land by Gardner for less than half of that amount, $416.25.[17]

Curtis opposed the BIA's proposed sale of the land for its timber value and was apparently working with a lawyer, S. H. Rosenthal, of Reno, to advocate for a good price for the part of the land taken for a highway right-of-way.[18] The Indian Agency was not pleased with Curtis's use of a lawyer, according to an April 1920 letter from the Greenville Agency to Colonel L. A. Dorrington: "I do not recognize the need of lawyers in these cases. I want to sell this allotment soon and I would like to have you put these facts before the heir there, Edward E. Curtis." The Greenville agent continues to explain that Sus-45 is part of a group of allotments that the agency would like to sell together so that Red River will be compelled to build a railroad spur out to the lands and log them all at once:

> If we sell the adjacent lands the Red River Lumber Company will run a spur track to them and cut the timber. If this allotment of Hank Wano's is not sold at that time it will probably be worth very little and the owner, after the tracks are taken away, as they will be after the other lands are cut over, will not be able to sell at all, I am afraid. The Timber will deteriorate and parties from Susanville will steal wood from it until there is not much left.[19]

The Greenville Agency further noted that the land was "so worthless that there is no value at all placed upon it by the Cruiser, so you can readily understand it would be no place for any kind of a home." The agent concludes the letter by stating that he is offering his help to Curtis to make the best decision on the land.[20]

A second letter, dated November 1920 to Dorrington of Reno, Nevada, asks Dorrington to try to get Curtis to sign the sale papers and indicates conflict between the state and local governments and the federal government over Indian allotments on the public domain:

> There is no use of his standing out for more money. The state can condemn his half of the land and probably get it for less than the amount we have asked. The State

and County of Lassen fought us to a standstill in this matter, claiming we were holding them up on this right of way, even taking the matter to Congress because Coe had promised or told the State Highway Commission that these rights of ways through Indian lands would be donated by the Indians. This happened to be our first fight in behalf of the Indian allottees and we thought we did mighty well in getting this much for crossing a part of this allotment. Please advise the man Curtis and Rosenthal this is their last opportunity to sign. If the deed is not signed at this opportunity I will take the matter up with the Office to divide this allotment and cut Curtis loose from any benefit at all of any Government administration.[21]

As such, while the agency saw itself as fighting the state on Indians' behalf, it did not like dealing with proactive heirs that questioned its opinions about when, how, and to whom the land should be sold.

Another example of allottee assertiveness in challenging various Indian Service designations of value is found in the allotment of Henry John Jenkins, Sus-33, located in Mountain Meadows. Jenkins's land was held for cancellation in 1902, the cancellation order was revoked in 1903, and the land was ultimately sold to Red River in 1914. The allottee exercised a great deal of agency in managing the sale of the allotment in order to fund improvements on private land he had purchased near Janesville, on the southwestern side of Honey Lake Valley. Two years passed from the time of Jenkins's petition to sell in 1912 to the sale in 1914, and, in that time period, there is evidence of internal discrepancies regarding the value of the allotment within the Office of Indian Affairs. When Jenkins first petitioned to sell his allotment in June 1912 it had been appraised at $1,200, primarily because of its timber value. Red River offered $1,200 for the land in February 1914; Jenkins accepted the offer in March, but the Office of Indian Affairs rejected the sale in April 1914, citing that the petition for the sale approved by the Office in June 1913 was contingent on the land not being sold for less than $1,373. The supervisor from Roseburg wrote back on May 2, 1914, noting that the allotment had actually been advertised for $1,200, so Red River had made a fair bid, and he felt the timber was not worth any more than $1,200. The sale was approved on May 29, 1914, with Red River as the sole bidder.

The "Report on the Cash Sale of Allotted Indian Land" explained the lack of competition for the land as follows: "Timbered land near holdings of this company and no one else cares to purchase land in that vicinity for the reason that they would have to take the price offered by the Company; the sale should be approved." As such, Jenkins's land sold for less than an amount the agency had agreed on, and this was justified both because of an evident Office of Indian Affairs' error in advertising but also because Red River already owned so much land in the vicinity—"several thousand acres adjacent," according to the superintendent's 1913 report—which supported the sale.

The value of the multiple Jenkins allotments was generally disparaged by the timber cruiser Gardner, who, as was later investigated, worked simultaneously for both buyer (Red River) and seller (the Indian Office). In his 1918 appraisal of Sus-162 (Ellen Jenkins), he wrote that "most of the timber is of very medium age and size and very fair quality—Land mostly poor quality and little feed."[22] In 1920 Ellen Jenkins's heirs sold the land to Red River for the price of $22.70/acre.[23] Similarly, when her relative Ike Jenkins/Jay Side petitioned to sell his land, it was deemed by the agency "valuable only to Lumber Co.,"[24] and in his appraisal, Gardner wrote, "Land useless, save for timber growth."[25] On Harry Jenkins's allotment (Sus-167), the two appraisers differed in their opinions of the value of the land: in 1912 the cruiser Murphy deemed it generally "all good land and good logging," and valued it at $5,000.[26] Just six years later, in 1918, the cruiser Gardner found the land "badly bug infested" and dropped the value to $4,157,[27] or approximately $26/acre, which became the selling price to Red River in 1920.[28]

For Henry Jenkins, however, the sale of Sus-33 was valuable for investment in his home on two acres near Janesville, which he had "bought from a white man for $100" in 1909.[29] His two acres were productively "in orchard and cultivation," and the superintendent agreed that "he should be allowed to sell and use a good portion of the proceeds in the purchase of other land, farming implements &c. He is a good worker and should be encouraged."[30] However, after the land allotment sale, Jenkins had trouble accessing the proceeds and inquired with Matron Edith Young more than once in the spring of 1915 about money to fund his fruit trees, horse boarding, and home improvements. As such, even after being allotted, purchasing a home in fee simple, and successfully selling his allotment (even if at a lower price than the agency approved), Jenkins still dealt with a maze of government bureaucracy and paternalistic oversight in order to access the funds in his Individual Indian Monetary account.

Indeed, BIA oversight over the lives and lands of allottees was extensive,[31] including determinations of competency of allottees, appraisal and sale of allotments, and management of allottees' funds to purchase new lands and homesites that were out of the region valuable for timber and hydroelectric development and more suited to facilitating the agricultural enterprises that were the aim of the original Allotment Act. In 1910 George Peconam (Sus-34) petitioned for a fee patent on his allotment, located in Mountain Meadows.[32] Attorney W. C. Keegin of Holcomb & Keegin in Washington, D.C., wrote to the commissioner of Indian Affairs in support of Peconam's petition in October 1910, noting that Peconam showed "competency . . . to transact his business affairs," and that the price he wished to sell the land for, a mere $1,600, was "just and reasonable."[33] However, Horace Wilson appraised Peconam's land less than two years later in May 1912 and found it worth $4,000, principally for the timber.[34] A July 1912 report by the superintendent on the petition for sale noted that Peconam wanted to sell the land because "it is timber land and not suitable for a home," and he wanted to use the profit from the sale to buy a "farm in Honey Lake Valley." He also noted that "a great many white people have sold timber land in this vicinity" for $6–$10/acre.[35] Also in July 1912, a review of the petition for the sale of the land by the Roseburg superintendent noted that any land purchased by the BIA for Peconam with the proceeds from the allotment sale would also be placed in restricted status—that is, like allotments, it could not be sold without the agreement of the secretary of the Interior.[36] In December 1913, the BIA office in Washington, D.C., reported that Peconam had accepted the sale. The clerk noted with some disappointment that other allottees within the group of allotments the agency was trying to sell (namely, Henry Wilson, Sus-278, and Joe Wilson, Sus-29), declined to sell, and attributed their refusal to a "malicious influence" "exerted by a rancher living in the vicinity of these persons," indicating the BIA belief in its wisdom to make the best deals for Indian allottees.[37]

In the report on the sale of George Peconam's allotment, the reason for going with the sole bid from Red River of $4,000 is explained in part by the high value of the land: "Value too high to be handled by small investor; this company owns all, or practically, all, timber in the vicinity of this land; I do not believe a better price would be offered by readvertising."[38] The sale was confirmed and a fee patent issued to Red River on January 27, 1914. By December 1914, the Roseburg Agency had nearly completed the purchase of 320 acres of agricultural land near Susanville for the Peconam family, for an average price of $31.50/acre.[39] However, the sale appears to have been delayed, as evidenced by a letter on Peconam's behalf from the BIA field matron Edith M. Young, asking about the purchase of the farm and indicating Peconam's desire to begin working the land.[40] Wilson directly wrote to Peconam, referencing Young's letter and stating that the sale would be completed soon.[41] On April 7, 1915, a telegram to Wilson reported completion of the sale,[42] and noted the land would be held in restricted status for the Peconams. This transaction exemplifies both the oversight of the BIA over Indian affairs as well as ongoing Indian advocacy to ensure benefit from sale. It also raises questions as to why the BIA allotted nonarable lands that did not fit the act's mission and then facilitated the sale of those lands and purchased other, higher-value lands more attuned to that agricultural mission. While the initial allotments were sold for an average of $22.66/acre, these other replacement lands were purchased for $31.50/acre.

Red River, the purchaser of Peconam's allotment and many others, was accused of buying the Northern California lands for unreasonably low prices. However, Red River biographer Robert M. Hanft claims that "the land, despite the beauty of the forest on it, really had no value" and Walker's "purchase was to give it value" (1980, 17). As such, the land's worth is only revealed when it is purchased by a non-Indian corporation and its resources transformed into profit. This limited notion of value does not consider the multifaceted, nonmonetary values of the land for Maidu and other Indigenous people. As Laura Pulido and Nicole-Marie Cotton argue, strategic devaluation of the land is embedded in institutionalized racism: "Racism, as a material and ideological system that produces differential meaning and value, is harnessed by capital in order to exploit the differences that racism creates. In this case . . . devalued communities, places, and people . . . enable firms to accumulate more surplus than would otherwise be possible" (2016, 15). In sum, the rhetoric was that Indian people, who were not yet citizens at this time, were not properly "using" the land, and thus its value was only realized by non-Indians purchasing it and putting it to use; a process facilitated by federal agencies.

Federal agency employees were deeply involved in this discussion of value, some ostensibly trying to gain as many benefits as possible for Indian allottees and others trying to be very specific about which uses of land would lead to specific values per acre. In the example of Sus-231, the allotment of William Dick, the Department of the Interior would not approve sale because the land was not reappraised following a letter from the director of the U.S. Geological Survey that discussed its immense power-site value:

> [The] land has value for water-power purposes because of its location within the Big Meadows reservoir site on the North Fork of Feather River.
>   . . . [The] Great Western Power Company has acquired title to most of the lands within the flowage of the Big Meadows reservoir and has secured permits

necessary to the development of power in the section of North Fork of Feather River between the Big Meadows reservoir and the Big Bend plant. . . . While the Big Meadows dam is now constructed to a height of 63 feet only, provision has been made to increase the height ultimately to 110 feet, and to utilize almost the entire fall of this section of the river in the ultimate development of approximately 500,000 horsepower. When the dam is raised to a height of 110 feet the land in question will be required for flowage purposes.

The value of this land is represented by the increased number of horsepower which may be developed and the increased number of acres which may be irrigated as a result of the regulation of the flow of the North Fork of Feather River by means of this reservoir.[43]

Drawing on proposals from GWP and a U.S. Forest Service report on the power production potential between Big Meadows and Big Bend in the Feather River Canyon, the director of the U.S. Geological Survey calculated approximately how much additional power GWP would be able to generate from the development of reservoirs at Big Meadows and Butt Valley, and determined a minimum value of $10/horsepower for undeveloped power sites. This translated into $50/acre for the William Dick allotment, or approximately $8,000—far more than the bid of $2,760 from Red River.[44] However, all of this debate over the value of the allotment and timber and conflict between the sellers, Indian Office, and U.S. Geological Survey, meant that Dick's allotment did not ultimately sell until after his death in 1920, thus benefiting his heirs but not him directly.

Indeed, differential evaluations of allotments led to conflict between agencies such as the BIA and U.S. Geological Survey, as well as the various companies interested in purchasing the lands. In the 1919 petition to sell Emma Thomas's allotment to benefit her aged mother Cora Roy, Superintendent Edgar Miller described the land as "very poor grazing land," "more valuable to GWP than anyone else," and within the GWP power site and scheduled for inundation.[45] A 1914 appraisal by Charles Gardner that described the same land as "best adapted for forest growth and grazing" and possessing 25 acres of "good grass," worth $2,680.[46]

A 1915 appraisal by C. E. Dunston, supervisor of forests, found the land to include 25 acres of "excellent meadow land" with the remaining absolute forest land, worth $2,650.[47] Red River's Clinton L. Walker bid on the land in 1916, offering $5,560, and the bid was initially accepted but then declined. As a 1917 apologetic letter from Hauke explains, Red River's offer of $34.75/acre was too low because of the allotment's location within the power site: "The land has been appraised by the Geological Survey at an average price of $50 an acre for reservoir purposes, exclusive of the agricultural value."[48] In his 1918 appraisal, Irvine Gardner ranked the land as having no agricultural value, just 10 acres of good grazing land and the rest of the possible grazing land as "poor" to "very poor," with some value as a power site and the majority of the land valuable for three types of timber (yellow pine, sugar pine, and fir, with attention to the relative worth of each), worth $4,697.50,[49] now *below* the Red River bid that had been rejected by the Indian Office the previous year. Despite Hauke's letter regarding foregrounding power-site value, Irvine Gardner found the land best suited for "forest reproduction." The ultimate sale price on Emma Thomas's allotment was $5,192.50 and, as Miller responded (in template language found on many other allotments) to the question of why a sole bid (from GWP) was acceptable in the sale of the land, "This land is worth more as a power site to G.W.P. Co. than it would be for any other purpose. Rejection of bid would not benefit Indian."[50] Gardner and Miller regularly evaluated land sold to GWP as of little value unless utilized by that company.

While it did not help Emma Thomas's family, generally the decision by the U.S. Geological Survey to place a higher value on allotments within power sites meant higher prices on land for Indian allottees in Big Meadows.[51] However, such determinations came too late for those who had already had their lands canceled and flooded, as discussed in chapter 2. As the supervisor in Roseburg wrote to the commissioner of Indian Affairs in 1915:

> Your Office will remember that I took up the sale of these allotments . . . for the reason that the Power Company had condemned several Indian allotments under the Act of March 3, 1901 (31 Stat., L. 1058-1084), and, as shown in my [1912] report . . . the Indians had . . . received but very little for their allotments under the condemnation proceedings, and I was of the opinion that I could get more for the Indians for their allotments by having the lands appraised and selling them under existing regulations.[52]

Of the 164 allotments totaling 25,200 acres in Big Meadows, Butt Valley, Mountain Meadows, and Humbug Valley, 90 were sold for an average price of $4,394, or $27/acre for a 160-acre parcel. The highest sale price was $35,000 (to Mason & Haeger, Inc., in 1950) and the lowest was $684 (to Red River in 1921).

Thirty-five of these allotments were sold to Red River or Clinton Walker for an average consideration of $2,875 per allotment, and 19 were sold to GWP for an average of $5,121 per allotment. Nine allotments were sold to other timber companies for an average of $10,754, but this average is artificially high due to the fact that three of these sold in the 1950s, when prices were higher. Of the remaining 74 allotments, 10 were relinquished between 1894 and 1902 and 45 were canceled.

Another factor that slowed transactions on allotments, yet sometimes benefited allottees and heirs, was the presence and valuation of minerals on the land. If there was concern that an allotment had mineral or hydro-production value, it would have to be assessed by the U.S. Geological Survey before the sale could be approved. A 1912 report on the mineral character and power-site possibilities of Fannie Jenkins's allotment (Sus-170) found that, although the land had been included in Power Site Reserve No. 245, "more recent information" found that "the land is without value for power purposes," and recommended revoking its withdrawal.[53] The same report found possible mineral value and recommended a "field examination," which Superintendent Horace Wilson took issue with: "These Indians have had these allotments a long time and have received no benefit whatever from them. . . . I am now wondering whether or not these Indians will be required to keep these allotments for an indefinite period of years simply because the land may contain some mineral. The Director of the U.S. Geological Survey speaks of a field examination. When will such field examination be made?"[54] Wilson also voiced concern regarding the lack of protection for Indian allottees if their land was found to have a mineral deposit, alluding to a law that enabled the establishment of a mining claim if valuable minerals were thought to be present, regardless of land-ownership status.

In the north arm of Indian Valley, sale negotiations on two allotments with some mineral value took place over a nearly 40-year period (1912–1950), during which time at least one of the parcels was used as a "tailings dump" by the Engel Mining Company. Jim and Alice Henry petitioned to sell the allotments of Charley Henry (Sus-369) and Nelson Henry (Sus-173) in 1912. Both petitions described the land as timbered and "not suitable for a home." However, the U.S. Geological Survey found that the land might contain valuable minerals (gold and copper). The Indian Office recommended selling both allotments but retaining mineral rights:[55] in April 1913, Assistant Secretary of the Interior Lewis Laylin suggested a clause reserving "to the grantor for a period of twenty-five years . . . all right to the oil, gas, and minerals found to exist within the limits of the land covered by this deed." However, if no exploration was made within five years, the reservation would lapse. Despite interest from potential purchasers including Red River, H. R. Neel Lumber Company of Sacramento, the Calvada Lumber Company, and local ranchers and timber operators, the two allotments did not sell until 1950, to two local lumber companies.

The full value of allotments in timber and minerals was rarely realized for the allottee. Up in Mountain Meadows, Frank Bully's mother, Jennie Toby, petitioned for the sale of his land due to its timbered character, which was "of no source of income" to her.[56] When Susanville matron Edith Young inquired on Jennie's behalf whether the funds from the allotment sale would be forthcoming, Superintendent Charles E. Coe of the Indian Service replied that the land had been advertised "for some time without any bids having been received" and would be advertised again in 1917. On October 7, 1914, Supervisor Wilson wrote to the commissioner of Indian Affairs to request authorization to sell the allotment on behalf of the heirs. He explained that the land had been appraised both by Murphy in May 1912, who valued the pine on the allotment at $2/thousand, and by Charles Gardner in 1914, who valued it at $1/thousand. Wilson also looked at the land and felt that $3,970 was too high a price and suggested selling it for $3,000. He also encouraged the sale specifically to Red River due to the nearby location of their mill and the fact that "the Company practically owns all the land in that vicinity. . . . I do not believe that there would be any other bidder for the land except [Red River], as timber buyers do not often bid on land surrounded by the holdings of a large company."[57] In his November 21, 1914 response, Second Assistant Commissioner Hauke suggested raising the appraisement to $4,445, based on the rate of $2/foot, as nearby allotments had sold for. He noted: "I do not think it would be fair to the Indian heir, notwithstanding her poor physical condition, to offer to sell the land described in this petition for less than its apparent value as based upon facts before the Office." However, a 1918 appraisal by Irvine Gardner valued the land at just $2,050, and Jennie Toby accepted an offer from Red River for that amount on January 20, 1920. The report on the sale, signed on December 16, 1920, justified the sole bid from Red River on the basis that again it was the "only Lmbr. Co. operating in vicinity and worth more to them on account of inaccessibility to others. Not in the best interest of Indian to ready."

On July 31, 1920, Assistant Commissioner E. B. Merritt in the Office of Indian Affairs, Washington, D.C., wrote to Miller inquiring "under what authority" the allotment was sold for $2,050 instead of $4,445. Merritt examined the conflicting appraisals completed in 1912, 1914, and 1918, which listed amounts of timber on the parcel differing by 900,000 feet. He argued that trespass must have occurred and asked whether the agency had collected trespass damages. On August 5, 1920, the Forestry Division wrote to Irvine Gardner regarding the allotment, warning "the Office believes we are way low on price," and requesting a formal response. He reiterated the importance of an accurate cruise by Gardner: "If your cruise is wrong, we are wrong and it is possible the Indian is wronged—a thing you do not wish to happen."

On October 19, 1920, Red River transmitted a defensive letter to Miller, arguing that the company paid a fair price for the land and that the Indian Agency was an inefficient business partner. They threatened not to undertake further transactions with the agency if the agency felt that it could "re-evaluate" sale prices after purchase, at its discretion. The company also stated that it had not been unfair in its dealings with the agency: "We have not, at a sale picked out a few easy logging chances and bid on them leaving the isolated tracts to be purchased at our convenience several years from now, but have taken the whole intermingled bunch of allotments and will have to carry a lot of them a good many years before they are available."[58] On the following day, Gardner penned a letter to Miller, stating that he had met with Fletcher Walker of Red River regarding the sale price of Frank Bully's allotment, and Walker would not budge on the accuracy of the appraisal and the price paid. Walker indicated that the land had burnt the previous summer, further justifying the lower price. Gardner stood by his appraisal, and referenced a declining market, arguing that "if we sell our scattered timber lands to [Red River] or to anyone else who will bid more, we will have to make good terms to induce a sale. . . . [I] feel now we should try and make a clean-up of these lands, the good selling the bad, and advertising groups as you did in Pit River Power sale."[59] The Forestry Department then wrote to the commissioner, noting that sales would be more difficult if the agency persisted in reevaluating the value of allotments after sales were complete. The author also indicated that Red River was a valuable partner, "probably the only purchaser for Indian timber in any considerable amounts." However, he also articulated, "Please understand that we are interested in getting the most money for the Indian and in no way favor either [Red River] or any other prospective purchaser, but we should be allowed to sell on advertised or understood values with no additional come back for more money."[60] On November 1, 1920, with no report yet from Gardner, the Forestry Department indicated to the commissioner that he had discussed it briefly with him in person, noted full faith in Gardner, and attributed his delay to timber cruising before the winter season commenced. On November 2, 1920, the Forestry Department further indicated their support for the sale, noting that they had been on the land and found much of the timber dead or dying, and felt strongly that the sale should go through "if we wish to do business further with Red River and dispose of our other timber land." A November 3, 1920, letter from the Forestry Department to the commissioner further encouraged the sale, noting that the land could "deteriorate or burn up" and that they had no practice of refunding the purchaser when allotments burned. Indian Affairs commissioner Cato Sells transmitted the fee patent to Red River on February 2, 1921.

THE IMPORTANCE OF ACCESS

Following Jesse Ribot and Nancy Peluso's theory of access, one may have a legal right to property but lack the means (or the "bundle of powers") to benefit from it (2003, 173). Ribot and Peluso define access broadly as "the means by which a person can benefit from things" (156). While allottees likely saw the land as part of a web of relationships and associated responsibilities rather than a "thing," this theory is applicable here because non-Native notions of property define the construct of allotments and the oversight provided by the Indian Agency. For the agency and buyers competing for allotments, as well as allottees endeavoring to glean some benefit from these parcels, the valuation of land was linked to its accessibility—that is, both its location (its proximity to processers and markets) and the means of managers to extract its value. Sale of allotment lands was often justified based on the land's accessibility to an existing timber operation that had the ability to efficiently harvest the timber on the land. Further, location of lands relative to nearby corporations generally cemented those corporations' monopolies and their ability to offer low prices for remaining allotment lands—for either grazing or timber. Presaging what would be a common issue with the utility and value of allotments, the allotment of Sam Johnson in Dixie Valley (Sus-228), in the part of the Pit River homeland that is within Lassen County, was listed as valuable to a particular company because it was "within the boundaries" of that company. This language mirrors that used regarding allotments in Big Meadows and Mountain Meadows justifying sale to Red River.

The Report on Allotment 228 further notes that "the allottee cannot and will not improve his land," and "nearness to the Clark Co.'s land increases its value 20%."[61] Allottees were often chastised by the agency for thinking that their land would be worth more than the appraised value. According to U.S. Indian service clerk A. A. Bear, allottee Dick McClelland (Sus-240) had considered the allotment valued at "the ridiculous figure of $3,000," but "as a matter of fact were it not for the fact that it is in close proximity to the Clark ranch, it would be utterly impossible to sell it for any figure. . . . My appraisement [of $550 is] the extreme limit of the amount which the Clark Co. will pay, and probably in excess of that amount."[62] The company purchased the land for $550 in 1914, or just $3.44/acre.

In the 1913 superintendent's report on Sus-228, it appears that Captain Nelson Johnson's allotment was already at least partially landlocked by a private company, and the BIA and the company could then determine that it was in the allottee's "best interest" to sell to that nearby landowner. Indeed, the 1914 report on the sale justifies selling to the sole bidder Jas. Snell, noting that "the land is included within the ranch owned by the bidder, and is valueless to any other person."[63] Snell also bought numerous other allotments in the area in the ensuing years, including Sus-247 and Sus-248 (owned by Belle and Emma Jerry) in 1928, paying less than $500 for each 160-acre allotment.[64]

BIA agents were aware that companies were compelling either the allottee or the agency to petition to sell. In the superintendent's report attached to the petition for the sale of McClelland's allotment Sus-240 in Dixie Valley, in response to the question as to whether the purchaser "has used influence with the allottee to have the land offered for sale," the supervisor answered affirmatively and explained that the allotment "lies within the Clark Co's ranch, and they desire it in order to [straighten] their boundaries."[65] As late as 1939, the Clark Company was leasing remaining allotments for grazing, and McClelland's son Roy suspected that the company had moved a fence in order to encompass a watered section of his sister Lulu's allotment (Sus-242): "There used to be some good meadow land on one of these allotments but now the fence has been moved back so that all of the meadow is in the C.W. Clark Co.'s field." As Roy McClelland wasn't certain about this, the superintendent of the Sacramento Indian Agency requested that a field officer go meet with him and go out together to the land to "check the lines on the two allotments where he suspects the fence has been moved."[66] No further report of the results of their investigation is available, but allotments 241 and 242 were sold to T. E. Connolly in 1950.

Connolly was also interested in the nearby allotment of Bill McClelland (Sus-249), which the Clark Company was leasing to avoid trespass because they were obliged to cross it with their cattle.[67] In a lengthy letter to a BIA Appraiser in 1957, Connolly argued that the Sus-249 heir Charles Buckskin was being taken advantage of by a local non-Native man who said he was married to Buckskin's sister. Connolly inferred that Buckskin needed help managing his affairs.[68] Less than one month later, the BIA confirmed Buckskin's fee patent, ostensibly washing its hands of any obligation to the land and the allottee.[69] In his reply to Connolly, the BIA realty officer explained the history of the land and let Connolly know that Buckskin's fee patent had been approved earlier that month by the BLM and that a patent in fee would be issued to Buckskin directly. As such, it appears from the documents available that would-be purchaser and large landowner Connolly knew before Buckskin that Buckskin was to receive a fee patent to the 160-acre allotment, and would therefore be able to sell it.[70]

INVESTIGATION OF INDIAN AGENCY EMPLOYEES MILLER AND GARDNER

Red River and the Greenville Indian Agency were in frequent communication regarding the value of Indian allotment lands in both the Maidu and Pit River homelands. In July 1919, Superintendent Miller wrote to Clinton Walker of Red River, evidently responding to Walker's inquiry regarding the sale of two allotments in Butt Valley (Mattie Gould, Sus-238, and Albert Gould, Sus-239). Red River had purchased Sus-239 in May 1919 and was working to purchase Sus-238. Miller reminded Walker that "these allotments . . . are sold subject to the approval of the Indian Office and the Secretary of the Interior," indicating that perhaps Red River was waiting for the confirmation of sale of Sus-239 and wanted to push forward in purchasing Sus-238. Miller continued his letter by indicating concern about the prices the agency was receiving for the allotments, and framed his administration as getting better prices for Indian lands than the recently abolished Roseburg Agency:

> All of the lands have been recently appraised under my administration. . . . I was
> not at all satisfied with the prices gotten by the Roseburg Office and our sales

and recent appraisements corroborate my judgment in the matter. Lands you have been interested in, some you had deposited money on and sale turned down have brought over twice as much as you offered. In some cases our appraisements have been three times over the former appraisements and we have been able to sell the land at the appraised valuation. It is my belief that much land has been sold at too low a figure.[71]

Despite these concerns, in December 1919, Clinton Walker wrote to Miller inquiring in part about the Williams allotments (Sus-200–206) between Crescent Mills and Taylorsville and advocating for a lower price for them. According to Walker, they had been advertised several times and the company was interested, if the agency was willing to give them "an option . . . to purchase them at the prices at which they have been advertised."[72] Walker concluded his note by calling Irvine Gardner's attention to the "fire risk which is very hazardous" and "which should be taken into account when appraising the lands."[73] Fire risk was often referenced in order to bring the price of allotments down. Ultimately, three of the allotments were sold to Red River and four were sold to a competitive bidder, Senator H. S. Horsman.

The allotments that Miller was concerned about selling too low were often allotments that had been appraised by Gardner, an independent timber cruiser who appraised allotments in the Susanville series (in Plumas and Lassen Counties). In a March 5, 1920, letter to the commissioner of Indian Affairs, Gardner describes his work to "clean up" Maidu and Pit River lands for the benefit of the Indians by working closely with Red River to sell Indian allotments. He described Red River as a generous company that bought lands it "did not particularly want" but agreed to purchases because it was difficult to log nearby without trespassing. He framed himself as working tirelessly and thanklessly to make the sales work by clustering groups of allotments for efficient conveyance to Red River in order to achieve maximum benefit for the Indians. He explained that the work to "close up all deals regarding timber" is intense in the Burney/Goose Lake area, in the Pit River Canyon, and in Indian Valley, with lands belonging to the Williams family between present-day Crescent Mills and Taylorsville.

However, as indicated by correspondence later that year, it is clear that some agency employees were not as enthusiastic about pushing forward the sale of Indian allotment lands, particularly when the allottees did not want to sell. In an October 25, 1920, letter to Clerk W. S. Kreigh, Redding District, Superintendent Miller reflected on a situation along the Pit River in which an Indian person refused to sign sale papers to PG&E for an allotment he or she had an interest in:

> Those who refuse to sign must not be forced to sign for the matter of their homes is involved and I do not blame them a bit for not signing until it is made plain to them they will get at least as good a home before signing away their present home, many of which have been occupied for years. There is a moral obligation in this sale not in others—the matter of seeing that these Indians get a home other than the one they sell—for you know that it is unfortunate they have to sell and that most of them have been settled on these lands as homesites for years. We should feel obligated to really see that homes are in sight for these Indians before they are dispossessed. I feel that it is not a good thing at all to disturb Indians with homes occupied for years, as these, and that we are, in a way, walking backward in our work to sell such homes, but this land was needed in a big industrial project and if the whites had them they would have to give them up the same as our Indians. I feel that it is the thing to do under the circumstances, but would impress upon you that we are morally involved.[74]

However, further south in Maidu country, Gardner remained particularly fervent regarding the benefits of a group sale to the timber company: "Four of these claims were advertised for four years at a price of $4,587. . . . It would be a shame to refuse an offer of $12,662 for these four and nearly $16,000 with the two additional when the Indians desire to sell so badly wanting to get a home this Spring."[75] Gardner listed heirs to the Williams allotments as Doc Williams, his son Ridlon, and his daughter Mrs. Monroe, who was married to a white man and living "here in Westwood." According to Gardner, who was trying to usher the sale through of the timberland on the slopes of Mt. Hough, "They have made all their plans and tell me they have been trying to sell for $7,000." The reader, in this case the commissioner, is left to conclude that the Indians are getting a much better deal than if they negotiated the sale themselves (which they are prevented from doing due to the federal trust status of the land)—going from $7,000 to between $12,000 and $16,000, depending on the number of allotments sold. Thus, Gardner's text underscores the important role of the agency and of himself as the appraiser in looking out for allottees' interests.

Turning to allotments in and around the city of Susanville, Gardner is more explicit in his arguments for the sale of the lands to the timber company in groups of allotments. He notes that the appraisal prices have increased 300 percent and that maintaining these higher appraisals can be best achieved by sale "in a block." This is because lands were "so scattered that no one could possibly log some individually to profit." This argument underscores the need for a large corporation to log the lands rather than individual timber managers, mirroring current issues in forest management policy, in which there is little room for small companies or individuals to profitably harvest timber. Gardner's argument for efficiency also notes that grouping the lands for sale and subsequent management by one owner would allow "all timber land both good and bad [to] be cleaned up." He underscores Red River's largesse in purchasing land of relatively inferior timber quality at a relatively high price, noting the historical context that "all timber land that an Indian gets was through the oversight of the Sierra Lumber Company who picked up all what they deemed timberlands in this territory 20 years before the first allotment was made." As such, Gardner again portrays himself as a savior, working in the best interest of the allottees and attempting to negotiate the best deals for their apparently subpar timberlands with a generous company that is already working in the area.[76] There is not discussion of whether the allottees will readily receive the proceeds of the sales. As is typical, these proceeds will be managed by the BIA and meted out to allottees following approval of their specific requests. There is also no mention of whether Red River's bids on Indian lands are comparable with amounts offered on lands with other owners. Gardner is also silent on his role with Red River and with the agency, stating simply that "Miller will agree with him."

Again, a March 9, 1920, letter from Miller to the commissioner of Indian Affairs indicates a different view of Gardner's efforts to sell the lands to Red River. As Miller notes with some evident frustration, "Mr. Gardner . . . seems to take an unusual interest in the administrative affairs of this jurisdiction and is always very eager to sell lands after they are appraised." He indicates agreement with the overall strategy of sale to Red River, noting that they are "probably the only buyer," and that they will buy groups of lands, which saves the agency "much expense and work," and "[get] the money for many needy Indians without waiting to go through the tedious public sales." Miller also indicates an eagerness to sell the Williams allotments in Indian Valley and Pit River allotments in Burney. However, his assessment of Gardner indicates a clash of personalities, as well as a significant level of mistrust. As Miller writes, Gardner works on his own will, is "hard headed," and thinks he knows best what to do.[77]

In November 1921, Gardner was placed on furlough by the agency, and a subsequent investigation revealed that he had been accepting favors from Red River while he was employed by the BIA: "It appears that while actively employed in our services you lived in a house, without the payment of rent, provided by the Red River Lumber Company, and that you also accepted and had the free use of an automobile in your work furnished by said company, which was one of the principle purchasers of Indian lands."[78] The commissioner of Indian Affairs asked that Gardner resign effective November 14, 1921, the date of his furlough. Gardner resigned on September 11, 1922.[79]

While Gardner had been on furlough, in June 1922 he had submitted charges against Miller to the commissioner of Indian Affairs,[80] accusing him of selling lands at too low a price to PG&E. Identifying himself as "Cruiser at Large on Furlough," Gardner summarized some of these charges in a letter to the supervisor of the U.S. Indian Service, Horace Wilson: "[Miller] has not a single friend among any of the Indian tribes with which he is connected and I know nearly every one personally. . . . I was advised to keep out of the PG&E as they . . . had fixed matters with [the] Office. . . . All negotiations were made by E. K. Miller direct and had I been given a chance we would have in certain case[s], I am sure, secured more."[81] On July 21, 1922, Inspector Roberts and Supervisor Wilson wrote to Miller, informing him that complaints had been levied against him by Gardner and requiring him to respond to a list of 22 questions, particularly regarding the sale of allotments on the Pit River.[82] In his opening response to the complaints levied against him by Gardner, Miller immediately turned the tables on Gardner and accused *him* of being a corporate insider with PG&E, as well as Red River:

> Mr. Gardner was told not to meddle with the P.G. & E. Pit River sale because I could not trust him to keep Government business in his head and not peddle it. He had approached the P. G. & E. about the sale of these lands before I had any idea that company wanted them and I wired the Office to take neither his nor anyone else's judgment [*sic*], that I wanted a chance to go into the matter before recommendations went in from this office . . .
>
> The PG&E officials did not care to have anything to do with Gardner [on] account of his being so closely connected with the Red River Lumber Company . . .
>
> . . . Gardner knew all the time of the power project, talked it and repeatedly stated to me and to others that all the valuation those Pit River Indian lands had was power project value. He even went so far as to arrange a conference in S.F.

with the P. G. & E. officials for me to go there with him, at the expense of those officials, in an effort to talk trade in conjunction with the Red River Lands along the river. He was flatly told by me that under no consideration would I attend or have anything to do with such a meeting.[83]

Miller completed his full response to Roberts on August 7, 1922. The following overview of the questions and Miller's responses is provided because of their importance in illuminating how the agency justified its process of valuing and selling allotments to partners in the timber and power industries.

Roberts asked Miller who had appraised the allotments along the Pit River that were sold to the Mt. Shasta Power Corporation and what Miller's opinion of was of the honesty and qualifications of the appraiser to ascertain the value of the land for power purposes. Miller responded that Gardner had done the first appraisements and he generally had faith in his work, but "in some instances, as in this Pit River Project, [the appraisals were] deemed low by myself and raised. . . . In his power-site land valuations I believe he has been low on all of them. His power-site valuations in the Great Western Power project was raised $15.00 an acre by me." This statement indicates that Gardner was involved in land sales both to Red River and PG&E along both the Feather and Pit Rivers, firmly establishing that he had an impact on the divestiture and restitution (or lack thereof) of both Pit River and Maidu lands.

When pressed further on whether Gardner was "crooked," Miller responded that there were "suspicious circumstances" involving Gardner, particularly regarding his relationship with Red River, and he asked Gardner to respond to accusations made against him in the report, but Gardner was furloughed before a full investigation could commence. Roberts became more detailed with his questions, asking if Miller knew that Red River had given Gardner a house and a car while he was working for the U.S. government. Miller responded that he had warned Gardner that this would draw criticism and brought it to the attention of the agency officials. He added that he "repeatedly clashed with Gardner about these matters," revealing a power struggle between the two men and the lack of an agency response to an employee (Gardner) receiving favors from a prominent purchaser of Indian lands.

Roberts focused several questions on the appraisal and sale of lands along the Pit River, asking first if Miller had approved Gardner's appraisals and if he was qualified to do so. Miller responded that he did not approve the appraisals, although he did raise them in conference with Indian Service employee W. S.

Kreigh, and he consulted other knowledgeable parties, including members of the State Water Commission. The commission, however, was less than helpful, apparently telling Miller that "there was no precedent or authority for placing such values. . . . Such values varied with every project and . . . no two men agreed on such values." One wonders if the commission stood to gain from the development of these upstream projects and was, as such, hesitant to propose any minimum prices on the acquisition of lands necessary for hydropower development.

Roberts was also concerned with the price that Red River got for lands along the Pit River, compared to the price that was paid for Indian allotments. Miller responded that he did not know at the time of sale about the agreement between Red River and the Mt. Shasta Power Company, in which the latter company paid less for Red River lands based on an agreement to provide future power to them. Miller dismissed this as between the two companies, adding, "Of course, such a contract for the Indians was not possible." Regarding the condemnation suit that awarded C. L. Walker of Red River $40,000 for 160 acres along the Pit River, far more than was ever paid for Indian allotment lands, Miller responded that this award had "no connection with the sale of the Indian lands within that project," and continued to assert "that the Indians got a good, honorable full value for their lands at the time they sold them and that any attempt to hold up any company in such a project would be detrimental to us, to the Government, and to the Indians. It is absolutely unfair and unjust to compare these prices under these awards to the prices we got for the Indian lands two years before." He went on to speculate on the "peculiar circumstances" surrounding the hefty settlement to Clinton Walker, including the improvements that Walker had put into his land and the prime location of the lands, yet also accusing Walker of milking the process to get more than the land was worth: "The lands of Clint Walker were purchased by him to do just what he accomplished—hold up the Power Company for a big price. His lands were more valuable than any in the project excepting the Red River lands; he could have developed a power project himself with 111 feet fall on his own land, he being right on the bend of the river. This made his lands much more valuable than the Indians' and in a class by themselves." Miller concluded defensively that "the Indians got full value, for their lands were worth really nothing except as they might be valued within some power proposition. It should be remembered that alone these Indian lands could not be used for a power project and, if necessary, the Company could go further upstream and leave them out all together." Again, Miller used the language and the concept of "value" to understate, and wholly disregard, the value of Indian lands to Indian people. Instead, he framed the power company's development proposition as something Indian people and the agency managing their lands should be grateful for.[84]

Indeed, when asked if he or the Indian Office was responsible for the sales of the Indian allotments to the power company, Miller said that the power company initiated the sale, but that he and Kreigh saw the sale as "a good chance to make better off these Indians" and followed their usual prescription to "fully protect the Indians." As he reported, the sale proceeded through normal steps of Indian Office approval, and the shorter time period of advertisement (30 days instead of 60 days) was under Indian Office instruction. This indicates a broader problem of paternalism, bias toward development, and lack of Indian representation in the approval process within the Indian Office. However, Miller frames himself and Kreigh as just doing their jobs within the constraints of mandates from higher administration.

Miller asserted more agency, but when Roberts asked him about another detail of the sale—the requirement that bidders purchase all of the allotments in a group, rather than a single allotment or a subset of them—he was quite proud of this plan, stating, "I am responsible for the manner of selling the lands in group." He did this

> in order to sell the poor with the good in groups, protect the Indians in group valuations and allow people to bid unharrassed by grafters wishing to get hold of a key piece simply to hold up an entire project and prevent the other lands selling at any price. We have found this plan very successful in a number of groups besides water projects, such as grazing lands with one allotment with a big spring on it and none on the others; it would be foolish to sell the water and not the adjacent lands, and eminently unfair to those Indians owning the lands without water. If these lands had been placed on the market without that proviso we would still have on our hands lands purchased by the Mt. Shasta Power Company, with no valuation and no chance to sell, because they were not to be used and had no real power valuation, but in group form they had to be taken with the others.

In the next chapter, I will examine how this practice facilitated the formation of large land monopolies, as timber and power companies and large ranching interests were encouraged to buy groups of Indian allotments, thus quickly amassing large holdings with the support of the agency. The strategy of grouping allotments also occasionally led to friction between the agency and PG&E—for example, in instances in which the company and the agency were able to get allottees' signatures to sell lands the company wanted most—but they had a more difficult time getting signatures for the sale of lower priority lands in the same group. Miller approached this challenge by coordinating meetings directly between PG&E company representatives and individual allottees, in situations in which the allottees did not trust the agency.

Roberts was concerned with the amount of sales to PG&E versus other bidders and any behind-the-scenes agreements that may have occurred to encourage such sales. Roberts asked Miller to explain a statement in a letter that he had written to PG&E that a trip with the representatives of the company "did the work." Miller responded that the trip had been successful in facilitating direct communication between PG&E and allottees who were considering sale of their allotments:

> We mentioned [to Bob and Sarah Wolfins] the fact that the Indians would not be dispossessed, that the company said and agreed that the Indians could remain on their lands as long as they wished, or until they got other places, and when they left they could take what of their improvements they desired. . . . Bob said that he understood this but had heard it only [through] us, not direct from any official and asked outright and plainly that we bring an official of the company to him and to some of the other Indians to tell them that direct. . . . We met other Indians the same day who asked the same thing of us. We thought it a good idea to have a man designated by the company visit the Indians and tell them directly the attitude of the company and make promises to them we could hear and tie them to. It was also understood that this man was to tell the Indians they would be given work on the project and that the Indians would be given preference everything else being equal. It meant a whole lot to the Indians to have a Company man tell them these things to their faces and it was good business in the interest of the Indians. . . . The trip was a great success and made things easier understood by the Indians and by us, too. It put the Indians right up against the company men who told them [directly] their intentions and made them promises we could hold them to. This trip practically cleaned up those holding out on signing, except the Aubles and Bentons, and made for a better feeling in every way, especially among the Indians, who seemed at first to distrust the company.

According to Miller, the Indian agents paid their own expenses on the trip, but rode in a PG&E company car.

Roberts was also concerned about a statement by Miller about "making capital for [PG&E] out of the friendship of the Indians." Miller had a harder time explaining this statement but argued that he meant "capital to the Company as well as to the Indians," in that, by getting the Indian people and the company to know one another, benefits would come to both parties. Benefits to the Indians would consist of work opportunities and the ability to stay on their lands and/or remove their improvements if they chose to leave. For the company, the cooperation of the Indians would make it easier for them to do their work. He also alluded to benefits for the agency, in that the company could provide support to the Indian people during the winter time "when they are isolated and needing help and attention." Exemplifying the blurring between the role of public and private entities in Indian affairs in the early twentieth century, it seemed as if Miller saw the company as filling the roles the agency was not able to provide in a large jurisdiction in inclement weather. Indeed, he opined further on the challenges of his role to lead the school and the agency in a large and understaffed area: "This jurisdiction is a very large and mountainous one, far too large for one man to handle and get over it carefully each year. . . . In the winter it is practically impossible to get into the greater part of this inaccessible Indian country."

The packet Miller submitted to Roberts responding to the charges included a statement from Clerk Kreigh. Regarding the sale of Indian allotments on the Pit River, Kreigh explained that the Competency Commission had come in 1919 to grant allottees fee patents to their land, but he had just learned that power development was planned on the Pit River, so he requested that the commissioners not grant any fee patents to allottees on the River because he felt "that the Indians would not understand the power proposition," and it was in their best interest for the agency to "sell these lands for them." He then offered an example from Henry and Lewie Wool, in which the agency was able to get them an additional $4,900 more for their land than they would have gotten from their own negotiation with the power company. When Miller described this situation further, he gave additional detail, explaining that those they "held . . . as wards" got more money for their land than those who had been declared competent and dealt directly with the Mt. Shasta Power Company: "Those given patents in fee . . . Ada Bowers, Mabel Bowers, and Joe Bowers . . . got way below what we would have gotten for them had the Competency Commission not turned them loose before the sale. I believe they got around $8,000 for <u>the three pieces</u> of land. Compare this with the prices we secured from the same company for similar land. This shows beyond question the necessity for protection of every sort in such groups."[85] For lands they sold, Miller and Kreigh described themselves as working with allottees to use the proceeds to buy property and arable land, often with restrictive clauses in the deed.

Kreigh also offered more detail on how the agency advertised lands along the Pit River: by "sending out 800 posters to post offices, banks, corporations and individuals in all of the northern part of the state as far as the bay. . . . [They] also advertised in the SF Chronicle, the Sac Bee and the Redding Searchlight." Kreigh also enumerated the number of homes and autos the agency purchased for allottees in the Redding District with land sale revenue.[86] Finally, he responded to the issue of Red River getting so much money for their land along the Pit, agreeing that the land had special characteristics for power value, specifically, "[Walker] owned the river on both sides of a large bend in the river, and if he could have acquired title to the river in the angle he would have developed on his own land a power project by tunnel with a fall of 111 feet." While Kreigh did not offer information on whether the Indian lands also had such characteristics,[87] Miller did, drawing on State Water Commission records to explain that the fall of the Pit River along the Indian lands was 130 feet, and could not be developed except along with other lands.[88]

Miller concluded his statement with numerous anecdotes about similar prices received along the Pit River for lands by white landowners. He described PG&E as being direct and clear about their intentions with his agency, the Office of Indian Affairs in Washington, D.C., and allottees. Regarding the large price paid for Walker's lands, he characterized Walker as "a land speculator pure and simple . . . looking after his own interests." He described Gardner as "more foolish or 'crazy' than dishonest," but an "efficient" cruiser and appraiser who should remain in the woods, rather than trying to "but in" on administration.[89] For his own part, he described himself as perhaps imperfect, but focused on goals of Indian progress: "I am not infallible, and it may be [my] judgment in certain cases can be successfully questioned, but I know that my honesty can not be." On August 28, 1922, Commissioner Chas Burke wrote to Miller, accepting his explanation and quoting the report of the Inspector, which recommended that Miller be fully, freely and emphatically freed of the charges which have been proffered against him of having acted in collusion with the PG&E Company in Selling Indian lands at a lower price than they should have been sold for, and that he be commended for the fair, able, and energetic manner in which he conducted all his dealings during the period when the sale of these lands were under consideration. I believe that he is entitled to this action as a mere matter of justice to a public servant who has been unjustly censured.[90]

As such, following the independent investigation of these dueling complaints, Burke effectively absolved Miller of any accusation of wrongdoing, but summarily dismissed Gardner from the agency.

Investigation regarding Supervisor Wilson's role in the land sales to PG&E continued after Miller was acquitted, in part due to Miller's allusions to the fact that certain papers in connection with PG&E were missing from the Greenville office files after Wilson borrowed them. Wilson remained defensive, and continued to accuse Miller of selling lands with hydropower value to PG&E for "far less than white people received for their lands located near the Indian lands."[91] However, the agency continued to defend its employees against any wrongdoing in the sale of lands to the hydroelectric companies on the Pit River. In an unsigned, undated letter to a Mr. Daiker, an unknown investigator defended the actions of the agency:

> Every action taken by the Superintendent in sales to the Mt. Shasta Power Corporation and PG&E Co., were under instructions from this Office and the Department. Private sales are not allowed in cases like these, and the order of this Office to sell all to one person or corporation, with a bid on each tract, was made to prevent a hold up of a public utility, and to make certain a sale of tracts least desired by purchasers. . . . The company was excavating on its own land and needed some covered by the advertisement, at once. In fact it was allowed, at its own risk, to commence at one point where a failure would hinder, and temporarily stop work. Their bids were far in excess of appraisements. The Office and the Department knew exactly what it was doing when it sold the lands.[92]

In sum, the agency saw itself as simultaneously protecting Indian interests and enabling the company to develop a public works project. While this investigation focused on the Pit River in particular, no similar investigation of underselling or backroom-dealing took place on the Feather River or in the Almanor Basin, where lands were canceled and condemned, sometimes with no restitution to allottees. This book, and associated maps and allotment databases delivered to the Maidu Summit, attempts to begin that inquiry.

REFLECTIONS ON THE IMPORTANCE OF VALUE

Any discussion of the sale and management of Indian allotment lands is not complete without attention to concepts of value, which involve the value or worth of the lands and waters in question, the characteristics of the entities charged with estimating and determining value, and the moral values and principles that guided the administration and sale of allotments at the turn of the twentieth century. Discussion of value in these contexts reveals agency and corporate actions guided both by greed and disingenuous approaches to Indian communities, as well as by an oppressive paternalism.[93] The (nonmonetary) value Indian people hold for their homelands cannot be overstated; in these regions, descendants of the allottees whose lands were implicated in sales to power and lumber companies remain in their homelands. For many Maidu today, owning property may be out of reach due to the high land values. Through tracking how lands have been valued over time, we can better understand the creation and production of large landowning interests that continue to hold Indian lands,[94] as well as the importance of windows of opportunity when land values are reconfigured to emphasize conservation or restitution.[95]

4

MONOPOLIES

BUILDING ON the study of value in the previous chapter, this chapter investigates how and when former allotment lands in Plumas and Lassen Counties were purchased or otherwise acquired by large landholding interests (public and private), and how Native allottees negotiated their rights with these large landholding entities. I explore Indigenous engagement (as employees, owners, petitioners, partners, etc.) over time with large industrial and conservation landowners, respectively, drawing on examples from specific allotment histories. I look for examples that might inform how descendants of allottees and these companies, if they continue to have a presence in the region, might address history and work together productively.

THE RED RIVER LUMBER COMPANY

How and why did the Red River Lumber Company come to own so many Indian allotment lands, and so much Maidu and Pit River land in general, in the northeastern Sierra? The story is one of complicity and privilege, as federal agencies and private companies supported one another in claiming and processing natural resources of the West. The iconic leader of Red River was Thomas Barlow Walker, son of an Ohio immigrant who perished on his way to California in 1849 to explore the gold fields. The biographer and historian Robert M. Hanft describes Walker as a self-made businessman who pursued college education, military service, and sales of farm equipment, all to little effect, and eventually built an empire in the Minnesota timber industry (1980).

In 1862 Walker was hired by George B. Wright to survey a tract of federal land. During this time, Walker noted where the timber was, and this was also perhaps his first exposure to the vast mineral, timber, and hydrological wealth on land claimed by the federal government. After two decades of working in a timber partnership called Butler Mills & Walker Company, Walker founded Red River in 1884, in Crookston, Minnesota, where he had established a mill. The family-owned company was named after the Red River, which forms a border between Minnesota and North Dakota (Hanft 1980, 14; *Mississippi Valley Lumberman* 1944).

Unpublished material compiled by biographer Clara Nelson includes reference to early accusations of land fraud against Red River, in which the company was said to encourage settlers to file for timber under the Timber and Stone Act of 1878 and then sell it to the Company, to describe dry and timbered land as "swampy" in order to obtain it for lower prices, and to obtain timbered land by dishonestly filing a mineral claim.[1] In an undated treatise entitled "Looters of the Domain," Walker is noted as having no less than 50 charges of fraud against him in 1902. The author expressed frustration with the inaction of the GLO in 1907, whose Commissioner Ballinger "said he would make no effort to investigate the Walker [entries] unless the California State Mining Bureau should furnish the Gen. Lan [*sic*] Office with specific charges of fraud. . . . And why should a state office call the attention of the Goft. [*sic*] Official to matters affecting the public domain of the U.S."[2] Walker admitted that timber had come from public lands, but it was not timber cut by Red River employees but by contractors that then sold logs to Red River. It appears that Walker's later solution was to buy as much timberland as possible, so that all timber product came from Red River's lands. While all of the methods by which he obtained the land are unclear, Walker began to amass lands with timber and potential mineral wealth.

In 1889 just two years after the passage of the Indian Allotment Act (1887), and perhaps anticipating that accessible timber supply in Minnesota would eventually be exhausted, Walker began exploring options for purchasing lands in Northern California. According to Hanft, Walker began buying properties in California in 1894. From the allotment records in Plumas and Lassen

Counties, the earliest Red River purchase of allotments took place in 1912, with the majority purchased between 1914 and 1920. Walker eventually became one of California's largest landowners.[3] A 1924 article in the San Francisco Chronicle describes Walker as the sixth wealthiest man in the country, owning nearly 500,000 acres in California and the same amount in Minnesota, and the founder of a company (Red River) that "has cut more timber than any other in the United States" (*San Francisco Chronicle* 1924).

Similar to his strategy in Minnesota, Walker purchased lands that other timber operators may not have been interested in because of their distance from markets. In order to resolve this issue, Walker worked closely with rail and other transportation providers to build the infrastructure to move the timber once harvested. When he began work on a mill in Westwood, California, in 1913, he brokered a deal with Southern Pacific Railroad to construct an additional 135 miles of track in exchange for a guarantee of shipping Red River lumber on Southern Pacific tracks. The railway was completed in February 1914 by a subsidiary, Fernley & Lassen Railway (Hanft 1980, 47). In August 1914 the fledgling Red River mill increased its capacity, powered by what would today be called a biomass plant, which created power from wood chips (57).

Rather than buying huge blocks of land that included land without timber, Walker purchased timberlands alone as much as possible, resulting in "scattered and irregular" holdings. This matched the configuration of timber on the landscape, yet also may have contributed to his problems with trespassing on other's properties. A 1913 letter from Greenville Indian School's W. S. Campbell described a visit from Henry Snayden, who told him that "the Walker people, who are conducting extensive operations in cutting lumber in Lassen county," were very close to the allotments of Frank Bully (Sus-53) and Mary Dokesim (Sus-123). Campbell encouraged A. A. Bear to look into this, adding that maybe they "will not cross over the line, but it might be well to watch them a little."[4]

Like many non-Native historians, Hanft calls 1890s northeastern California "a vast empty land," despite the dense Native population of Maidu and Pit River, as well as nearby Paiute, Washoe, and Shoshone. From 1894 through 1913, Walker—through his son Clinton, who was in charge of cruising and field work—purchased lands in Northern California. Often, Red River was the only bidder on Indian allotment lands. On the 1914 report of the sale of allottee Indian Bob's land (near Diamond Mountain, southwest of Susanville, California), when asked to justify why the sale to T. B. Walker should proceed in the absence of competitive bids, the BIA replied that the land was "valuable only on account of the timber, no person other than the purchaser, who represents Red River, is so situated as to make the land desirable. The sale should be approved, not readvertised."[5] On a 1929 report of the sale of allottee Jennie Williams's land, also near Diamond Mountain, the reason for selling the allotment to Red River Lumber over Lassen Lumber and Box Company was even briefer, limited to "nothing to be gained by readvertisement."[6]

According to Hanft, the first tree cut by Red River was felled in September 1912, with a ceremonial first cut by Clinton Walker's eight-year-old daughter, Harriet (Hanft 1980, 48). Red River also purchased its first Indian allotments in Plumas County in 1912: Clinton Walker purchased the 160-acre Big Meadows allotment of Maggie Jenkins (Sus-168) for $1,755 in August 1912 and the 160-acre allotment of Roxy Peconam northeast of Chester for $937.50 in December 1912. The Walkers continued purchasing allotments in Plumas and Lassen Counties until at least 1928. According to my research on Indian allotments in Plumas and Lassen Counties, Red River and heirs purchased 96 allotments, a total of 14,932 acres.[7] Ultimately, Hanft reports that Red River holdings were over 1.25 million acres in Northern California.

Red River's expansion in Westwood reached its height during World War I, about 1917, with 1,700 employees (74). The quintessential "company town," Westwood had a company store, company celebrations, and herds of beef and milk cattle to supply the town's needs. In 1919 Red River continued to expand in response to what Fletcher Walker termed a "strong demand for California lumber," which was becoming "a satisfactory substitute for the exhausted former supply of Minnesota and Canada" (79).

The interaction between the two large companies, Red River and GWP, and the BIA and the railroad companies, is complex. On at least two occasions, employees from GWP (the supervising carpenter George Peltier and physician Fred Davis) left that company to join Red River in Westwood (48, 54). As detailed in chapter 3, on one occasion an employee of the BIA (Irving Gardner) worked for both the BIA and Red River at the same time, and, upon dismissal from the BIA, went to work for Red River.

The interaction between Red River and the federal government extended beyond specific interactions with both the BIA and the U.S. Forest Service to broader agreements that provided Red River with favorable shipping rates when the Railroad Administration took over rail lines during World War I (78). While other companies suffered from Railroad Administration increases in freight fees, Red River held a competitive advantage because its rates remained significantly lower than other shippers, and they were able to maintain their operations.

Red River accelerated its monopoly over the region as it acquired more land, because it became the only likely buyer. According to a letter from the timber cruiser Charles Gardner enumerating appraisals on several allotments between Greenville and Susanville: "I have based my values on conditions found in that vicinity—where the County records show the Red River Lumber Co own practically the entire surrounding territory—This timber Co. which owns 800,000 acres in the vicinity is the only possible bidder on the allotments above mentioned and I have endeavored to make my appraisals at a figure that would bring fair returns to the owners—and a bid from the Lumber Company."[8] Similarly, as the Report on Sale of Doc Williams's allotment (Sus-200) in 1923 reads, the sole bid from Red River was accepted because "the purchaser is the only party located in a position to use the timber. Owns much of the adjoining property."[9] The same thing happened to Linda Williams's allotment (Sus-205), because "they have option on timber in adjoining in the forest reserve,"[10] and "nearly all timber lands in this vicinity are owned by the Red River Lumber Co., who own ranches adjoining this property. . . . And timber must go out across their land."[11]

Red River stood to gain particularly in this instance, as Doc Williams wanted to sell multiple Williams allotments at once. The Indian Agency had also for several years been invested in trying to sell all of the allotments together to support the construction of a sawmill that would contribute to local economic development. The seven parcels near Taylorsville totaled 957.9 acres, and the majority of their appraised value was in the timber.[12] Two bidders, both with adjacent lands, competed for the Williams allotments: Red River and former congressman H. S. Horsman. While Horsman bid more, he apparently bid late, so Red River's bids were accepted on three allotments (200, 202, and 203—Doc, Harry, and Lincoln Williams), and Horsman's on four (201, 204, 205, and 206—Annie, Lents, Linda, and Ridlon Williams).[13] Edgar Miller advocated for this situation, describing the importance of Red River's role to the agency:

> One serious thing to bear in mind is that we are almost entirely dependent upon the Red River Lumber Company for our market in getting rid of these lands and that no offense should be given them to make them decide to purchase no more Indian timber or lands. . . . Their money has helped many a poor Indian family into a good home and saved many others from conditions worse than bad and in

no way that I know of have they attempted to take any advantage of being in the independent position they are.[14]

Indeed, even as the Indian Agency was tasked with carrying out the trust responsibility to Indian people and protecting their interests, Red River, one of the largest lumber producers in the nation, was seen as a necessary partner, and one that the agency wanted to take care not to offend.

Miller personally intervened to develop an agreement between Horsman and Red River, by taking Horsman over to meet with Fletcher Walker regarding these lands. He reported in a subsequent letter to the commissioner of Indian Affairs that the men were congenial and agreeable to the arrangement, even as they were each attentive to protecting their respective interests.[15] In this instance, the agency facilitated the sale and attempted to stay on good terms with the largest landowners and buyers, possibly to the detriment of the Indian allottees whose interests they were supposed to be protecting.

THE RED RIVER LUMBER COMPANY AND MAIDU
LEGACIES OF RESISTANCE

In 1920 Red River acquired the allotment of John Peconam (Sus-6), a patriarch of a large Maidu family. John Peconam was married to Roxy Peconam, and the two of them had eight children, and their numerous descendants today are members of Susanville Indian Rancheria and Honey Lake Maidu, as well as other tribes. One in particular, Ron Morales, son of Leona Peconam Morales, hosts the Susanville Bear Dance.[16] John Peconam passed away in 1901, Irvine Gardner appraised his 150-acre allotment in October 1918,[17] and his heirs petitioned to sell it in December 1919. The petition indicated some urgency to sell to Red River, as "land worth the price of lumber only. If sold now can get better price than anyone else will give. Company will not want to lay tracks over again after this district is logged for a few allotments."[18] John Peconam's allotment was sold for the appraised value of $2,206 (roughly $14/acre) in December, 1920, to the sole bidder, Red River. As with other reports on allotment sales to the company, the report argued that selling to the sole bidder was permissible because Red River was "now logging in the vicinity and worth more money to them while they have tracks laid than later—No one else would pay this price for this land."[19] As many "heirs who could be found" accepted the sale in June 1920,[20] and the superintendent wrote to the commissioner of Indian Affairs in

July requesting that the sale be finalized and the proceeds distributed to the heirs.[21] The sale was completed in December 1920 and a fee patent was issued to Red River on January 28, 1921.[22]

Despite the apparent "success" of the 1920 sale, the Peconams had previous difficulty with Red River. In June 1914, Red River trespassed on Peconam's land and burned a structure. A Red River representative wrote a letter to Supervisor Wilson in Susanville arguing that the cabin was on land "belonging to the company, and not on the Indian allotment."[23] However, a 1919 report shows that Red River was responsible for the damage and also trespassed on the allotments of Ella Mack (Sus-129), Ollie Mack (Sus-131), and Maggie Butler (Sus-420). On the Mack and Butler allotments, Red River was assessed damages for illegal timber harvest, but on the Peconam allotment, Red River had destroyed buildings, and was also assessed $620 in damages.[24]

Following the sale of John Peconam's allotment to Red River, the Peconams questioned whether Red River had ever actually been assessed damages for the destruction of the structures. In a March 1922 letter, Miller inquired of Gardner whether the appraisement, which read, "Timber $1,586, buildings $620; a total of $2,206," included or did not include the value of the buildings burned: "Please make a statement . . . of the fact that you made the building entry for the damages account of the burning of the buildings and that there were no buildings at the time of appraisement."[25] Gardner replied a few days later that "criminals were staying" in the "old barn and shack on this land," and a Red River employee was "instructed to clean up all these places . . . and the buildings were destroyed at that time." He explained further that his $620 line item pertained to the buildings and was "double their value from the best information I could get." He also noted that Red River had already "straightened up the matter."[26] However, Gardner himself had placed on furlough by the agency and asked to resign in November 1921, due largely to questions about his simultaneous employment with Red River.

Roxy Peconam, wife of the late John Peconam and an heir to his estate, wrote to Miller in December 1922, irate about the lack of payment for the destroyed structures: "Your check of 76. cts received. And I want to say to you Mr. Miller that I have $600, six hundred that was due me as damages/ for distroying [sic] my property at Westwood. And if this money is not payed [sic] me at this time I will have an attorney to file suit for same. And investigate the whole of my dealings with you about all of our allotments undersold all the way through."[27] Miller replied politely yet defensively three days later, explaining that the fees due for trespass and destruction of the buildings had been "collected with the purchase price," divided among the nine legal heirs, and that "this office will be glad to explain to any reliable representative of yours these matters, and we are always ready to defend ourselves from any unjust attack."[28] In February 1923, Miller expressed additional frustration with the Peconams over the matter of the burned buildings, noting that the $620 had been received from Red River, and paid to the heirs: "This has been explained to them about forty times." He suggested that they ask the company "about the matter if they do not believe what this office tells them." He then reiterated Gardner's opinion that the price for the buildings was generous.[29]

In August 1954 Roxy Peconam inquired again about the status of the allotment sale and proceeds, via her daughter Leona (Peconam) Morales and F. G. Collett, executive representative of the Indians of California, Inc. Collett wrote to the BIA on Morales's and Peconam's behalf, noting that Roxy Peconam received only a small amount for the burned buildings (including the lumber, machinery, and other property inside of them), but "she was never paid for timber taken out by Red River Lumber Co., nor did she agree to sell the land."[30] The office replied shortly afterward, explaining the history of the heirs' petition to sell in 1920, the sale (including the valuation for the burned buildings) later that year, and the issuance of a fee patent to Red River on January 28, 1921.[31] In August 1955 Collett wrote to the BIA Realty Office again on the Peconams' behalf, noting that the Peconam heirs believed that they had only sold the timber, and that the allotment was still in trust.[32] No reply is on file from the BIA regarding this assertion. As this snapshot of Peconam family history with Red River shows, controversy over appraisal, terms of sale, and collection and disbursement of trespass damages and sale proceeds all continued to be fraught matters decades after the BIA declared the transactions complete and issued fee patents to Red River.

While it liquidated assets in 1944 and the mill at Westwood burned in 1956, because of its purchase of so many Maidu allotments and ancestral lands, Red River continues to have a presence in the Maidu homeland. The brief case studies of interactions between allottees and the company reveal an enterprise that worked closely with the Indian Agency to commoditize Plumas and Lassen County forestlands. At the turn of the twentieth century, these headwaters regions were being turned to the production of water and power to serve downstream communities, at the expense of Maidu and Pit River families and communities that still have not received adequate restitution for the impacts of this process. These case studies also reveal that allottees figured out ways to work within the system imposed on them by the agency and the corporations to gain some measure of value from their lands, remain in Maidu country if they chose to do so, and hold the agency and the companies publicly accountable for their transgressions on Indian land. However, Red River was only one of several large interests that Maidu allottees had to contend and negotiate with; others included GWP, the Forest Service, and cattle companies.

THE GREAT WESTERN POWER COMPANY

According to a brief promotional history of GWP written by the company itself, GWP incorporated in 1915, consolidating three preexisting companies (the Great Western Power Company, City Electric Company, and Consolidated Electric Company).[33] By 1920 GWP was providing power to "31,615 domestic, agricultural, and industrial customers in some 15 counties of Northern California" (Coleman 1952, 275). To keep pace with demand, GWP was adding infrastructure in the San Francisco Bay Area to distribute the power issuing from facilities in the Feather River Canyon, including the Caribou and Las Plumas Plants. In 1924 it reported serving more than 30 cities, including San Francisco, Santa Rosa, Sacramento, Oakland, Richmond, and Martinez, with a combined population of more than 1.4 million people. By 1929 it reported a 6.9 percent rate of return on its electric production.[34]

GWP extolled the power production and storage capacity of its principal property, Lake Almanor, "an artificial lake formerly known as Big Meadows" that "regulates the flow of the north fork Feather River." The company expressed its pride in controlling "the most important rights to the waters of this stream," enabling it to plan for Almanor's expansion. Indeed, according to their lawyers, GWP held the rights to Lake Almanor water and the "principal waters" of the north fork Feather River "in perpetuity." GWP can be seen as building a water monopoly in Northern California, as it also owned the majority of stock and operated the properties of the California Electric Generating Company, as well as held the majority of the shares of the Western Canal Company, which oversaw the diversion of Feather River water to agriculture after it had been used for power production. In a striking convergence of interests between colonial development mechanisms, the "rates of the Company and the issuance of its securities" remained under the jurisdiction of the California Railroad Commission.

The company predicted that demand would only grow, as California's develop-ment "has been and will in the future be predicated upon hydroelectric power."[35]

Between 1907 and 1912, PG&E operated 11 hydropower plants, but not all were in production at any given time. These included plants on the Yuba, Mokelumne, and Sacramento Rivers and their tributaries.[36] PG&E also contin-ued to grow, its gain in gross revenue up 157.6 percent and its gain in number of customers up 101.6 percent between 1915 and 1925 (Coleman 1952, 280). By 1922 there were only three major gas and electric utilities in California: GWP, PG&E, and San Joaquin Light and Power. GWP, after rebuffing an attempted purchase by PG&E, decided to strengthen its position by purchasing San Joaquin Light and Power in 1924. In 1925 the consolidated GWP and San Joaquin Light and Power Companies were purchased by the North American Company, a New York–based investment firm (291–94). By 1927 it was bringing electricity to "more than 300 Northern California communities" and rapidly acquiring smaller local and regional utility companies and their associated properties (280).

One competitor company that became part of GWP was the Oro Electric Corporation. This company, incorporated in 1911 to include the Oro Water, Light and Power Company, which served primarily Oroville, had plans to build a hydroelectric plant at Yellow Creek, a tributary of the north fork Feather River that traverses Humbug Valley, or *Tasman Koyom*. The Oro Electric Corporation also placed a dam on Butt Creek below Almanor Dam. GWP opposed this move, asserting its senior water rights to Butt Creek (posted in 1902), and even-tually blew up the company's Butt Creek Dam. In the conflict that followed this bold destruction, PG&E ultimately bought out the Oro Electric Corporation and retains the land on both Yellow Creek and Butt Valley to this day, subject to conservation easement held by the Feather River Land Trust in Butt Valley, and subject to pending land transfer to the Maidu Summit Consortium & Conservancy in Humbug Valley, with an accompanying conservation easement held jointly by the California Department of Fish and Wildlife and the Feather River Land Trust. Water rights will remain with PG&E.

In a 1930 hearing regarding PG&E's proposal to purchase GWP stock, a "Testimony on Value" noted that GWP held a "minor use permit," also termed a "license," "right of way or easement," from the Federal Power Commission dated November 18, 1925, and effective through December 31, 1968, to flood 1,001.2 acres of government lands in the Lake Almanor Basin. Only 671.19 acres covered by the permit were below the 4,500' contour line (the maximum flood line), a small portion of the 29,000 total acres below the line, the majority of which were in private ownership by the company.[37] The hearing materials clarified that the development of the reservoir and the generation of power each required a set of permissions: water rights to control, divert, and store water (and later release it for power production) derived from the state (appropriated by the company as early as 1890) and recognized by the federal government, and federal permits to pass over or build on U.S. government lands (but not to take or divert water) for the purposes of power production.[38] While the company also held federal major permits to operate the Caribou plant and other plants in the Feather River Canyon, these permits "in no way relate[d]" to the Almanor permits—although their operation would be assumed to be dependent on the operation of the reservoir.[39]

GWP was able to establish its principal storage reservoir at Big Meadows (Lake Almanor) and grow based on the acquisition of Mountain Maidu individual Indian allotments, via both cancellation (in part in Plumas Superior Court) and purchase. The land for the power site at Big Meadows (Powersite 234) was identified by the Executive Order of November 23, 1911. However, even lands included in the power site might still belong to the allottees if the trust patents to those lands had been issued prior to the 1911 withdrawal. It was this fact that enabled the sale of Indian allotments even after the establishment of the power site reserve and perhaps contributed to removing the oversight of the U.S. Geological Survey sometime around 1915.[40]

Such was the case for allotment 231, discussed briefly in chapter 3, which was trust patented to William Dick in 1907 yet included in the area withdrawn in 1911. After Dick's death in 1919, his heirs (or the Indian Office) petitioned to sell his land, noting that it was "within the powersite of GWP and will become flooded after completion of project." According to a 1920 memo from the assistant commissioner of the GLO, because "the trust patent issued prior to the date of withdrawal, patent in fee should issue without any reservation."[41] The land was then sold to Great Western Power Company, with the justification for accepting the sole bid being that it was "within powersite of G.W.P. Co."[42]

This action was contrary to the advice of the director of the U.S. Geological Survey. In a 1912 letter rejecting petitions to sell allotments 233 and 234 (belonging to Harry and Andy Dick, respectively), he explained that the lands were within the flood area of the expanding reservoir, calculated the value of the reservoir and the importance of including the land in Power Site Reserve #234 (approved November 23, 1911) and recommended that "no sale of this land be approved or trust or fee simple patent be issued as regards the land, to the end that the title to lands valuable for power purposes may be retained in the United States."[43] However, perhaps unbeknownst to the director of the U.S. Geological Survey, trust patents on the allotments in this area had generally already been issued to allottees by the GLO and the BIA.

In a 1912 letter to the commissioner of Indian Affairs, Roseburg supervisor Horace Wilson tried to mediate between the Office of Indian Affairs and the U.S. Geological Survey. He noted that the Office of Indian Affairs recommended sale of allotments 233 and 234 based on their timber value,[44] but the U.S. Geological Survey denied sale based on their location in the power site. Based on his visit to the land, he observed that the dam was progressing: "It will be a very large one, and the area to be flooded is said to be the second largest in the world," inundating "quite a number of Indian allotments" in the process.[45] According to Wilson, he had been aware of this for some time and already sought the Office of Indian Affairs' advice on a letter he received from GWP's attorney Guy Earl, in which GWP offered to either buy the allotments, or, "if they could not purchase . . . condemn [them] under the laws of the State of California." Wilson asked the Office of Indian Affairs if GWP could, in fact, condemn the lands, or if he should continue to try to sell them, or if the government would intervene to retain the land because of its power-site value. Wilson also countered the Office of Indian Affairs' opinion that the timber was valuable on the land because of its inaccessibility, noting that GWP had tried to "give this timber to any company that would take the timber out of Big Meadows and so far no one has accepted their offer" because of the lack of "transportation facilities" and "the reason that it would probably cost . . . more than the timber and lumber would be worth to transport it to the markets." In contrast, however, Wilson said he had "heard a rumor" that Red River planned to build mills and/or a railroad into the area to remove the timber. Still, he felt the sale of the timber would be "impossible" and asked for direction from the office on how to proceed.

These differences in perceptions of value and competing roles of different jurisdictions led to wildly different appraised values of the land: for example, in 1912 Andy Dick's allotment (Sus-234) was appraised at $1,600, with the majority of the value in the timber; in 1914 it was appraised by Deputy Forest Supervisor Otto Swenson as worth $930; also in 1914 it was appraised by Charles Gardner as worth at $2,255, with the land worth just $750 and the timber $1,505; in 1916 it was appraised by C. E. Dunston for $4,550, with the land worth $480 and the timber worth $4,070, but Red River's 1916 bid of $4,550 was rejected by the

Office of Indian Affairs in 1917. A 1918 appraisal by Irvine Gardner included the value of powersite flowage at $20/acre, increasing the value of the parcel to $5,655. The land was sold to GWP in 1920 for $8,055.

In a 1915 letter in which the director of the U.S. Geological Survey determined the value of the remaining lands within Big Meadows based on their power-site potential, he urged:

> In view of the great and primary value of this reservoir for power purposes and the small area of land remaining within it which is subject to public control, I regard it as highly desirable from the standpoint of the public interest that title to this and other land included in the reservoir site should remain in the public. I would therefore recommend that the land be not disposed of except with the reservation of the water-power rights to the United States and, if this can not be accomplished, that action on this matter be suspended until the enactment of legislation which would permit of the disposal of the tract with a reservation of the water-power rights to the United States.
>
> It is evident from the record that if the tract is disposed of at the present time as recommended by the Commissioner of Indian Affairs[,] fee title will almost immediately pass to the Great Western Power Company without restriction or the possibility of regulation in the public interest, a result which is understood not to be in accordance with present Departmental policy as regards lands valuable for water-power purposes.

The director concluded his statement with the advice to at least sell the land for an amount that included the value of its power production potential.[46] By 1915, however, an order had been issued "discontinuing the practice of calling upon the Geological Survey for reports prior to the approval of petitions for sale," thus effectively removing the Survey's oversight from the process of selling lands with hydropower production potential.[47]

GWP's ability to condemn Indian allotment lands came into question when the Indian Office made an error with the allotment of Maggie Bacala (Sus-179) / Maggie Butler (Sus-420). The office apparently double-allotted Maggie Bacala/Butler, given that she went by different names. The allotment to Bacala (179) was made in 1894 but never patented to her and subsequently condemned and flooded for GWP's reservoir purposes. There is little information on this land and the cancellation proceedings. When Indian Service Clerk A. A. Bear examined this apparent error in 1913, he raised the question of GWP's title to

Sus-179, "For I don't believe that a condemnation proceeding of Public Land would secure them a fee patent for the land."[48] In a 1922 overview of the case, the assistant secretary of the Department of the Interior, F. M. Goodwin, explained that

> the Western Power Company, a corporation organized under the laws of the State of California, finding itself in need of certain lands in connection with the development of its activities . . . instituted condemnation proceedings pursuant to a provision found in the act of March 3, 1901 (31 Stat., 1058-1084), which reads:
>
> "Lands allotted in severalty to Indians may be condemned for any public purpose under the laws of the State or Territory where located in the same manner as land owned in fee may be condemned, and the money awarded as indemnity shall be paid to the allottee."
>
> The title so acquired was confirmed in the power company by the act of May 5, 1908 (35 Stat., 100), which stated that "all the interest of the United States in and to the land in the Susanville land district in the State of California . . . aggregating in all 890 acres[,] is hereby relinquished, released, and confirmed to the Western Power Company."[49]

The statutes invoked are highly significant, as they indicate the way in which the federal and state legal apparatuses supported the development of a private monopoly held by the emerging power company. Many Indian lands in Big Meadows were condemned in 1902, eventually flooded, and are now owned by PG&E.

The letter goes on to note that the power company paid $540, "which was retained, on deposit, to the credit of the heirs of Maggie Bacala," as she had already passed away. Allotment application 420 was approved after her passing with a trust patent issued in 1908. The Department of the Interior then assisted the heirs in selling Sus-420 to Red River in 1921. Returning to the matter of the initial allotment of Sus-179, Goodwin argued that the land had already passed to the power company and, as such, "it was beyond the power of this Department to impair or disturb the right to such lands then vested in the power company." As such, the Congressional Act overrode the operation of the federal agency (in this case, the BIA within the Department of the Interior) to secure lands for Indian people. Further, according to Goodwin, the power company had made a payment, but the payment had been deposited in the U.S. Treasury as "miscellaneous receipts" and never reached the family of Maggie Bacala.[50] Regardless, Goodwin informed the commissioner of the GLO "to note on the records of your office . . . 'Application not perfected; title to those lands confirmed in Western Power Company, act of May 5, 1908.' On this showing the case will be considered as closed."[51]

From Indian Service communications, it appeared that the local employees of the agency found themselves trying to facilitate sales of lands within their jurisdiction to the company in the face of inevitable inundation. A 1913 letter from Greenville Indian School's W. S. Campbell, for example, asked for assistance in finding allottees (or their heirs, if allottees were deceased) Charlie Bacala (180), Neva Thomas (184), and Ellen Wano (301), because their lands were "within the reservoir site of the Great Western Power Company's dam" and needed to be sold to the company.[52] Campbell didn't know whether the allottees were living, where they were, or if any process had begun to sell the lands.

The Indian Office held a monopoly of its own over individual allottees' funds, treating them as wards of the agency, making moral judgments on their behavior, and meting out monies in response to small, distinct requests. However, when it came to protecting Indian lands from trespass, the agency was often unable to be effective. As such, Indian people received the brunt of the agency's oversight and attempted control over their lives, and very little protection from incursions by outside interests. In one example, Harrison Dibble (Lee) wrote to Superintendent John Rockwell in 1943 to inform him that stray cattle had been trespassing on his allotment and that of two of his family members for three weeks. He requested assistance, noting the agency's previous communication that any trespassing cattle were to be apprehended, impounded, and retained until the owners paid $1 per head to claim them. He regretted that he "had no way or means to impound these cattle" and could not even get close enough to discern the brand "due to the wildness of the stock." His request for help in the matter was met by a terse reply from Rockwell, who concluded that he could not get an employee to the land "to make a trespass case" and offered the solution of leasing the allotments, "which will automatically take care of the trespass situation." As such, the response from the agency was to lease or rent the lands out to a cattle rancher or other landholder, typically non-Indian, who would be able to keep trespassing cattle off of the land, utilize it, and pay rent to the agency, which would then disburse it to Lee as it deemed appropriate. These solutions continued to disempower the Indian landowner; the partnership was between the agency and a possible lessee, and the Indian landowner was reduced to waiting for possible proceeds to be reduced at the agency's discretion.[53]

The BIA strategy of getting trespassers to formally lease or buy the land they were trespassing on was also applied in the case of Belle Fox. When her land was trespassed on, the agency went about looking for the offending "sheep men" and helping them to arrange the "necessary lease."[54] Allottees themselves were often eager to sell land, as they did not have the means to develop cattle or timber enterprises, often traveled for work, and had a difficult time accessing the lease proceeds from the Indian Office. As recorded in Wild Bill's 1941 petition to sell his allotment (Sus-457): "This land is good for nothing but grazing and cannot be used for anything else and is innacces able [sic] from a road. I have not been able to live on this Allotment due to have to work on the ranches elsewhere for a living and the small amount of grazing lease does me very little good."[55]

Many times, the cancellation of the lands was not communicated to allottees, who found themselves suddenly without even the small land area of their allotment. One descendent of allottees, Levi Tom, wrote several letters to the BIA—at least one in 1938, 1949, and 1961, inquiring what happened to the canceled allotments of his father Ike Tom (Sus-160) and his relatives Bob Schaffer and Emily (Emma) Shaffer (Sus-151). In his October 1938 reply, then Sacramento Indian Agency superintendent Roy Nash stated that "these two [allotments], with several other Indian allotments in that vicinity, were condemned by decree of the Court in favor of the Western Power Co."[56] Superintendent Nash repeated this explanation to Shafer Tom, and Sacramento Area Office realty officer Britton Clair repeated it to Levi Tom in a 1961 reply.[57] In none of these replies did the agency offer compensation or alternative land options.[58]

Records show that GWP sometimes operated outside of BIA regulations and negotiated directly with individual Indian allottees. For example, a February 1, 1913, letter from the Greenville Indian School superintendent to the Department of the Interior, U.S. Indian Service, notes that GWP "made settlement" for their lease payment directly with John and Ellen Jenkins, heirs to the Harper Jenkins allotment (165). Per the lease agreement made in October 1911, GWP was to lease allotment 165 for $240/year, for not more than three years, in order to quarry stone on the allotment for use in building the dam and temporary housing for dam builders. GWP gave the Jenkins "provisions and supplies amounting, as per receipts furnished, to total amount of rent due" under the lease. The superintendent told GWP that this was not proper protocol and that cash was to be paid directly to his office in the future, but he did not require GWP to remit cash value to the agency that the company had already paid to the allottee in goods. General language in the lease agreement indicates BIA support for GWP activities. For example, in the November 3, 1911, Certificate of Supervising Officer approving the lease, Superintendent Campbell writes that "the proposed lessee is a corporation engaged in an important public enterprise that is worthy of encouragement, and in my judgment the presence of the said lessee will be beneficial to the Indians."

GWP's enterprises upstream also supported the expansion of valley agricultural monopolies, as the company's system contributed to the regular delivery of water and power downstream and was envisioned as fitting into a larger system that would reduce the risk of catastrophic flooding. Interest in the safety and efficacy of the dam at Big Meadows was apparent from the earliest days of the project. J. D. Galloway, an engineer who had worked on the dam for GWP, called the dam at Almanor "the most important structure on the entire system of the power company."[59] Galloway left GWP in 1925 due to differences of opinion in how the dam should be constructed. He noted in a spring of 1928 visit that the spillway was unsafe and should be repaired:

> It is my belief that only a few hours would be necessary for the stream to cut back to a point where it would undermine the material of the dam, thus releasing the waters in the reservoir and resulting in the complete destruction of the dam.
>
> It would not be difficult to visualize the results of the breaking of this dam with 1,300,000 feet of water stored in the reservoir. Everything in the canyon for 75 miles would be completely wrecked, including the Western Pacific Railroad and the three power houses of the power company at Caribou, Bucks Creek, and Las Plumas. The effect of the water would be felt in the upper reaches of the San Francisco Bay and the destruction of cities and farm areas between the mouth of the canyon and the bay would be great. It would undoubtedly destroy completely the City of Oroville and probably cause great damage in Marysville.[60]

In response to a report on "Unusual Conditions at Big Meadows Dam" from September 24, 1929, including seepage and the design of the lower end of the spillway, the State Engineer's Office initiated an investigation of the dam in December 1929.[61] Prominent private agricultural interests including George Springer of the Alameda Sugar Company, W. T. Ellis of Marysville, P. N. Ashley of Woodland (farmer, and former engineer of Yolo County), and Jesse Poundstone of Grimes visited the site in November of the same year to ensure that the dam was functioning well and effectively to deliver water for agriculture in the Central Valley and mitigate flood risk.[62]

SALE OF GWP HOLDINGS TO PG&E

Appraised at $3,683,750 in 1930, GWP's property at Lake Almanor was the most valuable of all of the company's properties (worth $6,406,000 all together).[63] While the appraisal was based on a value of $125/acre, a review of property values in GWP's Feather River Water Power Project by the consulting engineer C. J. Rhodin reported a cost to the company of $37.50/acre (including overhead). Rhodin also examined the company's holdings of "mountain grazing land and meadow land" in nearby Indian Valley, worth $75–$125/acre. Additional examination of GWP's assets and liabilities revealed that the cost of hydropower production per kilowatt hour on the Feather River, examining the Caribou and Las Plumas Powerhouses specifically, averaged 3.4 mills/kWh between 1926 and 1929, making it more cost effective than the production of power at other facilities, including Hetch Hetchy at Newark (4.876 mills/kWh), the California

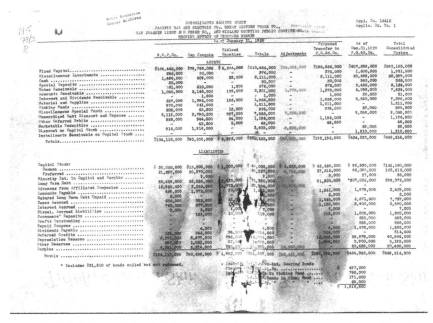

FIGURE 11. This consolidated balance sheet, dated January 31, 1930, shows the effects of the proposed merger that would establish PG&E as the major power producer and provider in Northern California. Note that GWP represented the majority of assets, and the greatest of these was Lake Almanor, at the headwaters of the Feather River Power system. (Filed in Erwin Cooper papers, Box 12, WRCA.)

Oregon PG&E plant at Cottonwood (4.5 mills/kWh), and even East Bay Utility District (average 3.75 mills/kWh).[64]

In 1930 PG&E purchased the North American Company's majority interests in GWP, San Joaquin Light and Power, Midland Counties Public Service Power Corporation, and the Fresno Water Company (Coleman 1952, 295). While it took another eight years to buy out all of the minority interests in San Joaquin Light and Power, and another 18 years to buy out North American completely, the 1930 purchase was a watershed moment celebrated by the company: "By this final major consolidation, P.G. and E had fulfilled its destiny. It had reached the peak of its long climb to a point when it could give to all Northern California, with only minor exceptions, the benefits of gas and electric service by one integrated system, administered by one company" (296).

The monopoly still in place today was completed more than 80 years ago. As with the success of most private enterprises, PG&E and predecessor companies were greatly aided by public blessing, in the form of hydropower reserves initially and later through state regulation as quasi public-private utilities: "Those benefits under state regulation were to be the economic advantages of adequate supply of light, heat, and power to communities, to industry, and to agriculture, provided with maximum efficiency at minimum cost to the consumer" (296). The initial developers and investors in the projects purchased by PG&E often moved into positions of power in the new company. As such, the corporate mergers simply reshuffled established powerful interests. One of the Earl brothers, who had conceived of and developed the Lake Almanor Project, took a seat on PG&E's board of directors following the 1930 purchase (297).

By 1931, PG&E served nearly 80 percent (46 of 58) of California's counties, more than 2.75 million people, with 1.27 million customers purchasing gas, electric, water, and steam (309–10). It was during the Depression in the early 1930s that the company was broadsided by public regulation, and fought it in the courts. The State Railroad Commission ordered a reduction in gas rates in 1933, exercising "for the first time in 22 years . . . regulatory power over gas and electric rates." The case was in the courts for five years before it was upheld, and PG&E began the onerous work of refunding customers more than $6 million in 1938 (310). However, PG&E's fortunes were already looking up by 1934, and it had voluntarily reduced gas rates in 1936 (perhaps as something of a concession agreed on by multiple interests), and the energy needs in World War II vastly increased PG&E's plants, projects, and sales.

The postwar boom in energy needs continued for PG&E, according to Coleman, and the company added two more hydro powerhouses on the North Fork Feather River in 1949 and 1950, bringing the total to five. The company planned to add four more, at Butt Valley, Caribou (#2), Belden, and Poe (336). Although PG&E's development and expansion was facilitated by public processes (such as condemning land for hydropower), PG&E has also continually fought against ongoing attempts to deprivatize utilities, in the courts and the boardrooms. According to Coleman, PG&E's positioned itself as "a staunch defender against political invasion of a business successfully created and maintained by individual initiative and developed according to the needs of a growing state" (320). With some notable exceptions (such as the Sacramento Municipal Utility District), PG&E has generally retained a monopoly on power production and distribution in northern California (321).

Perhaps the biggest "threat" to PG&E's market dominance was the development of the CVP, broached in 1930 in the State Water Plan, approved in 1933, and funded (to construct Shasta Dam) by President Franklin Delano Roosevelt in 1935. The CVP was a popular solution to offset Depression-era unemployment and was ostensibly focused on irrigation and flood control rather than power generation (326). The Bureau of Reclamation retained control over power generated at Shasta Dam. PG&E's monopoly was criticized in the context of a contract between PG&E and the government for power generated from the Shasta Dam Project. Under this "wartime contract," the federal government received 3.33 mills/kWh from the company, whereas under sale to public agencies, the government would receive 5 mills/kWh. Further, cities buying power from PG&E paid more than 7 mills/kWh, indicating that PG&E was making a profit. The contract, aimed to make power available for wartime industries, was set to terminate in 1947. When the facility was fully built out, additional transmission lines would have to be built, and a 1943 editorial argued that they should not be owned by PG&E, but by the public.[65]

Further resistance to PG&E having a predominant role in the conveyance and distribution of CVP power came from the California Farm Research and Legislative Committee. In a 1955 statement, Executive Secretary Grace McDonald cited agricultural economist Varden Fuller, calling for "distribut[ing] the power developed through public channels" and warning that "if the control of either the land or the power slips away, so that the increased income is not in the hands of those who are expected to pay the construction charges, it is inevitable that financial chaos and gross inequities result." In an examination of PG&E's access to federal power, alongside contracts with federal, state, and local agencies, McDonald voiced her committee's agreement with Senator Richard Neuberger of Oregon in his opposition to the sale of falling water to a private utility "on the grounds that it would be against the public interest and a violation of reclamation law . . . developed by a half century of congressional action." The California Farm Research and Legislative Committee specifically opposed PG&E's [bid] to purchase and distribute the power generated by the Trinity River system, arguing in part that this would jeopardize the CVP's main purpose, to "transfer water at the lowest possible cost from areas of plentiful supply to wealth-producing farm communities threatened with destruction because of lack of sufficient irrigation water."

PG&E seems to have continued its struggle against state regulation, which, according to PG&E reports to stockholders as well as public presentations, acted to curtail PG&Es ability to meet state energy needs and promote state economic development. In a 1979 statement before the Joint Committee on the State's Economy, PG&E vice president of planning and research Nolan Daines voiced frustration with the California Energy Commission's lower predictions of demand and therefore lack of support for construction and expansion of generation facilities, as well as conservation-minded require-ments to reduce oil use:

> Until priorities change from absolute protectionism to a realization of the need to accept facilities even if there is some effect upon the environment, we seriously question whether the present siting process will result in having the necessary electric generating facilities approved and completed in time to meet the load growth in the 1980s and replace gas and oil fuel in accordance with national priorities. (Daines 1979)

Today, most Northern Californians do receive PG&E power, but few are aware of the history of how PG&E acquired so much land and water rights on which to place power generation and transmission facilities. The conflicted utility deregulation process in the 1990s and the subsequent bankruptcy pro-ceedings in the late 1990s, along with PG&E's threat to sell off many of its landed holdings, returned PG&E policy and operation to the public eye. These processes also brought some of the Indian lands that provided a foundation for the company's growth back into reach, but that is the subject of chapter 5. At this point, we can note that PG&E grew as a monopoly from the early twentieth-century expansion of GWP and Red River, which was built on the backs of Indian allotments and facilitated by state and federal agencies.

AGENCY COMPLICITY AND AGENCY MONOPOLIES

Thus far, this chapter has focused on the ways in which private enterprises were able to grow in pursuit of designated "public goods"—for a very narrow public that did not include Indian allottees. However, public (state and federal) entities were also able to grow their land holdings from decisions made about Indian allotments. Sometimes both public and private parties gained from a single allotment. For example, in 1946 the superintendent of the Sacramento Indian Agency, John Rockwell, wrote to the commissioner of Indian Affairs in Chicago to request advance authority for PG&E to begin construction on a power line across the allotment of Charley Phillips (Sus-324), located near Dixie Valley in Lassen County.[66] The request reveals that Phillips's allotment had already granted a right-of-way of six acres to Western Pacific Railroad and was leased by a lumber company, which had employee cottages and a mill operation on the site. The company relied on timber from the National Forest lands bordering the allotment and supported the extension of the line, which would purportedly service their facilities on the allotment. The allottee was deceased as was one of his heirs, and the probate process for the heir was not complete, but there was urgency to the request, as PG&E desired to get the line done as soon as possible to "service new customers in the vicinity of Little Valley." No reply is on file, but what is striking is the number of corporate (lumber company, PG&E) and agency (Forest Service) players that stood to benefit from approval of the request on the single allotment, which was not necessarily benefiting Indian individuals.

THE U.S. FOREST SERVICE AND ALLOTMENTS

The BIA and the National United States Forest Service attempted to mete out small parcels to other Indian individuals and families living on what became Forest Service land. According to a 1909 Forest Service census and a 1912 Forest Service report of Indian people living on or near the national forest, Indian people in Plumas County either lived on their allotments, private ranch land (perhaps working for a rancher), land purchased by a white male who had married an Indian woman, or established individual, family, or group settlements on what the U.S. government deemed the "public domain." The 1909 census consisted of two lists; one included seven individuals and families living on the Plumas National Forest, and the second included 39 individuals and families who lived within the National Forest, but on allotments or other private land. The agency recommended granting "some form of permit" to families living on, or on inholdings within, the young national forest.[67] The 1912 census included six individuals and families living on or along the middle fork of the Feather River, most with established orchards and some stock and engaged in wage labor. One head of household surveyed located near Cascade in Butte County, John Kennedy, reportedly stated that he did not want any allotment, as he mined full time and raised a garden for subsistence.[68]

Despite Kennedy's statement, the assistant district forester L. A. Barrett included him on a list of "Indians on the Plumas Forest [that] may be entitled to an allotment on the land they are now occupying." This list of just eight individuals and heads of household consisted mostly of individuals living along the Middle Fork Feather River[69] and was in response to a request from Greenville Indian School superintendent Campbell for a list of Indians living within the National Forest, as the Indian Office wanted to provide them with allotments.[70] In 1918 six small allotments (the largest was 52 acres, and most were about 20–25 acres) were approved for heads of household and individuals, and two more were approved in 1924 and in 1933.[71] However, it appears that the Indian Office did not transmit this information to the Forest Service, according to a 1920 impatient request from Barrett for information as to whether the allotments had been approved and what their boundaries were.[72] This is partially due to the fact that the GLO provided final approval and issued the trust patent, and apparently did not provide that information to the U.S. Forest Service.[73] Another request to the BLM as recently as 1976 for copies of the trust patents on these same allotments indicates that the Forest Service may have either misplaced or was still lacking complete information on them.[74]

Despite work on the middle fork of the Feather River to approve Indian allotments for people long settled on what became United States Forest Service land, the agency also had a role in divesting Indian lands. Upstream in the Genesee Valley, Bill/Billy Baker applied for Sus-418 in 1894, but the allotment was held for cancellation in 1901 and the entire township was withdrawn in 1902 for the Diamond Forest Reserve and placed in permanent reservation based on proclamations of July 1905 and October 1906.[75] In a 1910 letter, the commissioner of the GLO explained to the Forester of the U.S. Forest Service that he received an application for the reinstatement of the allotment, including an affidavit from Baker that he moved onto the land in 1896 and had a house, barn, and six acres of cultivated land, including an orchard. According to the affidavit, Baker

> has lived continuously on the land for more than 13 years, never being away at work for more than a few months at any one time, and never knew that the land did not belong to him until he was told, three years since, by US Forest Rangers Joe Cook and William Stark, that his allotment had been canceled, and on being directed by them to remove from the land, he complied with the order. He makes affidavit that he never relinquished the land, or consented to its cancellation, and that the relinquishment purporting to have been made of the entry was not signed by him.[76]

Additional information from the author Pat Kurtz indicates that Baker and his family had built a home on the property, which had been burned by white men, and then built another home before moving to Indian Valley (2010, 63). The commissioner asked if the Forest Service objected to the allotment's reinstatement. Later that month, Assistant Forest Ranger E. V. Clark replied, explaining that Baker had actually not settled on his allotted land but on 40 acres owned by Pierce Evans: "Through Mr. Evans, Rangers Stark and Cooke ran out the Indian's line and found the mistake. It was then that the Indian was requested to move from the land and simply for the reason that Mr. Evans wished to use the land himself."[77] According to Clark, Baker's original allotment was still vacant but completely forested: "It is practically impossible to make a living on the ground." He noted that the allotment was similar to others in the region in its character so, if it were a homestead, he would "positively protest its patent," but, given that it was an allotment and that many others nearby were similar forested, he requested guidance. No additional correspondence is available in the BIA file at the National Archives. According to Kurtz, in 1926 Baker's son inquired with the Indian Agency about his father's allotment and was told that corroborative affidavits from others familiar with the case would have to be secured before a replacement allotment could be considered (2010, 64). The land, including Baker's allotment, remains in Forest Service ownership today.

THE INDIAN AGENCY, LESSEES, AND TRESPASSERS

The Indian Agency attempted to simplify the sale and management of allotments by working directly with other agencies, as well as with potential corporate purchasers and lessees. This could take the form of facilitating repetitive lease transactions or group sales. As discussed in chapter 3, the work to "group" allotments and sell several at one time was favorable to both timber and hydroelectric companies as well as large grazing and ranching interests. The Walker family of Red River was active throughout Plumas and Lassen Counties in both purchasing and leasing allotments: Rosa Jim's father, Captain James Buchanan's land was sold in 1950 to Floyd Edward Walker, and at least nine of his heirs at the time of sale leased their land to Fletcher Walker.[78] In 1922 Greenville superintendent Edgar Miller explained that allotments 387 (Electra Fox), 455 (Harry Lee), 456 (Mayfield Lee), 720 (Little Jack Fox) and 1009 (Long John / John Long) had been grouped for a cattle ranch in Ash Valley, Lassen County. A seller had been identified, prominent rancher J. J. Fleming, who "practically controls Ash Valley" through owning land and leasing Indian lands. As Miller described, many Indian people who worked for Fleming and the Indian Office felt sure of his fairness as a businessman. Ultimately, allotments 387, 388, 455, 456, 720, and 1009 were sold to Fleming, even though the heirs of Harry Lee (455) initially resisted the sale because they felt the price was too low. Miller described what he felt were the options for the Indians: live on the land or sell the land to Fleming, who already likely leased their land or whom they worked for. He felt that the sale of the land to Fleming would "protect" their interests.[79]

Miller was proud of the effort to group and either lease or sell allotments, extolling the virtues of this strategy in a March 1922 letter to the commissioner of Indian Affairs:

> It was at my suggestion Gardner reported on such groups where water was involved. This was in order to get the highest possible price for all the group when they were sold and to allow the leasing to be intelligently done so there would be no trouble over water holes between cattle and sheep men. This grouping idea has been also carried out in saw-mill sites, water projects, etc. It has worked to great advantage to the Indians.[80]

Appraiser Irvine Gardner also advocated for the strategy; in a letter to Miller regarding allotments 433, 434, 435, 1012, and 310, near Madeline, which were also to be sold as a group, he argued that since allotment 435 was the only parcel with water, none of the other parcels could be sold without it: "If these cannot be sold in a group I want note made that except for 435 any appraisals should be cut in two."[81] He mentioned three possible buyers—J. J. Fleming, Geo. Williams Jr. and Sr., and Pyramid Land and Stock Company— all of which were amassing land monopolies in the region, due in no small part to the strategy of purchasing Indian allotments in groups.

Similarly, at least five Indian allotments totaling 770 acres were sold to James Snell in the Dixie Valley area of Lassen County.[82] According to the report on the sale of Belle Jerry's allotment (Sus-247), "The C. W. Clark Company for which Mr. Snell is the manager owns practically all patented land in this vicinity and no one else would be interested."[83] Because of his influence and the amount of land he owned, Snell was able to be selective—in 1925 he bid on three allotments (247, 248, and 1032), but he refused to buy them unless all three allottees (or their heirs) agreed to sell. The Indian Office did not challenge Snell on this condition, apparently because he planned to build a dam and partially flood these allotments, but the allotments themselves did not come with any individual water rights to the stream.[84] The lands were sold to Snell in 1928.

While the Indian Agency attempted to be attentive to potential trespass issues on Indian lands in a wide jurisdiction, this took the form of offering trespassers deals on purchasing Indian lands in order to remedy their infractions. The BIA's role in supervising these transactions sometimes led to confusion among allottees and even local agency employees regarding which allotments remained in trust, who could use them, and at what times. As an illustration of this, in 1937 the Office of Indian Affairs, Field Service, field nurse Florence S. McClintock wrote to Superintendent Nash on behalf of the Bayley family, noting that "the Bayley family had always thought that they retained all the allotments 436 to 442. It was quite a surprise to them to know that 436, 441, and 440 were cancelled. Now they do not know where the lines are of the lands that they still retain."[85] She mentioned an heir's concern about incursions on what she thought was the allotment of her grandmother Ally Bayley, including a ditch and a road crossing, and requested a survey of the lands to delineate "just what is Government land, and what is not." However, no reply to her request is included in Bayley's allotment file.

In January 1940, Superintendent Nash wrote to Victor Christensen, ranch manager of the H. C. Cattle Company in the town of Likely, to inform him that the agency was advertising allotments near Likely for lease between 1940 and

1941. Nash noted that Christensen had bids on leases on four allotments in 1939 (Dick Rogers, Sus-403; Allie Bayley, Sus-437; Alice Pete, Sus-465; and Cilian Pete, Sus-464) but never completed a lease agreement or paid, yet grazed cattle on the land anyway. As such, Nash requested "some payment should be made for trespass . . . before we will consider a bid." The lease price was $0.10/acre, or $64 annually, for all four allotments. Nash also reminded Christensen that he had previously inquired about leasing these lands, along with that of Fannie Allen, Sus-454. He noted that the office did not have the policy of contacting Indian landowners if there is an interested purchaser but rather would "wait until the Indians themselves make the request for sale."[86] However, it appears that there were no qualms about contacting potential purchasers and giving them necessary information on the land, such as the appraised value, and encouraging them to consider purchase.

Indeed, leasing allotments was a long-term endeavor for the agency, which advertised, administered, and collected fees for leases on the allotment of Rosa Jim, for example, from at least 1899 through the land sale in 1951.[87] During this period, agency staff were actively engaged in finding lessors: for example, in 1936 Nash sent a letter to Frank Carroll of Susanville responding to an apparent lead on finding long-term lessors of the allotments of Rosa Jim (Sus-765), Jane Jim (Sus-654), and Mary Reavis (Sus-711). While the agency attempted to make leasing more efficient by grouping leases, it was unable (or unwilling) to give leases the close oversight that would prevent trespass and ensure benefits to the allottees. The agency had advertised all of these allotments for lease "but received no bids, although it had been reported to [them] that both of these allotments were being used by stockmen in that section."[88] A 1940 note from Flora George, one of Rosa Jim's heirs, also indicated trespass.[89] While the agency refused a bid of $6 per year (far below the minimum of $16), the agency field representative John Rockwell said that "it will be better to accept the offer and get something out of the place rather than to let it lie idle and collect absolutely nothing. As the property is unfenced, it will probably be grazed over by wandering bands of stock anyway."[90] Two years later, the agency field representative sent a letter to Flora George Wilson detailing the lease rate and the number of heirs and their respective shares, and noted, "We are endeavoring to settle possible trespass . . . and will let you know if we are able to collect anything."[91] As such, the agency was well aware of trespass, but could or did not actively investigate or prosecute it and continued to correspond with potential lessors in hopes of securing even minimally paid leases for the allotments within its jurisdiction.[92] However, even when leases were in place, there is evidence that payments did not reach allottees: In 1950 long-term lessors Christensen and the H. C. Cattle Company wrote to the agency to inquire about renewing their leases on the allotments of Allie Bayley (Sus-437), Cilian Pete (Sus-464), and Alice Pete (Sus-465), noting that "the Indians of the estates refuse to sign any lease as they have not gotten their money from the last two years."[93]

STATE COMPLICITY

In 1938 the National Reclamation Association wrote to all "Western Reclamationists," encouraging irrigation-project proponents to study the Natural Resources Committee's revised 1937 report on "Drainage Basin Problems and Programs," which allocated almost $50 million annually for irrigation for six years.[94] The report described California's needs as "control and redistribution of its water supply for domestic and industrial uses and for irrigation," highlighted the need for adequate water for agricultural development in the Central Valley, and lauded the recommendations for projects in the 1931 State Water Plan (46–47).

The largest potential beneficiaries of federal and state water projects in California are large agricultural interests in the central and southern San Joaquin Valley. From the 1950s through the present, agricultural corporations have continued to fight the concern to avoid "unjust enrichment" of valley landowners who receive subsidized water from upstream public projects. As late as 1981, a *Chronicle* article entitled "Another Try for Water Law Reform" described a Senate Bill to reform the 1902 Reclamation Act to "make it easier for farmers to own large amounts of valuable federally-irrigated land in western states." Rather than being limited to owning only 160 acres of federally irrigated land and having to live on or near that land, individual farmers would now be able to own up to 1600 acres and lease up to 1600 more "while receiving low-cost water from federal irrigation projects," and would not have to live near their land. While this proposed bill pertained more to California's federal CVP, it also implicated the SWP, as the shared federal and state facilities at the San Luis Rey Reservoir in the south San Francisco Bay Area meant that federal restrictions could apply to downstream users (*Chronicle Washington Bureau* 1981).

REFLECTIONS ON MONOPOLIES

In his hopeful treatise, the Pawnee attorney and scholar Walter Echo-Hawk reminds us that American values are built on justice, human rights, and striving for equality, and with tools like the UNDRIP, America can come to terms with times when it has strayed from its goals and develop healing policies of reconciliation (Echo-Hawk 2013). This book aims to contribute to that process by documenting times when American ideals strayed from larger goals of equality, setting in motion cascading inequalities that must now be addressed and mitigated. In this chapter, I have attempted to show how the administration of public domain allotments in a culturally, ecologically, and economically important headwaters region of California led to displacement of Indian people as well as to the consolidation and enrichment of non-Indian corporate interests and the expansion of public conservation. Public conservation both excluded Indian people from the management of their homelands—those places central to the continuance and maintenance of their world—and simultaneously supported the growth of extractive industries by permitting regulated harvest. Through conceptualizing even public lands as monopolistic when it comes to the seizure of Indian lands, we may begin to envision a more just arrangement, in which Indian lands are returned to and/or comanaged with descendants of the first families of this region.

5

MAKING INTERVENTIONS

The Federal Energy Regulatory Commission (FERC) Hydropower Relicensing and Stewardship Council Processes

The story is about the particular depth of pain caused by Indians' land loss and the ensuing paths that contemporary Indians take to resist, return, and heal. One of those ways is to hold accountable those responsible for the loss.

—KRISTEN A. CARPENTER, "CONTEXTUALIZING THE LOSSES OF ALLOTMENT THROUGH LITERATURE"

The hydroelectric projects have caused a large cultural disruption by making the Maidu people landless and totally without secure access to traditional cultural sites in these areas, including family burial sites. When you have 110 different families having to relocate to different areas in different directions it can't help but have an effect on their culture and way of life.

The dams and hydro projects have . . . stopped the salmon, eels, snapping turtles . . . from traveling up the rivers and streams. They have taken away the way of life that went with the harvesting and gathering of these resources. There were fishing villages, gathering sites, gathering ceremonies, songs, etc. that were lost. These projects changed the culture and way of life completely by taking away the land the people lived on and their resources . . . that they harvested for food and ceremonial use.

—LORENA GORBET, MAIDU CULTURAL AND DEVELOPMENT GROUP VICE CHAIRMAN, LETTER TO THE CONTROL BOARD

THE MAIDU Cultural and Development Group submitted the above comments in 2005 in response to the Control Board's scoping process for the Upper North Fork Feather River Hydroelectric Project Water Quality Certification. The Control Board is a regulatory state agency tasked with ensuring that water bodies are managed in ways that uphold their designated beneficial uses. Despite the MCDG's strong words in 2005, there is little attention to Maidu rights and cultural resources in the Control Board's Draft Environmental Impact Report released in 2014, which focuses on how to retain the North Fork Feather River as a coldwater fishery. While the Central Valley Region of the California Regional Water Quality Control Board designated the North Fork Feather River as a coldwater fishery (California Regional Water Quality Control Board, Central Valley Region 2016, Table 11-1), Maidu drew on their much longer relationship with the watershed to challenge this designation:

> We also question why the North Fork Feather River is being designated only as a cold-water river rather than a warm water fishery and a coldwater fishery, as we used to gather eels, snapping turtles and other warm water species within the North Fork watershed. The river was traditionally cold in the winter but warmer in the summer with the fish that needed the cooler water moving upstream to the shaded pools in the streams of the watershed. (Gorbet, letter to the Control Board)

Maidu Traditional Ecological Knowledge of the river system is generously shared by Maidu elders but not incorporated into the final Control Board study of alternatives to manage one of the most important rivers in the state. This process of selective listening on the part of the agencies is emblematic of the frustrations inherent in Maidu participation in environmental review processes that are not designed to *hear* and meaningfully respond to or act on their concerns.[1]

This chapter focuses on Maidu participation in the FERC Hydropower Relicensing and Stewardship Council land conservation planning processes as key sites of Indigenous intervention in water policy in the face of either agency disregard or limited agency attempts at inclusion without attention to history and its contemporary ramifications. Both of these processes began in the early 2000s, and Maidu participation represented a continuation of Maidu organizing and activism to stop unauthorized uses of their homelands and waters.[2] The FERC and Stewardship Council processes also began just around the time of the formation of the Maidu Summit Consortium, which consolidated much of the Maidu activism in Indian Valley, Big Meadows, Mountain Meadows, Butt

Valley, and Humbug Valley (all headwater regions of the SWP) with the exception of the work of the Honey Lake Maidu, which chose not to participate in the summit yet continues to actively work on site protection issues, particularly in the Mountain Meadows and Susanville areas.

Maidu participation in legal and regulatory processes regarding hydropower management and conservation in the upper watershed of the SWP is characterized by persistence. Maidu representatives navigate a bureaucratic maze of steps and requirements firmly based in European-derived perspectives on natural resources use and management. Maidu continue to challenge the institutional barriers to achieving any mitigation from the FERC relicensing proceeding on the Upper North Fork Feather River Project. There are also at least three other FERC relicensing proceedings—Oroville (2100), Poe (2107) and Rock Creek-Cresta (1962)—that are also key sites of Maidu intervention and participation, but their analysis is beyond the scope of this book. While the Upper North Fork Feather River relicensing process is ongoing nearly 15 years after PG&E submitted its initial application to FERC in 2002, opportunities for achieving some of the long-requested mitigations to hydropower impacts on Maidu became available primarily in the parallel Stewardship Council land divestiture process, which began with the 2003 Settlement Agreement between PG&E and the California Public Utilities Commission. The work of the council is discussed in both historical and contemporary contexts, and an update is offered on Maidu advocacy to receive restitution and lands.

This chapter reaches back to the analysis in chapter 3, examining the structures of value in place today, specifically the ways in which conservation value is assigned to the same lands once so highly valued for timber and hydropower potential at the turn of the century. The chapter concludes with reflection on the ways in which Maidu people continue to successfully challenge institutionalized marginalization of their histories and contemporary rights to steward their homelands.

MAIDU INTERVENTION IN THE PROJECT
NO. 2105 FERC RELICENSING

The loss of ceremonial sites and other traditional cultural properties as a result of the three dams and related facilities of the 2105 project area continue to create cultural disruption and related impacts for the Maidu. It continues to be our position that these

lands were originally taken from our ancestors in a manner that would not be considered
legal today. . . . No group has been impacted longer or has a more long-standing right
to be represented in the new license process than the Maidu.

—LETTER FROM REINA ROGERS, SECRETARY OF THE
BOARD OF DIRECTORS, MCDG, TO RANDALL LIVINGSTON,
LEAD DIRECTOR, HYDROPOWER GENERATION
DEPARTMENT, PG&E, MARCH 12, 2003

The FERC is an agency directed by up to five presidentially appointed commissioners who serve staggered five-year terms. Among FERC's duties is the licensing of nonfederal hydropower projects that are "in the public interest" (FERC 2014). These licenses may last up to 50 years and must reflect a broader plan for the river that benefits "commerce . . . [utilizes] water-power development . . . [provides] protection, mitigation, and enhancement of fish and wildlife . . . and [benefits other] public uses, including irrigation, flood control, water supply, and recreational and other purposes."[3] The FERC process does not foreground protection of cultural resources as a central goal of watershed planning, and in this way, not much has changed since the GWP projects were developed on the North Fork Feather River at the turn of the century and the SWP was developed in the midcentury. FERC's licensing process includes study, analysis, and public comment on all aspects of the project, and the Control Board must issue a water quality certification under Sec. 401 of the Clean Water Act (33 USC §1341) in order for FERC to grant a license.

The focus of the 2105 relicensing application is the Upper North Fork Feather River Project, located in the heart of the Mountain Maidu homeland and generating 1,171.9 gWh. The project covers 30,032 acres of PG&E lands as well as 1,024 acres of federal lands (the U.S. Forest Service and BLM), and includes three dams and reservoirs (Lake Almanor, Butt Valley, and Belden Forebay) and five powerhouses. A fourth dam, Indian Ole Dam, named after Ole Salem, impounds a seasonal reservoir at Mountain Meadows (with a capacity of 23,952 acre-feet), which has been used by PG&E since 1924 and owned by the company since 1945 but was operated without a permit until 1989.[4] The Hamilton Branch Powerhouse is powered by water from the Mountain Meadows Reservoir, but "because of its size and its age it is exempt from FERC license requirements" (SWRCB 2014). In 1989 PG&E filed an application with the Control Board to appropriate water at the Indian Ole Dam, and multiple parties protested, including the California Department of Fish and Game. In 1990 the Control

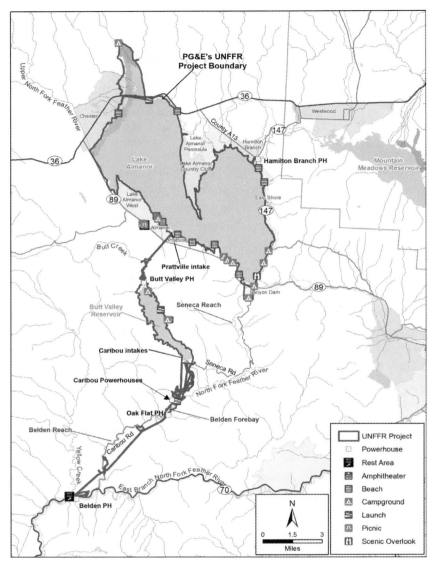

MAP 4. Overview of the Upper North Fork Feather River Project, FERC Relicense Application 2105. (Courtesy of the State Water Resources Control Board Upper North Fork Feather River Hydroelectric Project, Draft Environmental Impact Statement, November 2014.)

Board approved PG&E's application, subject to terms and conditions suggested by the Department of Fish and Game, including regulations on the timing of water drawdown from the reservoir and requirements to maintain minimum levels in Mountain Meadows to protect resident fish and wildlife (SWRCB 1990). The current PG&E license application to FERC for the Upper North Fork Feather River Project (#2105) focuses on continuing to operate the project as-is, with the addition of 34 acres of U.S. Forest Service land at Caribou and Belden in the Feather River Canyon.[5]

The heart of the Upper North Fork Feather River Project is the heart of the Mountain Maidu homeland. The impacts on Mountain Maidu people from the development of the hydroelectric project came in waves that continue today. Big Meadows was home to at least nine large Mountain Maidu villages and still contains numerous plant stewardship sites and significant cultural places that were not inundated by the reservoir.[6] Maidu land and water rights were disregarded completely until the passage of the Allotment Act in 1887, which enabled some Maidu to acquire limited land title, but the subsequent development of Big Meadows into Lake Almanor at the turn of the century ushered in a new era of displacement by both hydroelectric and timber companies bent on acquiring all Maidu land, including the allotments held in trust for the Maidu by the BIA.

FERC's *Final Environmental Impact Report* on the Upper North Fork Feather River Project is generous in its assessment of GWP, describing how it "had to acquire some allotments from Maidu landowners when it bought up property for its UNFFR hydroelectric project" (FERC 2005, 3-305). However, as previous chapters show, GWP did not always buy—it was able to condemn land and gain title without evidence of payment. Even when it did buy the land, the money went into Individual Indian Monetary accounts managed by the BIA that were difficult for Maidu allottees to access.[7] While FERC does admit that "it is a historical fact that some Indian allotments were acquired by Great Western Power when it obtained rights and easements for the original UNFFR hydroelectric project," it insists that, contrary to tribal assertions of their ties to the area and the illegality of land transfers, there are "no tribal lands (as defined in 36 CFR Part 800.16(x)) . . . within the project boundaries," (FERC 2005, 3-320) and "PG&E owns 30,032 acres out of the 31,060 acres within the FERC project boundary." The commission concludes somewhat defensively, "Land title is a legal issue to be resolved in the courts and not an environmental issue to be reviewed under NEPA or Section 106 of the NHPA" (FERC 2005: 3-324).

However, it is that land, whose very characteristics and formations illustrate Maidu history, that continues to generate significant profits for PG&E and benefits to millions of downstream users.

Indeed, FERC requires the managers of its largest (more than 1,500 kWh) licensed projects to report on the amount of electricity generated. PG&E has 25 such licensed projects that generated a total of 5,519,196,657 kWh in FY 2016, of which 1,486,618,873 kWh, or approximately 25 percent, are projects on the North Fork Feather River (Cresta, Rock Creek, Belden, Butt Valley, Caribou 1, Caribou 2, Oak Flat, and Poe) (PG&E 2016). The Upper North Fork Feather River Project at Lake Almanor alone generates 1,171.9 gWh of electricity annually (FERC 2005, 1-1), and PG&E operates 11 powerhouses between Lake Oroville and Lake Almanor (FERC 2005, 1-3). As such, power generated from the North Fork Feather River Projects, made possible by PG&E's largest reservoir at Lake Almanor, continues to be significant for the company. The North Fork's importance increases when you add in the power generated and water stored by the SWP (initially called the Feather River Project) facilities on the river, including its largest facility, at Lake Oroville, and a smaller upstream facility at Antelope Lake, east of Lake Almanor. The importance of the Feather River, and the Upper Feather River in particular, cannot be underestimated in the water power and conveyance system of the state of California.

UPPER NORTH FORK FEATHER RIVER PROJECT NO. 2105: BACKGROUND

The Upper North Fork Feather River Project was last licensed in 1955. In 2002, two years before the license was set to expire in 2004, PG&E filed an application with FERC to relicense the project. In 2003, following FERC's acceptance of the application, 17 parties submitted motions to intervene in the relicensing proceedings, including the MCDG. In 2005 FERC issued its *Final Environment Impact Statement* on the project. In 2014 the Control Board issued its *Draft Environmental Impact Report* regarding issuing a water-quality certification under Sec. 401 of the Clean Water Act (33 USC §1341). In order to obtain a water quality certification, the project must have a sufficient level of water quality to protect beneficial uses of water determined by the Control Board.[8] A designated beneficial use of the North Fork Feather River is cold freshwater habitat. In 2006 the U.S. Environmental Protection Agency found that North Fork Feather River water temperatures were high, and the Control Board determined that causes included "hydromodification and flow regulation"—the impact of PG&E's projects in and above the Feather River Canyon.[9] Both of the Control Board's two alternatives include proposed "thermal curtains" upstream that would send cooler, deeper water from the bottom of Lake Almanor downstream (SWRCB 2014, Chapter 4, "Project Alternatives"). The MCDG, the Maidu Summit Consortium and Conservancy, the Greenville Indian Rancheria, and the Susanville Indian Rancheria have consistently opposed the thermal curtain because of the possible physical impacts of its construction on a highly culturally sensitive area, and they recommend instead supporting a holistic, long-term, integrated approach foregrounding upstream restoration to cool the waters that feed the North Fork Feather River.[10]

At the time of their formal intervention in the relicensing process in 2003, the MCDG represented several Maidu groups, including the United Maidu Nation, Maidu Elders of Indian Valley, Maidu Veterans of Plumas County, Roundhouse Council Indian Education Center, and Plumas County Indians, Inc.[11] The MCDG had long voiced frustration with a consultation process that privileged consultation with federally recognized tribes.[12] Due to the nonratification of treaties made with California Indians in 1851 and 1852, state policies of outright extermination, the establishment of parcels of land for "homeless California Indians" in the early decades of the twentieth century that many Maidu did not choose to move on to, the termination of tribes in the 1950s and 60s, and their re-recognition in the 1980s, many Maidu are not members of local federally recognized tribes in Greenville, Susanville, and Oroville. As MCDG coordinator Farrell Cunningham wrote in 2002:

> It is estimated that only 10% of California's Native inhabitants are represented by "recognized" tribes. For example, the Maidu tribe, the largest tribe in California, is politically unrecognized by the US Federal Government. This means that a strict adherence to Section 106 federal cultural consultation protocols essentially dis-enfranchises the majority of the descendants of the aboriginal inhabitants of the 2105 license project boundary area and prevents them from meaningfully engaging with PG&E to protect their cultural heritage and to seek mitigation for ongoing cultural disruption that will result from the operation of the facilities under a new license.[13]

Cunningham also argued that Maidu groups continue to apply for federal recognition, and could likely be granted recognition within the new license period of 30 years, so the company should be consulting with both recognized and petitioning tribes.

The final environmental impact statement issued for PG&E's Upper North Fork Feather River Project (centered around Big Meadows / Lake Almanor) includes acknowledgment that a key issue in the relicensing includes "protecting cultural resources," but, following the staff's recommendation to relicense the project, no additional measures are offered in the abstract to reach this goal (FERC 2005, 1-3). A 2005 programmatic agreement between FERC and a California State Historic Preservation Officer regarding the 2105 License—with Greenville and Susanville Rancherias, the MCDG, and Honey Lake Maidu all invited to concur—simply states that annual reports will be provided about cultural resource management activities and a Historic Properties Management Plan will be developed.[14] MCDG was very clear in the supportive letters attached to its motion to intervene in 2003 (and in a 2002 letter) that an appropriate condition of approval for the license would be permanent cultural easements for Maidu people to access cultural places on the landscape:

> Project facilities and project facilities management continue to create the negative impacts to "cultural integrity," to the "cultural condition" of TCPs by denying Maidu access to these sites for cultural practices that could reverse . . . the disproportionate burden that this minority cultural group currently bears as a result of the continued operation of these hydroelectric projects. License conditions that grant cultural easements which enable Maidu to maintain cultural heritage over the course of the license period as well as additional mitigation for cultural disruption will begin to limit perpetuation of cultural degradation and cultural disruption.[15]

However, the *Final Environmental Impact Statement* maintains cultural resource management as a duty primarily of PG&E, the U.S. Forest Service, the Advisory Council on Historic Preservation, and the State Historic Preservation Officer, and did not accede any cultural easements to Maidu people, organizations, or tribal governments (FERC 2005, 3-319–3-320).

As part of the relicensing process, PG&E is required to identify all historic and cultural properties within the area of potential effect and conduct cultural resource studies and consultation pursuant to Sec. 106 of the National Historic Preservation Act.[16] From Maidu perspectives, both the law and PG&E's

perspective on what constitutes a culturally important property are limited, and limiting. Maidu responses to PG&E's work on cultural resources from Susanville and Greenville Rancherias[17] and the MCDG criticized the company for narrowly defining the area of potential effect and circumscribing the size and importance of cultural sites. As Gorbet wrote on behalf of the MCDG in 2005: "A MCDG priority is Maidu site protection. By sites, we don't just mean the burial sites. We mean all the sites whether burial, village, sacred, ceremonial, or gathering. We have gathering sites for food (both plants and animals), for medicine plants, and for basketry materials. We are concerned with all these aspects of site protection. . . . Native American monitors . . . reported that there were artifacts and sites everywhere around the lake and that the survey crews said that whole areas should be declared as sites and protected." (Gorbet, letter to the Control Board). Company policies and the federal and state statutes present a different (and problematic) definition of cultural places and mitigation from the Maidu. This is reflective of a colonial redefinition of all aspects of the world as discrete resources that can be separated, measured, and valued. This is in contrast to Indigenous worldviews, in which places on the landscape are connected to one another, to human beings, to nonhuman beings, and to past, present, and future.

In 2002 comments on PG&E's draft Traditional Cultural Properties report, the Greenville Rancheria requested that PG&E provide "areas for gathering among the Maidu for ceremonies, education, and plant gathering," but PG&E responded that they had an existing permit process that anyone could apply to in order to utilize PG&E lands. When the tribe requested fee waivers to recreational areas, PG&E responded that such waivers would be "discriminatory against other groups." Finally, when the tribe asked for "a map of Indian allotted land prior to the flood of 1913" for educational purposes, PG&E responded that allotments were only "property boundary designations" and did not fall under the definition of Traditional Cultural Properties promulgated by the National Park Service (Parker and King 1998), and therefore were outside of the scope of the Traditional Cultural Properties study. Further, PG&E stated that it had limited information on allotments and referred the Maidu to the BLM office in Sacramento.[18] Indeed, PG&E denied all other Maidu requests, including a request for Maidu monitors to protect cultural resources from both construction crews and tourists, a cultural center along the lake, an extension of the area of potential effect beyond the FERC project boundary,[19] and a study of Native plants.

In 2003 in a powerful and comprehensive letter to PG&E, Gorbet introduced a new Mountain Maidu group, the Maidu Summit, which included the MCDG, two federally recognized tribes (Greenville Indian Rancheria and Susanville Indian Rancheria) and the petitioning Tsi'Akim Maidu (Taylorsville Rancheria), and cultural-protection organizations for specific places, including the Tasman Koyom Cultural Foundation, Mountain Meadows Preservation Association, and Stivers Indian Cemetery Association. The creation of the Maidu Summit underscored the unity of Maidu community members, organizations, and tribes in the request for analysis and mitigation of the ongoing cultural disruption wrought by the hydroelectric project at Lake Almanor. In the letter, Gorbet describes the 2105 project area as a hub of the Maidu homeland; a place known for its rich plant and animal resources and abundant springs; a place that Maidu people traveled to from miles around for large bear dance ceremonies; a place where evidence of Worldmaker's journey is imprinted on the landscape; and a meeting place for trade and exchange between people from throughout the Maidu homeland.[20] All of this was not only violently disrupted, but *submerged* by the seizure of the land by non-Indians and the creation of the GWP reservoir, now PG&E's Lake Almanor: "Looking at Lake Almanor, Butt Valley Reservoir, Hamilton Branch, and Mountain Meadows Reservoir we can intuit that a large ecological disruption has occurred in these areas. A land base that was once meadow, forest, stream, springs, and ponds, is now water—a series of large reservoirs. No baseline was established so most of the ecological effect will go undocumented in a scientific way." This ecological disruption cannot be delinked from cultural disruption: "As a result of the creation of the first 2105 project, in the 1900s, Maidu social fabric was ripped." Even as they document these ruptures, Maidu community representatives also emphasize their ongoing resilience and survival, in their homeland, and in their commitment to bring lands back into Maidu ownership.[21]

The MCDG letter further details how the land was acquired by GWP and Red River, with the support of the Indian Agency, offering a more detailed explanation of allotment history, its particular impact on Maidu, and the scope of allotments in the 2105 Project area than is found in any of the PG&E license application documents and studies. MCDG contends that 73 allotments (11,039 acres) were directly impacted by the 2105 Project and an additional 36 (5,664 acres) are located on nearby PG&E lands (Mountain Meadows and Humbug Valley), and documents the ways in which the allotments were canceled, often without Maidu knowledge, assent, or benefit. In response, PG&E argues that its predecessor companies acquired all former Indian allotment lands by legal means, and encourages MCDG to address its concerns and requests to the Department of the Interior, the BIA, and the Plumas County Superior Court.[22]

In their 2003 letter to FERC, the MCDG also requested analysis of and specific mitigation for eight allotments in particular, now either inundated or partially inundated by the lake, deemed "USA Withdrawn" with unclear title to PG&E.[23] The MCDG offers clear suggestions for forms the mitigation could take: cultural easements for ceremony and traditional land stewardship, land donations, financial support to maintain donated lands, funding for a Maidu museum, funding for a Maidu cultural community center, or, at minimum, an inclusive consultation process with nonfederally recognized Maidu community members as well as federally recognized Maidu tribes.[24] PG&E argued that it already paid a fee to FERC for use of federal lands and did not feel that "*additional* compensation to the Maidu" was necessary.[25]

While PG&E again did not accede to any Maidu requests, the Maidu members of the MCDG and the Maidu Summit continued to press them at Stewardship Council meetings, which began in 2004 in Chester, near the shores of Lake Almanor. It was in the Stewardship Council process that these repeated Maidu requests finally gained some traction. The Stewardship Council broadened the audience that heard these arguments from just PG&E to federal and state agencies, private conservation groups, citizen protection entities like the California Public Utilities Commission, and the Native American Heritage Commission, all collectively tasked with developing a public-interest conservation plan for former and current PG&E lands throughout California. There was still resistance among the council board members to Maidu arguments for social and environmental justice at the headwaters, and Maidu had to continue to voice their history and position to the council for approximately 10 years before gaining land through the process, but, ultimately, they will be receiving almost 3,000 acres of land in Humbug Valley and around Lake Almanor.[26] Despite its challenges, the Stewardship Council process offered more opportunities for Maidu voices to be heard and supported than the FERC relicensing process.

PACIFIC FOREST AND WATERSHED LANDS STEWARDSHIP COUNCIL: A BRIEF OVERVIEW

The Stewardship Council was formed following a 2003 agreement between PG&E and the California Public Utilities Commission. California's largest private utilities, PG&E and Southern California Edison, had unsuccessfully attempted to comply with required utility deregulation, divesting themselves of certain fossil-fueled power-generating facilities and purchasing electricity wholesale. Rather than increasing profits, the companies were paying for electricity that was not always available, leading to brownouts in California cities in the late 1990s. PG&E asserted that, as a result of the energy crisis beginning in May 2000 and because its retail rates were frozen, it was unable to recover approximately $9 billion of electricity procurement costs from its customers, resulting in billions of dollars of defaulted debt and the downgrading of its credit ratings by all the major credit rating agencies.[27] As a result, PG&E filed for Chapter 11 bankruptcy protection in April 2001. The California Public Utilities Commission and PG&E litigated competing plans of reorganization through the federal bankruptcy proceeding, resulting in the approval of the Land Conservation Commitment, under which PG&E would permanently protect approximately 140,000 acres of watershed lands associated with its hydroelectric generation facilities. A key component of the settlement agreement was the creation of the Stewardship Council in 2003, which was charged with making recommendations for the divestiture of those 140,000 acres.

PG&E would retain various rights to the lands in question, including outright ownership of 67,000 acres essential to their utility operations, which would be preserved by conservation easements held by a second party. PG&E would also retain rights, including certain water rights, to the remaining 75,000 acres, which would be available for divestiture to new owners, subject to conservation easements held by a third party. All of the lands were to be managed for a set of six beneficial public values: protection of fish, wildlife, and plant habitat; preservation of open space; outdoor recreation; sustainable forestry; agriculture; and protection of historical and cultural resources (Pacific Stewardship Council 2007).

The cultural and historical beneficial public value guiding the Stewardship Council land divestiture indicates the potential for attention to Indigenous cultural importance of sites. The settlement agreement and stipulation note that the former PG&E lands may be donated to "public entities or qualified conservation organizations," and the Stewardship Council interpreted the term "public entity" to include tribes, making tribes eligible to gain fee title to the lands.[28] Further, although not specifically enumerated in Stewardship Council policy, under SB-18, federally recognized or unrecognized tribes can hold conservation easements on these lands. However, as of 2017, no tribes have been chosen as conservation-easement holders.

The settlement agreement and stipulation that formed the Stewardship Council are completely silent on the history of these lands, their ongoing cultural and environmental importance to California Indians, and the potential to return these lands to the California Indians that they were directly taken from a century ago. California tribal representatives have repeatedly framed the Stewardship Council divestiture as an environmental justice issue, citing the history of these lands (which often surround valleys, or lie along rich river canyons), as village sites, burial areas, important plant stewardship sites, culturally important places, and Indian allotments before they were taken for hydropower development to serve the needs of the expanding state of California.[29] The MCDG has been working for many years to track and map the history of these lands in order to make it extremely clear that they were/are Maidu lands and to assert that the council's process is a prime opportunity to give them back.

Initially, no California Indian representatives were seated on the Stewardship Council board. As outlined in the 2003 settlement agreement, the board was to consist of representatives from PG&E, the California Public Utility Commission, the California Department of Fish and Game, the Control Board, the California Farm Bureau Federation, and three public members named by the California Public Utility Commission. Following public comments, membership was expanded to include one representative each from the California Resources Agency, the Central Valley Regional Water Quality Control Board, the Association of California Water Agencies, the Regional Council of Rural Counties, the California Hydropower Reform Coalition, the Trust for Public Land, the Office of Ratepayer Advocates, the California Forestry Association, and a joint liaison from the Federal Department of Agriculture–Forest Service and Department of Interior–BLM.[30] When the council began holding public meetings around the state in 2004 to get feedback on how to oversee the divestiture, tribal representatives and allies repeatedly stood up and expressed outrage at their lack of representation on the board.[31] In response, the council requested that Larry Myers (Pomo), then–executive secretary of the Native American Heritage Commission, join the board. In 2008 the council also elected Ken Tipon (Pomo) to serve as an alternate for Myers. Although Myers retired from the Native American Heritage Commission in 2010, he continues to serve on the board.

The council conducted public outreach and scoping meetings around the state from 2004 to 2007 (Pacific Stewardship Council 2007), organized the land into 11 watersheds and 47 planning units, created a plan to begin with four pilot planning units (Pacific Stewardship Council 2008) and then to move in stages through the remaining lands, and published a land conservation plan in 2007 (Pacific Stewardship Council 2007). The council's goal was to complete the conservation-easement assignment on all 140,000 acres and land-divestiture process on 75,000 acres by 2013, but the work is ongoing as of April 2018.

The Stewardship Council has an application/qualification process for both fee title holders for the lands as well as conservation-easement holders. All applicants in the Stewardship Council process were encouraged to complete formal land stewardship plans on parcels of interest. When the Maidu Summit, a consortium of nine Mountain Maidu groups, organizations, and tribes (federally recognized, petitioning, and federally unrecognized) initially submitted its land stewardship plans for PG&E lands located in the Maidu homeland in 2007, they were able to write freehand, following some guiding questions. In 2009, two years after the Summit had submitted the land stewardship plans for these parcels around Lake Almanor and in Humbug Valley, they were asked to complete a detailed statement of qualifications regarding their solvency as an organization and their ability to steward these lands. While Stewardship Council staff clarified that the statement of qualifications was required for all donees and easement holders,[32] at the time of request the Summit volunteers perceived it as a change in the process, leaving some community members feeling as if they were being asked to provide additional materials and/or go through additional steps that were not required from other applicants.[33]

In order to receive a donation of the lands, in some cases tribes were encouraged to either form coalitions with conservation nonprofits and/or agencies or to form their own conservation nonprofits. Eligible nonprofits, however, were required to have extensive experience with land conservation and management. Tribal nonprofits focusing on the application of traditional ecological knowledge, despite the depth of this approach to land management, were not seen as possessing the land management expertise of a non-Native land trust formed as recently as the 1980s or 1990s. In order to increase its eligibility, the Maidu Summit applied for and received nonprofit status in 2010.

After additional application work, in a historic Stewardship Council meeting in 2013, the council recommended the transfer of 2,325 acres of land in Humbug Valley to the Maidu Summit. This was followed by recommendations in 2014 and 2016 that the Summit receive an additional 641 acres on the shore of Lake Almanor. Since the original 2013 recommendation, the council has awarded funds to the Summit to complete their land management plan with the help of private environmental consulting firms, and land transaction work is ongoing as of April 2018. Easements on all lands transferred to the Summit will be held by the Feather River Land Trust, which has a long-stated commitment and a formal memorandum of understanding to partner with the Summit.

These recommended transfers of land are highly significant not only for the Maidu but also because they provide a ray of hope for other tribes seeking lands in the Stewardship Council and other processes. Out of the 38,500 acres of land to be recommended for divestiture by the Stewardship Council—to entities ranging from federal (U.S. Forest Service) and state (California Department of Forestry and Fire Protection) agencies to a local resource conservation district—4,708 acres (or approximately 12 percent) have been recommended for transfer to three tribal entities (the Potter Valley Tribe in 2012 and 2014, Pit River Tribe in 2015, and Maidu Summit in 2013, 2014, and 2016).[34] While donees for at least 8,000 acres remain to be selected, thus far the lion's share of the land will be donated to state and federal agencies—approximately 12,600 to CAL FIRE, 5,000 to the U.S. Forest Service, and 6,200 to the University of

FIGURE 12. Maidu Summit Consortium and Conservancy board members and supporters after the November 14, 2013, Stewardship Council meeting in which the council recommended the transfer of 2,325 acres of Humbug Valley to the Maidu Summit. (Photo by Jane Braxton Little.)

California.[35] From a historical perspective, the state has already had numerous opportunities to obtain this Native land free or cheaply; for example, in 1950 the State of California Department of Fish and Game purchased 880 acres of allotments in Lassen County, including lands in Honey Lake and Long Valley areas, for just \$4.32/acre, at a total cost of \$3,807.50 to the agency.[36] As of June 2017, the council is still working through the recommendation process, and more lands may be transferred to tribes and to the University of California.

Given that all lands in the Stewardship Council process will be protected by conservation easements held by a third party, it is worth noting that, as of June 2016 Stewardship Council data, on the 136,742 acres on which the easement holders have been recommended, all will be held by just 13 non-Native conservation entities, including one state conservation agency (the California Department of Fish and Wildlife) and one resource conservation district (Western Shasta RCD),[37] despite the fact that tribes can hold conservation easements, and at least one tribe (Greenville Rancheria, 2009 proposal for the Bucks Lake Planning Unit) and one Native land trust (Native American Land Conservancy, in support of the initial application of the Maidu Summit) applied to hold conservation easements.

INTERVENTIONS AND TRANSFORMATIONS

In the Stewardship Council process throughout California, California Indian people are applying to get restricted title to lands that were taken from their ancestors. In the FERC relicensing process discussed in this chapter, Maidu are intervening to negotiate license conditions that provide some access to and/or compensation for power company lands that were taken from their ancestors. The parameters of both of these processes don't address how these lands came to be part of PG&E's upstream holdings and are now part of the Stewardship Council land divestiture, nor do they permit a full recognition and response to the fact that "the material, spiritual, philosophical, and social culture of the Maidu remain tied to this landscape."[38] Even with these challenges, Native participation is essential, because both processes represent rare openings—to regain Native land title and Native access to land that has been kept from Native people for the last 100 years, and to continually assert Native American history and relationship to the land in the public record. Indeed, these upstream land- and waterscapes were, are, and will always be Native land.

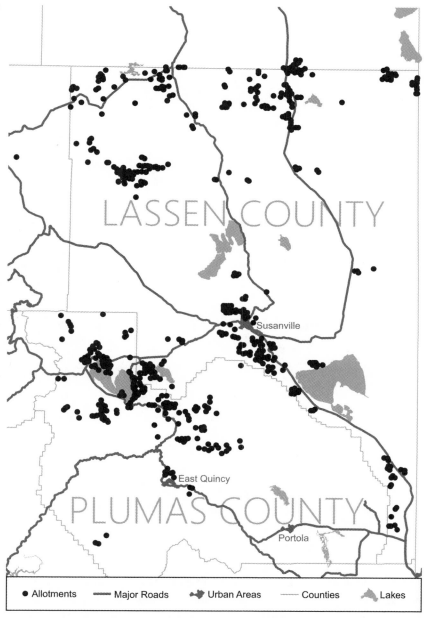

LASSEN COUNTY

Susanville

East Quincy

PLUMAS COUNTY

Portola

● Allotments　━━ Major Roads　🔺 Urban Areas　──── Counties　🔺 Lakes

MAP 5. General locations of historic Indian Allotments within present-day Plumas and Lassen Counties. Cartography by Michele Tobias, University of California, Davis, based on research by Beth Rose Middleton, Lorena Gorbet, and other partners. Shared with permission from the Maidu Summit Conservancy.

CONCLUSION

Toward a More Just Landscape at the Headwaters

"Don't forget," Fleur seems to tell us contemporary lawyers, the story should be about *"restoration, getting the land back, and justice."*

KRISTEN CARPENTER, "CONTEXTUALIZING THE LOSSES OF
ALLOTMENT THROUGH LITERATURE"

An epistemology of spirit encourages us all to be of service. . . . In that way, our research is bound in meaning and inspired by service to others or to our natural environment. . . . See your work as a . . . sacred object . . . for your family, your community, your people—because it is.

MANULANI ALULI MEYER, "INDIGENOUS AND AUTHENTIC: HAWAIIAN
EPISTEMOLOGY AND THE TRIANGULATION OF MEANING"

N THIS final chapter, I reflect on the multifaceted research methods aimed at achieving a central goal of this research, which is improving the inclusion of Native nations, communities, organizations, families, and individuals in environmental policy-making. I discuss the historical and contemporary institutional exclusion of Indigenous histories and the ways in which this exclusion bars decision-makers from being duly informed about the essential nature of Indigenous involvement in determining the future of ancestral Indigenous lands. The chapter concludes with the beginnings of a vision for policy reform that leads to enhanced Indigenous futures on the SWP and other sites of Indigenous land/water divestiture around the nation.

I began this work as a volunteer, working alongside MCDG staff Lorena Gorbet and Farrell Cunningham, *yatam*, as they continued to assert Maidu history and Maidu rights to be at the table and to gain mitigations in ongoing projects determining the future of their homeland. The project began with listening to Gorbet and Cunningham, as well as many others, including Franklin Mullen, Ron Morales, Marvena Harris, Melany Johnson, Lily Baker [*yatam*], Beverly Ogle, Warren Gorbet, Marvin and Joyce Cunningham, Ben Cunningham, Trina Cunningham, Taras Gaither, Vivian Hansen, and Carol Hall as they talked about the history of the land, the seizure of the allotments and, in various ways, their resistance to the latest entity trying to stop their access to the land (for medicinal, food and basketry plants, tending ancestral places, tending cemeteries, gathering for ceremony, etc.). While I knew that the allotment period was only one very small snapshot of the length and breadth of Maidu history in the North Fork Feather River region, I focused on that era because of the extensive documentation available on the time period in relationship to the development of the area.

As I continued visiting the archives and reviewing allotment files, I found that they contained numerous other stories that revealed, for example, the oppressive nature of paternalism when the BIA refused to send funds (derived from land sales) to families with ill children, hand-drawn sketches of the land- and waterscapes from more than 100 years ago, and detailed explanations of the steps taken to solidify the expansion of monopolies for timber, grazing, hydropower production, and conservation. I was interning with MCDG and the Maidu Summit in the early and mid-2000s, when the Stewardship Council land-divestiture process began. The founding documents and initial structure of the council exemplified the ways in which the Maidu and other Indigenous people throughout California continue to be excluded from formal roles in natural resource policy-making on their own ancestral lands. Alongside MCDG's ongoing research, my allotment research became useful in the process of applying for Stewardship Council lands, as we worked to share with the council how recently PG&E had gained title to the Maidu lands and how Maidu people were still dealing with collective landlessness, partially from the effects of those transactions. MCDG had been using its own allotment data already to inform FERC of these same issues in the ongoing relicensing applications for the hydroelectric projects along the North Fork Feather River.

When I began to turn more attention to the broader context in which the cancellation and sale of the majority of allotments took place, I saw that many Native nations around the United States had suffered similar extreme and violent displacement from hydroelectric development, although this generally occurred later in the twentieth century, as funding and infrastructure for public works projects increased. During a cultural monitoring training held at Susanville Indian Rancheria in the mid-2000s, I met Caleen Sisk, chief of the Winnemem Wintu, and, over the next several years, I was able learn more about the impact of the development of the federal CVP on her nation and her people's ongoing struggle to stop the proposal to raise Shasta Dam, at the headwaters of the CVP. Along with learning about the inundation of Winnemem Wintu sites by the CVP, I was involved with the first Tribal Water Summit (2009) and increasing tribal participation in DWR's State Water Plan process, and I realized that the California SWP was just downstream of and fully integrated with PG&E's management of the Upper North Fork Feather River Projects. The SWP, the largest state water conveyance system in the United States, is privately owned at its headwaters, and the site of massive and ongoing Maidu displacement.

This situation exemplifies four points, which I will expand upon in this chapter: (1) the Indigenous histories that frame some of the largest public works projects, which impact all downstream Californians on a daily basis, are largely unknown; (2) contemporary natural resource education and policy-making contributes to the perpetuation of institutionalized racism by being ignorant of this history; (3) public conservation programs, agencies, and processes are as complicit in the denial of Indigenous rights as corporate development; and (4) natural resource policy-making and planning can be transformed with attention to history, a commitment to justice, and a commitment to inclusion. As Farrell [*yatam*] wrote in the first iteration of the Maidu Summit's land management plan proposal for the lands available through the Stewardship Council process in the upper Feather River watershed: "We should be even more frightened of living in a world where the foundation of injustice is honorable and the perpetuation of that injustice acceptable. . . . We must make a future of justice." To me, these words were a call to action. I was compelled to write this book to contribute to that future of justice.

INDIGENOUS HISTORY AS A FOUNDATION FOR ENVIRONMENTAL POLICY

I obtained a doctoral degree in environmental science, policy, and management from the University of California, Berkeley, where I also took courses in the Department of City and Regional Planning, School of Public Health, and Boalt Hall School of Law. While my home department at the University of California, Davis, is Native American Studies, in 2016 I also began to serve on the faculty of the Ecology Graduate Group, specifically in the area of environmental policy and human ecology. While we who work on environmental science and policy work on issues that are central to the sovereignty, identity, culture, and community of Native nations, *none of the courses of study in environmental policy at either of these institutions require a Native American Studies course or any engagement with Native communities or nations.* This seems to me to be a fundamental problem and one that contributes to ongoing displacement and disenfranchisement of Indigenous peoples; students who graduate with degrees in environmental policy, planning, and management may have no knowledge of Indigenous peoples and their deep, ongoing, and multifaceted relationships to the land and water.

The Maidu were initially excluded from the process of deciding how their homeland would be managed at the turn of the century by virulent racism, which included denial of citizenship and due process. In 2016, as I wrote this text, Indigenous water protectors from around the world and their allies gathered at Standing Rock Sioux Nation and were tear gassed, sprayed with water cannons, and shot with rubber bullets by heavily armed law enforcement as they prayerfully and peacefully resisted the progress of an oil and gas pipeline slated to cross their water source and their homeland. That struggle by Dakota and Lakota people along the Missouri was the latest in nearly 80 years of resistance to stop government projects from trampling on the rights of upper Missouri Basin tribes. Effectively, the water protectors said "Enough." Meanwhile, American land management institutions, and the educational institutions that educate the future leaders of those agencies, perpetuate and legitimize the deep injustices that characterize historical relations on American land and water by not educating our students about these histories, relationships, and contemporary realities. Educators must foreground Indigenous histories of land and resource development and introduce students to community members with whom they can collaborate to create more just environmental policies and policy-making processes. If we do not, we are undoubtedly perpetuating institutionalized racism.

When Maidu Summit members asserted that the process of divesting PG&E lands for conservation should consider how the lands came into PG&E ownership, and consider environmental justice, the council responded that they had to follow the steps mandated in the settlement agreement. In public meetings, board members stated directly that the process was not about justice, it was about conservation and managing the land for a set of beneficial public values. I would contend that if the process is not about justice, it is about injustice, because burying the fact that the majority of the land was outright stolen, and a small part of the land (the allotments) sold or condemned to power companies in a time of great duress for California Indian people—a time when they were subject to BIA oversight that was rife with paternalism and double-dealing, and when they had neither rights of citizenship nor self-representation—continues to legitimize that process. Whether the land is sold for development or donated to a public or private conservation entity, if this recent history of how it came to be part of the process is not acknowledged, Indigenous rights and Indigenous humanity continue to be denied.

Examining and questioning the foundations of natural resource decision-making is a first step to developing more just processes and policies in the present. Given that the land that underlies the private hydroelectric projects at the headwaters of the SWP is Maidu land that was unjustly taken from Maidu people, opinions of a diverse representation of Maidu people should be central to any decisions made about that land going forward. Maidu people have various relationships with and commitments to that land that extend further back in time than those of any other party, and those relationships should be respected in every decision and decision-making process. If there is land to be transferred from the company that seized it from Maidu people, Maidu should have preference to receive those lands and should be involved in every land transfer and the planning and management of lands within their homeland. This relationship with Indigenous peoples should happen everywhere the Stewardship Council process is taking place. This is a radical shift in values that is based on an awareness of the ramifications of history, a commitment to justice, and a commitment to inclusion.

RESEARCH PRODUCTS AND CONSIDERATIONS

This project involved several research products that were developed principally for Maidu people and are, as such, not reproduced here due to privacy concerns.

These include an Excel database categorizing information on allotments and a map of allotments in ArcGIS, which can also be used in a web-based platform. With the support of the Yocha Dehe Endowed Chair in California Indian Studies at the University of California, Davis, two research assistants, Sandra Gutierrez (Purepecha) and Deserea Rose Langley (Shoshone, Paiute), scanned documents associated with the sale and establishment of allotments, and Michele Tobias and Alex Mandel of the Geospatial Consulting Service enabled the scanned files to be linked to the shapefiles of the allotments to create a web-based map on a private platform. The data for hosting this information will be provided to the Maidu Summit and to Greenville and Susanville Rancherias. Digital files of allotment paperwork, the Excel database (which contains information on location, name of allottee, date of allotment, character of land, cancellation, and land sales), and shapefiles will also be provided to Greenville and Susanville Rancherias, the Maidu Summit, and other Maidu organizations and individuals. I will also print a limited number (due to funding constraints) of copies of the map to provide to community members without computer access.

These research products are listed above to outline a method for approaching ways to understand, visualize, and apply data on Indigenous land history. Because of its interest to a range of community members, with different levels of computer access and savvy, the data must be provided in a variety of formats to serve different users. This raises a range of challenges, including the difficulty of acquiring funding required to transfer the data to descendants without computer access.

GOING FORWARD: A PRAXIS OF INTERVENTION

In California, it is rare to find an individual, family, or business south of Oroville that does not rely on either SWP or CVP water. These two massive systems transformed the land- and waterscape of the state, with far-reaching consequences for Indigenous peoples, as well as for ecosystems such as the beleaguered Sacramento–San Joaquin Delta. Whether you live in California or another state, it is important to know where your municipal water and power comes from, and where the water comes from that feeds the systems (food production and otherwise) that you depend on, and when the conveyance and development systems that bring that water to you were built, and how, and by whom. Generally most of us live in a place where a large public or private project is responsible for bringing us our water. These projects come with many consequences. They are only construed as beneficial because the models that enabled them left out key constraints, such as Indigenous rights, human rights, and the health of nonhuman relatives.

The process of solar development offers a good example: while it may be just as effective to put solar panels on the roofs of houses, particularly in sunny regions of the state, private companies with public support and funding have emphasized building huge solar projects in the desert, where they trample on Indigenous cultural landscapes and impact birds, fish, and wildlife. The models encouraging the development of these huge projects in the Southern California deserts focus on the amount of electricity that can be produced in a concentrated area and whether it can be efficiently transported to large centers of consumption, like the Los Angeles basin. Imagine if respect for the cultural vitality and cultural landscapes of desert Native nations and the lives of tortoises and desert birds were given the same levels of consideration as efficiency and profit? What if the history of how these desert lands, the homeland of Cahuilla, Serrano, Chemehuevi, southern Paiute, and Kumeyaay peoples, came to be under the ownership of the BLM (previously known as the GLO) was foregrounded, and the leadership of representatives from the cultural practitioners within these nations was central to the decision-making process?

In this text, I invited readers to accompany me on a walk through time and space in Maidu country in the northeastern Sierra, from a time period in which individuals received allotted lands on the public domain to when they had those lands canceled and fought for some measure of restitution from either the cancellation or sale, and both public and private entities became monopolistic landholders on the backs of Indigenous peoples who were divested of their homelands. Those past policies led to current situations in which Indigenous peoples still are collectively landless while the descendants of those who developed either conservation or corporate monopolies remain landed. There are long histories of Indigenous resistance, at every stage in the process, and contemporary Maidu calls for land restitution as "just compensation" for all that was taken or water protectors' calls to stop oil and gas pipelines under the Missouri and elsewhere, are the contemporary expression of years of opposition to policies and policymakers that have disregarded their humanity. The frameworks of decision-making for the lands and waters we depend on are flawed, limited, and act to perpetuate institutionalized injustices. My own research into

Maidu allotments at the headwaters has attempted to bring awareness to this history and support intervention and compensation to Maidu, Pit River, and other upstream allottees. I invite us all, in our own ways, to participate in that intervention. How do we bring awareness to histories on the lands and in the waters that underlie the present configuration of ownership, management, and decision-making? How do we change the inputs into the models to ensure justice becomes more important than profit?

There are key points in time when intervention can make a significant difference. In the context of the SWP, the upper headwaters lands on the Feather River were developed for hydroelectricity by predecessor companies to contemporary PG&E beginning around 1900. A key point of intervention following this painful history was the development of the SWP in the 1950s, with the bond that funded the project passing in 1960. What if, in the studies leading up to the project, the agencies were attentive to how that upper headwaters infrastructure was developed and committed to find a way to not reinforce similar displacement with Oroville Dam? In contrast, Concow Maidu sites, villages, and cemeteries were flooded for the Oroville project—reproducing the same pattern that the private enterprise had followed upstream.

In the late 1990s and early 2000s, there was another key point when intervention could have occurred, when the California Public Utilities Commission and PG&E reached a settlement in 2003. The settlement admirably spells out conservation protections for these upper watershed lands owned by the utility company but is silent on Indigenous peoples' rights, the histories of those lands, and the relationship between traditional environmental knowledge, Indigenous stewardship, and land restoration. At this time, the parties to the agreement could have insisted on Indigenous land and water restitution, on foregrounding Indigenous knowledge and stewardship in order to restore the watershed, and on centering Indigenous participation in the land planning and divestiture process. Instead, the council was formed with little to no Native participation, and only the advocacy of Indigenous people around the state led to the appointment of the founding Native American Heritage Commission secretary, Larry Myers (Pomo) to the council, and it has been a struggle over the last decade, and continues to be a struggle, to get some of the lands transferred to tribal entities.

The relicensing proceedings for the hydroelectric projects on the North Fork Feather River are another key, and ongoing, point of intervention. These licenses allow the projects to continue to operate for periods of 30 to 50 years. Decisions made on the projects today impact the next two generations, at least. While the Poe and Rock Creek–Cresta relicensing proceeded with Maidu participation, but with minimal concessions being made, the Almanor and Bucks processes are ongoing and remain key sites where FERC and the Control Board could increase their acknowledgment of Maidu history, Maidu rights, and Maidu demands to gain compensation in the process. Maidu resistance to the thermal curtain, and traditional knowledge about the temperature of the river and the species that lived in the river prior to its development, should be centered in the relicensing proceedings.

Statewide, we are also at a critical juncture with the twin tunnels projects, now folded into the "California WaterFix" project under the DWR. This project would take water out of the Sacramento River in up to two huge tunnels, bypassing the delta to convey the water south. While the delta is certainly in need of improved management and restoration, the tunnels are another massive infrastructure project that will come with enormous costs for Indigenous histories in the soils where the tunnels will be placed, and have the dangerous potential to further impact the delta by rerouting the majority of water past it. This is a point where the voices of Indigenous peoples whose homelands will be crossed by the proposed tunnel should be foregrounded.

Tools that might be used in these contemporary points of intervention include cultural-conservation easements, the development of Indigenous-led land trusts to hold land in conserved status, and the creation of innovative cross-sectoral, Indigenous-led cultural land-conservation partnerships. The transfers to tribal entities by the council reveal use of two of these tools: first, the Maidu Summit Consortium and Conservancy is a recognized nonprofit Native American land trust, one of a growing group of Native land trusts that hold up to 10,000 acres of land in conserved, culturally and environmentally protected status.[1] Second, both the Pit River Tribe and the Summit have developed innovative collaborative partnerships for conservation management with non-Native state agencies and conservation nonprofits. However, while cultural resources protection may be folded into conservation easements, I have not seen the application of specifically cultural-conservation easements—formal, legal agreements held by Indigenous entities that would enable access, stewardship, and protection of culturally important places by Indigenous peoples—in the council process or the FERC relicensing. There is much potential for the development and application of innovative conservation tools to facilitate transfer of lands or interests in lands to original peoples.

It is through long-term, detailed research into histories of land and water management and policy, and listening to those who would tell their stories and their families' stories of the impacts of these policies, that one can discern continuities in the political-economic frameworks that have governed natural resource decision-making. From these patterns, one can find points of intervention and advocacy to foreground the protection of Native lands, cultural values and communities, and environmental sustainability. This work helps link past to present to future, calling attention to patterns of exclusion and potential points to intervene to create more just futures with the lands and waters that sustain us.

ACKNOWLEDGMENTS

I AM GRATEFUL to the Maidu Culture and Development Group staff and leadership, particularly Lorena Gorbet and Farrell Cunningham [*yatam*] for introducing me to the issues in allotment history in the upper watershed. This project aims to contribute in multiple ways to the ongoing work of the MCDG and the Maidu Summit Consortium and Conservancy, as well as to other Maidu groups and organizations. All royalties will be donated to the Maidu Summit, MCDG, and Maidu We'ye.

I am thankful to those who taught me about issues of tribal land and water rights and hydro development in other watersheds, particularly Judy LaDeaux and Chief Caleen Sisk. Thanks are due to those who helped me learn how to work with ArcGIS software, including Michael DeLasaux, Zeke Lunder, Maggi Kelly, and Josh Fisher. Many entities and individuals have provided information to the project, including the Susanville Indian Rancheria, Honey Lake Maidu, Pacific Watershed Lands Stewardship Council (Jessica Daugherty and Heidi Krolick), David Sandino, Leah Wills, and archivists at the National Archives and Records Administration, Pacific Region (particularly Deborah Osterberg and John Seamans), in Washington, D.C., and at the Minnesota Historical Society. The cartographic work would not have been possible without Michele Tobias and Alex Mandel. Several students have also contributed to this project, most recently Deserea Langley and Sandra Gutierrez, both PhD students in Native American Studies at the University of California, Davis.

Multiple funders have also provided support, most recently the Yocha Dehe Endowed Chair in California Indian Studies, but also the University of California President's Faculty Research Fellowship in the Humanities and the University of California, Berkeley, Center for Race and Gender Graduate Research Fellowship. I am also grateful to the University of California, Davis, and the Department of Native American Studies for granting me a quarter of sabbatical leave so that I could complete this book.

A depth of gratitude is due to supportive friends and mentors, including those who read this text and provided comments, encouragement, and suggestions. All my thanks to my family—particularly my son, my husband, and my mother—for bearing with my long work hours and multiple archive trips, and having faith in the potential of this project to contribute to justice.

TIMELINE

THE FOLLOWING *timeline includes both significant dates discussed in the text and events that were important to people in Mountain Maidu country. The timeline attempts to place both land and water decisions in Maidu country in the context of water resources development in the state and the nation, with a focus on tribal concerns. Sources include interviews, newspaper articles, court cases, statutes, environmental studies, and archival documents.*

1812   General Land Office (GLO) created, moved into the Department of the Interior in 1849.

1824   Bureau of Indian Affairs (BIA) established in the War Department, moved to the Department of the Interior in 1849.

1830   Epidemic, illness, and disease strike Mountain Maidu settlements. Disease may have traveled up the Feather River Canyon from contact with whites in the Central Valley and Sierra foothills.

1850   J. Goldsborough Bruff (a member of Peter Lassen's 1850 prospecting party) writes in his journal that "Indian lodges were numerous in [Indian] Valley and villages probably edged the entire valley."

1850   Act for the Government and Protection of Indians legalizes indentured servitude [effective slavery], denied self-representation.

1851   California Land Claims Act: all persons who claimed California lands were required to submit their claims for review and approval within two years or they would pass into the public domain.

1851–52 Treatymaking by Commissioners Wozencraft, Barbour, and McKee with approximately one-third to one-half of California Indian tribes. Eighteen treaties agreed to throughout the state, reserving 7.5 million acres of land for California Indians.

1852   First white settlements in Indian Valley (near Greenville and Taylorsville).

1873–78 Early comprehensive studies to begin systematic planning for the development of California water resources: Presidential Commission investigating the Central Valley and Sierra Nevada (1873) and maps produced by California State Engineer William Hall (1878).

1878   Timber and Stone Act (Forty-Fifth Congress, Session 2, Ch. 151, 20 Stat.89): land considered unarable sold for $2.50/acre in 160-acre parcels.

1884   Red River Lumber Company founded by Thomas Barlow Walker.

1887   General Allotment / Dawes Act (with 1889, 1907 amendments), allotting qualified Indian heads of household to file for individual 160-acre or smaller allotments, which would be held in trust by the BIA for the allottee for 25 years or until the allottee was deemed competent to sell.

1891   26 Stat. 794, 794-96 amended the Dawes Act to enable leasing of allotments if the allottee could not work due to age or disability.

1894   T. B. Walker begins buying California properties.

1902   Bureau of Reclamation established within the U.S. Geological Survey, separated as an independent agency in 1907.
        Earl brothers and Julius Howells file for water rights on the Upper North Fork Feather River.

1904   Pacific Gas and Electric (PG&E) established (incorporated 1905).

1905   Forest Service established.

1906   Great Western Power Company (GWP) established.
        Burke Act or Forced Fee Patenting Act amended the Allotment Act to give the secretary of Interior power to decide if Indians could be declared "competent" and issued fee title to their allotments.

1905   Discovery of 18 treaties negotiated with California Indians 1851–52, not ratified, and placed under injunction of secrecy by the Senate.

1908   PL-109, "An Act to relinquish, release, and confirm the title of
        certain lands in California to the Western Power Company," relin-
        quishes 890 acres to GWP.
        Big Bend Powerhouse completed by GWP.
        Winters v. US (207 U.S. 564) affirms Indian water rights based on
        the date of establishment of trust land and the amount of practically
        irrigable acreage.

1910   Roseburg Indian Agency established to serve nonreservation Indians
        in southern Oregon and Northern California. Closed in 1918.
        Act of June 25, 1910, Ch. 421, §1, 36 Stat. 847 authorized withdrawal
        and reservation of lands for water-power sites and other purposes.

1911   Greenville Indian Industrial School becomes Greenville Indian
        Industrial School and Agency. In 1923 the Greenville Agency
        becomes a subagency of the Sacramento agency.
        Executive Order identifies power-site at Big Meadows.
        Oro Electric Corporation incorporates.

1912   First Plumas allotment purchased by T. B. Walker / Red River Lum-
        ber Company.
        Public Utilities Act authorizes the State Railroad Commission
        (became the California Public Utilities Commission in 1946) to
        regulate utilities in unincorporated California (extended to all of
        California in 1915).

1914   GWP completes dam at Canyon Dam and began filling Lake
        Almanor.
        Congressional authorizations to buy lands for "homeless California
        Indians" (also in 1915, 1921–23).

1916   Greenville Indian Industrial School superintendent Edgar Miller
        writes to commissioner of Indian Affairs to find out why so many
        allotments under GWP's reservoir were canceled with no payment.

1920   Federal Power Commission established.
        Federal Water Power Act (41 Stat. 1063, 16 USC 791-823).

1921   GWP completes Caribou Powerhouse on the North Fork Feather River.
        State of California authorizes comprehensive statewide water
        resources investigation.
        Public sales of Indian lands at Greenville Agency.

Commissioner of Indian Affairs asks timber cruiser Irvine Gardner to resign, effective November 14, 1921. Gardner resigns on September 11, 1922.

1922   Greenville Indian Agency superintendent Edgar Miller investigated and exonerated.

1923   Land for Taylorsville Rancheria bought from heirs of Old Allick (Sus-212).

Sacramento Indian Agency created, later subsumed into Central California Agency and became the Sacramento Area Office of the BIA.

1924   Indian Citizenship Act.

Land for Susanville Indian Rancheria bought from Fannie Taylor.

Butt Valley dam completed, reservoir filled.

1928   GWP completes Bucks Creek Powerhouse.

California Indians Jurisdictional Act authorizes California attorney general to sue the federal government on behalf of tribes whose lands were stolen following nonratification of treaties 1851-52. Settled in 1944, $5 million paid for 7.5 million acres.

1930   PG&E purchase of GWP.

1931   California "State Water Plan" formally recommends the construction of Oroville Dam.

1933   Tennessee Valley Authority Act.

Central Valley Project Act of 1933 (Chapter 1042, California Statutes 1933).

Construction of Grand Coulee Dam on the Columbia River begins, completed in 1942.

Construction of Bonneville Dam on the Columbia River begins, completed in 1937.

1934   Indian Reorganization Act officially ends the Allotment Act, includes provisions for establishing new reservations and getting land for individual Indians and tribes.

1935   Public Utility Act of August 26, 1935 (49 Stat. 838, 16 USC).

1937   Rivers and Harbors Act (Public No. 392, Seventy-Fifth Congress, 1st Session) reauthorizes funding for the Central Valley Project (CVP), work begins on the CVP.

1941   CVP, Acquisition of Indian Lands, Public Law 198, Chapter 334, S. 1120, July 30, 1941.

California State Legislature adopts plan to build Oroville Dam.

1944   Red River Lumber Company liquidates assets.

Flood Control Act, 58 Stat. 887, Ch. 665, December 22, 1944.

1945   Shasta Dam completed.

California State Legislature passes State Water Resources Act and establishes a governor-appointed State Water Resources Board.

1946   U.S. Indian Claims Commission Act creates Court of Claims, Indians of California bring claim for aboriginal California lands.

Bureau of Land Management created from the merger of the GLO and U.S. Grazing Service.

1948   American Declaration on the Rights and Duties of Man adopted by the 9th International Conference of American States in Bogota, Columbia.

1950   Rock Creek Powerhouse completed by GWP.

1951   California State Legislature and State Water Resources Board fund three-phase (1951, 1955, 1957) State Water Plan.

1953   Construction completed of Garrison Dam, flooding the majority of the agricultural land of the Three Affiliated Tribes of the Fort Berthold Indian Reservation Termination.

House Concurrent Resolution 108, Termination Act, articulates Congressional policy to terminate Indian tribes.

Public Law 280 transfers all criminal and some civil jurisdiction over California tribes from the federal to the state government.

1955   Federal Power Commission issues license to PG&E for the Upper North Fork Feather River Project.

1956   California Department of Water Resources created.

1958   California Rancheria Termination Act Rancherias terminated and land divided among the people who "were using them."

1960   California State Water Project approved.

1967   California State Water Resources Control Board established.

1969   PG&E completes Belden Powerhouse.

1974   International Indian Treaty Council established.

1977   Congress reorganizes the Federal Power Commission to form FERC.

1985   Indian Creek Hydroelectric Project plan abandoned, largely because of the failure to adequately consult with Maidu and fulfill the cultural resources analysis.

1988   San Luis Rey Indian Water Rights Settlement Act (PL 100-675).

1994   Executive Order 12898, "Federal Actions to Address Environmental
        Justice in Minority Populations and Low-Income Populations,"
        requires that each federal agency develop strategies for achieving
        environmental justice.

1996   Executive Order 13007 (1996), "Indian Sacred Sites," calls federal agen-
        cies to avoid impacting sites and to accommodate tribal access to sites.

2001   Rock Creek Cresta relicensed.
        PG&E files for Chapter 11 bankruptcy protection.

2002   Creation of Maidu Summit organization.
        PG&E begins application to FERC for relicensing Project 2105
        (Upper North Fork Feather River).
        FERC 2105 relicensing of the dam at Lake Almanor releases a report
        on traditional cultural sites in the Almanor Basin.

2003   Settlement agreement between the California Public Utilities
        Commission and PG&E creates the Pacific and Watershed Lands
        Stewardship Council.
        Maidu Cultural and Development Group (MCDG) granted inter-
        venor status in 2105 relicensing process.

2004   Mountain Maidu and others reprimand the Stewardship Council
        board of directors for lack of Native representation. The council
        responds by inviting Larry Myers of the Native American Heritage
        Commission to join the board.
        California Senate Bill 18 passes, acknowledging that federally recog-
        nized or unrecognized tribes can hold conservation easements.

2005   FERC issues Final Environment Impact Statement on Project 2105
        (Upper North Fork Feather River).

2006   U.S. Environmental Protection Agency finds that North Fork
        Feather River water temperatures were too high.

2007   Maidu Summit submits first application for PG&E lands available
        through the Pacific Watershed Lands Stewardship Council divesti-
        ture process.
        UN Declaration on the Rights of Indigenous Peoples agreed to by
        the UN General Assembly, supported by the United States in 2010.

2008   Soboba Band of Luiseno Indians Settlement Act, PL 110-297.

2009   Maidu Summit submits Statement of Qualifications to receive land donations through the Pacific Watershed Lands Stewardship Council divestiture process.

2010   Maidu Summit Consortium and Conservancy receives nonprofit status.

2011   Executive Order B-10-11 passed by Governor Jerry Brown in California, requiring that each state agency engage in tribal consultation.

2012   Stewardship Council Board votes to transfer 723 acres to the Potter Valley Tribe.

2013   Stewardship Council Board votes to transfer 2,325 acres of land in Humbug Valley, or Tasman Koyom, to the Maidu Summit.

2014   State Water Resources Control Board issues Draft Environmental Impact Report issuing a water quality certification under Sec. 401 of the Clean Water Act (33 USC §1341).
       Stewardship Council Board votes to transfer 219 acres to the Potter Valley Tribe.
       Stewardship Council Board votes to transfer 441 acres to the Maidu Summit.

2015   Stewardship Council Board votes to transfer 850 acres to the Pit River Tribe.

2016   Stewardship Council Board votes to transfer 200 acres to the Maidu Summit.

NOTES

INTRODUCTION

1. In his investigation of cartography and Indian land cessions in the United States, geographer Imre Sutton acknowledges that it is commonly known that Indian lands were regularly sacrificed for the creation of hydroelectric projects (2002).

2. The public agencies that contract with the DWR to receive water from the SWP are the Alameda County Flood Control & Water Conservation District, Zone 7; Alameda County Water District; Antelope Valley–East Kern Water Agency; Casitas Municipal Water District on behalf of the Ventura County Flood Control District; Castaic Lake Water Agency; Central Coast Water Authority on behalf of the Santa Barbara County FC&WCD; City of Yuba City; Coachella Valley Water District; County of Kings; Crestline-Lake Arrowhead Water Agency; Desert Water Agency; Dudley Ridge Water District; Empire-West Side Irrigation District; Kern County Water Agency; Littlerock Creek Irrigation District; Metropolitan Water District of Southern California; Mojave Water Agency; Napa County FC&WCD; Oak Flat Water District; Palmdale Water District; San Bernardino Valley Municipal Water District; San Gabriel Valley MWD; San Gorgonio Pass Water Agency; San Luis Obispo Co. FC7WCD; Santa Clara Valley Water District; Solano County Water Agency; and Tulare Lake Basin Water Storage District.

3. According to current policy, in order to engage in a formal government-to-government relationship with the United States government, Native Americans must be recognized by the federal government as Indigenous nations. The federal government recognizes Native American tribes in three ways: by administrative

action as outlined in 25 CFR, Part 83, which outlines the regulations and process that a tribe must follow to apply for federal recognition via the Office of Federal Acknowledgment (BIA, DOI); by congressional legislation, such as HR846 (2000), the Graton Rancheria Restoration Act; or by federal court decision. Many authors have critiqued the inherent coloniality of the system by which the federal government chooses to recognize or not recognize Native nations. See, for example, Tolley 2007; Gunter 1998; Paschal 1991; Goldberg and Champagne 1996.

4. For example, according to 1982 research by California State University, Long Beach, geographer Rodney Steiner on the largest landholders in California, 67 large landowners in California each own more than 25,000 acres, and 19 of these own more than 75,000 acres. In noncontiguous holdings, PG&E held more than 250,000 acres at the time of the study, the T. B. Walker heirs (of the Red River Lumber Company, which was an aggressive purchaser of Indian allotments) held more than 25,000 acres, the Southern Pacific Railroad—the largest landowner in California—held more than 2 million acres, and Standard Oil held more than 260,000, mostly obtained from the railroad. See Steiner 1982.

5. The patriarch of the Cross family, Martin Cross (Mandan, Hidatsa) served as chairman of the Three Affiliated Tribes from 1944 to 1946 and 1950 to 1956 and helped to found the National Congress of American Indians. See VanDevelder 2004.

6. As VanDevelder describes the sentiment of farmers in the Missouri Basin around 1960, "Farmers were beginning to suspect that irrigation had been nothing more than a cruel ploy all along. They had been duped into playing obedient pawns in the battle between two federal agencies fighting for control of the Missouri River. After the first dams were built and flooding ceased in downstream states, no one in Washington seemed much inclined to spend billions more dollars on irrigation projects" (2004, 177–78).

7. See VanDevelder's discussion of Constance Elizabeth Hunt's study *Down by the River* (2004, 83).

8. The Army Corps of Engineers supported the Pick Plan, designed by Colonel Lewis Pick, which included the massive Garrison Dam, and the Bureau of Reclamation supported the plan designed by engineer Glenn Sloan, which included a network of smaller dams and reservoirs. President Roosevelt approved the Flood Control Act in 1944, which included elements from both plans and became known as the Pick Sloan Plan. Tribes were not consulted throughout this process of deciding the future of their lands and communities. See VanDevelder 2004; Lawson 2009, xv.

9. See, for example, Sammon 2016; Navajo 2016; Whyte 2016.

10. See, for example, Reyes 2002; Harden 1996. I would also like to acknowledge a striking presentation entitled "Fallout: Repercussions of the Dam Raise" about the impact of the dam on her family, community, and nation by Sim Hay Kin Jack, a member of the Colville Confederated Tribes and a PhD student in Native American studies at the University of California, Davis (Jack 2016).

11. Frederick Ike Sr., Yakama, in Ulrich 2007, 16.

12. William Yallup Sr., Yakama, in Ulrich 2007, 26.

13. See, for example, Garrett 2009.

14. Reginald Winishut, in Ulrich 2007, 23.

15. There are many corollaries between the story of California's water development and Richard White's accounting of the story of railroad development across the United States. As White explains, railroads were built ahead of demand, with public subsidies, and acted to enrich a small group of businessmen: "Entrepreneurs obtained great fortunes, but they created inefficient, costly dysfunctional corporations. . . . They built railroads that would have been better left unbuilt. . . . They set in motion a train of catastrophes for which society paid the price" (2011, xxvi).

16. There is extensive documentation in academic, news, and government sources of the pollution and associated health impacts in California's Central and San Joaquin Valleys. See, for example, London and Huang 2012; Barboza 2013, 2014; Cole and Foster 2001, preface and chapter 4.

17. For an overview of the state and federal statutes and processes that enabled the seizure of California Indian lands and the following limited opportunities (via the 1928 Jurisdictional Act and the development of the Court of Claims in 1946, respectively) that enabled California Indians to assert land claims and demands for restitution, see Flushman and Barbieri 1986; Sutton 1985.

18. According to Sutton, the claims processes dealt more with land, leaving water to litigation (1985, 220). Following Hundley (1978), the landmark *Winters* decision left unanswered whether tribal-reserved water rights were reserved by tribes as "a reservation of rights not granted" or reserved by the government for tribes—a granting of a right upon the establishment of the reservation. The response to this question might help legally establish in Western courts whether tribes were due restitution for water rights taken when lands were taken.

19. The 1988 San Luis Rey Indian Water Rights Settlement Act (PL 100-675) involves the La Jolla, San Pasqual, Pauma, and Pala Bands of Mission Indians, who were promised up to 16,000 acre-feet per year, made available by conservation and water transfers from the All-American Canal (see Colby, Thorson, and Britton 2005). The 1988 Settlement Act could only become effective after the United States, the involved tribes, and two local entities reached their own settlement agreement, which happened in December 2014 (see Subcommittee on Water 2015). All parties then supported H.R.1296, to modify and clarify the 1988 Settlement Act. As of September 22, 2016, H.R.1296 passed the House and on September 26, 2016, it went to the Senate (see H.R.1296—"To amend the San Luis Rey Indian Water Rights Settlement Act to clarify certain settlement terms, and for other purposes"—online at https://www.congress.gov/bill/114th-congress/house-bill/1296). The two other water rights settlements achieved in California were the Soboba Band of Luiseno Indians Settlement Act, PL 110-297 (2008), which ratifies the 2006 Settlement Agreement between the Soboba Band, the federal government, and 3 non-Indian water districts to secure Soboba's water supply and provide funding for tribal

economic development and water development (see H.R.4841—110th Congress: Soboba Band of Luiseno Indians Settlement Act); and the Pechanga Water Rights Settlement, which is Subtitle D in PL 114-322, Water Infrastructure Improvements for the Nation (WIIN) Act, signed December 16, 2016.

20. See the International Indian Treaty Council n.d.; Mohawk 1982.

21. The American Declaration of the Rights and Duties of Man was adopted by the Ninth International Conference of American States in Bogota, Columbia, in 1948. The Dann sisters drew on the declaration (particularly article 2, stating that all people are equal under the law; article 18, affirming the right to a fair trial; and article 23, affirming the right of each person to property) to counter the U.S. Claims Commission decision that denied them their aboriginal land rights to their Western Shoshone homeland in Nevada (*Mary and Carrie Dann v. United States 2002*).

22. In 2012 the executive director of the Indian Law Resource Center, Robert Coulter, called the UNDRIP (agreed to by the UN General Assembly in 2007 and supported by the United States under President Obama in 2010) "one of the most significant developments in international human rights law in decades" and explained how he and others had long advocated for the declaration "on the premise that domestic law was terribly inadequate to protect indigenous peoples' rights" (Indian Law Resource Center 2012). In 2011 the Yocha Dehe Wintun Nation and Cortina Band of Wintu in California invoked the declaration to establish a conservation and cultural easement on a site slated for development in the eastern San Francisco Bay area. In 2012 the Winnemem Wintu Tribe of Northern California invoked the declaration as one of many supporting laws and policies that should enable them to hold their Women's Coming of Age Ceremony on the McCloud River in peace and dignity (see Mulcahy 2012). For a comprehensive overview of the hopeful significance of the UNDRIP, see Echo-Hawk 2013.

23. Regarding the opportunities and shortcomings of the UNDRIP, see Champagne 2016.

24. This includes Executive Order B-10-11 (2011) by Governor Brown in California, which requires that each state agency engage in tribal consultation. Many state agencies have also written and adopted their own tribal engagement policies.

25. This includes Executive Order 12898 (1994), "Federal Actions to Address Environmental Justice in Minority Populations and Low-Income Populations," which requires that each federal agency develop strategies for achieving environmental justice, and Executive Order 13007 (1996), "Indian Sacred Sites," which calls on federal agencies to avoid impacting sites and to accommodate tribal access to sites.

26. See Theodoratus Cultural Research 1986; Middleton 2014.

27. For accounts of the violence and terrorism against California Indians, see, for example, Heizer 1993 (originally published in 1974); Gould 1990; Hoopes 1975; Johnston-Dodds 2002; Lindsay 2012; Trafzer and Hyer 1999.

28. See Schneider's (2010) discussion of nineteenth- and twentieth-century Pomo strategies of pooling wages from agricultural labor to buy lands.

29. Translated from Maidu to English as "head man" (K. Anderson 2015, 260).

30. Translated from Maidu to English as a respectful term one uses when speaking about a person who has passed on. As Karen Anderson explains, speaking about Farrell Cunningham, "According to his custom, we avoid saying the names of those who have passed on. If his name must be pronounced, it should be followed by 'yatam.'" (2015, 3).

31. Translated from Maidu to English as "edible root, Yampa" (K. Anderson 2015, 175).

32. Translated from Maidu to English as "big time" (K. Anderson 2015, 228), this was actually a Bear Dance, which may be more specifically termed *panom weda* (275).

33. See, for example, the struggle to make the Marine Life Protection Act (MLPA) process accountable to Indigenous peoples whose ancestral lands include the California coast, exemplified by the "MLPA Tribal Takeover," available at https://www.youtube.com/watch?v=inpAE-rOkXc. For two distinct perspectives on navigating the MLPA process to achieve tribal rights, see Rosales 2012–13 and Yurok Tribe 2011.

34. For a powerful discussion of the impact of the doctrine of discovery and the need to dismantle it, see the 2013 lecture "Enduring Impact of the Doctrine of Discovery," given by Chris Peters, executive director of the Seventh Generation Fund, at the Lyng v. Northwest Indian Cemetery Protective Association (1988): 25 Years Later conference that Cutcha Risling Baldy and I organized at the University of California, Davis, available on YouTube at https://www.youtube.com/watch?v=3Nsu59_vW54; for an overview of the history, falsity, and impacts of the doctrine, see Newcomb 2008.

35. See, for example Williams 2012; Echo-Hawk 2010.

36. Tuck and Yang are unapologetic and unwavering in their definition of decolonization as "incommensurable" with business as usual: "Decolonization eliminates settler property rights and settler sovereignty. It requires the abolition of land as property and upholds the sovereignty of Native land and people. . . . Decolonizing the Americas means all land is repatriated and all settlers become landless. It is incommensurable with the redistribution of Native land/life as common-wealth" (2012, 26, 27).

37. For an account of the role of the Northern California Indian Association and attorney C. E. Kelsey in unearthing the unratified treaties and advocating for restitution and lands for California Indians, see Miller 2013a. See also Miller 2013b; Flushman and Barbieri 1986; Hoopes 1975.

38. President Theodore Roosevelt called it "a mighty pulverizing engine to break up the tribal mass." From the "First Annual Message" on December 3, 1901.

39. See Washburn 1975. As David Chang describes, "Allotment combined the making of land into private property and the taking of that property from [Indians]" (2011).

40. Bobroff (2001, 1601) articulates similar sentiments about the meaning of land to Indian people, their responsibilities to it, and the impossibility of reducing it to a product that could be bought and sold, despite the pressures of allotment.

41. Collier, John, memorandum, The Purposes and Operation of the Wheeler-Howard Indian Rights Bill, Hearings on H.R.7902 before the Senate and House Commit-

tees of Indian Affairs, 73rd Cong., 2nd Sess. 15, 15–18, 1934; see also Ruppel 2008; Bobroff 2001, 1610.

42. The 1894 General Indian Appropriations Act expanded the reasons for leasing to "inability" to work, and extended the terms of farming, grazing, business, and mining leases, and then reverted to the original terms of the 1891 act by the General Indian Appropriations Act of 1897 (see Poindexter 1994, 68).

43. According to Bobroff, the Burke Act played a prominent role in the transfer of 23 million acres of Indian lands through "the issue and subsequent alienation of fee patents" (2001, 1610).

44. This facilitated increasing alienation of Indian lands; as Bobroff explains, "With other Indians seldom having money to purchase these lands (and with allotments un-mortgagable), an additional 3.7 million acres, often of the best lands, passed to non-Indians" (2001, 1611).

45. According to comments on this manuscript received from Heidi Krolick (on August 8, 2017), Stewardship Council executive director, tribes that are entitled to hold conservation easements under California Civil Code Sec. 815.3(c) may receive title to these lands. This includes all federally or nonfederally recognized tribes in California (the latter must be on a contact list maintained by the Native American Heritage Commission to protect cultural places).

46. I mapped as many allotments as possible that are located within the boundaries of Plumas and Lassen Counties.

47. I am inspired by the reflective allotment cartographic work of Mark Palmer (Kiowa), who also discusses issues of confidentiality, respecting the privacy of family members, and working to protect the identity of descendants of allottees. See Palmer 2011, 41.

CHAPTER 1

1. In a 1783 letter to James Duane, George Washington discusses post-Independence Indian policy, opining that the Indians would disappear in the face of American expansion: "The gradual extension of our Settlements will as certainly cause the Savage as the Wolf to retire; both being beasts of prey tho' they differ in shape."

2. Bulletin 132-88, the twenty-sixth edition of *Management of the California State Water Project*, refers to President Grant's commission as the first systematic planning for the development of California water resources. This was followed by a series of maps and reports published by the state engineer William Hall in 1878 to support systematic water resources development of the Central Valley. Filed in the Malca Chall Research Collection, issue/copy 62, call no. MS, WRCA, UCR.

3. U.S. Statutes at Large, XXV, 1887–1889, 619; 10th Annual Report of the USGS (1889), 1–80; Sterling 1940.

4. Lawrence, Nordeen, and Pumphrey 1963; Sterling 1940.

5. For example, the allotment of Willie Charley (Sus-312), was included in Power Site Withdrawals Nos. 234 (S/2 SE/4 Sec. 29, NW/4 NE/4, Sec. 32, made by the Department of Interior on November 23, 1911) and 245 (NE/4 NW/4, Sec. 32, made by the Department of the Interior on February 15, 1912).

6. Title 43, Public Lands, chapter 6, "Withdrawal from Settlement, Location, Sale, or Entry." Act of June 25, 1910, Ch. 421, §1, 36 Stat. 847 authorized withdrawal and reservation of lands for water-power sites and other purposes.

7. Specifically, this includes funds received from public lands sold in the states of Arizona, California, Colorado, Idaho, Kansas, Montana, Nebraska, Nevada, New Mexico, North Dakota, Oklahoma, Oregon, South Dakota, Utah, Washington, and Wyoming. According to the Bureau of Reclamation's "Brief History," Texas was added to the list in 1906.

8. Department of the Interior, General Land Office, 1901; see also Rowley 1996, 100, which describes Newlands as working closely with Frederick Newell of the U.S. Geological Survey in 1900 to develop a "national irrigation bill that could be funded from the sale of public lands."

9. Many authors have documented the breadth and depth of California Indian land stewardship and its importance in creating and sustaining unique and complex California ecosystems that depended on human interaction and intervention. See, for example, Anderson 2005; Lopez 2013; Long et al. 2016.

10. In 1913 Newlands argued that only white people should be able to become citizens and further that "we should write the word white into our constitution" (Rowley 1996, 143).

11. Rowley discusses the process leading up to the successful development of the Newlands Project and the construction of the Derby Dam in *Reclaiming the Arid West* (1996). Multiple court cases detail the impacts of the Derby on the water rights of the Pyramid Lake Paiute Tribe, including *Pyramid Lake Paiute Tribe of Indians v. Morton* (354 F. Supp. 252, 1972), *Nevada v. United States* (463 US 110, 1983), *US v. Orr Water Ditch Company, et al.* (914 F.2d 1302, 1990), and *US (Plaintiff) and Pyramid Lake Paiute Tribe (Petitioner-Appellant), v. Orr Ditch Water Co., et al.* (United States Court of Appeals, Ninth Circuit, No. 07-17001, 4/7/2010). January 2016 marked the beginning implementation of the Truckee River Operating Agreement (TROA), to which the Pyramid Lake Paiute Tribe is a signatory. The TROA is based in the 1990 Truckee-Carson-Pyramid Lake Water Rights Settlement Act. University of California, Davis, Native American studies PhD student Amber Bill is currently working on writing the first history of water litigation and negotiation at Pyramid Lake written from the point of view of a Pyramid Lake Paiute tribal member.

12. Department of the Interior, Office of Indian Affairs n.d., 2. One egregious violation in California is the example of the former superintendent of Indian Affairs in California, Edward F. Beale, who purchased the Tejon Reservation in Southern California. See Frank, Geyla, and Goldberg 2010, 36.

13. The figure of 25,200 acres is derived from records on 164 individual Indian allotments located within the townships of 26N-29N, between the ranges of 6E and

9E; this area encompasses Mountain Meadows, Big Meadows, Butt Valley, and Humbug Valley.

14.   Statement filed in Sus-150, RG75, NARA, Pacific Region.

15.   In an April 7, 1922, letter to Commissioner Chas Burke, Gardner described Bob's landlessness, requested some restitution for him from the public domain, and concluded "this is a bad case and I have promised to help the old man." Letter from Irvine Gardner to the commissioner of Indian Affairs, Chas Burke, April 7, 1922, filed in Sus-150, RG 75, NARA, Pacific Region.

16.   W. H. Spaulding, assistant secretary of GWP, to Edgar Miller, April 13, 1922, filed in Sus-150, Robert Shafer, RG75, NARA, Pacific Region.

17.   Edgar Miller to GWP, Attention W. H. Spaulding, Secretary, April 17, 1922, filed in Sus-150, Robert Shafer, RG75, NARA, Pacific Region.

18.   Edgar Miller to the commissioner of Indian Affairs, May 2, 1922, filed in Sus-150, Robert Shafer, RG75, NARA, Pacific Region.

19.   Douglas Clark, area realty officer, Sacramento Area Office, BIA, October 11, 1956.

20.   C. L. Graves, acting superintendent, California Indian Agency, to Carl Salem, September 24, 1947.

21.   Letter from Douglas Clark (signed for James B. Ring, area director), Sacramento Area Office, to Rose Salem, May 10, 1951.

22.   See, for example, Lorena Gorbet, Board of Directors, MCGD, to Magalie Salas, secretary at FERC, "Re: In the Matter of Relicensing of the Upper North Fork Feather River Project 2105. Request to the FERC to analyze and address the following impacts to the Maidu Indians in the 2105 Environmental Impact Statement," November 24, 2003. The letter details the history of allotments and their unjust cancellation in the area of the hydroelectric project at Big Meadows and requests just compensation for all that was lost.

23.   See also the California Public Utilities Commission's "CPUC History and Organizational Structure," available online at http://www.cpuc.ca.gov/history/.

24.   All towns and counties mentioned in this book are in California unless indicated otherwise.

25.   According to Coleman's history of PG&E, the "Bucks Creek Powerhouse is distinguished as having the highest head of any hydro plant in the Western hemisphere" (298).

26.   J. D. Galloway to James Black, general manager, GWP, March 9, 1935, filed in John Debo Galloway Papers, Box 10, Folder 46.

27.   See John D. Galloway papers, WRCA, UCR.

28.   It was originally enacted as the Federal Water Power Act of June 10, 1920 (41 Stat. 1063, 16 USC 791-823). The Public Utility Act of August 26, 1935 (49 Stat. 838, 16 USC) made the 1920 act part 1 of the Federal Power Act.

29.   16 USC, Title 16, Chapter 12, Subchapter I, Sec. 797(e).

30.   According to the hydraulic engineer Fred Pyle (1935), the city had an average growth rate of 1,000 people per year since the establishment of the pueblo of San

Diego in 1769, but this spiked again in the 1920s and 1930s, and the city increased by more than 85,000 people between 1923 and 1935.

31. "Schedule showing estimated cost of properly establishing the Capitan Grande Indians permanently upon lands to be purchased for them," August 19, 1922, filed in Hiram Newton Savage Papers, Box 8, Folder 40. WRCA, UCR.

32. Estimate by the supervising engineer Herbert V. Clotts, August 19, 1922.

33. *La Mesa, Lemon Grove & Spring Valley Irrigation District v. The City of San Diego*, in the District Court of the United States, Southern Division of the Southern District of California, September 29, 1930, filed in Hiram Newton Savage Papers, Box 8, Folder 40, WRCA, UCR.

34. Bill to amend 40 Stat. L. 1206 of February 28, 1919.

35. "San Diego River Project—Mission Reservoir Basin—Riverview Zone: Reservoir, Dam and Roads, Lands, Rights of Way," June 29, 1932, filed in Hiram Newton Savage papers, Box 8, Folder 40, WRCA, UCR.

36. SWRB 1951, 2. The language of opening up "surplus lands" for settlement was also a common argument used by proponents of allotting Indian reservations. See, for example, a 1903 editorial that appeared in the *Missoulian*, a Montana newspaper, advocating for opening up "valuable" "surplus lands" on the Flathead Reservation to settlers, discussed in Smith 1979.

37. Galloway to Black, October 29, 1924, filed in John Debo Galloway Papers, Box 10, Folder 46, WRCA, UCR.

38. Galloway to Black, "Re: Sacramento Municipal Utility District—Power Plants," September 3, 1926, filed in John Debo Galloway Papers, Box 10, Folder 44, WRCA, UCR.

39. Letter from Galloway to Emory Wishon, vice-president and general manager, GWP, September 2, 1927, filed in John Debo Galloway Papers, Box 10, Folder 44, WRCA, UCR.

40. President Roosevelt revised the report and sent it to Congress in 1938. In 1939 the National Reclamation Association compiled and distributed the irrigation sections of the report to its constituents, encouraging readers to use the report to advance their irrigation projects and "further the development of their section of the West," according to a letter from F. O. Hagie, secretary-manager, National Reclamation Association, to "Western Reclamationists," March 3, 1938.

41. Statutes of 1945, Chapter 1514.

42. These are State Water Resources Board Bulletins No. 1 ("Water Resources of California," 1951), 2 ("Water Utilization and Requirements of California," 1955), and 3 ("The California Water Plan," 1957). Overview available in Division of Water Resources Staff 1955. Filed in Cooper MS 76/10, Box 8, WRCA.

43. As Banks argued, "Exportation of water to areas outside of those in which the waters originate is not something new. . . . But the problem has always been here— the problem of assuring that you will have adequate water when and where you need it in the future" (1956, 1–2).

44. See overview in Banks 1960, 1.
45. See SWRB 1951, 59. See also p. 63 regarding specifics on the impact of the Shasta Reservoir on downstream flood control and p. 64 regarding the comparative benefits of the Shasta Reservoir on the Upper Sacramento and the proposed Oroville Reservoir on the Feather and mid to lower Sacramento, respectively.
46. SWRB 1951, 61, 71. The area had been famously termed the Peach Bowl after it produced $10 million in peaches in 1947.
47. Press Release—JA—1009, Governor Edmund G. Brown, September 15, 1966, filed in MS 76/10, Box 8, WRCA.
48. Press Release—DT—1198, Edmund G. Brown, Governor, November 5, 1966, filed in MS 76/10, Box 8, WRCA.
49. GWP built the Big Bend Powerhouse in 1908, Caribou Powerhouse in 1921, and Bucks Creek Powerhouse in 1928, and after the consolidation with PG&E in 1930, PG&E built Rock Creek Powerhouse in 1949 and Cresta Powerhouse in 1950. PG&E also built the Hamilton Branch Powerhouse on Lake Almanor's east shore. PG&E c. 1957.
50. As of 1957, PG&E was working on the Butt Valley Powerhouse, Caribou Two Powerhouse, and Poe Powerhouse. PG&E c. 1957.
51. As of 1957, PG&E was planning a powerhouse at Belden, but it was not yet scheduled for construction. PG&E c. 1957.
52. According to its 1956 Annual Report, the company was relying on census data that forecasted that California would be the most populous state in the nation by 1965.
53. Paul S. Taylor to Fred A. Seaton, secretary of the Interior, July 9, 1960, filed in Goldberg papers, MS 85/2, Box 4, Folder 25.
54. Taylor to Seaton, July 9, 1960.
55. "Nothing in this Act shall be construed as affecting or intended to affect or to in any way interfere with the laws of any State or Territory relating to the control, appropriation, use, or distribution of water used in irrigation." Reclamation Act / Newlands Act of 1902, 57th Congress, Session 1, Chapter 1093, Section 8.
56. Congressional Record, p. 7052, May 11, 1959, in Taylor to Seaton, July 9, 1960.
57. Banks 1960, 10, referring to PL 86-488, 74 Stat. 156.
58. House Resolution No. 293, J. W. Thursby, senior economist, July 22, 1960, "Study of 'Unjust Enrichment,'" filed in B. Abbott Goldberg papers, MS 85/2, Box 3, Folder 10.
59. See Leland O. Graham to Governor Edmund Brown, November 1, 1959, 15–20, filed in B. Abbott Goldberg papers, MS 85/2, Box 3, Folder 10.
60. Graham to Brown, November 1, 1959: Exhibit G.
61. House Resolution No. 293, June 18, 1959, California Assembly Daily Journal, 5769–70.
62. Clair Engle, chairman, Committee on Interior and Insular Affairs, U.S. House of Representatives et al., to Edmund G. "Pat" Brown, attorney general, February 4, 1957, filed in B. Abbott Goldberg papers, MS 85/2, Box 3, Folder 10, and reprinted in *California Law Review* 772 (1957).

63. Graham to Brown, November 1, 1959: "Exhibit C: Landownerships in Excess of 10,000 Acres, State Service Area, San Joaquin Valley Portion, Kern County, CA," August 7, 1959. For more information on the history of the Tejon Reservation and how it was effectively discontinued (but never formally terminated), see Frank and Goldberg 2010. According to Steiner (1982, 319), Tejon Ranch was one of the largest landowners in California, with total holdings in excess of 75,000 acres.

64. Graham to Brown, November 1, 1959, 2–4.

65. Garrigus, Charles B., "Statement of Policy," Hearing, Sept. 25, 1959, Assembly Interim Committee on Water, cited in Graham to Brown, November 1, 1959, 14.

66. Milton S. Baum, informal memo re: unjust enrichment, October 14, 1959, in Graham to Brown, November 1, 1959, 18.

67. Graham to Brown, November 1, 1959, 28–34.

68. In these recommendations, Graham to Brown, November 1, 1959, 40–43, follows David Weeks (UC-Berkeley), Revision of Manuscript Sturm-Baum-Tukunaga-Thurs 8/25/1959, "Equitable Distribution of Benefits and Costs from State Water Development Projects," October 15, 1959.

69. State Water Resources Board (1957) Bulletin No. 3, "The California Water Plan."

70. Joe S. Bain to J. N. Spaulding, general superintendent, Department of Water Systems, PG&E, June 6, 1960, filed in Joe Staten Bain Papers, Folder 13, p. 3.

71. Interview with John F. Bonner, Engineering Department, PG&E, December 20, 1960, filed in J. S. Bain papers, Folder 14.

72. Interview with Bart Shackleford, PG&E, May 19, 1961, filed in J. S. Bain papers, Folder 14, WRCA.

73. "PG&E Water Sales Contracts," sourced from PUC Hydraulics File, dated 10/24/60, and "Memo to JSB from ik," entitled "P G & E," dated November 7, 1960, both filed in J. S. Bain papers, Folder 14, WRCA.

74. "Power Contract Between West Stanislaus I.D. and P.G. & E.," sourced from PUC App. 3201, Dec. #45512, April 21, 1953, filed in J. S. Bain papers, Folder 14, WRCA.

75. "Conduct: 1. Expansion, Investment—Water & Power," November 10, 1960, filed in J. S. Bain papers, Folder 14, WRCA.

76. PG&E 1954 Annual Report, 6.

77. "Conduct: 3. River Management," November 10, 1960, 5, filed in J. S. Bain papers, Folder 14, WRCA.

78. Lorena Gorbet, project coordinator, MCDG to Magalie R. Salas, secretary, FERC, December 15, 2005, "Re: FERC Project No. 2105-089 Environmental Impact Statement Comments."

79. Department of the Interior (H. P. Dugan, Regional Director), Department of Water Resources (Harvey O. Banks, Director) (May 16, 1960), "Agreement between the USA and the DWR of the State of California for the Coordinated Operation of the Federal Central Valley Project and the State Feather River and Delta Diversion Projects," filed in Cooper MS 76/10 Box 8, WRCA, UCR.

80. Fred G. Aandahl, acting secretary of the Interior, to Jerome F. Kuykendall, chairman, Federal Power Commission, November 5, 1953.

CHAPTER 2

1. Petition for Sale of Inherited Indian Land of Allottee Harper Jenkins (Sus-165, d. 1901), June 15, 1912, filed in Sus-161, John Jenkins, RG75, NARA, Pacific Region. The petition also notes that the land was leased by GWP at a rate of $240/year, to expire on August 1, 1914.
2. See letter from Lorena Gorbet, on behalf of MCDG, to Magalie Salas, FERC, November 24, 2003.
3. A second alternative was a 110-foot dam, which would flood 23,250 acres, of which approximately 3,000 were federal public lands under government control.
4. Prepared by North State Resources for the State Water Resources Control Board's *Upper North Fork Feather River Hydroelectric Project Draft Environmental Impact Report*, secs. 6.12–17; C. L. Baker and T. Bakic 2001.
5. "Great Western Power Company of California: 7% Cumulative Preferred Stock," advertisement, June 20, 1924, filed in Erwin Cooper Papers, Box 12, MS 79/2, 7, WRCA.
6. The Walker family owned the Red River Lumber Company.
7. Superintendent C. H. Ashbury to Superintendent Horace Wilson, December 9, 1911, filed in Sus-161, RG 75, NARA, Pacific Region (hereafter simply Sus-161).
8. Wilson to Ashbury, December 13, 1911, filed in Sus-161.
9. C. F. Hauke, second assistant commissioner, BIA, to W. S. Campbell, superintendent, Greenville Indian School, February 18, 1913, filed in Sus-161.
10. A. R. Bidwell, division superintendent, GWP, to W. S. Campbell, superintendent, Greenville Indian School, October 1, 1912, filed in Sus-161.
11. Hauke Campbell, February 18, 1913, filed in Sus-161.
12. Bidwell to Campbell, "Subject: Jenkins Lease Payments," March 6, 1913, filed in Sus-161.
13. Campbell to the commissioner of Indian Affairs, forwarding petitions for sale of land, June 19, 1912, filed in Sus-161.
14. Appraisal for Sus-161 (John Jenkins) by Joseph Murphy, June 6, 1912, filed in Sus-161.
15. E. B. Merritt, assistant commissioner, Office of Indian Affairs, to Charles McChesney, superintendent, Greenville Indian School, April 9, 1915, filed in Sus-161.
16. George Hall was frequently one of two individuals who contributed affidavits corroborating the competency of Indian allottees to conduct their own affairs and have their allotments put into trust status. Given that he was a timber cruiser, it is likely that he would have an interest in the availability of these lands for purchase.
17. McChesney to the commissioner of Indian Affairs, April 4, 1916, filed in Sus-161.
18. Petition for Sale of Inherited Indian Land, Sus-161 (John Jenkins), signed by heirs and witnesses on August 1, 1920, filed in Sus-161.
19. "Report on Cash Sale of Indian Allotment Land When Patent in Fee Is to Be Issued to the Purchaser," approved by the GLO on December 17, 1920, filed in Sus-161.
20. Certificate of Appraisement, Sus-161 (John Jenkins), dated September 1918 and approved by Superintendent Wilson on November 21, 1918, filed in Sus-161.

21. F. G. Collett to Douglas Clark, BIA, Sacramento Area Office, July 1, 1954, filed in Sus-161.

22. Clark to Collett, July 20, 1954, filed in Sus-161.

23. See, for example, Honey Lake Maidu's web page "Ko'domyeponi: The Worldmaker's Journey," http://www.honeylakemaidu.org/photos/maiduFINALlores.pdf; Theodoratus Cultural Research 1986; Dixon 1905; U.S. Forest Service 1994.

24. This is a difficult statistic to ascertain, as private land ownership data (i.e., from a search engine like ParcelQuest, or from county records) does not list race or tribal membership. The 2012 BIA data on trust land ownership by tribes shows that the amount of land held by the two federally recognized tribes in the project focus (Plumas and Lassen Counties) is less than 1,500 acres.

25. Ashbury to the commissioner of Indian Affairs, September 11, 1915, filed in Sac-45, Joseph Taylor, RG75, NARA, Pacific Region.

26. Described as T29N R10E, Sec. 18, E/2 SW/4, SW/4 SE/4, and Sec. 19, NE/4 NW/4.

27. Arthur/Sargent Salem was allotted SUS-197, encompassing the NW/4 of Sec. 29, Township 27N, Range 9E, on April 3, 1894, while Lou was allotted Sus-196, encompassing the N/2 of the of the NE/4, the SE/4 of the NE/4, and the NE/4 of the NW/4 of Sec. 30, Township 27N, Range 9E, on April 3, 1894.

28. Cancellations of public domain allotments are frequently attributed to Commissioner Letter G, or just "G," referring to the Preemption Division (Division G) of the General Land Office (now known as the Bureau of Land Management). According to the guide to federal records in the National Archives and Records Administration (NARA) regarding the records of the BLM, Division G was established in 1867, acquiring responsibility for preemptions from Division "D," Private Land Claims Division, and has been known as the Preemption Division since 1877. Division G "adjudicated and adjusted land grants to states and corporations," "handled preemption claims by entrymen and corporations on the public domain," and "adjudicated contest cases between preemption claimants and corporations." See https://www.archives.gov/research/guide-fed-records/groups/049.html#49.3.8.

29. Ole Salem to the Commissioner of Indian Affairs, December 16, 1921.

30. Salem to the commissioner of Indian Affairs, December 16, 1921.

31. Edgar Miller, U.S. Indian Service, Greenville, California, to the commissioner of Indian Affairs, January 5, 1920, filed in Sus-14, RG 75, NARA.

32. Irvine P. Gardner, cruiser at large, to the commissioner of Indian Affairs, January 12, 1921.

33. As Ole related in his letter of December 16, 1921, "I want to put up some sheds and cow barns where I can put hay and fence a lot of hill land for pasture so my cows will not run away and be stolen by white people who use this Mount Dyer pasture, to run lots of sheep and cattle all summer."

34. Per the Dawes/Allotment Act of February 8, 1887 (24 Stat., 388).

35. Salem to Indian commissioner, December 16, 1921.

36. Hauke to Salem, January 10, 1922.

37. Gardner to Miller, February 15, 1923.

38. Miller to the commissioner of Indian Affairs, February 20, 1923. See also depositions received by the Greenville Indian Agency of February 19, 1923.

39. Acting assistant commissioner of the GLO JMM [illegible], to the commissioner of Indian Affairs Burke, dated November 15, 1923.

40. Hauke to the secretary of the Interior, November 27, 1923.

41. Hauke to William Spry, commissioner of the GLO, August 31, 1925.

42. Application by Ole Salem for a Patent in Fee, under Act of May 8, 1906, 34 Stat., 182, December 28, 1927, signed by Irvine Gardner, notary public, Lassen County.

43. Report on Application for a Patent in Fee to Ole Salem, on Sus-1079, located in the SE/4 of Sec. 27, T28N, R8E, signed by Superintendent Dorrington, n.d.

44. See Transmit Patent from Commissioner Chas Burke, Office of Indian Affairs, to Dorrington, as well as Receipt for Patent on Allotment 1079, signed by Ole Salem, June 1, 1927.

45. Form from the Sacramento Indian Agency, signed by agency superintendent Dorrington, sent to the commissioner of Indian Affairs, approved by the assistant commissioner and assistant secretary, dated March 20, 1928.

46. Dorrington to the commissioner of Indian Affairs, June 16, 1930.

47. Memorandum from Hooper, January 30, 1931.

48. Merritt to Dorrington, July 9, 1924, filed in Sus-1037, RG75, NARA, Pacific Region.

49. Sections 21 and 22 of Township 36N, R 7E.

50. "To enable an Indian allottee to demonstrate his good faith and intention the issuance of trust patent will be suspended for a period of two years from date of settlement."

51. As explained in a May 9, 1921, letter from Assistant Commissioner Bruce (GLO) to the Register and Receiver, Susanville, California, in the file for Ole Salem.

52. See letter from Dorrington to the commissioner of Indian Affairs, September 18, 1925, filed in Sus-1037, RG75, NARA, Pacific Region.

53. As quoted in a June 15, 1928, letter from Dorrington to the commissioner of Indian Affairs.

54. Dorrington to the commissioner of Indian Affairs, September 18, 1925.

55. E. B. Parrott, assistant commissioner, GLO, to Burke, November 3, 1925, filed in Sus-148, RG75, NARA.

56. Ned Bogunda, signed and notarized statement "In Re: Rose Meadows (Salem) land," March 2, 1928, filed in Sus-1037, RG75, NARA, Pacific Region.

57. Dorrington to the commissioner of Indian Affairs, June 15, 1928.

58. The act reads, "All the lands which may hereafter be designated or selected by such US surveys for sites for reservoirs, ditches, or canals for irrigation purposes . . . hereby reserved from sale as the property of the US, and shall not be subject after the passage of this act, to entry, settlement, or occupation until further provided by law." See F. F. Lawrence, C. E. Nordeen, and H. L. Pumphrey 1963.

59. Hauke to Spry, February 6, 1922, filed in Sus-312, RG75, NARA, Washington, D.C.

60. Hauke to the secretary of the Interior, April 23, 1923, filed in Sus-312, RG75, NARA.

NOTES TO PAGES 87-91   209

61. See letter from the superintendent to Eli M. Peazzoni, June 15, 1920, which clarifies that the GLO was responsible for canceling the Bill allotments.

62. Binger Hermann to "Gentlemen," taken from the Susanville Land Office by Gardner, dated November 9, 1901.

63. See letter from Assistant Commissioner G. H. Temple to "Sirs," taken from the Susanville Land Office by Gardner, n.d., and the note made by Gardner from the Susanville Land Office.

64. See letters from Eli Bill, or Eli Piazzoni, to Miller, received April 29, 1918, and July 23, 1915, respectively.

65. Richard Henry Pratt to the commissioner of Indian Affairs, date illegible, possibly 1915.

66. Gardner to Miller, December 11, 1919.

67. Hauke to Miller, January 20, 1920.

68. E. G. Scammon, land department manager, Red River, to Dorrington, May 31, 1926.

69. Dorrington to Scammon, June 1, 1926.

70. Dorrington to the commissioner of Indian Affairs, August 9, 1927.

71. Hauke to Dorrington, September 25, 1927.

72. Dorrington to Peazzoni, September 29, 1927.

73. Memorandum from Mae Hooper, Sacramento Indian Agency, to Superintendent Roy Nash, "Re: Cancellation allotments in Plumas County, later taken into the Plumas National Forest," July 21, 1938.

74. Nash to Piazzoni, July 21, 1938.

75. Letter on behalf of James B. Ring, acting area director (singed by Douglas Clark for Ring), to Rosie L. Walker, June 6, 1950. The letter concludes, "Since there is no suitable land on the public domain at the present time which is available for allotment, we do not have any remedy to suggest."

76. Application for a patent in fee, signed with Jack Mullen's right thumb mark, dated March 27, 1928.

77. Letter from Office of Indian Affairs commissioner Burke and assistant secretary Edwards to Dorrington, April 25, 1928.

78. "Petition for the Sale of Land by Original Allottees," Sus-1044, Mandy Roseberry, filed in Sus-1044, RG75, NARA, Pacific Region.

79. See, for example, Nash to E. C. Bonner, Alturas, January 16, 1939, and the announcement that the agency was taking bids on a list of allotments, February 20, 1929, filed in Sus-1044 RG75, NARA, Pacific Region.

80. Florence S. McClintock, field nurse, BIA, to John D. Rockwell, superintendent, Sacramento Indian Agency, "Re: Mandy Roseberry Baldnegro's and Lucinda Roseberry's allotments," December 20, 1943, filed in Sus-1044, RG75, NARA, Pacific Region.

81. Rockwell to McClintock, December 30, 1943.

82. Mary Roseberry to Rockwell April 17, 1944.

83. Rockwell to Roseberry, April 19, 1944.

84. Petition for the Sale of Inherited Indian Land, Report of the State Director, September 9, 1949, filed in Sus-1044, RG75, NARA, Pacific Region.

85. Receipt for Patent, Allotment Sus-1044, August 11, 1950, issued July 28, 1950.

86. McClintock's role and activities are discussed in Cahill's seminal work on the strategies of intimate colonialism practiced by the BIA, *Federal Fathers and Mothers*.

87. *Cobell v. Salazar*, 573 F.3d 808 (D.C. Cir. 2009).

88. Under the Burke Act, the secretary of the Interior was enabled to take an allotment out of trust without the allottee's approval. Taking the allotment out of trust or issuing a fee patent removed all restrictions on sale and placed the allotment in a taxable status (Burke Act, May 8, 1906, 34 Stat. 182).

89. Hauke to Wilson, February 24, 1916, filed in Sus-1052, RG75, NARA, San Bruno.

90. Wilson to the commissioner of Indian Affairs, March 16, 1916, filed in Sus-1052, RG75, NARA, San Bruno.

91. Little Pete Thomas, Pittville, to Miller, April 2, 1920, filed in Sus-1052, RG75, NARA, Pacific Region.

92. Miller to Thomas, April 7, 1920, filed in Sus-1052, RG75, NARA, Pacific Region.

93. Superintendent O. H. Lipps, Sacramento, to John Anderson, Greenville, dated March 17, 1932, filed in Sus-1052, RG75, NARA, San Bruno.

94. James B. Ring for Walter V. Woehlke, State Director, California Indian Agency, to Walter Mendibourne, September 3, 1948.

95. The land was referred to as "undeveloped" on the Petition for the Sale of Inherited Indian Land, Sus-409, September 9, 1949, and as most adapted for grazing on the Certificate of Appraisement, Sus-409, August 19, 1921. The final sale price is included on a September 8, 1950, memorandum re: Sale of Restricted Indian Land to the commissioner of Indian Affairs from the chief, Branch of Land, BIA. All filed in Sus-409, RG75, NARA, Pacific Region.

96. "Petition for the Sale of Inherited Indian Land," July 1916, filed in Sus-131, RG75, NARA.

97. "Certificate of Appraisement," October 1918, filed in Sus-131, RG75, NARA.

98. C. Rap Garvey, forest assistant, U.S. Indian Service, Roseburg, Oregon, to Charles E. Coe, supervisor, Roseburg School, November 18, 1916, filed in Sus-131, RG75, NARA.

99. "Petition for the Sale of Inherited Indian Land," December 3, 1919, filed in Sus-131, RG75, NARA.

100. Clerk to John McClellan, "In re: complaint of trespass," June 21, 1913, filed in Sus-1051, RG75, NARA, Pacific Region.

101. Clerk to Paul States, Doyle, "Timber tres-pass. Allotment Fred John," August 11, 1913, filed in Sus-1051, RG75, NARA, Pacific Region.

102. Clerk to H. or A. J. Doyen, August 16, 2013, filed in Sus-1051, RG75, NARA, Pacific Region.

103. Geraint Humphreys, general counsel, to Fortier, 1941.

104. Humphreys to E C. Fortier, December 29, 1941.

105. Rockwell to Humphreys, February 2, 1943.

106. Memorandum from the associate engineer E. B. Skiff to the district engineer Fortier, July 28, 1943.

107. Skiff to Fortier, July 28, 1943.

108. Humphreys to Fortier, August 25, 1943.

109. While he agrees with this as a moral stance, the geographer Imre Sutton acknowledges that, following the unratified treaties and the records associated with the Land Claims Act, it is legally very difficult to recognize aboriginal title in California (2000, 136–37).

110. Fortier to Rockwell, July 28, 1943.

CHAPTER 3

1. Following what Pulido and Cotton (2016, 15) have described as the operation of racial capital to facilitate corporate expansion.

2. I draw on W. E. B. DuBois's (1986) idea of double consciousness here, where he refers to the ways in which the person forced to deal with colonial laws, values, and norms always simultaneously sees himself both as the would-be colonizer sees him and as he sees himself. I thought of DuBois through reading Shoemaker 2017, 537.

3. GLO, Susanville, May 21, 1902, filed in Sus-293, RG75, NARA, Pacific Region.

4. Certificate of Appraisement, signed by Irvine Gardner and Edgar Miller, June 17, 1918, filed in Sus-293, RG75, NARA, Pacific Region.

5. C. F. Hauke to Charles Blazey, December 3, 1925, filed in Sus-1008, RG75, NARA, Pacific Region.

6. F. W. Coppersmith to J. J. Fleming, May 8, 1922, filed in Sus-1009, RG75, NARA, Pacific Region.

7. See, for example, the introduction to the Dawes Act, which states: "The President of the United States be, and he hereby is, authorized, whenever in his opinion any reservation or any part thereof of such Indians is advantageous for agricultural and grazing purposes, to cause said reservation, or any part thereof, to be surveyed, or resurveyed if necessary, and to allot the lands." U.S. Statutes at Large, Vol. XXIV, February 8, 1887.

8. Letter from the chief clerk to the secretary of the Interior, through the commissioner of the GLO, November 13, 1919, filed in Sus-1059, RG75, NARA, Pacific Region.

9. Statement by Frank Norman to Gardner, September 15, 1919, filed in Sus-1059, RG75, NARA, Pacific Region.

10. Certificate of Appraisement for the allottee Bob Mack, Sus-35, from Roseburg, Oregon, agency, dated May 15, 1912. The appraiser states, "Land not much value after timber is off."

11. Certificate of Appraisement for Bob Mack, Sus-35, Susanville Series, Roseburg, Oregon, dated November 7, 1915. Appraiser found the land worth $280 and the timber $1,105.

12. Certificate of Appraisement for Bob Mack, Sus-35, Susanville Series, Greenville, dated October 29, 1918.

13. Petition for the Sale of Inherited Indian Land, dated December 3, 1919, signed October 27, 1920.

14. Form of Acceptance of Sale of Land by Allottee or Heir, and Affidavit of Vendor, for the allottee Bob Mack, No. 35, Greenville Agency, dated October 27, 1920.

15. Petition for the Sale of Inherited Indian Land, regarding Sus-45, Hank Wano, signed by Edgar Miller, n.d., National Archives, Pacific Region.

16. Appraisal by Joseph Murphy, dated May 27–28, 1910.

17. Letter from Greenville (presumably from the superintendent of the Indian School, but no signature legible) to L. A. Dorrington, April 15, 1920.

18. Letter, unsigned, but clearly from an Indian Agency employee, to L. A. Dorrington, dated November 16, 1920.

19. Greenville (superintendent) to Dorrington, April 15, 1920.

20. Greenville (superintendent) to Dorrington, April 15, 1920.

21. Indian Agency employee to Dorrington, November 16, 1920.

22. Certificate of Appraisement, Sus-162, Ellen Jenkins, dated September 17–18, 1918, filed in Sus-162, RG 75, NARA, Pacific Region.

23. Report on Cash Sale of Inherited Indian Land, Sus-162, Ellen Jenkins, approved by the Department of the Interior on December 28, 1920, filed in RG75, NARA, Pacific Region.

24. Report on Cash Sale of Allotted Indian Land, Sus-166, Ike Jenkins / Jay Side, approved by the Department of the Interior on June 10, 1922, filed in RG75, NARA, Pacific Region.

25. Certificate of Appraisement, Sus-166, dated May 23, 1921, filed in RG75, NARA, Pacific Region.

26. Allotment 167, Harry Jenkins, estimated by Joseph Murphy, June 14, 1912, and Certificate of Appraisement, Harry Jenkins, allotment 167, Roseburg, Oregon, agency, filed in Sus-167, RG75, NARA, Pacific Region.

27. Certificate of Appraisement, Sus-167, Harry Jenkins, Greenville agency, filed in Sus-167, RG75, NARA, Pacific Region.

28. Report on Cash Sale of Allotted Indian Land When Patent in Fee Is to be Issued to the Purchaser, Harry Jenkins, allotment 167, filed in Sus-167, RG75, NARA, Pacific Region.

29. Petition for the Sale of Land by Original Allottees, submitted June 21, 1912, filed in Sus-33, RG75, NARA.

30. Petition for the Sale of Land by Original Allottees, Report of Superintendent, filed February 1, 1913, filed in Sus-33, RG75, NARA.

31. Cahill (2011) refers to some of the same players, such as the field matron Edith Young, seen in the paperwork regarding the allotments that are the focus of this text.

32. See the letter from the superintendent in Roseburg, Oregon, to the commissioner of Indian Affairs, dated July 1, 1912. George Peconam was allotted this land in 1892 and a trust patent was issued in 1908.

33. W. C. Keegin to the commissioner of Indian Affairs, October 3, 1910.

34. Certificate of Appraisement, signed by Horace G. Wilson, Roseburg, Oregon, dated May 11, 1912.

35. Report of Superintendent, signed by Horace G. Wilson, nod., signed by Second Assistant Commissioner C. F. Hauke on July 18, 1912, and by First Assistant Secretary Lewis Laylin on Sept. 27, 1912.

36. Letter from superintendent in Roseburg, Oregon, to the commissioner of Indian Affairs, July 1, 1912.

37. Letter from Clerk "re: Susanville allotments 278, 34, and 82," to Supervisor Wilson, December 4, 1913.

38. Report on the Cash Sale of Allotted Indian Land When Patent in Fee Is to Be Issued to the Purchaser, signed by Horace G. Wilson on December 29, 1913, and agreed to by Laylin on January 14, 1914.

39. Letter from superintendent in Roseburg, Oregon, to the commissioner of Indian Affairs, December 23, 1914, filed in George Peconam, Sus-34, RG75, NARA.

40. Edith M. Young to Wilson, March 10, 1915.

41. Wilson to Peconam, March 15, 1915.

42. Western Union Telegram from Hauke to Wilson, April 7, 1915.

43. Letter from the director of the Geological Survey to the secretary of the Interior, October 5, 1915, filed in Sus-231, RG75, NARA, Pacific Region.

44. Letter from Clinton L. Walker to Wilson, February 16, 1916. In his indignant reply to the rejection of his bid, Red River's Clinton Walker argued that the land was flat, dry, at least two miles from the flood line of GWP's existing reservoir, and he did "not see how it was possible to consider it as a possible . . . Power Site." Filed in Sus-231, RG75, NARA, Pacific Region. Red River's bids on allotments 233, 234, and 181 were also rejected in the same time period, according to a February 19, 1917, letter from superintendent Charles Coe to Walker (filed in Sus-233). Red River's bid of the appraised value of $1,780 on allotment 233 (Harry Dick) was rejected in 1917 and the land was sold to GWP for $7,709.50 in 1920 (see Report on Cash Sale of Allotted Indian Land, filed in Sus-233, RG 75, NARA, Pacific Region).

45. Petition for the Sale of Inherited Indian Land, Emma Thomas, Sus-181, signed by both Edgar Miller and Irvine Gardner, with the thumbprint of Emma's mother and heir, Cora Roy, dated June 10, 1920, filed in Sus-181, RG75, NARA, Pacific Region.

46. Certificate of Appraisement, Sus-181, Emma Thomas, dated June 19, 1914, filed in Sus-181, RG75, NARA, Pacific Region.

47. Certificate of Appraisement, Sus-181, Emma Thomas, dated November 5, 1915, filed in Sus-181, RG75, NARA, Pacific Region.

48. Hauke to Coe, February 13, 1917, filed in Sus-181, RG75, NARA, Pacific Region.

49. Certificate of Appraisement, Sus-181, Emma Thomas, dated July 23, 1918, filed in Sus-181, RG75, NARA, Pacific Region.

50. Report on Cash Sale of Allotted Indian Land When Patent in Fee Is to Be Issued to the Purchaser, Emma Thomas, Allotment 181, filed in Sus-167, RG75, NARA, Pacific Region.

51. For example, the allotment of Neva Thomas (Sus-184) was appraised by Gardner in 1918 as being worth $4,242 (Certificate of Appraisement, dated July 26, 1918), but the land sold to GWP in 1920 for $6,042, or $50.35/acre (Form of Acceptance of Sale, July 26, 1920; Report on Cash Sale of Allotted Indian Land, August 5, 1920). Similarly, the allotment of Kate Thomas (Sus-185) was appraised by Joseph Murphy in 1912 for $2,000 (Certificate of Appraisement, June 19, 1912) in grazing and timber value, for $2,186.25 by Charles Gardner in 1914 (Certificate of Appraisement, June 13, 1914), and for just $1,265 by Otto F. Swenson in 1914 (Certificate of Appraisement, August 5, 1914), but sold to GWP in 1920 for $8,723.50 (Report on Cash Sale of Allotted Indian Land, August 5, 1920), given that it was within the power site and would become flooded. Filed in Sus-184, RG75, NARA, Pacific Region.

52. Letter from superintendent in Roseburg, Oregon, to the commissioner of Indian Affairs, February 15, 1915.

53. Letter from the acting director of the U.S. Geological Survey to the commissioner of Indian Affairs, July 5, 1912, filed in Sus-170, RG75, NARA, Pacific Region.

54. Wilson to the commissioner of Indian Affairs, July 23, 1912.

55. Across Indian Valley, the allotment of Ridlon/Bert Williams (Sus-203) had also been sold with mineral rights reserved. Descendants of the allottee were still able to gain revenue from the lease of these mineral rights many years later. Walter V. Woehlke, California Indian Agency, to Florence Uptegrove, Department of Social Welfare, Susanville, May 26, 1948, filed in Sus-206, RG75, NARA, Pacific Region.

56. Petition for the Sale of Inherited Indian Land, May 16, 1914, filed in Sus-53, RG75, NARA.

57. Wilson to the commissioner of Indian Affairs, October 7, 1914, filed in Sus-53, RG75, NARA.

58. Red River to Miller, October 19, 1920.

59. Irvine Gardner to Miller, October 20, 1920.

60. Forestry Department to the commissioner of Indian Affairs, October 25, 1920.

61. Petition for the Sale of Land by Original Allottees, Report of Superintendent, approved by the first assistant secretary of the Department of the Interior on October 6, 1913, filed in Sus-228. Similarly, the superintendent noted that nearness to the company's ranch increased the value of Dick McClelland's allotment (Sus-240) "fully 40%," filed in Sus-240. RG75, NARA, Pacific Region.

62. Letter from Clerk A. A. Bear, U. S. Indian Service, Department of the Interior, to Wilson, April 23, 1913, filed in Sus-240.

63. Report on Cash Sale of Allotted Indian Land When Patent in Fee Is to Be Issued to the Purchaser, approved by the first assistant secretary of the Department of the Interior on June 30, 1914, filed in Sus-228, RG75, NARA, Pacific Region.

64. Sus-247, obtained by Jerry Indian for Belle Jerry, was 159.93 acres, and Sus-248, obtained by Jerry Indian for his wife, Emma Jerry, was 159.2 acres.

65. Report of Superintendent, attached to the Petition for the Sale of Land by Original Allottees, April 12, 1913, Sus-240. While the superintendent gave a similar

response to the same question on the petition for sale of Dick's wife Agnes's land in 1913, her land was not sold to the company, and was not sold until 1950, after her death in 1937 (Sus-241).

66. Nash to U.S. Indian Service Forest Supervisor Henry Vance, June 23, 1939.

67. T. E. Connolly to James B. Ring, BIA, Sacramento, August 5, 1950, filed in Sus-249.

68. T. E. Connolly to Bruce S. Peaseley, Appraiser, BIA, Sacramento, August 17, 1957, filed in Sus-249.

69. Douglas Clark, Area Realty Officer, BIA, Sacramento, to Charles Buckskin, regarding fee patent #1174363, which Buckskin had requested in April 1957, filed in Sus-249.

70. Connolly to Acting Area Realty Officer H. Martin Molony, Sacramento Area Office, August 27, 1957, filed in Sus-249.

71. Miller to Walker, Piedmont, July 22, 1919.

72. Walker to Miller, December 10, 1919.

73. Walker to Miller, December 10, 1919.

74. Miller to W. S. Kreigh, October 25, 1920.

75. Gardner to the commissioner of Indian Affairs, March 5, 1920.

76. This is directly contrary to how Red River describes the timberlands of the region in its materials: in 1913 the Walker holdings in California were described as covering 600,000 acres "of the finest Sugar Pine, White Pine, Red Fir and White Fir in the world," and it was predicted that "there is no tract of pine lumber in America that will produce a greater percentage of upper grades of lumber than that owned by the Red River." From the working papers of the biographer Clara Nelson, on file at the Minnesota Historical Society, Box 9, call no. 149.B.12.6F.

77. Miller to the commissioner of Indian Affairs, March 9, 1920.

78. Commissioner Chas Burke to Gardner, c/o Red River Lumber Company, Westwood, August 25, 1922, filed in RG75, NARA, Washington, D.C.

79. Burke to Gardner, c/o Red River Lumber Company, September 25, 1922.

80. Miller to the commissioner of Indian Affairs, August 9, 1922, and August 18, 1922, filed in RG 75, NARA, Washington, D.C.

81. Gardner to Wilson, June 27, 1922, filed in RG 75, NARA, Washington, D.C.

82. Inspector T. B. Roberts and Wilson to Miller, July 21, 1922, filed in RG 75, NARA, Washington, D.C.

83. Miller to Roberts, Klamath Agency, Oregon, "An Answer to I. P. Garner's [sic] Letter to Horace G. Wilson," June 27, 1922, August 3, 1922.

84. This is in keeping with Pulido and Cotton's 2016 analysis of the ways in which racism is harnessed to produce lower values of land and labor, which then contribute to the growth of firms and the state.

85. Miller to Roberts, August 7, 1916.

86. "List of Homes and Automobiles purchased for Greenville Jurisdiction Indians in Period Between July 1, 1920–July 30, 1922." In his "An Answer to I. P. Garner's [sic] Letter to Horace G. Wilson, June 27, 1922," letter, Miller defends his policy of purchasing property for Indian people within his jurisdiction (August 3, 1922).

87. In a October 16, 1922, letter to the commissioner of Indian Affairs, however, Wilson argues that a white landowner received a substantial sum for lands with "far less fall of the river . . . than any Indian did . . . whose lands were sold by Mr. Miller for a much less consideration."

88. Miller to Roberts, August 7, 1916.

89. Miller to Roberts, August 7, 1916.

90. Burke to Miller, August 28, 1922.

91. Wilson to the commissioner of Indian Affairs, October 16, 1922.

92. Letter to Mr. Daiker, no date, no signature, filed with a letter from Mr. Daiker to Doctor Marshalk and Mrs. Rapley, dated September 28, 1922, both stamped as filed by J.M.S.

93. Jason Black (2007) explores the misguided, heavy-handed, and disingenuous paternalism that characterized the allotment period.

94. See Steiner 1982, who does not mention Indian lands specifically, but identifies the largest landowners in California, many of whom were purchasers of Indian allotment lands or lands taken from Indian people when the treaties were not ratified.

95. As Sutton emphasizes, regardless of the determinations of the twentieth-century land claims proceedings, quests for land restoration and access will continue, based on the need to protect cultural places and practices tied to those places and to achieve justice in a context of entrenched injustice (2000, 143).

CHAPTER 4

1. Clara Nelson working papers, Box 149.B.12.6F in the T. B. Walker Collection, Minnesota Historical Society.

2. "Looters of the Domain," in the working papers of Clara Nelson.

3. See, for example, Steiner 1982.

4. W. S. Campbell, Greenville Indian School, to A. A. Bear, U.S. Indian Service, Susanville, filed in Sus-184, RG75, NARA, Pacific Region.

5. Report on Cash Sale of Allotted Indian Land When Patent in Fee Is to Be Issued to the Purchaser, Sus-26, Indian Bob, RG75, NARA, Pacific Region.

6. Report on Cash Sale of Allotted Indian Land When Patent in Fee Is to Be Issued to the Purchaser, Sus-100, Jennie Williams, RG75, NARA, Pacific Region.

7. The company also leased many allotments, but recording duration and extent of allotment leases was beyond the scope of this study.

8. Chas Gardner to Horace Wilson, Roseburg, Oregon, November 1, 1913, RG75, NARA, Pacific Region.

9. Report on Cash Sale of Allotted Indian Land, August 9, 1923, filed in Sus-200, RG75, NARA, Pacific Region.

10. Report on Cash Sale of Allotted Indian Land, May 22, 1923, filed in Sus-200, RG75, NARA, Pacific Region.

11.   Petition for the Sale of Land by Original Allottees, Report of Superintendent, February 11, 1921, filed in Sus-205, RG75, NARA, Pacific Region.

12.   Miller to the commissioner of the Indian Agency, May 18, 1923, filed in Sus-206, RG75, NARA, Pacific Region.

13.   Chief Clerk C. F. Hauke, Office of Indian Affairs, Department of the Interior, to Miller, June 26, 1923, filed in Sus-200, RG75, NARA, Pacific Region.

14.   Miller to commissioner of the Indian Agency, May 18, 1923, filed in Sus-206, RG75, NARA, Pacific Region.

15.   Miller to commissioner of the Indian Agency, June 8, 1923, filed in Sus-206, RG75, NARA, Pacific Region.

16.   For more information on the family and their involvement with the *weda*, see Tolley 2007.

17.   Certificate of Appraisement of Allotment Sus-6 (John Peconam), appraisal by Irvine Gardner on October 7–8, 1918, signed by Superintendent Edgar Miller on November 21, 1918.

18.   Petition for the Sale of Inherited Indian Land, December 3, 1919.

19.   Report on Cash Sale of Allotted Indian Land When Patent in Fee is to Be Issued to the Purchaser, Susanville Series, signed December 20, 1920.

20.   See, for example, the Form of Acceptance of Sale of Land by Allottee or Heir, and Affidavit of Vendor, signed by heir Edith Peconam and duplicate documents signed by Inez Peconam and affixed with Roxy Peconam's and George Peconam's thumbprints, all dated June 24, 1920.

21.   Superintendent to the commissioner of Indian Affairs, July 14, 1920.

22.   See Report on Cash Sale, December 20, 1920, as well as Receipt for Patent, issued January 28, 1921.

23.   Letter from Red River representative [signature not legible] to Wilson, August 31, 1914.

24.   Following an appraisement of damages by Irvine Gardner, a report containing this information was sent to the commissioner of Indian Affairs on November 17, 1920.

25.   Miller to Gardner, March 3, 1922.

26.   Gardner, cruiser at large on furlough, to Miller, March 7, 1922.

27.   Roxy Peconam to Miller, December 5, 1922.

28.   Miller to Peconam, December 8, 1922.

29.   Miller to Frank Carroll, February 7, 1923.

30.   F. G. Collett, Executive Representative of the Indians of California, Inc., to Douglas Clark, real property officer, BIA, Sacramento Area, August 23, 1954.

31.   Clark to Collett, August 26, 1954.

32.   Collett to Clark, August 10, 1955.

33.   "Great Western Power Company of California" (advertisement), June 20, 1924, filed in Erwin Cooper Papers, Box 12, MS 79/2, 7, WRCA.

34.   "Great Western System, Electric Department: Income and Rate of Return Based on Rates Now in Effect Historical Cost Rate Base," Table 1, in "Great Western Power System: Income-Rate Base-Rate of Return for Great Western Power Com-

pany of California, California Electric Generating Company, Napa Valley Electric Company, Feather River Power Company, 1929." J. S. Moulton, January 1930, filed in Erwin Cooper Papers, WRCA.

35. "Great Western Power Company of California," (advertisement), June 20, 1924.

36. "Water Rights: PG&E Company, by Substitution Method," filed in MS 79/2, 28, WRCA.

37. As clarified on April 24, 1930, GWP owned 96.5 percent of the reservoir, and the U.S. government owned 3.5 percent. Memorandum re: testimony on value, April 24, 1930, filed in MS 79/2, 8, WRCA.

38. Memorandum re: testimony on value, April 24, 1930, filed in MS 79/2, 8, WRCA.

39. Memorandum re: testimony on value, April 17, 1930, filed in MS 79/2, 8, WRCA.

40. See, for example, the files for Sus-233 and Sus-234. In particular, see memorandum from Acting Assistant Commissioner John McPhaul, GLO, Department of the Interior, December 28, 1920, filed in Sus-234, and the letter from Hauke to Wilson, July 9, 1915, filed in Sus-233.

41. Memorandum from John McPhaul, December 28, 1920, filed in Sus-231, RG75, NARA, Pacific Region.

42. Report on Cash Sale of Allotted Indian Land When Patent in Fee Is to Be Issued to the Purchaser, approved by the assistant secretary of the Interior on December 30, 1920, filed in Sus-231, RG75, NARA, Pacific Region.

43. Letter from the acting director of the Geological Survey to the commissioner of Indian Affairs, July 5, 1912, filed in Sus-233, RG75, NARA, Pacific Region.

44. Under Sec. 15 of regulations approved June 23, 1911, for the sale of timber from Indian allotments.

45. Wilson to the commissioner of Indian Affairs, July 29, 1912, filed in Sus-233, RG75, NARA, Pacific Region.

46. Letter from the director of the Geological Survey to the secretary of the Interior, October 5, 1914, filed in Sus-231, RG75, NARA, Pacific Region.

47. Letter from Hauke to Wilson, July 9, 1915, filed in Sus-233, RG 75, NARA, Pacific Region.

48. Bear to Wilson, March 24, 1913, filed in Sus-420, RG75, NARA, Pacific Region.

49. Letter from F. M. Goodwin, assistant secretary, Department of the Interior, to the commissioner of the GLO, January 20, 1922, filed in Sus-420, RG75, NARA, Pacific Region.

50. This fact presages the class-action lawsuit *Cobell v. Salazar* (previously *Cobell v. Kempthorne* and *Cobell v. Norton* and *Cobell v. Babbitt*) regarding the mismanagement of Individual Indian Monetary Accounts. The suit was initially brought by lead plaintiff Eloise Cobell (Blackfeet) in 1996 and settled for $3.4 billion in 2009.

51. Goodwin to the commissioner of the GLO, January 20, 1922, filed in Sus-420, RG75, NARA, Pacific Region.

52. Campbell to Bear, October 13, 1913, filed in Sus-184, RG75, NARA, Pacific Region.

53. See letter from Harrison Lee to John Rockwell, April 9, 1946, and the response from Rockwell to Lee, April 17, 1946, filed in Sus-456, RG75, NARA, Pacific Region.

54. Lucas C. Neal, land and lease clerk, Greenville Indian Agency, to Amador Thrasher, April 25, 1923, filed in Sus-463, RG75, NARA, Pacific Region.

55. Petition for the Sale of Land by Original Allottees, Sus-457, RG75, NARA, Pacific Region.

56. Letter from Superintendent Roy Nash, Sacramento Indian Agency, to Levi Tom, October 3, 1938, filed in Sus-160, Ike Tom, RG75, NARA, Pacific Region.

57. Britton Clair, Area Realty Office, Sacramento Area Office, to Levi Tom, March 31, 1961, filed in Sus-160, RG75, NARA, Pacific Region.

58. In response to Levi Tom's November 16, 1949, letter, in which he asks about Indians "getting land back" through a "settlement," Area Director James Stewart mentions that the "claims case of the California Indians" has received an appropriation of $5,000,000, but has yet to be distributed, and "there is no legislation existing or pending which would permit the purchase of additional lands for the California Indians." J. M. Stewart, Area Director, California Indian Agency, Sacramento, to Levi Tom, Greenville, December 20, 1949, filed in Sus-160, RG75, NARA, Pacific Region.

59. Letter from John Galloway to James Black, general manager, GWP, March 9, 1925.

60. Galloway to Emory Wishon, vice president and general manager, GWP, April 20, 1928. Galloway reiterated some of these concerns and gave a history of the design and building of the dam, including his critique of Howell's plans and departure from the company in 1925 (only to be reemployed to work on the Bucks Creek Project) in a September 3, 1930, letter to PG&E vice president of engineering A. H. Markwart. Galloway and Markwart had previously worked together to produce a 1920 report estimating the cost to complete GWP's Caribou Plant.

61. W. G. B. Euler to Wishon, December 12, 1929.

62. Galloway to Euler, November 8, 1929.

63. Estimated Present Value of Lands and Rights-of-Way: Great Western Power Company of California, California Electric Generating Company, April 1930, filed in MS 79/2, 8, WRCA.

64. Cost of Hydro Power—Feather River, filed in MS 79/2, 8, WRCA.

65. The PG&E Contract, December 1943, pp. 87–88 filed in Malca Chall Research Collection, Issue 62, call no. MS 2001/1.

66. Rockwell to the commissioner of Indian Affairs, October 22, 1946, filed with Jack Mullen, Sus-41, at the NARA—Pacific Region, San Bruno.

67. L. A. Barrett, Forest Supervisor, Plumas National Forest, Forest Service, "Indians on National Forest Reserves in California," Quincy, March 2, 1909, FS files, NARA, Pacific Region.

68. Walter C. Robinson, Forest Ranger, District 7, Plumas National Forest, Forest Service, "Plumas Settlements—Indian Allotments," Meadow Valley, December 28, 1912, FS files, NARA, Pacific Region.

69. All in T22N and R5E or R7E.

70. Letter from Campbell Barrett, January 29, 1913, lists James Edwards, Pete Edwards, John Kennedy, Joe Taylor, Fannie Hall, Ed Wagner, Oscar Johnson, and French Billy, the latter two individuals living on the same parcel. This is followed by a response from Barrett to Campbell, January 31, 1913, FS files, NARA, Pacific Region.

71. Those allotments approved in 1918 were for James Edwards, Peter Edwards, Fannie Hall, Joseph Taylor, Ed Wagner, and Henry Flynn. The allotment surveyed and approved in 1924 was for Jim Lee, and located at some distance from the others (in T25N, R6E), see letter from John Plover, U.S. Surveyor General for California, to the District Forester, Ferry Building, San Francisco, "Indian Allotment Survey #274, Plumas National Forest, in unsurveyed T25N R6E M.D.M.," March 19,1924. The allotment approved in 1933 (after being "overlooked in the files of the General Land Office since 1916," according to Chief of Status J. E. B. [initials only given] in 1920) was for Harry Edwards. See Form 301B, FS files, NARA, Pacific Region.

72. Barrett, "Settlement—Plumas: Indian Allotments," August 12, 1920, FS files, NARA, Pacific Region.

73. Letter from C. H. Squire [?](illegible), acting assistant forester, Forest Service, to district forester, San Francisco, "Settlement—Plumas: Indian Allotments," August 26, 1920.

74. D. E. Everett, leader, Landownership Adjustment Group, Forest Service, to the state director, Bureau of Land Management, Sacramento, December 7, 1976, and a similar letter of December 14, 1976, requesting information on the Jim Lee allotment. The BLM responded to the first letter with copies of the patents enclosed on December 9, 1976 (see letter of that date from Heidi Faymire, California State Office, BLM, Sacramento, to Russell Rogers, Lands and Minerals Staff, United States Forest Service, San Francisco).

75. Assistant Commissioner Proudfit, GLO, to forester, Forest Service, "re: Reinstatement of Indian allotment within the forest reserve," November 5, 1910.

76. Proudfit to forester, November 5, 1910.

77. Assistant Forest Ranger E. V. Clark to forest supervisor, Quincy, November 30, 1910.

78. Lamore Jim, Imogene Stonecoal Sus-75, Eloise Stonecoal Sus-76, Ruby George Sus-174, Lucile Bill Stonecoal Sus-271, Barbara Stonecoal Sus-272, Esther Bill Stonecoal Sus-131, and Jimmie George Sus-117.

79. Miller to the commissioner of Indian Affairs, March 8 1922, filed in Sus-1009, RG75, NARA, Pacific Region.

80. Miller to the commissioner of Indian Affairs, March 8, 1922.

81. Gardner to Miller, n.d., filed in Sus-1009, RG75, NARA, Pacific Region.

82. Belonging to Wilson Harrow (Sus-76), Sam Johnson for Cap. Nelson Johnson (Sus-228), Dick McClelland (Sus-240), Jerry Indian for Belle Jerry (Sus-247), and Jerry Indian for Emma Jerry (Sus-248).

83. Report on Cash Sale of Allotted Indian Land, filed in Sus-247, RG 75, NARA, Pacific Region.
84. Letter from Superintendent L. A. Dorrington to the commissioner of Indian Affairs, January 24, 1928, filed in Sus-247, RG 75, NARA, Pacific Region.
85. Florence S. McClintock, field nurse, Field Service, Office of Indian Affairs, to Nash, June 23, 1937, filed in Sus-437, Allie Bayley, RG75, NARA.
86. Nash to Victor Christensen, ranch manager, H. C. Cattle Company, Likely, January 4, 1940.
87. For information on Rosa Jim, see letter from James B. Ring, Area Director, Sacramento Area Office, to Mrs. Mae P. Carmony, Likely, January 15, 1952. Ostensibly, proceeds from the lease were deposited in the Individual Indian Monetary accounts of her heirs.
88. Nash to Frank Carroll, Susanville, April 10, 1936.
89. Flora George to Nash, February 18, 1940.
90. Letter from John Rockwell, field representative in charge, Sacramento Indian Agency, to Flora George Wilson, Hat Creek, July 15, 1941.
91. Rockwell to Flora George Wilson, Hat Creek, February 5, 1942. Both the Rosa Jim (Sus-765) and Mary Reavis (Sus-711) allotments sold at a BIA land sale in May 1951, for $976 each, although they had both been appraised at $1,200 when they were put up for sale 30 years earlier in 1923.
92. Nash to Albert Metcalf, Termo, June 21, 1938.
93. C. B. Christensen, H. C. Cattle Company, Likely, to Ring, May 21, 1950.
94. Letter from F. O. Hagie, secretary-manager, National Reclamation Association, March 21, 1938.

CHAPTER 5

1. This may be changing as the California Environmental Quality Act was modified by AB-52 (Gatto 2014) to establish the category of Traditional Cultural Resource and what impacts to such a resource constitute a significant effect on the environment.
2. Previous struggles included participation in the analysis of the proposed Indian Creek Hydroelectric Project. Maidu effectively stopped the project by refusing to share cultural information necessary for the impact analysis and mitigation planning required by the FERC. According to Theodoratus Cultural Research, it was summertime when the studies were conducted and the information was needed but, according to Maidu tradition, stories are told only in the wintertime (1986, 73).
3. 16 USC §803(a)(1).
4. This project is referred to in the Upper North Fork Feather River Final Environmental Impact Statement as "the unlicensed Hamilton Branch project" (FERC 2005, 2.1.1.3).

5.   The primary reasons given for the addition of land are to continue slope stabilization and maintenance around the Caribou No. 1 and 2 penstocks and to increase access to project facilities along the road that runs from Caribou to Butt Valley. FERC 2005, 3.3.6.2, sec. 3, p. 275.

6.   Many of these places are now inundated by the reservoirs, and measures for their protection include relocation if they are ever exposed. See FERC 2005, sec. 3, pp. 299–304.

7.   For example, a December 15, 1922, letter from Greenville Agency superintendent Edgar Miller to an allottee details the types of requests she can make for the use of funds in her account: "This money can now be used by you for legitimate and proper purposes, such as subsistence supplies, medical attention, clothing, etc., as provided by Indian Office Rules and Regulations." Filed in Sus-109, Minnie Jackson (Ives), RG75, NARA, Pacific Region.

8.   The possible beneficial uses of water are municipal and domestic supply, agricultural supply, industrial service supply, industrial process supply, groundwater recharge, freshwater replenishment, navigation, hydropower generation, water contact recreation, noncontact water recreation, commercial and sport fishing, aquaculture, warm freshwater habitat, cold freshwater habitat, estuarine habitat, wildlife habitat, preservation of biological habitats of special significance (for rare threatened or endangered Species), migration of aquatic organisms (for spawning, reproduction, and/or early development), and shellfish harvesting. California Regional Water Quality Control Board, Central Valley Region, 2016.

9.   See SWRCB 2014, 1-1; State Water Board Resolution No. 2006-0079; California Regional Water Quality Control Board, Central Valley Region, 2016.

10. See, for example, Susanville Rancheria Resolution #SU-BC-23-2004, "Re: Opposition for Installation of Thermal Curtin at Lake Almanor," recorded by FERC, October 7, 2004.

11. Letter from Farrell Cunningham, coordinator for the MCDG, to Randall Livingston, PG&E, and Magalie R. Salas, secretary, FERC, November 27, 2002.

12. Cunningham to Livingston and Salas, November 27, 2002.

13. Cunningham to Livingston and Salas, November 27, 2002.

14. Programmatic Agreement Among the FERC and the CA-SHPO for Managing Historic Properties That May Be Affected by License Issuing to PG&E for the Continued Operation of the Upper North Fork Feather River Hydroelectric Project in Plumas County, California (FERC Project No. 2105-089), August 11, 2005.

15. Cunningham 2002, 5. See also letter from Rogers with the MCDG motion to intervene March 12, 2003, and letter from Leah Wills for Cunningham to Salas, June 20, 2003.

16. See letter from Alison MacDougall, cultural resources specialist, PG&E, to Salas, January 16, 2003, outlining PG&E's responsibilities regarding cultural resource documentation in the FERC relicensing process and progress toward meeting those responsibilities.

17. In an October 13, 2004, letter to the FERC Tribal Liaison, Greenville Rancheria chairperson Lorie Jaimes reiterated a request that the area of potential effect of the hydroelectric project be extended two miles outside of the current FERC boundaries, to which the company replied that these lands were outside of their control and that it was not clear that impacts of the project were directly affecting those areas. "Response to GR Comment 24," in the Upper North Fork Feather Relicensing Project Licensee Responses to Comments on Section E-4 (Historical and Archaeological Resources), recorded by FERC, December 23, 2002.

18. Greenville Rancheria requests in letter from Richard Thompson, tribal administrator, Greenville Rancheria, to Macdougall, September 13, 2002, and PG&E responses in Upper North Fork Feather Relicensing Project, recorded by FERC, December 23, 2002.

19. PG&E responses in the Upper North Fork Feather Relicensing Project, recorded by FERC, December 23, 2002.

20. Gorbet to Salas, "Re: In the matter of relicensing of the Upper North Fork Feather River Project 2105. Request to the FERC to analyze and address the following impacts to the Maidu Indians in the 2105 Environmental Impact Statement," November 24, 2003.

21. As the MCDG's letter continues, "The endurance of Maidu culture in the face of extreme adversity is also documented." Gorbet to Salas, November 24, 2003, 3. Similarly, a December 19, 2005, letter from Susanville Rancheria's tribal chairman Stacy Dixon to FERC calls the filling of Lake Almanor "catastrophic" for the Mountain Maidu, and describes Almanor, Butt Valley, and Mountain Meadows reservoirs as "drown[ing] a significant portion of the Mountain Maidu tribes' culture and history."

22. PG&E Upper North Fork Feather River Project, FERC No. 2105, Reply Comments, in response to MCDG November 24, 2003, comments, January 15, 2004.

23. As Gorbet argues, "Since the condemned Indian allotment lands still belong to 'USA' or 'USA Withdrawn' and not to PG&E and they are former Indian allotment lands still under government control we would like to see some type of just compensation to the Maidu Indian community for these formerly Maidu lands, now public domain lands, being used exclusively by PG&E." Gorbet to Salas, November 24, 2003, 8.

24. Gorbet to Salas, November 24, 2003, 7–10.

25. PG&E Reply Comments 2004, emphasis in original.

26. From 2004, when the first council meeting was held in Chester, to 2013, when the council recommended the transfer of PG&E lands in Humbug Valley to the Maidu Summit.

27. See CPUC Decision 03-12-035, 2003.

28. Heidi Krolick, electronic communication with the author, December 4, 2012.

29. Codding and Goode 2011; Scheck 2011; Little 2011a and b; Middleton 2010.

30. Public Utilities Commission of the State of California (December 18, 2003), Decision 03-12-035, "Opinion Modifying the Proposed Settlement Agreement of

Pacific Gas & Electric Company, PG&E Corporation and the Commission Staff, and Approving the Modified Settlement Agreement."

31. For a description of this action, see Middleton 2008.

32. Comments on the manuscript provided by Jessica Daugherty, director of land conservation, Pacific Forest and Watershed Lands Stewardship Council, August 7, 2017.

33. For some discussion of this, see Middleton 2013.

34. Stewardship Council, Summary of Fee Title Donee Recommendations, June 15, 2016, augmented by updated acreages provided by Jessica Daugherty, director of land conservation, and Lauren Faccinto, project manager, Pacific Forest and Watershed Lands Stewardship Council, August 4, 2017.

35. See Stewardship Council, Summary of Fee Title Donee Recommendations, June 5, 2016. The BLM was poised to receive 6,964 acres, but, as of June 2016, all BLM recommendations had been rescinded due to concerns regarding the Federal Power Act, Section 4E conditions.

36. See Sus-1051, RG 75, NARA, San Bruno.

37. The 13 recommended easement holders are Bear Yuba Land Trust (11,903 acres), Feather River Land Trust (35,744 acres), California Dept. of Fish and Wildlife (2,325 acres), Ducks Unlimited (7,940 acres, an additional 9,277 acres of easements were recommended, but the organization withdrew), Mendocino Land Trust (6,432 acres), Mother Lode Land Trust (7,111 acres), Northern California Regional Land Trust (11,756 acres), Pacific Forest Trust (15,029 acres recommended, but organization withdrew), Placer Land Trust (6,620 acres), Sequoia Riverlands Trust (696 acres), Shasta Land Trust (32,607 acres), Sierra Foothill Conservancy (3,559 acres), and Western Shasta RCD (4,849 acres).

38. Gorbet to Salas, November 24, 2003.

CONCLUSION

1. These include the Amah Mutsun Land Trust, the InterTribal Sinkyone Wilderness Council, the Native Land Trust, the Kumeyaay Diegueno Land Conservancy, the Native American Land Conservancy, the Sogorea Te Land Trust, and the Native Land Conservancy. I wrote about some of these organizations and their pathbreaking work in *Trust in the Land* (University of Arizona Press, 2011).

WORKS CITED

Anderson, Karen Lahaie. 2015. *Mountain Maidu Dictionary*. Self-published.

Anderson, M. Kat. 2005. *Tending the Wild: Native American Knowledge and the Management of California's Natural Resources*. Berkeley: University of California Press.

Baker, C. L. and T. Bakic. 2001. "National Register of Historic Places Evaluation, Upper North Fork Feather River Hydroelectric System, FERC 2105, Plumas County, California." Prepared for PG&E, PAR Environmental Services, Sacramento, California.

Banks, Harvey O. 1956. Filed in Erwin Cooper papers, Box 12, MS 76/10, WRCA.

———. 1960. "A Year of Progress and Decision." Presentation given at the Association of Western State Engineers.

Barboza, Tony. 2013. "San Joaquin Valley Officials Fight with EPA over Air Quality." *Los Angeles Times*, December 22, 2013.

———. 2014. "L.A., Central Valley Have Worst Air Quality, American Lung Assn. Says." *Los Angeles Times*, April 29, 2014.

Bell, Derrick. 1992. *Faces at the Bottom of the Well: The Permanence of Racism*. New York: Basic Books.

Black, Jason Edward. 2007. "Rememberances of Removal: Native Resistance to Allotment and the Unmasking of Paternal Benevolence." *Southern Communication Journal* 72 (2): 185–203.

Bobroff, Kenneth H. 2001. "Retelling Allotment: Indian Property Rights and the Myth of Common Ownership." *Vanderbilt Law Review* 54 (4): 1559–626.

Bonner, John F. 1959. "Teamwork in Water Work." Paper presented at the Section on Water Problems, Commonwealth Club of California.

Brosius, Peter, Anna L. Tsing, and Charles Zerner, eds. 2005. *Communities and Conservation: Histories and Politics of Community-Based Natural Resource Management*. Walnut Creek, Calif.: AltaMira Press.

Brown, Edmund G. 1960. "California Water Program Bond Issue." Transcript of NBC broadcast. Filed in Cooper MS 76/10, Box 8, WRCA.

Cahill, Catherine. 2011. *Federal Fathers and Mothers: A Social History of the United States Indian Service, 1869–1933.* Chapel Hill: University of North Carolina Press.

California Department of Water Resources. 1959a. "Summary Statement on the Water Problems of California and Current Programs for their Solution." Delivered to the Senate Select Committee on National Water Resources on November 19, 1959. Filed in Cooper MS 76/10, Box 8, WRCA.

———. 1959b. "Highlights of the California Water Plan." Filed in Cooper MS 76/10, Box 8, WRCA.

———. 2016a. "California State Water Project Overview." https://www.water.ca.gov/Programs/State-Water-Project.

———. 2016b. "California State Water Project Today." http://www.water.ca.gov/swp/swptoday.cfm.

California Regional Water Quality Control Board, Central Valley Region. 2016. *Water Quality Control Plan (Basin Plan) for the CA Regional Water Quality Control Board, Central Valley Region.* 4th ed. Sacramento River Basin and San Joaquin River Basin.

Carpenter, Kristen A. 2006. "Contextualizing the Losses of Allotment Through Literature." *North Dakota Law Review* 82 (3): 605–26.

Chairman of the Board and N. R. Sutherland (president). 1958. "To Our Stockholders: Report of the Directors of Pacific Gas and Electric Company." In PG&E Annual Report 1958.

Champagne, Duane. 2016. "UNDRIP and Plurinationalism Can Accommodate Indigenous Political Needs." *Indian Country Today*, August 7, 2016.

Chang, David. 2011. "Enclosures of Land and Sovereignty: The Allotment of American Indian Lands." *Radical History Review* 109:108–19.

Chronicle Washington Bureau. 1981. "Another Try for Water Law Reform." November 6, 1981. Filed in Theodore C. Wellman papers, Box 4, Issue 110, call no. MS87/2, WRCA.

Codding, Ryan F., and Ron W. Goode. 2011. "California Indians Could Regain Ancestral Lands." *San Francisco Chronicle*, November 27, 2011.

Colby, Bonnie G., John E. Thorson, and Sarah Britton. 2005. *Negotiating Tribal Water Rights: Fulfilling Promises in the Arid West.* Tucson: University of Arizona Press.

Cole, Luke, and Shelia Foster. 2001. *From the Ground Up: Environmental Racism and the Rise of the Environmental Justice Movement.* New York: New York University Press.

Coleman, Charles M. 1952. *PG&E of California: The Centennial Story of Pacific Gas and Electric Company, 1852–1952.* New York: McGraw-Hill.

Committee on Irrigation of Arid Lands. 1901. "Reclamation of Arid Lands: Report to Accompany H.R. 14241." Fifty-Sixth Congress, 2nd session, Report No. 2927.

Daines, Nolan H. 1979. "Impact of Anticipated Electric Energy Shortage on the State's Economic Growth." PG&E Report No. 8. Filed in Theodore C. Wellman Papers, Box 4, Issue nos. 110, 112, 119, call no. MS87/2, WRCA.

Darling, Arthur B., ed. 1937. *The Public Papers of Francis G. Newlands.* Vol. 1. Washington, D.C.: W. F. Roberts.

Department of the Interior, General Land Office. 1901. "Construction of Reservoirs, etc.: Report to accompany S. 5833." Fifty-Sixth Congress, 2nd Session, Report No. 2308.

Department of the Interior, Office of Indian Affairs. N.d. "Indian Lands for Sale Under Government Supervision."

Department of Water Resources. 1959. "Before the CA Water Commission—Statement of DWR Concerning the Assignment of Applications Nos. 5629, 5630, 14443, 14444 and 14445—December 4, 1959."

Director of Water Resources Special Study Group. 1959. "Policy Recommended for Adoption to Implement the State Water Resources Development System." Filed in B. Abbott Goldberg papers, MS 85/2, Box 3, Folder 10.

Division of Water Resources. 1931. Bulletin No. 25: Report to the State Legislature.

Division of Water Resources Staff. 1955. California Department of Public Works, for the Assembly, California Legislature. "Water Problems of California and Plans for Their Solution." April 28–30, 1955. Filed in Cooper MS 76/10, Box 8, WRCA.

Dixon, Roland. 1905. *The Northern Maidu*. New York: American Museum of Natural History.

DuBois, W. E. B. 1986. *The Souls of Black Folk*. Library Classics of the United States. New York: Viking.

Echo-Hawk, Walter R. 2010. *In the Courts of the Conqueror*. Golden, Colo.: Fulcrum.

———. 2013. *In the Light of Justice*. Golden, Colo.: Fulcrum.

Ellison, William H. 1913. "The Federal Indian Policy in California: 1846–1860." Thesis, University of California.

FERC (Federal Energy Regulatory Commission). 2005. *Final Environmental Impact Statement*.

———. 2014. *Strategic Plan, 2014–2018*. https://www.ferc.gov/about/strat-docs/FY-2014 -FY-2018-strat-plan.pdf. Flushman, Bruce S., and Joe Barbieri. 1986. "Aboriginal Title: The Special Case of California." *Pacific Law Journal* 17 (2): 391–460.

Frank, Geyla, and Carole Goldberg. 2010. *Defying the Odds*. New Haven: Yale University Press.

Garrett, Bradley L. 2009. "Drowned Memories: The Submerged Places of the Winnemem Wintu." *Archaeologies* 6 (2): 346–71.

Gaworecki, Mike. 2016. "IUCN to Create New Category of Membership for Indigenous Peoples' Organizations." *Mongabay*, September 13, 2016. https://news.mongabay .com/2016/09/iucn-to-create-new-category-of-membership-for-indigenous-peoples -organizations/.

Gilmer, Robert. 2013. "Snail Darters and Sacred Places: Creative Application of the Endangered Species Act." *Environmental Management* 52 (5): 1046–56.

Goldberg, B. Abbot. 1964. "Statement in Opposition to AJR 2 and S. 1275." Paper presented at the California Senate Committee on Water.

Goldberg, Carole, and Duane Champagne. 1996. "Status and Needs of Unrecognized and Terminated California Indian Tribes." In *A Second Century of Dishonor: Federal Inequities and California Tribes*. Report prepared by the UCLA Native American

Studies Center for the Advisory Council on California Indian Policy (Community Service / Governance / Census Task Force Report).

Gould, Janice. 1990. "History Lesson." In *Beneath My Heart: Poetry by Janice Gould*. Ithaca, N.Y.: Firebrand Books.

GWP (Great Western Power Company). 1930. *Estimated Present Value of Lands and Rights-of-Way*.

GreenInfo Network. 2015. California Conservation Easement Database: California Conservation Easements Summary, April 2015.

———. 2016. California Protected Areas Database: CPAD Statistics, June 2016.

Gunter, Dan. 1998. "The Technology of Tribalism: The Lemhi Indians, Federal Recognition, and the Creation of Tribal Identity." *Idaho Law Review* 35 (1): 85–123.

Hanft, Robert M. 1980. *Red River: Paul Bunyan's Own Lumber Company and Its Railroads*. Lassen County Historical Society.

Harden, Blaine. 1996. *A River Lost: The Life and Death of the Columbia*. New York: W. W. Norton.

Heizer, Robert F. 1993. *The Destruction of California Indians*. Lincoln: University of Nebraska Press.

Hesselman, George J., ed., 1914. *Decisions of the Department of the Interior in Cases Related to the Public Lands*. Vol. 42: March 17–December 31, 1913, Washington, D.C.

Hoopes, Chad E. 1975. *Domesticate or Exterminate*. N.p.: Redwood Coast.

Houston, Will. 2017. "Klamath River Dam Removal Plan on Track as Administration Shifts." *Eureka Times Standard*, February 28, 2017.

Howard, Brian Clark. 2016. "River Revives After Largest Dam Removal in U.S. History." *National Geographic*, June 2, 2016.

Hundley, Norris, Jr. 1978. "The Dark and Bloody Ground of Indian Water Rights." *Western Historical Quarterly* 9 (4): 454–82.

Indian Law Resource Center. 2012. *United Nations Declaration on the Rights of Indigenous Peoples*. http://indianlaw.org/sites/default/files/Declarations_Booklet_2012 _LRSpreads.pdf.

International Indian Treaty Council. N.d. "IITC: A Voice for Indigenous Peoples." http://www.iitc.org/about-iitc/.

Jack, Sim Hay Kin. 2016. "Fallout: Repercussions of the Dam Raise." Paper presented for the class Indigenous Ecological Law and Policy.

Jacoby, Karl 2003. *Crimes Against Nature*. Berkeley: University of California Press.

Johnston-Dodds, Kimberly. 2002. *Early Laws and Policies Related to California Indians*. Sacramento: California Research Bureau, California State Library.

Kelley, Klara, and Harris Francis. 2001. "Indian Giving: Allotments on the Arizona Navajo Railroad Frontier, 1904–1937." *American Indian Culture and Research Journal* 25 (2): 63–91.

KFYR TV. 2016. "Standing Rock Sioux Tribe Releases Statement Addressing Escalation at DAPL Protest Site." http://www.kfyrtv.com/content/news/Standing-Rock-Sioux -Tribe-responds-to-law-enforcement-escalation-at-DAPL-protest-site-398966791 .html.

Kurtz, Patricia. 2010. *Mountain Maidu and Pioneers: A History of Indian Valley, Plumas County, California, 1850–1920.* Bloomington, Ind.: iUniverse.

Lawrence, F. F., C. E. Nordeen, and H. L. Pumphrey. 1963. *History of Land Classification Related to Waterpower and Storage Sites.* USGS Survey Circular 400. Rev. ed.

Lawson, Michael. 2009. *Dammed Indians Revisited: The Continuing History of the Pick-Sloan Plan and the Missouri River Sioux.* Pierre: South Dakota Historical Society Press.

Lind, Neeta. 2016. "News Timeline of Standing Rock Water Protectors' Resistance to Dakota Access Pipeline." *dailykos,* October 11, 2016.

Lindsay, Brendan. 2012. *Murder State: California's Native American Genocide, 1846–1873.* Lincoln: University of Nebraska Press.

Little, Jane Braxton. 2011a. "Maidu Group Vies with State to Oversee Humbug Valley." *Sacramento Bee,* April 18, 2011.

———. 2011b. "California Tribe Competes with the State to Restore Its Homeland." *High Country News,* September 22, 2011.

———. 2014. "The Humbug Partnership." *Boom.* https://static1.squarespace.com/static/5693c8c42598idaa9801282f/t/56a67eb2bfe873441ae66359/1453751986824/Boom-MagazineThe-Humbug-Partnership-%C2%BB-Boom-Magazine1.pdf.

London, Jonathan K., and Ganlin Huang. 2012. "Cumulative Environmental Vulnerability and Environmental Justice in California's San Joaquin Valley." *International Journal of Environmental Research and Public Health* 9:1583–608.

Long, Jonathan W., et al. 2016. *Restoring California Black Oak Ecosystems to Promote Tribal Values and Wildlife.* USDA Forest Service, PSW Research Station, General Technical Report 252.

Lopez, Valentin. 2013. "The Amah Mutsun Tribal Band: Reflections on Collaborative Archaeology." *California Archaeology* 5 (2): 221–23.

Meyer, Manulani Aluli. 2008. "Indigenous and Authentic: Hawaiian Epistemology and the Triangulation of Meaning." In *Handbook of Critical and Indigenous Methodologies,* edited by Norman K. Denzin, Yvonna S. Lincoln, Linda Tuhiwai Smith. Los Angeles: Sage.

Middleton, Beth Rose. 2008. "We Were Here, We Are Here, We Will Always Be Here: A Political Ecology of Healing in Mountain Maidu Country." PhD diss. University of California, Berkeley.

———. 2010. "Towards a Political Ecology of Healing." *Journal of Political Ecology* 17: 1–28.

———. 2011. *Trust in the Land.* Tucson: University of Arizona Press.

———. 2013. "Just Another Hoop to Jump Through? Using Environmental Laws and Processes for Indigenous Rights." *Environmental Management* 52 (5): 1057–70.

———. 2014. "ChuChuYamBa / Soda Rock: Toward an Applied Critical Geographic Perspective on Traditional Cultural Properties (TCPs)." *Human Geography* 7 (2).

Miller, Larisa K. 2013a. "The Secret Treaties with California Indians." *Prologue* 45 (3–4): 38–45.

———. 2013b. "Primary Sources on C. E. Kelsey and the Northern California Indian Association." *Journal of Western Archives* 4 (1): 186–93.

Mississippi Valley Lumberman. 1944. "Red River Lumber Co. Sells Westwood Holdings to Fruit Growers Exchange." December 8, 1944.

Mohawk, John. 1982. "Directions in People's Movements." In *Native Peoples in Struggles.*

Mulcahy, Gary (Winnemem Wintu Government Liaison). 2012. "BIA Meeting will End Chief Sisk's 24-Day Fast." Winnemem Wintu, July 9. http://www.winnememwintu .us/tag/u-n-declaration-on-the-rights-of-indigenous-peoples/.

Nagle, Mary K. 2013. "Nothing to Trust: The Unconstitutional Origins of the Post–Dawes Act Trust Doctrine." *Tulsa Law Review* 48 (1): 63–92.

Natural Resources Committee. 1938. *Drainage Basin Problems and Programs.* As revised by the president in 1938 and distributed by the National Reclamation Association in 1939.

Newcomb, Steven. 2008. *Pagans in the Promised Land: Decoding the Doctrine of Christian Discovery.* Golden, Colo.: Fulcrum.

Northwest Power and Conservation Council. 2013. "A Guide to Major Hydropower Dams of the Columbia River Basin." https://www.nwcouncil.org/energy/ powersupply/dam-guide.

Ogle, Beverly Benner. 1998. *Whisper of the Maidu: My Indian Ancestors of the HumBug Valley.* Self-published.

Ornelas, Roxanne T. 2014. "Implementing the Policy of the U.N. Declaration on the Rights of Indigenous Peoples." *International Indigenous Policy Journal* 5 (1): 3.

Pacific Stewardship Council. 2007. "Land Conservation Plan: Volume 1." http://lcp .stewardshipcouncil.org/Vol_1/toc.htm.

———. 2008. "Volume 3, Pilot Process." http://stewardshipcouncil.org/documents/ Volume%20III%20Pilot%20Process_Adopted%203.26.08.pdf..

———. 2015. "Summary of Watershed Lands to be Retained by PG&E." http://www .stewardshipcouncil.org/Users/rwhite/Desktop/Summary%20of%20watershed %20lands%20retained%20by%20PG&E%206.12.2013%20EXCEL.pdf.

———. 2016. Summary of Fee Title Donee Recommendations.

Palmer, Mark H. 2011. "Sold! The Loss of Kiowa Allotments in the Post-Indian Reorganization Era." *AICRJ* 35 (3): 37–57.

Parker, Patricia L., and Thomas King. 1998. *Guidelines for Evaluating and Documenting Traditional Cultural Properties.* National Register Bulletin 38, U.S. Department of the Interior, National Park Service, Washington, D.C.

Paschal, Rachael. 1991. "Comment: The Imprimatur of Recognition; American Indian Tribes and the Federal Acknowledgement Process." *Washington Law Review* 66 (1): 209–28.

Peinado, J. Carlos, dir. 2006. *Waterbuster.* VisionMaker Video.

Peters, Chris (executive director of 7th Generation Fund). 2013. "Enduring Impact of the Doctrine of Discovery." Lecture given at *Lyng v. Northwest Indian Cemetery Protective Association* (1988): 25 Years Later, University of California, Davis, King Hall School of Law.

PG&E. 1954a. "Operating Review." In PG&E Annual Report 1954.

———. 1954b. "Report of the Directors of PG&E: To the Stockholders." In PG&E Annual Report 1954. Filed in J. S. Longwell (MS 80/12), Box 1, Folder 2.4.

———. 1956. "Highlights of the Year's Operations." In PG&E Annual Report 1956. Filed in WRCA, Hans Albert Einstein (MS 80/8), Box 5, Folder 15.2.

———. c. 1957. *Feather River Development*. WRCA, Hans Albert Einstein (MS 80/8), Box 5, Folder 15.2.

———. 1958a. "The 1959 Financial Story." PG&E Annual Report 1958.

———. 1958b. "Revenues and Sales." In PG&E Annual Report 1958.

———. 1959a. "Serving—Today and Tomorrow." In PG&E Annual Report 1959.

———. 1959b. "To Our Stockholders." In PG&E Annual Report 1959.

———. 2016. Statement of Gross Generation for FY 2016. Report given to FERC.

Poindexter, Mark D. 1994. "Of Dinosaurs and Indefinite Land Trusts: A Review of Individual American Indian Property Rights Amidst the Legacy of Allotment." *Boston College Third World Law Journal* 14 (1): 70–71.

Pulido, Laura. 2016. "Geographies of Race and Ethnicity II: Environmental Racism, Racial Capitalism and State-Sanctioned Violence." *Progress in Human Geography* 41 (4): 524–33.

Pulido, Laura, Ellen Kohl, and Nicole-Marie Cotton. 2016. "State Regulation and Environmental Justice: The Need for Strategy Reassessment." *Capitalism Nature Socialism* 27 (2): 12–31.

Pyle, Fred D. 1935. "El Capitan Dam and Reservoir." *Municipal Employee* 3 (8).

Reyes, Lawney. 2002. *White Grizzly Bear's Legacy*. Seattle: University of Washington Press.

———. 2006. *Bernie Whitebear: An Urban Indian's Quest for Justice*. Tucson: University of Arizona Press.

Rhodin, C. J. (consulting engineer). 1930. *Great Western System: Feather River Water Power Project, Review of Property Values*.

Ribot, Jesse, and Nancy Lee Peluso. 2003. "A Theory of Access." *Rural Sociology* 68 (2):153–81.

Rosales, Hawk (executive director of the InterTribal Sinkyone Wilderness Council). 2012. "Heeding Frickey's Call: Environmental Justice in Indian Country." *American Indian Law Review* 37 (2): 347–422.

Rowley, William D. 1996. *Reclaiming the Arid West*. Bloomington: Indiana University Press.

Ruppel, Kristen. 2008. *Unearthing Indian Land: Living with the Legacies of Allotment*. Tucson: University of Arizona Press.

Sammon, Alexander. 2016. "A History of Native Americans Protesting the Dakota Access Pipeline." *Mother Jones*, September 9, 2016.

San Francisco Chronicle. 1924. "TB Walker, State Lumber Magnate, Here." March 6, 1924.

Scheck, Justin. 2011. "Maidu Land Claim with Strings Attached." *Wall Street Journal*, November 15, 2011.

Schneider, Khal. 2010. "Making Indian Land in the Allotment Era." *Western Historical Quarterly* 41 (4): 429–50.

Shoemaker, Jessica A. 2017. "Complexity's Shadow: American Indian Property, Sovereignty, and the Future." *Michigan Law Review* 115 (4): 487–552.

Smith, Burton M. 1979. "The Politics of Allotment: The Flathead Indian Reservation as a Test Case." *Pacific Northwest Quarterly* 70 (3): 131–40.

Spence, Mark. 1999. *Dispossessing the Wilderness.* New York: Oxford University Press.

State of California, Department of Water Resources. 1959. *The Burns–Porter Act.* Filed in Cooper MS 76/10, Box 8, WRCA.

———. 1960. *Statement on the State Water Program.* Filed in Erwin Cooper papers 8, WRCA, University of California, Riverside.

———. 2014. "Project Alternatives Eliminated from Further Consideration." In the *Upper North Fork Feather River Hydroelectric Project Draft Environmental Impact Report.*

Steiner, Rodney. 1982. "Large Private Landholdings in California." *Geographical Review* 72 (3): 315–26.

Sterling, Everett W. 1940. "The Powell Irrigation Survey, 1888–1893." *Mississippi Valley Historical Review* 27 (3): 42134.

"Substantiation of the Feasibility of the California Water Project Proposed in the California Water Resources Development Bond Act." 1959. Filed in Cooper MS 76/10, Box 8, WRCA.

"Summary of Accomplishments of Water Program Funded Under the Provisions of SB 1106." N.d. Filed in Cooper MS 76/10, Box 8, WRCA.

Sutton, Imre. 1985. *Irredeemable America: The Indians' Estate and Land Claims.* Albuquerque: University of New Mexico Press.

———. 2000. "The Continuing Saga of Indian Land Claims: Not All Aboriginal Territory Is Truly Irredeemable." *AICRJ* 24 (1): 129–62.

———. 2002. "Cartographic Review of Indian Land Tenure and Territoriality: A Schematic Approach." *American Indian Culture and Research Journal* 26 (2): 74–75.

SWRB (State of California, State Water Resources Board). 1951. *Report on the Feasibility of Feather River Project and Sacramento–San Joaquin Delta Diversion Projects Proposed as Features of the California Water Plan.*

———. 1956. *The California Water Plan.*

SWRCB (State of California, State Water Resources Control Board). 1990. Decision 1626, Approving Application 26651, PG&E Company, Applicant, CA Dept. of Fish & Game and California Sportfishing Protection Alliance, Protestants. http://www.waterboards.ca.gov/waterrights/board_decisions/adopted_orders/decisions/d1600_d1649/wrd1626.pdf.

Theodoratus Cultural Research. 1986. "Cultural Resources of the Indian Creek Water Power Project: Plumas County, California." Submitted to Jones and Stokes Associates, Inc., Sacramento, Calif.

Tolley, Sarah-Larus. 2007. *Quest for Recognition: California's Honey Lake Maidus.* Norman: University of Oklahoma Press.

Trafzer, Clifford E., and Joel R. Hyer. 1999. *Exterminate Them! Written Accounts of the Murder, Rape and Enslavement of Native Americans During the California Gold Rush, 1848–1868.* East Lansing: Michigan State University Press.

Tuck, Eve, and K. Wayne Yang. 2012. "Decolonization Is Not a Metaphor." *Decolonization: Indigeneity, Education & Society* 1 (1): 1–40.

Ulrich, Roberta. 2007. *Empty Nets: Indians, Dams, and the Columbia River*. 2nd ed. Columbus: Ohio State University Press.

University of California. 1957. "Feather River Powerland: Tour Schedule." WRCA, Hans Albert Einstein (MS 80/8), Box 5, folder 15.2.

U.S. Department of the Interior, Bureau of Reclamation. N.d. "Grand Coulee Dam Statistics and Facts." http://www.usbr.gov/pn/grandcoulee/pubs/factsheet.pdf.

U.S. Forest Service. 1994. *An Ancient Trail of the Mountain Maidu Indians*.

VanDevelder, Paul. 2004. *Coyote Warrior: One Man, Three Tribes, and the Trial That Forged a Nation*. New York: Little, Brown.

Washburn, Wilcomb E. 1975. *The Assault on Indian Tribalism: The General Allotment Law (Dawes Act) of 1887*. Philadelphia: Lippincott.

White, Richard. 2011. *Railroaded: The Transcontinentals and the Making of Modern America*. New York: W. W. Norton.

Whyte, Kyle Powys. 2016. "Why the Native American Pipeline Resistance in North Dakota Is About Climate Justice." *Conversation*, September 16, 2016.

Williams, Robert. 2012. *Savage Anxieties: The Invention of Western Civilization*. New York: Palgrave Macmillan.

Yurok Tribe. 2011. *MLPA and Marine Resource Plan*. http://www.yuroktribe.org/government/tribalattorney/documents/2011.08.29_YurokTribe-FactualRecordtoCAFGC.pdf.

INDEX

Page numbers in *italics* indicate illustrations.

North American Company, 135, 145. *See
also* Great Western Power Company
(GWP); PG&E

Office of Indian Affairs, 27–28, 68, 99, 125–
26. *See also* Bureau of Indian Affairs
Ogle, Beverly, 36
OIA. *See* Office of Indian Affairs
Ornelas, Roxanne, 11–12
Oro Electric Corporation, 136, 188. *See also*
Great Western Power Company
Oroville Dam, 26, *41*, 42–50, *45*, *47*, 53, 189.
See also Oroville Reservoir
Oroville Reservoir, 26, 42–50, *45*, 65–66. *See
also* Oroville Dam

Pacific Forest and Watershed Lands
Stewardship Council. *See* Stewardship
Council
Pacific Gas and Electric (PG&E). *See*
PG&E
Palmer, Mark, 19
Peluso, Nancy, 112
PG&E: 2003 settlement with California
Public Utilities Commission, 19–20,
56–57, 165, 166–69, 181–82, 191 (*see also*
California Public Utilities Commis-
sion; Stewardship Council); acquisition
and holding of Native lands by, 14–15,
19–20, 22, 116, 118–26, 161–62, 165–67, 169;
acquisition of GWP holdings by, 34,
136, 144–48, 189 (*see also* Great Western
Power Company); bankruptcy of, 56,
167–68, 191; Bureau of Reclamation and,
63 (*see also* Bureau of Reclamation);
CVP and, 56, 146–47 (*see also* Central
Valley Project); growth and expansion
of, 34, 35, 53–56, *55*, 145–48, 187; hydroelectric power generation by, 5, 53, 55–56, 162;
hydropower systems of, 5, 53–57, *54*, 62,
136, 159–61, *160*, 204n49 (*see also* Great
Western Power Company; Upper North
Fork Feather River Project); land and

water rights of, 14–15, 57, 196n4; policies
and daily operations of, 61–63; public
regulation of, 145–46, 147; relicensing
proceedings for, 5, 11, 22–23, 64, 156–67,
160, 181–82, 190, 191 (*see also* Federal
Energy Regulatory Commission);
revenue streams of, 63; SWP and, 5 (*see
also* State Water Project). *See also* Upper
North Fork Feather River Project
Pick Sloan Plan, 7, 196n8
Pit River, 84, 112, 114–20, 123–25
Pit River (people), 12, 19, 24, 134–35, 171, 182,
192
Poindexter, Mark, 18
Potter Valley Tribe, 12, 171, 192
powerhouses: Belden Powerhouse, 190; Big
Bend Powerhouse, 34, 204n49; Bucks
Creek, 36; Bucks Creek Powerhouse,
189, 202n25, 204n49; Caribou Power-
house, 188, 204n49; Cresta Powerhouse,
204n49; Hamilton Branch Powerhouse,
204n49; Rock Creek Powerhouse, 190,
204n49
Prattville reservoir, 40
Public Law 280, 69, 190
Public Utilities Act (1912), 34–35, 188
Public Utility Act (1935), 189

railroads, 34, 130–31, 197n15. *See also* Southern Pacific Railroad; Western Pacific
Railroad
rancherias: California Rancheria Termination Act, 190; Enterprise Rancheria,
65; Greenville Indian Rancheria, 21, 163,
164, 165–66, 172, 179; Susanville Indian
Rancheria, 21, 163, 189; Taylorsville
Rancheria, 189. *See also* reservations
Reclamation Act (Newlands Act, 1903),
26–27, 58, 154, 204n55
Red River Lumber Company, 187, 188, 189;
acquisition of Native lands by, 15, 22, 36,
76, 79, 82, 86, 89, 101–112, 114–15, 127–35,
188, 213n44; Great Western Power

ABOUT THE AUTHOR

Beth Rose Middleton Manning is an associate professor of Native American studies at the University of California, Davis. Her first book, *Trust in the Land: New Directions in Tribal Conservation*, focused on Native applications of conservation easements.

WALKS THROUGH HISTORY
KENT

WALKS THROUGH HISTORY
KENT

John Wilks

First published in Great Britain in 1998 by
The Breedon Books Publishing Company Limited
Breedon House, 3 The Parker Centre,
Derby, DE21 4SZ.

Updated edition 2007

ISBN 978-1-85983-552-4

Printed and bound by
Cromwell Press, Trowbridge, Wilts

Contents

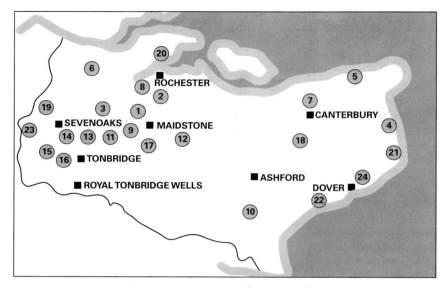

Key map to the walks

A brief historical introduction

Each walk in this book has been chosen not only because it is a pleasant walk in its own right, but also because it goes past sites which reveal the rich and varied history of the county. The walks are arranged chronologically, each walk having a major historical theme, and together they take the walker through 4,000 years of Kentish history. The purpose of this introduction is to show how each of the walks in this collection fits into the overall history of the county, a history that is very much shaped by Kent's proximity to Europe. For through migration, trade and invasion, Kent has had close contact with the Continent throughout its history.

In prehistoric times Britain was connected to continental Europe by a land bridge. It was across this bridge that Homo Sapiens first reached Britain, entering through its southeastern corner and gradually spreading north and west. Human remains and flint tools 200,000 years old have been found at Swanscombe near Gravesend, the earliest example of Kentish man. Britain only became an island around 6500BC, when the seas rose and flooded what is now the English Channel, breaking through the Straits of Dover. Initially this drastically reduced the rate of migration from the Continent, but gradually man perfected the building of canoes and leather-made boats, small craft that were nevertheless sturdy enough to allow him to cross the treacherous seas of the channel.

These early Stone Age men lived mainly in the open air, camping beside rivers and lakes and existing on what could be hunted or gathered. Consequently, they made little mark upon the landscape. Occasionally they used caves for temporary shelter, and evidence has been found in one such cave, at Oldbury Hill, (walk 3) that it was regularly used by hunters for seasonal refuge about 2001BC. But although the dwellings they built may have made no mark on the landscape, the tombs and trackways made by Stone Age man are still to be seen today. Collective tombs known as long barrows can be seen at the Coldrum Stones (walk 1) and at Kits Coty (walk 2). These tombs have more in common in their construction with Holland and Denmark than with the rest of Britain, evidence that there was regular contact across the seas. The ancient trackways of these people can still be followed, running for instance along the foot of the North Downs (walk 2).

During the Stone Age the population was very small and widely scattered, with between 10,000 and 20,000 people in the whole of Britain. Improved agricultural techniques and the use of metal for tools led to a rapid population expansion during the Bronze Age (2000BC to 700BC), and man became organised into tribes or clans. Burial was now by cremation, with the ashes interred in round barrows (walk 10). When climatic changes rendered large areas of the uplands and the north of the island uninhabitable, pressure upon the remaining land made inter-tribal conflict inevitable, with the new metal technology being pressed into service to provide weapons.

By the Iron Age, about 700BC onwards, Britain had regular contact with Europe, exporting corn, cattle, hides, gold, silver, iron, hunting dogs and slaves. The bulk of this trade was through Kent, already known by that name and already the most prosperous part of Britain. Towards the end of this period Kent was settled by the Belgae, a continental tribe driven from their homelands in Gaul (modern France and Belgium) by the increasing power of the Roman Empire. This powerful and warlike tribe built hilltop strongholds such as Oldbury Hill Fort (walk 3), for use in times of emergency, and maintained strong links with their continental cousins, both in terms of trade and militarily. By the middle of the first century BC, British mercenaries were fighting in Gaul against the Romans, and Britain was sanctuary to Rome's enemies.

The actions of the Belgae and other hostile tribes eventually provoked Roman intervention. Julius Caesar came twice to Britain, firstly in 551BC for a reconnaissance, then again in 541BC, this time with a much stronger force with which to subdue Rome's most prominent enemies. On both occasions Caesar landed in the vicinity of present day Deal (walk 21), the closest point to continental Europe where the flat open beaches offered easy landing. Caesar declared that Kent was the most civilised part of Britain, easily on a par with Gaul, and planted the seeds for Britain's incorporation into the Roman Empire. A century later Rome returned, this time bent upon the permanent occupation of Britain. An invading army landed at Pegwell Bay (walk 4), swept up through Kent, and overcame a British army at the Battle of the Medway (walk 8). Although the eventual subjugation of the whole of England 'would take many years, resistance in Kent was at an end, and for the next four centuries Kent reaped the benefits of being part of the Roman Empire. The Romans made Richborough their major British port (walk 4) and trade between Britain and the Continent flowed through Richborough and across Kent along the Roman road of Watling Street. Cities like Rochester and Canterbury and luxurious villas such as that at Lullingstone followed (walk 6). Initially citizens from the rest of the Empire came to Britain as soldiers, administrators and merchants, but gradually the local population took on Roman values and played an increasing role in the running of the province. A new Romano-British civilisation developed.

By the fourth century the survival of the Roman Empire was under threat. In Britain, Saxon pirates harassed the coastline. To counter this a series of strongpoints, the Forts of the Saxon Coast, were built, at such places as Richborough (walk 4) and Reculver (walk 5). Eventually, however, the Romans were forced to evacuate Britain in 410AD, and Kent was increasingly prey to the influx of warring bands of Saxons, Jutes, and Danes. The Saxon warlords Hengist and Horsa made the Isle of Thanet their base, from which they established the Saxon kingdom of Kent. Although Romano-British civilisation continued, Britain gradually reverted to a rurally-based tribal society. Political and economic control was increasingly in the hands of a landowning aristocracy, who were under little central control from a king. During this time Kent still remained relatively wealthy and reasonably civilised. The culture inherited from the Romans was not swept away, but forced underground.

Christianity had been imposed upon Britain by Emperor Constantine in the fourth century AD but was lost as a national religion when the Germanic tribes arrived, bringing their own religious beliefs. In 597 AD Pope Gregory sent St Augustine to Britain to convert the country back to Christianity. Augustine landed at Ebbsfleet and journeyed to the Kentish capital, Canterbury, where he was welcomed by King Ethelbert and his Christian Queen, Bertha. The King and his subjects rapidly converted to the returned religion, and Augustine established the Archbishopric of Canterbury as a jumping-off ground for the further spread of Christianity (walk 7).

From the eighth to the 10th centuries Kent, along with much of the rest of England, was increasingly harried by the Danes, until they were finally driven away by King Alfred. (The site of one of Alfred's campaigns can be seen near Appledore on walk 10.) Kent was soon incorporated into the Saxon kingdom of England and enjoyed a return to peace and prosperity. Settlements expanded further and further into the huge Wealdan Forest, which covered much of the interior of the county. Towns grew in size and wealth, and trade with Europe was re-established. There is little direct evidence of the Saxon period to be seen today. The Saxons only occasionally built castles (such as Leeds Castle, walk 12), and most of their churches and palaces have been incorporated into later buildings. However, many of the settlements in Kent date from this era, and their Saxon origins are denoted in placenames: the ending 'den' and 'ing' mean an enclosure, 'ley' refers to a clearing in the forest, 'ham' and 'ton' denote farms and dwellings.

In 1066 William, Duke of Normandy, invaded Britain with a small army, bent upon securing the English crown to which he had at least some legitimate claim. Unlike previous invaders, William did not land in Kent but in neighbouring Sussex. After defeating the English at Hastings, William's army marched around the coast of Kent, receiving reinforcements from Normandy en route, and marched up Whatling Street to London to receive his crown.

William's immediate need after the Battle of Hastings had overthrown the old Anglo-Saxon monarchy was to ensure that the population were subdued and that any revolts were nipped in the bud, and also to ensure that no other adventurer was able to invade from abroad. William saw to it that a castle was built in every county, town, and at points of strategic importance. The great castles at Rochester (walk 8) and Dover (walk 24) were started at this time.

The Normans brought with them the art of castle building to England. William gave his nobles a free hand to build private castles to defend their lands. In the years immediately following the conquest a rash of castles sprang up over England, a visible reminder to a cowed population of the power of their new masters. The initial castles were simple affairs, an earth mound with a simple wooden keep on top and a wooden palisade around the outside, known as 'motte and bailey'. Soon, however, these were replaced by more substantial stone-built castles, which provided bases of wealth and power (examples are seen at Eynsford castle, walk 6, and Leeds Castle, walk 12).

The Norman Conquest was essentially an aristocratic one and did not result in any mass influx of new settlers into England. Only 6,000 men accompanied William to England. William needed an army to defend his conquest and a nobility who could be guaranteed to defend his new kingdom. He achieved both these goals by taking the land of the defeated Saxon aristocracy and parcelling it out to his supporters, in return for which they were obliged to provide knights and men-at-arms when required. This system of rights and obligations based upon land tenure is known as feudalism. These Norman landowners, churchmen as well as secular barons, now had a vested interest in defending their new estates, and through them the integrity of the realm. The effects of the introduction of feudalism can be seen on the ground in West Malling and Offham (walk 9).

For the Normans, religion was as important as the sword. William was accompanied by his supporter Bishop Lanfranc, who was soon made Archbishop of Canterbury and the foremost churchman in England. During this early Norman period many Saxon religious buildings were extended or rebuilt in the Norman style. The great cathedrals of Canterbury (walk 7) and Rochester (walk 8) date from this time, as did many of Kent's fine old churches, monasteries and abbeys. (Both the church and abbey in West Malling, walk 9, date from this era.) The boundaries between church and state, between obligations and duties owed to and by each, were blurred during the Norman period. This culminated in the great conflict between King Henry II and his Archbishop Thomas Becket, which resulted in the murder of the latter in 1170 in Canterbury Cathedral, and Canterbury thus becoming a place of pilgrimage (walk 7).

The three centuries following the Norman Conquest were a period of consolidation. The Norman kings and barons had great holdings in land on both sides of the channel. While they developed the resources of their new holdings in Britain, they also continued to manage their old ones on the Continent, and in the process forged firm links of trade and travel between the two lands. This was also a time when the new relationship between the king and his barons was hammered out, for William had imposed the new concept that all land belonged to the king, to be given to his subjects in return for service. This view was alien to the established view that the king was only the first among his peers, and on several occasions the nobility resorted to arms against the encroachment of royal power. In 1216 the barons, aided by the French monarchy, revolted against King John, and Dover, Canterbury (walk 7) and Rochester Castles were all involved in the conflict. 1264 saw another Baronial revolt, this time led by Simon de Montefort against Henry III, and again Rochester Castle saw action (walk 8).

Apart from these large scale revolts against royal power by the nobility, there was often fighting whenever the king was weak, either with the nobility fighting each other or fighting their king as they jockeyed for position. Leeds Castle saw an example of one such comparatively minor skirmish in the reign of Edward II (walk 12). Kent was little involved in the last major conflict between the nobles, the Wars of the Roses, which largely ended with the accession of the House of Tudor in 1485.

By the 14th century Kent was the richest county in the land. Money poured in from pilgrims coming to Canterbury (walk 7), rich agricultural land abounded around the margins of the ever-receding forest, and the ports of the channel coast grew powerful and affluent as trade flowed between England and the Continent. Examples of this are seen at Sandwich (walk 4) and Appledore (walk 10). This was not to say Kent was peaceable: the interior of the county was still covered by the Forest of the Weald, settlements were still scattered and the roads between them were poor. Landowners who sought estates in the forest margin often had to fight to impose the law that enabled them to maintain those lands. The dangerous times these lesser landlords lived in is amply demonstrated by the existence of fortified manor houses across the county, such as Old Soar (walk 11) and Ightham Mote (walk 13).

The growing wealth of Kent was not bought without paying the price of social injustice. Feudalism continued to exist until well into the 15th century, and the peasants resented the numerous taxes and arbitrary fines that were imposed upon them without any redress. In 1381 this resentment spilled over as the Peasants Revolt. This started in Essex and in Kent, where the rebels under Wat Tyler attacked local landlords in places such as Appledore (walk 10), before capturing Canterbury Castle (walk 7) and marching upon London. Only after the rebels received promises of reform from young King Richard II did they disperse, only to see those promises rapidly broken and their leaders executed. In 1453 there was another revolt in Kent against the corruption and arbitrary exercise of power by the ruling classes, this time among the more well-to-do commoners. Led by Jack Cade they defeated a royal army at Sevenoaks (walk

14) and occupied London, before again being betrayed by broken royal promises.

During the 14th century Edward III allowed Flemish weavers who were fleeing from religious persecution to settle in Kent, bringing with them the skills needed to start a cloth industry. The villages and towns of the Weald flourished, raising sheep, weaving wool and digging the clay necessary for cleaning and dying the wool. The ports of the channel coast flourished as cloth swelled English exports, and organised themselves into a powerful league known as the Cinque Ports. In return for favourable import-export rights and tax concessions, the Cinque Ports supplied the monarch with ships in times of war and policed the collection of customs duties. Originally the Cinque Ports comprised the four Kentish ports of Dover, Sandwich (walk 4), Romney and Hythe, and Hastings in neighbouring Sussex, but they eventually incorporated another 20 ports along the channel coast. These included some such as Appledore (walk 10), which today are miles from the sea thanks to changes in the coastline.

Iron had been smelted in the Weald since Roman times, but it was initially of poor quality. The invention of water-driven smelting machinery changed this, and in the 16th century Kent became the industrial heart of England. Local iron was mined and smelted using the power of local streams and foundries burning charcoal from the Wealdan Forest. This Kentish iron was forged into tools and weapons that were in high demand in England and abroad. Traces of this industry can still be seen today at West Peckham (walk 17). Many towns in the Weald grew in importance and remained so until the technological developments of the late 18th century moved the industrial focus of England to the coalfields of the Midlands and the North.

By the middle of the reign of Henry VIII Kent was settled, peaceful and increasingly wealthy. Evidence of this prosperity can still be seen in towns such as Chiddingstone (walk 15), Penshurst (walk 16) and Chilham (walk 18). Better communications with London made Kent a favoured place for the homes of crown servants, who built country houses in the county, such as Lullingstone Castle (walk 6). The Tudor period saw the development and expansion of many huge estates across the county, with fine houses surrounded by extensive parks laid out for recreation and stocked for hunting (walk 14 visits one such estate, Knole House). Two of Henry VIII's wives, Anne Boleyn and Anne of Cleves, occupied Hever Castle (walk 15). Sir Philip Sydney, courtier, poet and soldier, the quintessential Elizabethan man, lived at Penshurst Place (walk 16).

The Civil War in the middle of the 17th century largely passed Kent by. There were minor skirmishes at Deal (walk 21), and there are reminders of the Commonwealth Period around Plaxtol, in the form of a rare commonwealth church (walk 11). Generally, however, the Stuart era in Kent was marked by continued tranquillity, with estates such as Chevening (walk 19) continuing to flourish.

Kent has always been in the front line against invasion from the Continent. The Romans, the Saxons and the Danes all invaded through Kent. The shores of Kent, which have changed their course considerably since Roman times, have been defended for 2,000 years against invasion. The Romans built the forts of the Saxon Coast to protect against Germanic invaders (walks 4 and 5). The Saxons under Alfred fought the Danes in its creeks and inlets (walk 10). The Normans, after entering through neighbouring Sussex, rapidly built strong castles in Kent to defend against future continental incursions. During the Hundred Years War the coast of Kent was raided several times by the French (walk 10). Henry VIII's foreign and religious policy made invasion from France again a possibility, and a line of strong modern castles such as Upnor (walk 20) and Deal (walk 21) were built all around the coastline. Henry's forts were never used in his lifetime, but one of them, Upnor, saw service during wars against the Dutch in the following century (walk 20).

Britain was at war against the French for most of the 18th century, and one of the heroes of that struggle, General James Wolfe, was born at Westerham, and is commemorated there (walk 23). This epic struggle culminated in the wars against the Revolutionary Government and its successor the Emperor Napoleon, from 1792 to 1815. Invasion from France, was once again threatened, with Kent in the front line. To counter this, extensive defences were built along the coastline, most especially the vulnerable area around Romney Marsh. Here the Royal Military Canal (walks 10 and 22) was built behind a line of coastal fortifications (visited at Hythe, walk 22). Deal (walk 21) was one of the major ports in England for the Royal Navy during the 18th and 19th centuries, and also profited from a flourishing trade in smuggling. During World War One the Dover Patrol was vital in keeping open Britain's communications with her army in France (walk 24). England was again threatened with invasion in 1940, and Kent saw a major part of a new type of war, this time one fought in the air during the Battle of Britain (walk 24).

From the cliffs above Dover (walk 24) one can look down at the bustling port, with its busy container terminal, and a constant stream of ferries crossing the channel. Around Hythe (walk 22) there are road signs pointing to the Channel Tunnel. Both are modern reminders of that proximity to Europe which has been a constant theme throughout Kent's history.

Advice to walkers

All but one of the walks in this collection cross countryside for at least part of their route. Although the terrain is not difficult or dangerous, it can become very wet and slippery in places, especially after a shower of rain, and walking boots or stout shoes are recommended for any of these walks. It is also recommended that you carry waterproofs, since the weather can change quickly even in Kent, and you could easily find yourself some distance away from shelter when the skies open, Remember that on some walks there may be occasional brambles, nettles or crops which scratch, so bear this in mind when deciding whether to walk in shorts. Directions for each walk are given in the text and a sketch map included to give an outline of the route. These sketch maps are not detailed enough to navigate by, and it is strongly recommended that you carry the relevant Ordnance Survey map, in case of difficulties or in case you wish to deviate from the route. The 1:50,000 series is perfectly adequate to walk from. Although all directions are accurate at the time of writing, features do occasionally change: a hedge or tree may disappear, a stile may be replaced by a gate. By comparing the written directions with the OS map it should be perfectly possible to find the correct route even if features have occasionally altered. All routes in this book use public rights of way or permissive footpaths when crossing private land. Again, the OS map will confirm the right of way in case of doubt. If a footpath or bridleway is shown on a current map, it is the duty of the landowner to maintain the route and you have a legal right to use it. However, it is sensible to show discretion and compromise rather than a rigid insistence on your rights: for instance, if at certain times of the year the route across an open field is not obvious or is obscured by crops, it may be better to walk around the perimeter of the field. Consideration for others is key when walking, and at all times remember the Countryside Code laid down by the Countryside Commission:

1. Enjoy the countryside and respect its life and work
2. Guard against all risk of fire
3. Fasten all gates
4. Keep your dogs under close control
5. Keep to public paths across farmland
6. Use gates and stiles to cross fences, hedges and walls
7. Leave livestock, crops and machinery alone
8. Take your litter home
9. Help to keep all water clean
10. Protect wildlife, plants and trees
11. Take special care on country roads
12. Make no unnecessary noise

I have indicated where refreshments can be obtained on each walk. On a number of the walks, refreshments are only available at the beginning or end. It is therefore advisable to carry a snack and, more importantly, something to drink with you, especially on the longer walks. Please note that the mention of the existence of a pub is not necessarily an endorsement of it! Convenient car parking places have been indicated for all walks. At the time of writing, most of these were free and there is adequate parking at most spots indicated. Should you have difficulty it is far better to find a different parking spot and make your way to the start of the walk on foot, rather than causing an obstruction with your car. Most importantly, remember you are visiting a place where other people live. Do not cause inconvenience to local people by parking across access to houses, farms, fields or churches.

WALK 1

The Coldrum Stones: Long barrows and mediaeval tracks

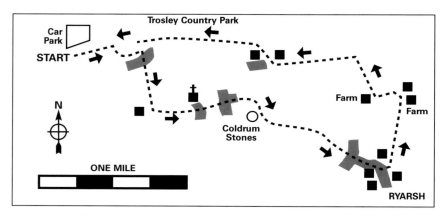

Distance: 6 miles
Map: OS sheet 177 or 188
Start and Parking: The walk starts from Trosley Country Park (grid ref: 633611). This is just to the east of the A227, nine miles south of Gravesend. There is ample car parking there.
Refreshments: None

Historical Background
During the Early and Middle Stone Age, or 'Neolithic' Period (roughly 4000BC to 2500BC), the idea of collective burial was traditional throughout the countries on the western seaboard of Europe. Communities went to huge efforts to build massive communal graves with the primitive tools of the day. These were then used for successive burials over a number of years, being closed and then reopened, until finally they were sealed permanently. The religious significance of this form of burial is not known, nor is it known why some individuals were thus buried but not the rest of the community. It is tempting to speculate that they were leaders of the community, but if so they were perhaps more likely to be religious leaders than political.

These collective tombs are known as barrows, either 'long' or 'round' dependent upon their shape, and are found across the whole of the British Isles and Western Europe. The actual design of the barrow alters according to region. The Coldrum Stones, which are the well-preserved remains of one of the earliest long harrows in Kent, are part of a group called the Medway Barrows. These are far more similar to tombs found in north-west Europe than to tombs found in the rest of Britain, arguing for a strong cultural connection across the North Sea.

The Walk
This walk starts in Trosley Country Park and descends the North Downs to visit the Coldrum Stones. It then goes through the pleasant countryside at the foot of the escarpment and returns along part of the Pilgrims' Way.

- With the toilets and visitors' centre on your left, go down the waymarked path to reach a cross track after a few yards.
- Turn left along the cross track for 350 yards. Ignore a marker for 'Blue Walks' on your right, but 10 yards later, at a post with seven waymarkers on it, turn right and descend steps through trees.
- Ignore side turnings and descend the path, which soon becomes stepped again.
- At the bottom of the steps ignore horse barriers ahead but instead turn left along the path.
- After a quarter of a mile turn right through a horse barrier, at a waymark. Cross a track, pass through another horse barrier, and descend to a lane.
- Cross the lane and enter the field opposite. Keep straight on down the right-hand edge of the field, keeping the fence and trees to your right.
- Pass through a kissing gate and continue straight on along an enclosed footpath. When the path ceases to be enclosed, keep straight on down the right-hand edge of a field.
- Where the fence on the right ends, keep straight on across the field, aiming to the left of houses seen ahead.
- Keep straight on with gardens on the right. When the gardens end, turn left onto a cross track.
- Follow the bottom edge of the field, aiming for a church seen ahead.

There are fine views of the North Downs on your left. An ancient Neolithic (Stone Age) trackway, later to become used in mediaeval times as the Pilgrims' Way from London to Canterbury, runs along the foot of the Downs. During the Stone Age, the whole of the countryside you are walking through would have been lightly wooded. Even by the Middle Ages, the agricultural land would not have been as extensive as it is today.

- Pass through a farmyard and into the end of a lane, with the church on your left.

The main claim to fame of the Church of St Peter and St Paul is an enormous pulpit said to have come from Westminster Abbey, and a collection of human and animal bones exhumed from the Coldrum Long Barrow. The church itself is largely Norman, built by Bishop Gundulph (see walks 8 and 9) around AD1100 on the site of a demolished Saxon church.

- Walk down the lane. Pass a house on the left after 30 yards and immediately turn left up the slope to a stile.

The Coldrum Long Barrow,
a communal grave from 3000BC.

- Keep straight on across the field, aiming for houses opposite.
- Exit the field into a lane. Cross over the lane and take the tarmacked track opposite, signposted 'Coldrum Long Barrow'.
- Pass through a parking area and continue down the track opposite.
- The track soon narrows into a footpath, passes through trees and emerges into a field. Keep ahead down the right-hand edge of the field. Where the hedge on the right ends, keep ahead over the field.
- Bear right with the path out of the field and down to a cross track. Turn right after 60 yards to Coldrum Long Barrow.

The Coldrum Long Barrow was a communal grave from the period 3000–2500BC. In structure it was a rectangular earthen mound, orientated roughly east–west, higher at the east where the entrance was. The interior of the tomb consisted of a burial chamber with drystone interior walls, covered with an earthen mound. This in turn was flanked by 24 large blocks of stone (known as sarsen stones), to act as a retaining wall or kerb around the mound. The largest stones flanked the entrance. These sarsen stones are not local in origin. It is possible that they are what are called 'erratic', boulders carried on the glaciers during the Ice Age and deposited many miles from their origin.

The construction of the barrow is a type common to tombs in the Medway area, but not found elsewhere in Britain. It is, however, very similar to tombs of the same age found in Western Europe, in particular the Hunebeds of Holland and Germany and the Dysse tombs of Denmark. This is strong evidence that there were close cultural links between the inhabitants of North Kent and those on the Continent, 5,000 years ago.

The Coldrum Long Barrow was in use over a considerable period, being opened at successive intervals as fresh corpses were interred. The remains of at least 22 people, of all ages and both sexes, were found inside. The communities who built the barrows were not settled in one place: they would move on every few decades once the land became exhausted. Consequently over time the barrows became further and further away from where the people now lived and required longer and longer journeys to bury the dead in them. This may be the reason why a barrow was eventually permanently sealed and abandoned.

- Pass the long barrow on your right and continue up the concrete drive for 100 yards. Where the drive turns right, keep straight on down a footpath to a cross track.
- Turn left down the cross track for 25 yards to a field gate between two stiles. Take the stile to the left of the gate and go down the left-hand side of the field, with trees on your left.
- At the end of the trees keep straight on, aiming for a stile in the trees ahead.
- Cross the stile and follow a path through woods to enter scrubland.
- Follow a clear path half-right through scrub land to a stile near the top right-hand corner.
- Cross the stile and turn left along a footpath to cross a footbridge and enter woodland.
- Follow the path as it winds through the wood to reach a lane.
- Turn right in the lane and then immediately turn left down Chapel Street.

- Follow Chapel Street for quarter of a mile to reach houses. Pass the first house on the left, and then immediately turn left up its drive, at a footpath sign. Keep ahead for 20 yards to enter a field.
- Turn left along an enclosed footpath towards the North Downs ridge, with gardens on your left.
- Cross a stile and continue straight on up the right-hand edge of a field.
- At the end of the field, turn right through a gap in the field boundary, then immediately turn left, to continue on the same line of advance, now up the left-hand edge of a field, with a drainage ditch on your left.
- After 100 yards cross a footbridge on the left and continue, now with the ditch on your right, to enter the next field. Continue in the same direction, still with a ditch on your right.
- Where the ditch on the right ends, turn left across the field, aiming for the corner of the wood ahead.
- At the corner of the wood, continue ahead, with the wood on your left. Bear right with the field boundary, then pass through a gap in the hedge on the left at a waymark.
- Turn right in the next field and walk up the right-hand edge, with trees on the right, to a stile.
- Cross the stile and walk up to a drive, in front of a large timber barn. Turn left along the drive, passing a second barn, and follow the drive to a T-junction beside a house on the right.
- Turn left down the drive towards a farm seen ahead. Pass a pumping station on your right, and just before a barn turn right up an enclosed track for quarter of a mile.
- At a T-junction turn left and follow a track, the Pilgrims' Way, for one mile along the foot of the downs. Ignore all turns to the right or left.

The Pilgrims' Way was the traditional route taken by mediaeval pilgrims travelling from London to Canterbury, to pay homage at the shrine of St Thomas Becket (see walk 7). Pilgrims' used to gather together for protection and travel in groups through countryside that in the 13th century was still forested and lawless. On one side pilgrims would have seen some agricultural land around the villages of Ryarsh and Birling. These would have been huge fields divided into strips and all growing the same crop, with stands of trees between them. On the other side would have been the dark, thick woodland sloping up to the top of the ridge. It is one such group of pilgrims that is immortalised in Chaucer's Canterbury Tales, *telling tales to pass the time and keep their spirits up.*

The Pilgrims' Way follows a much older trackway that has followed the foot of the North Downs since Neolithic times, where the chalk of the Downs meets the underlying clay and springs bubble out of the soil. Neolithic man followed this path, with its supply of fresh water, despite the thick forest it ran through. This supports the view that the threat of ambush by ones fellow man was much less then than in later times.

- The Pilgrims' Way track comes out at the end of a tarmacked road. Turn right between the gates of houses and enter an enclosed track.
- Climb steeply with the track. At the top of the slope, turn sharp left (signposted 'North Downs Way') and pass through a kissing gate beside a horse barrier, marked 'Entrance to Trosley Country Park'.
- Keep ahead along a broad track, ignoring all side turnings, for two thirds of a mile to reach the seven-waymarked post of your outward journey again (but with only four waymarks on this side) at the top of steps down to the left.
- Pass 'Post 3' on the left in 10 yards and follow the track, soon to reach the car park again up on your right.

WALK 2
Kits Coty: Stone Age graves and trackways

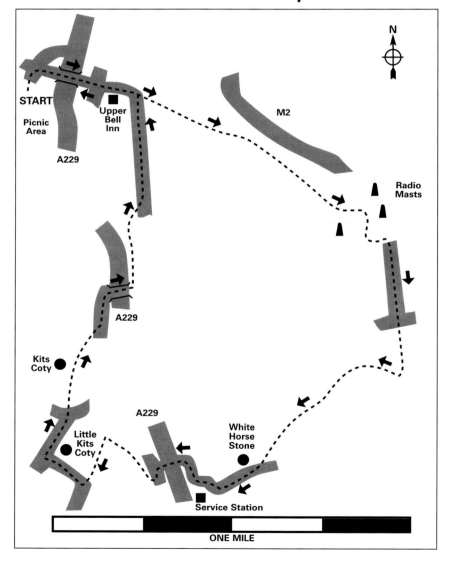

N

START

Upper Bell Inn

Picnic Area

A229

M2

Radio Masts

A229

Kits Coty

Little Kits Coty

A229

White Horse Stone

Service Station

ONE MILE

Distance: 4 miles

Map: OS sheet 178 or 188

Start and Parking: The walk commences from Blue Bell Hill Picnic site (grid ref: 743621). Blue Bell Hill is just off the A229 and very close to junction three of the M2, two miles south of Chatham and four miles north of Maidstone. If coming from the south (Maidstone) turn off the A229 just at the summit of the North Downs, following signs for Blue Bell Hill. From the north go to the roundabout where the A229 meets junction two of the M2, and then take a minor road south for half a mile, again signposted Blue Bell Hill. There is parking at the picnic site.

Refreshments: Public house at Blue Bell Hill.

Historical Background

The Stone Age or Neolithic era as a whole lasted from around 4000BC to 2100BC. The people of the Neolithic era had a very sophisticated culture: they lived in settled communities, made and used tools that were suitable for most everyday needs, cultivated the land and herded domesticated animals. They had well-developed religious beliefs and built lasting tombs for certain members of their community, probably those with religious status. Their social organisation was possibly tribal, but more likely based upon an extended family. Because the land was large and the population small (less than 20,000 people in Britain), they had no need for territorial expansion and by and large lived at peace with their neighbours. Their communities were not isolated but had far-reaching communications and limited trade, not only within Britain but abroad as well, and travel, although full of natural hazards, does not seem to have been threatened by their fellow man.

Neolithic people lived in settled but transitory communities. They would clear a patch of the all-pervasive forest, settle and cultivate it for a few years or even a few decades until the land was exhausted and the natural resources of the forest used up, and then move on and start again. Their homes were made of wood and their agricultural methods primitive, and so the only permanent mark they left upon the landscape were their stone and earth-built tombs and their long-distance trackways. That their architectural skills were considerable is demonstrated by the fact that their tombs still survive after 5,000 years: it was not that they could not build homes that were permanent, they simply had no need to.

The Walk

This walk goes through a region full of evidence of Neolithic man: the flint fields used for tools, the ancient trackways and the two tombs of Kits Coty and Little Kits Coty. It starts on top of the North Downs, descends steeply to travel through the rich arable land on the plain below, and finally re-ascends the ridge.

- From the entrance to the Blue Bell Hill picnic site car park, turn right into the road and after 100 yards cross over the A229 on an elevated road bridge.
- Follow the road to a crossroads at the Upper Bell Inn. Cross over and keep straight on up Mill Lane.

- Where Mill Lane bears right and becomes Warren Road, turn left behind a national speed limit sign to two stiles. Cross the right-most stile into an enclosed path, with a field on the left and stables on the right.
- Follow the enclosed path for 200 yards to reach trees.
- Follow the path through the trees along the edge of a field.
- At the end of the field cross a stile and continue along a clear path leading deeper into the woods. After 50 yards ignore a left turn, and 50 yards further on ignore a cross track and keep straight on, now with the M2 close on your left.
- Where the path emerges into a large field, keep ahead along the left-hand edge of the field, with the M2 still on the left for a short while.

There are numerous pieces of flint to be seen in this field, a common sight in many fields on the chalk uplands across Britain. Neolithic man made the majority of his tools from flint, and the availability of this valuable commodity was one of the attractions for settling on or near to the chalk ridges of the North and South Downs and the Ridgeway. In some areas of the country there were flint mines, and evidence that tools were mass-produced and traded with other communities. The flint upland here would have been worked just for the immediate needs of the local community.

- In the far corner of the field, turn right at the foot of a radio mast and continue along the field boundary, passing buildings and another mast on the left.
- Follow the field edge around to a tarmacked drive outside some gates. Turn right along the drive for 300 yards to reach a cross drive.
- Keep straight on over the cross drive and bear half-right along a marked footpath across a large field, aiming for the woods ahead.
- On reaching the woods, turn right along the track, keeping the woods on the left.
- In the corner of the field, where the field boundary turns right, turn left between two sarsen stones and follow the track into the woods.
- Keep straight on at a cross track and follow the path to reach a concrete 'North Downs Way' marker in the middle of a grove of yew trees.

There is no evidence that yew trees had any religious meaning to Stone Age men, but they did acquire a deep religious significance to man during the Iron Age, 700BC onwards. Deities were to be found in forests and groves, marshes, lakes, rivers and springs. Druids, religious leaders of great power, conducted services in groves, some of which may have been associated with human sacrifice. The yew tree has its blood-red berries fruiting at the time of Midwinter's Day, a time when the world was at its darkest and coldest, and thus had a special significance for ceremonies based around renewing the earth by calling the sun back. Yew trees and their berries became incorporated into the later Christian stories of Christmas.

- Soon start to descend the spur with the path, with views opening up to the left and then to the right. Ignore a left turn at a fence and continue down the spur, descending ever more steeply, soon using wooden steps set into the bank.

- At the bottom of the steps, turn right with the path and wind through trees for 50 yards to a cross track. Turn left down the cross track and in 30 yards pass through a horse barrier and down a few steps onto a trackway.
- Turn right and follow the trackway.

From Neolithic times a track has followed the North Downs, not along the summit but along the foot, where the chalk of the Downs meets the underlying clay and springs bubble out of the soil. The supply of fresh water was the reason for Neolithic man following this lower path, despite the thick forest it ran through. This supports the view that the threat of ambush by ones fellow man was much less then than in later times.

- In 100 yards pass an isolated sarsen stone on your right.

This stone is called the White Horse Stone, and it appears that it was being transported along the ancient track from the site of its excavation five miles to the east, to where the Kits Coty burial mound was being constructed, a mile west of here. How these huge stones were moved is unknown, but it is likely that ropes were tied around them and they were dragged by a human workforce, either on rollers or more likely using sledges. It is tempting to see the holes at either end of the stone as having been deliberately drilled into the stone to aid pulling, but there is no evidence for this. Why this stone was abandoned is unknown.

- Follow the trackway around the bottom of a field. Where the track becomes metalled, turn right and walk up towards the service station (being renovated at time of writing) seen ahead.
- Just before the service station, turn right down a metalled cycleway (signposted '17 Rochester') and follow it down and around to the left, to pass through a tunnel under the A229.
- Exit the tunnel and turn left at a T-junction. In 40 yards turn right onto a field path (signed 'North Downs Way')

This is still the same Neolithic trackway that you were on previously, but it is now called the Pilgrims' Way, used in the Middle Ages by pilgrims bound to Canterbury to worship at the shrine of St Thomas Becket (see walk 7).

- Follow this tree-lined footpath along the foot of the Downs for quarter of a mile to a cross track. Turn left down the cross track to reach a lane in 200 yards.
- Turn right into the lane and follow it for 350 yards to reach a road.
- Turn right along this busy road for 50 yards to reach Little Kits Coty, keeping an eye open for fast-moving traffic.

Little Kits Coty was a rectangular burial mound, of the same design as the Coldrum Long Barrow (walk 1). It was orientated roughly east–west, higher at the eastern end, where the entrance is, and sloping down away from the entrance. It had a single communal burial chamber lined with sarsen stones, buried beneath a mound of earth. This in turn was lined with sarsen stones that possibly acted as a kerb around the mound. This is one of a number of similar burial mounds or barrows found in the Medway area and the design has more in common with barrows found in Western Europe than those in the rest of the British Isles.

- After viewing Little Kits Coty, return to the road and walk along it with care for 300 yards to reach a road junction.
- Bear right around the bend for a few yards until you reach the Pilgrims' Way going off on the right. Cross the road at this point, turn left for 10 yards, then turn right onto a footpath on the right (signed 'North Downs Way').
- Climb the tree-lined track for 200 yards to the top of the slope, to reach Kits Coty on your left.

The imposing entrance to the Neolithic burial mounds of Kits Coty.

Kits Coty was a communal burial mound, built around 2200BC, and later than Little Kits Coty at the foot of the hill. Although this has been identified as a long barrow, it now appears more likely that it is the type of tomb known as a 'portal dolmen'. This is a small rectangular stone chamber, buried beneath a mound of earth, with the entrance marked by two huge upright stones capped by a sloping roofstone, which projects beyond the upright to form a sort of porch. As the mound subsides over the centuries, the roofstone collapses into the shape seen today.

By the time Kits Coty was built it had become the tradition to put burial mounds on high airy places. Whether this had religious significance or whether it was to give the mounds an additional use as a territorial marker, is unknown. Certainly by now communities were starting to become linked to specific geographic areas, and more permanent settlements with permanent territories were developing.

Those buried under the mound are more likely to have been people of religious importance, priests or shamans, than political leaders. The mound was named 'Kit's Coty' in the Middle Ages, meaning the house (or 'coty') of Kit, or Catigern, an Iron Age chieftain supposedly buried there. The mound is, however, far older than the Iron Age and there is no reason to believe it contains any such person.

- Continue up the trackway, ignoring side turns. Eventually climb some steps with a fence on your left to reach a road.
- Turn left along the road for 200 yards, passing the entrance to 'Beechcroft', then use a footbridge to cross the A229.
- On the far side of the footbridge, keep ahead up the right-hand side of the A229 for 30 yards, then bear off right up a footpath, initially parallel to the road but soon bearing away from it.
- Turn right with the footpath to climb over a stile and up through trees to reach a lane.

This lane follows the course of a Roman road, a spur that connected the Medway Valley with Watling Street, the main London–Dover road. Like all Roman roads, this would have had an all-weather surface which would have enabled travel to have continued regardless of the season of the year. The ancient Neolithic trackways along the foot of the Downs were reduced to quagmires in wet weather and effectively all communications ceased in the winter.

- Turn left in lane and follow it for a third of a mile, to where it swings left at a '30mph' sign. The lane is now Mill Lane again.
- Retrace your outward journey for a quarter of a mile by keeping straight on to reach the Upper Bell Inn, then crossing the crossroad and keeping ahead to reach the car park.

WALK 3
Oldbury Hill: Hill forts and trade routes in the Iron Age

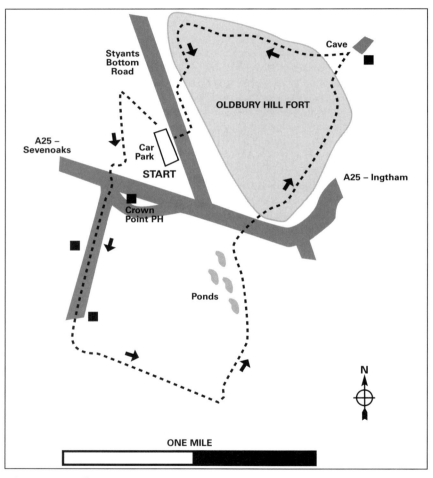

Distance: 4.5 miles
Map: OS sheet 188
Start and Parking: The walk commences from Oldbury Hill car park (NT), Styants Bottom Road, north off the A25 between Sevenoaks and Ightham (grid ref: 577558). If

coming along the A25 from Sevenoaks, pass Crown Point car park on your right: immediately beyond it on the left is a bus stop pull-in. Styants Bottom Road is a narrow lane immediately at the end of the bus stop. If coming from Oldbury, pass Coach Road on your left and immediately look for a National Trust signpost, pointing to the car park down a lane to the right. The concealed car park entrance is 200 yards down the Styants Bottom lane on your left. An alternative starting point is the Crown Point lay-by on the A25 (grid ref: 577559).

Refreshments: Available at the Crown Point public house near the start of the walk.

Historical Background

By the end of the Iron Age trade between the British tribes was extensive and trade goods came from as far afield as the Middle East and North Africa. A number of tribes had clans on both sides of the channel, and many tribes had strong cultural and trading links with their neighbours on the European mainland. Then, as now, most trade routes ran east–west from the harbours on the channel coast to the Thames Valley and beyond. Oldbury Hill stands upon one of the much rarer routes that ran north–south across the Weald, and it is the largest hillfort in Kent.

The first settlements upon Oldbury Hill were shelters established in caves by Palaeolithic hunters nearly 2,000 years ago, evidence of which can still be seen today. Towards the end of the Iron Age, around 100BC, a hillfort was constructed by local Wealdan tribes, both to provide shelter in times of trouble for their herds and people, and also to provide temporary shelter for traders. The fort was built on the top of Greensand Ridge, where two valleys running north–south through the steep-sided ridge provided a natural line of fortification. This fort occupied such an important strategic position that it was soon taken over by the Belgae, the foremost trading tribe of the time, which had a sturdy foothold in both southern Britain and northern Europe. The Belgae extended the site to cover 151 acres, and greatly improved its fortifications. Oldbury was soon of major importance to the Belgae. It was an extensive settlement in its own right as well as an important and strategically-placed trading post, and as such was defended fiercely but in vain against the advancing Roman legions in AD43.

The Walk

This walk travels along the wooded Greensand Ridge, following part of the ancient Iron Age trade route into Oldbury Hill Fort, to visit the fort itself.

- From the Oldbury Hill car park, proceed to the far end, passing under the overhead exit barrier. Immediately turn sharp left onto a bridle path.
- After 100 yards, at a crossing bridlepath, turn left, soon climbing steeply up to the A25.
- Turn left to the main road and cross with care to the uphill corner of the Crown Point lay-by. The Crown Point Inn lies below you in the dip, and a stone-faced cottage faces you. (If parked at Crown Point, your starting point is the top of the lay-by.)
- Follow the broad drive to the left of the stone-faced cottage at the top of the lay-by. The drive, soon tarmacked, continues for 600 yards to the end, passing a house to your left.

- Continue in the same direction along a bridle path, leaving leftwards from behind the house.
- Climb on the path to a gate. Turn left into a cross track beyond the gate and proceed, with steep drops down to Stone Street soon emerging on your right.
- After 600 yards, at the point where the trees on your left drop away into a hollow, turn left steeply downhill on a path through the woods.

You are now following the course of the old prehistoric road, which ran from the south coast near Pevensey to the Thames. It climbed from the Medway Valley around Tonbridge, crossed the ridge at the point you are now at, and then proceeded to the confluence of the Medway and the Thames, near present day Rochester. This journey, which forced the traveller to leave the open ridges and traverse the dark and forbidding forest, could easily have taken two days, especially if stock were being driven. However, overnight comfort and protection was near at hand, in the form of Oldbury Camp, a mile ahead down the path.

- Continue ahead and down when joined by another track from the right, eventually passing a series of small pools to your left.

Pools have existed beside the path since prehistoric times, and would have provided welcome watering holes for travellers and stock, just driven over the high ridge behind.

- Look for a path to your right, leading off opposite the fourth pool, and follow this out to the A25. This path can be hard to find in the summer undergrowth, but if it is missed, do not worry; just follow the main path you are on until the A25 is reached.
- Turn right along the A25 and cross the road to a bus stop pull-in on the opposite side of the road. (The junction of the A25 and Coach Road is visible, 50 yards further along the main road, on the right.) Behind the bus stop is a National Trust sign board.

You are now at the southern gateway of Oldbury Castle, with its ramparts, two and a half miles long, towering above you. Two thousand years ago these ramparts would have been bare earth, not wooded as today, and a strong wooden gate would have been present to bar progress if necessary. The gate was always the weakest part of a fort, and most forts would have had one or at most two gates. Oldbury had two. The gate itself would have been a movable wooden structure, often a pile of logs, inside intricate earth ramparts that defended it. These ramparts are clearly visible here at Oldbury's southern gate.

- Facing the sign board, take the right-hand path, climbing above the A25 on your right, for 150 yards.
- Still climbing, turn left with the path. Fifty yards beyond the corner, turn right at a cross track through a barrier and up a few natural steps.
- Follow the broad track ahead along the lower ramparts.

Today the view is obscured by trees, but 2,000 years ago the ramparts would have been clear, with views commanding the surrounding countryside. The banks would have been more precipitate than today and a strong wooden palisade would have faced downhill, giving further protection in times of trouble.

- Ignore a waymarked track on the left, and keep straight on with drops to your right.
- Keep straight on at a cross track.
- After a further 150 yards, you come to a waymarked cross track with a steep path dropping through a cutting to your right. Ignore this downhill track, but take the track next to it, the rightmost of two straight on tracks.
- After 50 yards, bear right at a junction.
- Go down steps and through a cleft in the rock.

The ramparts of Coldbury Castle Hill Fort.

At the bottom of the steps, look to the left behind a fallen tree, up a bank. The cave you see is one of several rock dwellings on the hill occupied by the Palaeolithic hunters who pre-dated the castle by many centuries. These dwellings were more than just a temporary overnight shelter, and were occupied for many weeks at a time during the hunting season. Formed by natural erosion within the sandstone, the floor would have been covered by rushes and skins to provide some measure of comfort.

- After looking at the rock dwelling, continue down the path. Turn right around a garage, and up the bridleway to the side of the house.
- Go straight ahead up a steep and sunken track, passing back through the ramparts to a cross track, encountered earlier, at the top of the slope. Now go straight on along the bridleway.
- Continue along the bridleway, passing a National Trust board to your left and orchards through the trees to your right.

You soon pass near the site of an ancient spring, which drains into a pool on your left. This spring provided drinking water for the fort in times of siege, and lay immediately beside the north–south road, along which you entered the fort and which continues towards present day Rochester.

- After 600 yards you come to a junction of paths. Ignore those to left and right, and take the left-most of the three that go straight on.
- After 50 yards, turn sharp left with the path. You are now at the most spectacular part of the fortifications, walking between two sets of ramparts.

Again, none of the woods which fill the vista would have existed. To your right, clear views would have commanded the surrounding countryside. To your left, within the inner rampart, would have been a vast open space, covering 150 acres. In times of peace, the hillfort would have been an administrative and commercial centre for the tribe, and would have had huts for the regular inhabitants, stockades and temporary accommodation for passing traders. The bulk of the tribe would have lived in outlying farms in the countryside beyond. There was a flourishing iron-working industry nearby, and the produce of the forges would have been traded here.

In times of war, the fort would have provided emergency shelter for the neighbourhood, and in the centre was plenty of open space to house the cattle of the surrounding farms. It is still just possible to make out the occasional outline of a hut circle or a grain pit amid the oak groves and chestnut coppices that now cover the site, and it is rewarding to wander through the middle of the old fort and let your imagination loose.

- After 300 yards, turn right down some wooden steps. Keep straight ahead at the foot of the steps.

- Just before a lane is reached, turn left onto a cross track. Follow the track for 300 yards to join the lane opposite Oldbury Hill car park.
- If you started from Crown Point, cross the lane and immediately before the overhead barrier of the car park exit, turn up a bridlepath to the right. Now follow the first instructions of this walk to return to Crown Point.
- Sandwich experienced a renaissance in the early 16th century, when an influx of Flemish refugees brought weaving skills into the town, and also brought land reclamation skills that re-opened water channels and drained marshland, facilitating market gardening.

WALK 4

Richborough and the Roman invasion of Britain

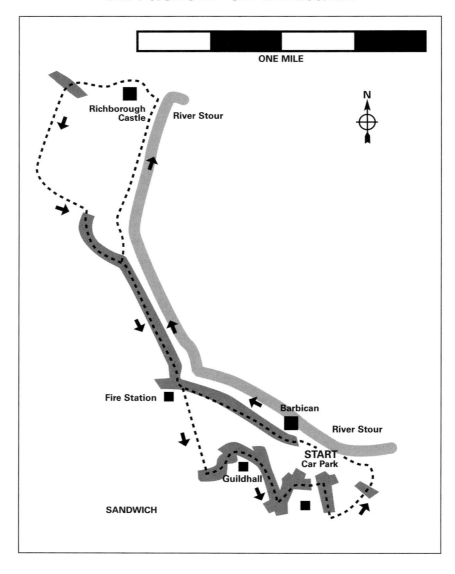

ONE MILE

N

Richborough Castle

River Stour

Fire Station

Barbican

River Stour

START
Car Park

Guildhall

SANDWICH

Distance: 4.5 miles
Map: OS sheet 179
Start and Parking: The walk commences from the old quay in Sandwich (grid ref: 334582). Sandwich is on the A256, seven miles south of Ramsgate and six miles north of Deal. There is ample pay-and-display car parking on the quay itself.
Refreshments: Public houses, shops and cafés in Sandwich.

Historical Background

In AD43, 50,000 Roman troops landed at Richborough and swept up through Kent to conquer Britain for the Emperor Claudius. A fort was built at Richborough, soon to be replaced by a flourishing town, the main entry into Britain for the next two centuries. Deteriorating military conditions led to the town being demolished to make way for a strong fort around AD250. This was built to command the southern entrance of the Wantsum Channel, an area of mud flats and creeks separating the Isle of Thanet from the mainland. For 150 years Richborough was a vital link in the string of forts built to protect the Saxon shore. Although it continued to be used by the British even after the Romans abandoned Britain in AD410, Richborough gradually sank into disuse.

In its place the town of Sandwich developed a mile to the south. Sandwich was an important town in Saxon times, and in the Doomsday Book of 1086 it was ranked the fourth most important town in England, after London, Norwich and Ipswich. Its prominence increased still further with the arrival of the Normans. Sandwich was one of the original Cinque Ports (from the french 'cinq' or 'five'), who were granted lucrative trading advantages by the Crown in return for providing boats for use by the king in time of war or national emergency. The town flourished until the 14th century, when the silting up of the harbour led to a gradual decline in its trade.

The Walk

This walk goes around the historic old town of Sandwich, one of the best preserved historic towns in England, and across the fenlands of the Stour estuary to the mighty Richborough Castle.

● From the Old Quay car park, with the river on your right, walk along the old quay towards the bridge. Do not cross the bridge, but pause at the end of it and look at the gatehouse, or 'barbican'.

Initially Sandwich stood at the head of a small inlet, emptying into the Wantsum Channel. It was thus protected from the worst of the seas and had easy access across the channel, north and south along the English coast, and inland through rivers and creeks. It also had good road access up the Roman Watling Street, to Canterbury and beyond. Its name means 'town built on the sands', an eloquent statement of its original position.

The old quay was the harbour-front of Sandwich in its heyday. A huge fishing fleet operated out of Sandwich in the Middle Ages: the town paid a rent of 40,000 herring a year to Canterbury Cathedral in 1086. In addition, as one of the original five Cinque Ports, the merchant vessels trading from Sandwich were among the most prosperous in Britain. They traded for wines, silks, spices and other luxury goods across the whole of Europe with produce brought from all over the British Isles, either around the coast or down the road from Canterbury and London.

Sandwich's sheltered harbour, with ready access to the Continent and to London, was a favourite entry and exit point for travellers. A key character in the Kentish story, Thomas-à-Becket, left England into exile from Sandwich in 1163, and landed on this quay on his return seven years later.

Initially Sandwich had no town walls. The houses facing the harbour were stoutly built for defence, and this was reinforced by churches built initially as mini fortresses. The Barbican was not part of the original town defences. It was added in 1539, at the same time that Deal, Walmer and Sandown Castles were built, as part of the line of coastal defences built by Henry VIII to give protection against the French.

- Turn left from the end of the bridge and pass through the Barbican gateway, and then turn right in front of the Admiral Owen public house, to go down Strand Street.
- Go down Strand Street, ignoring side turnings.

Originally the river was much wider, with a bank or 'stronde' along its southern side. This 'stronde' or 'strand' became the main street in the town, with narrow gaps at intervals between the close packed houses to allow passage onto the only dry road leading inland. These gaps became the narrow side streets you see today.

Strand Street has the greatest collection of timber-framed buildings found anywhere in England. Some of the best examples are 'The Weavers', home to Flemish refugees from religious persecution who settled in Sandwich in the early 16th century (opposite Kings Yard) and 'The Pilgrims', two early 15th-century merchants houses (at the junction with Harnet Street).

- Where Harnet Street joins from the left keep straight on, passing St Mary's Church.

Prior to 1380 Sandwich had no town walls. Part of its defences were churches built as fortresses to provide sanctuaries as well as places of worship. The Church of St Mary the Virgin had such a dual purpose, and was severely damaged during French raids in 1217 and in 1457.

The church had a long and eventful history. It was originally given as a nunnery by Ethelbert King of Kent, who had married a Christian princess, Bertha, and was inclined towards the Christian religion. It was Ethelbert's ready conversion that so eased St Augustine's mission in AD697 (see walk 7). The nunnery site was used by the Normans to build a fortress church. This was damaged by an earthquake in 1578, undermining the foundations to the extent that the tower collapsed in the next century and the church was abandoned until very recently.

- Follow Strand Street past the magnificent Manwood Court to reach Gallows field.

Gallows Field was just outside the Canterbury Gate through the town walls, which were built in 1380. It was an execution site for felons and was used up until 1792, when two deserters from the army were hanged.

- Turn right into Richborough Road, opposite the Kent Fire Brigade Station.
- Go up Richborough Road. Continue to follow the lane through fields and past isolated houses.
- Where the lane bends left, just before passing under the elevated road bridge of the A256 and by a level crossing sign, go right through a kissing gate beside a metal field gate.
- Keep straight on along a broad track, with the River Stour to the right, soon passing under the A256.
- Continue ahead, still with the river on your right and soon with a railway to your left.
- After two thirds of a mile cross a stile and over a sluice gate.
- At a T-junction, where the river bends sharply to the right, turn left and cross over the railway track.

The walls of Richborough fort can now be seen ahead of you.

- Carefully cross the railway track, and cross a stile on the other side of the railway. Do not cross a second stile immediately on your left, but instead turn right. Pass to the right of outbuildings and onto a track.
- Turn left with the track and climb a slope, with garden of a house on your left.

Richborough was the foremost port in Roman Britain. The temporary fort built in AD43 to protect the beachhead of the Roman invasion was demolished as the rapid pacification of Kent made it redundant. Richborough grew into a major military and naval supply base, in the centre of which stood a huge triumphal arch, straddling the way from the port to Watling Street and the rest of Britain, a symbolic entrance into the new Roman province. Soon a port named Rutupiae grew up under the protection of the fort, with warehouses and merchants dwellings growing up around the harbour, and taverns, hostels, baths and an amphitheatre being added as the town flourished. Imports and exports flowed through Rutupiae, which became the gateway to Britain.

Rutupiae flourished as a commercial centre for 200 years. By the middle of the third century pirate activity was seriously interrupting trade, and raids from Gaul on to the coast were becoming common. Much of the town centre was demolished and rebuilt as a strong castle, to provide a secure base for dealing with these raiders. It was surrounded initially by a double and in places triple line of ditches and ramparts, with immense stone walls inside these. Richborough Castle commanded the southern end of the Wantsum channel, while Reculver commanded the northern (see walk 5).

The harbour and much of the surrounding town were lost beneath the sea, which covered the flat lands you have walked across from Sandwich. The remainder of the town was largely lost beneath the third-century fort, whose walls, ditches and ramparts you see before you. Inside these walls are to be found traces of the fort buildings, and the foundations of the immense arch that dominated the town.

Richborough Castle, the gateway to the
Roman province of Britannia.

Richborough Castle is open from 1 April to 30 September, 10am–6pm. There is an admission charge, but it is free to members of English Heritage.

- Continue along the track, following it as it bends left along the castle walls and then right towards houses ahead.

The course of the old Wantsum Channel can be seen as the flat land to the right. Behind the power station seen in the distance is Ebbsfleet, where St Augustine landed in AD597 on his mission to convert Britain back to Christianity (see walk 7).

- Join a flinty track and keep straight on, passing a row of houses on your right, to reach a lane.
- Cross the lane and enter a field opposite. Follow the footpath down the right-hand side of the field, keeping the field boundary on your right.
- Pass into a second field and keep straight on, still with the field boundary on the right.
- At the bottom of the field enter the next field and bear quarter left across the next field, aiming for a marker post 100 yards away in the middle of the field.
- At the marker post turn left and walk with a drainage ditch on your right.
- Cross a stile by a gate and keep straight on down an enclosed path. In 50 yards ignore a turning to the right and then very shortly ignore one to the left.
- Keep straight on along the top of a bank. Do not descend but keep ahead into a field.

- Keep straight on across the field, aiming at a gate to the right of some brick and concrete pillars seen ahead.
- Cross a stile by the gate and into a lane. Turn right along the lane and follow it as it winds through fens, until in a quarter of a mile it crosses the railway and then passes under a road bridge.
- This is Richborough Road again. Follow it back to Gallows Field. On reaching the main road again, cross the road and turn left in front of the fire station.
- After 50 yards turn right down The Butts.

Norman feudalism was based on the concept that everyone, from the richest lord to the smallest farmer, held land in exchange for providing military service. In reality, it was the nobility who provided the professional soldiers, and their retainers were conscripted when required, with little or no training in the arts of war.

This altered in the middle of the 14th century, under the demands of the Hundred Years War. England had developed a weapon which was to dominate the battlefields of Europe for 200 years, namely the longbow. In skilled hands this weapon could drive a metal tipped arrow through the thickest armour at a range of 250 yards. To ensure this skill existed a form of military service was introduced: every commoner was required on pain of fines to practice with the longbow for two hours every week, after the Sunday church service was finished. An area was set aside for this practice, usually waste ground abutting the town walls, and named after the straw targets used, known as 'butts'.

- Stay on the concrete pavement to the right of the drive and walk along the old town wall.

The town walls in Sandwich were built comparatively late, in 1380. The advent of gunpowder had rendered the previous defences – fortified churches and strong houses – useless, and so the town was encircled with walls, stone built on the northern, seaward side, and here on the west and south, an earth embankment topped with a wooden palisade and fronted by a deep ditch.

The influx of Protestant refugees fleeing from religious persecution in Flanders during the late 15th century brought with it not only weaving skills but also skills in hydrodynamics. The marshes outside the town were drained, land reclaimed for arable use, and a clean water supply provided to meet the town's needs.

- On reaching a road turn left and follow the road, passing St Thomas' Hospital on your left.

St Thomas' Hospital is a comparatively new building, but there has been a hospital on this site since 1392. This was not a 'hospital' in todays meaning of the word, but rather a 'hospice', providing shelter for the poor rather than medical care. This is one of three founded in Sandwich by wealthy benefactors in the 13th and 14th century, and is named after Thomas Becket.

- At a mini roundabout, turn right. 50 yards later turn left and walk ahead to a T-junction in front of the New Inn. Turn right here to reach the square in front of the Guildhall in 10 yards.

The Guildhall was the central council chamber of mediaeval Sandwich, and reflects in its name that local government was the domain of the merchants' guilds. It served as a courtroom as well as a council chamber, and assizes were held here until 1951. The present building dates from 1579 and contains largely unaltered architectural features from the Elizabethan and Stuart periods.

Guided tours are available Tuesday–Thursday, 11.30am and 2.30pm, and Fridays 11.30am, in season.

- Pass in front of the Guildhall and along New Street. Almost immediately turn left down Austins Lane and then turn right into King Street.

St Peter's Church is another of the Norman fortress churches of Sandwich. Like St Mary's, it was badly damaged in the French raid of 1217.

- At a road junction at the Post Office continue ahead to reach a cross roads. Here turn sharp left down The Chain.
- In 60 yards turn right and keep ahead to St Clements.

St Clement's has a superb Norman tower chancel and central nave. The nave aisles were added in the 15th century. Unlike St Mary's and St Peter's, this church escaped the ravages of French raids, being in the corner of the town furthest from the sea. Since 1948 it has been the Parish Church of Sandwich.

- Pass through the churchyard, with the church on your right. Leave the churchyard and turn right up a no through road, with the rear of the church on your right.
- Keep ahead up this road to reach the town walls again.
- Turn left on to a tarmacked path along the town wall.

The ditch and rampart that formed the landward side of the town walls can clearly be seen here. The rampart you are walking along would have been topped with a wooden palisade.

- Cross a road and continue along the wall, now fenced on your right and called The Bulwark.
- Turn left with the wall and follow footpath back to the quay and the car park.

WALK 5

Reculver: Roman forts and Saxon churches

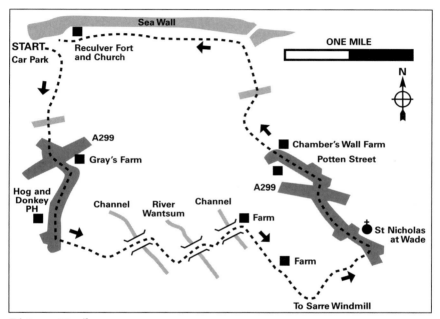

Distance: 10 miles

Map: OS sheet 179

Start and parking: The walk commences from the car park of Reculver Country Park (grid ref: 225693), at the end of a minor road, clearly signposted from the A299 Thanet Way.

Refreshments: Pubs and cafés around Reculver Country Park: Hog and Donkey pub two miles along the route: pubs and shop at St Nicholas at Wade.

Historical Background

In Roman and Saxon times, the coastline in this part of Kent was very different from today. Thanet was still an island, separated from the mainland by a sea channel, called the Wantsum Channel, which connected the Thames estuary and the English Channel. This was a desolate landscape of tidal marshes and mud flats, between one and three miles wide, with a winding stretch of navigable water running through it. The Romans built two forts to command this channel, Richborough at the southern end (see walk 4) and Reculver at the northern end. These were part of a series of forts constructed to control the estuaries and navigable waterways of Britain's south-eastern coastline, known as the Saxon Coast.

The fort at Reculver was originally nearly a mile from the sea (the present church stands almost in the middle of the old fort), but during the intervening centuries the coastline has encroached and over half the fort is now submerged. At the same time the Wantsum Channel has silted up, and gradually dried out, and the area has gradually been reclaimed as agricultural land. The Romans built Reculver around AD200 and garrisoned it until Roman authority collapsed towards the end of the fourth century, after which the fort fell into disuse.

In AD669 Egbert, King of Kent, gave the land to Christian missionaries and by AD692 there was an important monastery on the site. The church survived the troubled eighth and ninth centuries with very little damage. Although the monastery had ceased to exist by the 10th century, the church remained as the parish church of the area until the end of the 18th century, by which time the sea had encroached so far that the inhabitants of the parish moved to drier ground.

The church was partially dismantled to provide building material for a new parish church at Hillborough and the rest left to the mercy of the sea, but in 1809 Trinity House bought the remains, primarily the twin towers, as a navigation aid for vessels entering the Thames estuary.

The Walk
This walk follows part of the old Saxon shoreline and crosses the now reclaimed Wantsum Channel, an area of sea in Roman times. It returns along the coast to visit the remains of Roman and Saxon Reculver.

- Leave the entrance to Reculver Country Park car park and, facing the King Ethelbert Hotel, turn right down the road. After 100 yards, behind a pillar box and telephone kiosk and just before the café, turn left up a no through road signposted to 'Reculver Caravan Site'.
- Where the concrete drive turns into the entrance to Reculver Caravan site, continue straight on down an enclosed track between parts of the caravan park.
- After 200 yards and just before a gate, where the track emerges into open fields, turn right past a power line and follow the path alongside a water channel.
- Continue straight on across the top of a field. Carry straight on, with a channel on your right, along the side of a field to a footbridge.
- Cross the footbridge and continue on alongside the channel to reach a gate on to a drive.
- Pass through the gate, turn right along the drive for 10 yards, then turn left along a concrete drive to pass under the railway. Follow the concrete drive gently uphill for 400 yards to reach a lane.
- At the lane, turn left for 10 yards to reach a T-junction, then turn right down the road signposted 'Marshside'.

- Follow the road for 250 yards as it swings left and then crosses the A299 Thanet Way by a road bridge, with the Roman Galley Hotel to your left.
- At a T-Junction on the far side of the road bridge, turn left. Follow this quiet lane as it swings right and downhill through Grays Farm, and then through Little Greys. Continue along the lane once it has levelled out, now with a water channel along the left side, passing the remote Hog and Donkey public house on your right.

You are now walking along what in Roman times was the shoreline. To your right the land slopes gently upwards; to your left is what used to be the Wantsum Channel, a flat expanse of water, reeds and mud flats stretching over a mile before reaching the opposite shore, just discernible as a slight rise at what is now St Nicholas at Wade.

- Four hundred yards past the Hog and Donkey, where a small lane branches off to the right, turn left across a bridge over the channel and through a field gate onto a bridle path.
- Continue along the bridle path as it winds through fields. After 800 yards, fork left at a junction.
- Continue for another half mile along the bridle path as it winds through fields, with bushes and trees along the path edges for many sections, to reach a gate.
- Pass through the gate, cross a dyke by a tractor bridge, and turn right onto a permissive path along the top of the dyke.
- Continue along the dyke, with the channel to your right, for 600 yards, passing two wooden footbridges across the channel. 20 yards after passing the second footbridge, turn left onto an adjoining bridle path.
- Follow the bridle path between fields, with intermittent hedges and spinneys on your left, maintaining generally the same direction, to reach a concrete bridge across a water channel.

You are now crossing the River Wantsum. Until now all the fenland you have crossed since leaving the lane by the Hog and Donkey was tidally submerged in Roman and Saxon times. You are now crossing the navigable channel that ran through the marshes and mudflats of the Wantsum Channel.

- Cross the bridge and follow the winding metalled drive to cross a second bridge.

You have now reached what in Saxon times was the far shore of the Wantsum Channel.

- Cross this second bridge and follow the drive, passing a farm on your left. As the drive swings leftwards, ignore bridges on your right, but a few yards further on, opposite a cottage, turn right onto a bridle path.
- Follow the bridle path, with hedges on the right and soon with a channel on right. After 400 yards, ignore a bridge on your right and continue straight on, with the channel on your right. Where the path leaves the channel, continue straight ahead along a clear path across a field, towards farm buildings.

- Just before farm buildings, where the main bridle path turns left, keep straight on along a lesser track. After 20 yards, where this track turns left into the farmyard, go straight on through a gate onto a grassy track. Follow this track for a few yards as it bends to the left.
- Although the right of way now goes into the corner of the yard ahead, follow the permissive diversion by aiming half-right through the small caravan parking area in front of you. Pass between caravans and leave through a narrow gate in the middle of the hedge in front.
- Continue straight on in the same direction, along a clear bridle path in front of you. Follow the bridle path, soon with a hedge on your right, as it bends around field boundaries, for 600 yards.
- Where a tarmacked path joins from the left, turn left onto a tarmacked path and follow it slightly uphill across a field.

If you wish to visit Sarre Windmill, a working windmill and animal farm open to the public, continue straight on along the bridle path at this point.

Sarre Windmill is open daily 10am–5pm.

- Follow the path, initially tarmacked, for 800 yards across fields, ignoring a bridle path leading off to the right. On the outskirts of St Nicholas at Wade the path reaches a turning circle at the end of a cul-de-sac, with a strategically positioned bench.

Sitting on the bench you are afforded fine views over the Wantsum Channel and of Sarre Windmill. Although the Wantsum Channel was navigable from north to south, there were also fords which crossed the marshes from the Kentish mainland to the Isle of Thanet. One such ford was just in front of you, running left to right, from where Sarre Windmill now stands to Upstreet on the Kentish side of the channel.

- Follow the tarmacked path around the left-hand boundary of a field, and then across a second field to enter a recreation field.
- Continue straight on along the right-hand edge of the recreation field. The path soon becomes enclosed, and shortly passes through a gate to reach a road.
- Turn left for 20 yards up the road to reach a T-junction.
- Turn left at the T-junction and proceed along the main street of St Nicholas at Wade, passing between two public houses and shortly passing the church on your right.

The church of St Nicholas is 13th century with an early 14th-century tower. Inside are arches in the chancel dating from around AD1200 and an interesting wooden staircase leading to a lobby above the porch.

- One hundred yards past the church, at a junction of roads, fork right down Court Road.
- Continue along the road for half a mile, ignoring turns to left and right.

● The road crosses the A299 Thanet Way via a road bridge, from the top of which there are fine views.

The twin towers of Reculver can just be seen on the skyline, above the sea wall that now demarks the limit of the reclaimed fenlands.

● Cross the A299 and follow the road to a T-junction, where you turn left, signposted 'Potten Street'.
● In 200 yards, where the road swings right at Potten Street, continue straight on. Follow the lane for a further 400 yards to pass through Chambers Wall Farm.
● Immediately after passing the farm, where the lane swings left, turn right across a small bridge onto a concrete track.
● Follow the concrete track for half a mile. Where the concrete ends, bear right, with a hedge on your right, soon to join a track along the top of a dyke, with the water channel to your left.
● Continue along the dyke for 600 yards to cross the railway.
● On the far side of the railway track, turn right with the track to the top of the dyke, then immediately cross the dyke and descend leftwards to pick up the continuation of the track you have been following. Turn right onto the track and go along the top of the dyke, with a water channel on your left.
● After 600 yards the track reaches a metalled path along the top of a sea wall. Turn left along this path, with drained marshes on your left and the recently reclaimed lagoon on your right.
● After 200 yards the path reaches the coast.

Reculver Towers can be seen in front of you. Trinity House, the body responsible for ensuring safe navigation around Britain's coasts, bought the towers in 1809 to save them from demolition, on the grounds that they provided a distinctive landmark for shipping entering the Thames estuary. Their domination of the landscape can clearly be seen for the remainder of this walk.

● Follow the sea wall for one and a half miles, with Reculver Towers getting ever closer to you.

The beach on your right was used during World War Two as a testing ground for many weapons, among the most well known of which was the 'Bouncing Bomb', designed by Barnes Wallis and used in the famous Dambusters' raid. A complete prototype bomb was dug up from this beach in the summer of 1997, where it had lain since being tested over 50 years earlier.

If you look to your left as you walk along the sea wall you will be able to clearly distinguish both shores of the old Wantsum Channel.

● The path eventually reaches Reculver.

A Saxon church stands behind the Roman fort of Reculver.

You are now passing through what used to be the Roman port. The sea was a mile to your right and the fort was on the headland ahead of you, which provided a sheltered anchorage.

● Turn left along the foot of the old Roman fort.

On your right is a surviving section of the Roman fort wall. Clearly visible are the layers of flint and mortar alternated to provide the wall with extra strength.

● At a T-junction, turn right through the east gate of Reculver fort.

The Roman fort at Reculver was nearly 600 square feet, surrounded by walls 15 feet high and 10 feet thick. It was built upon a natural rise of land, and the rubbish accumulated during two centuries of occupation raised the level of the fort still more. It had a garrison of around 1,000 men, and it contained all the facilities necessary for their comfort, including barracks, bath-house and a temple. Over the intervening centuries the sea has advanced by a mile, and swept away the north and west walls of the fort. A pathway leading from the east gate still follows the course of the surviving east and south walls. Nothing remains to be seen of the buildings inside the fort.

● Follow the path, passing the church on your right.

Much of the church has been demolished, either eroded by the sea or pulled down for building materials. The oldest part of the church is the nave, built in AD669. The bottoms of these Saxon walls still survive. The church was small, with an aisle-less nave and rounded chancel, a design typical of early churches in Kent. The original walls and the eighth-century extension are marked out on the ground.

The church was remodelled in the 12th century. The twin towers were added, with a main west entrance between them. They were originally topped with wooden spires, but these blew down in 1818. Although the stairs up to the third storey of these towers survive, they are no longer open to the public.

Both the church and the fort are open to the public at any reasonable time.

● Follow the path to emerge above the car park.

The ruins of Herne Bay Pier can be seen out to sea, in front of you and to your right. The pier was destroyed by storms in the early 1980s, but the pier head survived and still stands, now isolated half a mile out to sea.

WALK 6
The Darenth Valley:
2,000 years of commuters

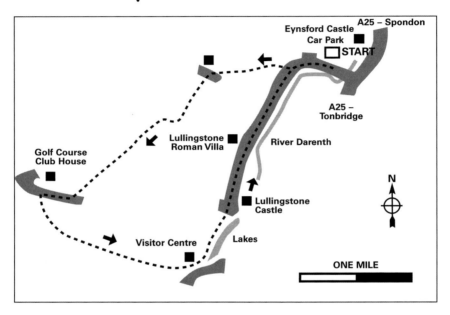

Distance: 5.5 miles

Map: OS sheet 177

Start and Parking: The walk commences in Eynsford village (grid ref: 539656). From the A225 from London, turn right across a hump-backed bridge in the village centre, in the direction of Lullingstone Villa and Castle. Park in the public car park behind the Plough Inn, Lynsford.

Refreshments: Pubs, tearoom and a shop in Eynsford: Clubroom of Lullingstone Golf Course opens to the public: soft drinks and snacks at Lullingstone Castle Visitors' Centre.

Historical Background

Today the charming Darenth Valley, especially its northern end around Eynsford, Shoreham and Otford, is often thought of as being a dormitory for London commuters. Although there is still a considerable amount of local employment in the area, it is true that a considerable percentage of the working population take advantage of the easy access into London to work in the city while living in a green and pleasant valley.

What is less frequently realised is that this area has in a very real sense been a home for London 'commuters' throughout the ages. True, prior to the Industrial Revolution and the arrival of the railway in the middle of the last century, the bulk of the population worked where they lived. But for wealthy courtiers, civil servants and merchants, whose public life revolved around the capital, the Darenth Valley has provided a pleasant and sheltered place to live within easy distance of London for 2,000 years. A Roman civil servant working in Londinium bought a farm at Lullingstone and converted it into a magnificent villa; a Norman baron built a castle as his home at Eynsford, conveniently close to the capital; a Tudor courtier built a mock castle at Lullingstone and installed a tiltyard for the entertainment of his monarch and his peers.

The Walk
This walk goes through the lovely countryside of the upper Darenth Valley, passing some splendid examples of Roman, Norman and Tudor architecture. It follows the river to return under one of the most spectacular 19th-century railway viaducts in south-east England.

- Leave the car park behind the Plough Inn and turn right along the lane, walking upstream alongside the Darenth, away from the village centre.
- Continue through the village, past Home Farm on the left and ignoring a right-hand turn to Crockenfield.
- Houses finally fade away to an open valley. Look for the last house on the right, Meadow View. Fifty yards past Meadow View turn into a field at a footpath sign beside a gate on the right.
- Proceed diagonally across the field, ascending towards the top of the railway viaduct which can be glimpsed through the trees to your left.

The arrival of the railway in the 1840s brought the Darenth Valley within commuting distance of London as never before. Eynsford, Shoreham and Otford all expanded from being essentially agricultural communities to providing homes for the more affluent workers in the city. The viaduct to your left is a splendid example of Victorian civil engineering and will be seen to its full later in the walk.

- At the top of the field, cross the railway line with great care and follow the clear path through the next field to a stile leading onto a drive.
- Cross the drive and follow the path through the third field, making for the bottom corner of a fourth field. Fine views over the Darenth Valley open up to your left.
- Enter the fourth field and continue your general line of advance, along the bottom of the field. The grey roof of the building now housing Lullingstone Villa can just be glimpsed in the trees at the bottom of the slope.
- Cross a stile and turn right into an enclosed path. Proceed up hill for 100 yards, and then turn left into an open field.

- Continue straight ahead along a clearly defined path which follows the top of the Greensand Ridge. This path marks the western boundary of the Tudor deerpark that adjoined Lullingstone Castle. There are fine views down into the Darenth Valley to your left, looking across the old deerpark.

Deer still roamed this park until the end of the last century, and oaks survive which were planted in Tudor times. Until the Middle Ages deer had freely grazed the woodland of England, and were the sole property of the king under the Laws of the Forest. By the end of the 15th century the forests had shrunk under encroachment by agriculture and the heavy demand for wood to provide charcoal. Increasingly the greater landowners would enclose large swathes of land and stock them with their own deer herds, especially bred and managed to provide hunting for the landowner and his guests. Continuing deforestation meant that soon deerparks were the only habitat for these once free-roaming animals.

- Follow the path down into a dip, with a golf course to your left, and up the other side. Bear slightly left to enter the woods ahead.
- Climb up through the woods by gentle wooden steps. In the right season a mass of bluebells are to be seen. After 200 yards emerge onto the side of the golf course.
- Proceed straight ahead, following the somewhat indistinct path along the right-hand edge of the golf course.
- At the end of the golf course, ignore the broad path directly ahead and bear slightly left to enter the woods.
- Wind through the open woodland, full of bluebells in May. The path often divides and reunites, but continue your line of advance, with the open golf course visible through the trees to your left.
- Join a broader track, and continue in the same general direction, still with the golf course to your left. Ignore cross tracks and continue forward.
- Eventually your path reaches a horse barrier. Pass through into a broad track and turn left.
- Cross between two fairways and keep straight ahead into the woods.
- Proceed through open woods, ignoring a cross track and continuing until you reach a tarmacked horse ride at the end of the woods. Turn right onto the tarmacked path, but look at the fine view down the valley to your left, once all deerpark but now a golf course.

This shows an interesting change in land use. Once the preserve of the local landowner, for he and his friends to go hunting for recreation, the land is now open for recreation to the general public.

- After 250 yards, turn left at public footpath sign (FP 206). (The clubhouse of Lullingstone Golf course is clearly visible to your right, and is open to the public for refreshments, reached by following the tarmacked path around.)
- Follow the footpath away from the golf course and down into woods. At the bottom of the slope, carefully cross the fairway and follow the broad path ahead up into the open woods on the other side of the valley.

- At a cross track, continue straight on, ignoring all turns to right and left.
- Emerge from the woods at the top of a dry valley falling away to your left. Continue straight on uphill, with fence and trees to your right.
- Re-enter the woods, and follow a broad track straight ahead, eventually passing through a horse barrier, to footpath signposts. Here go straight on (signed to 'Visitors' Centre').
- After 100 yards, take the right-hand fork, and follow the path downhill. You shortly emerge at the top of a wide meadow, with fine views down into the Darenth Valley, and with the Lullingstone Visitors' Centre clearly visible at the foot of the slope.
- Continue down the slope to the Visitors' Centre (refreshments available).
- Pass to the right of the Centre, to a stone bridge across the river. Do not cross the bridge, but just before it turn left onto a footpath along the riverbank.
- Follow this pleasantly shaded footpath along the river, with the old deerpark to your left, soon to reach a man-made weir and lake.

This lake was constructed in Tudor times to provide fish for Lullingstone Castle and was used in Stuart times by the owners, the Hart family, for recreational fishing. The lake also provided water for a silkworm factory, run by the Hart family and their successors the Dyke family for many years.

- Pass through the car park of Lullingstone Castle, to a tarmacked drive. Here turn left, in front of the castle.

Although there has been a manor of Lullingstone since Domesday times, the current manor house dates from the reign of Henry VII, when it was built by Sir John Peche. A prominent courtier, Sir John took a leading part in the Royal Jousts of 1494, at which he won the prize, a golden ring with an inset diamond, which was presented to him by the king's younger daughter Margaret. A favourite of the king, Sir John became Sheriff of Kent in 1495, arresting the pretender Perkin Warbeck and being knighted for his part in the Battle of Blackheath in 1497. Sir John also went on to become a close companion of Henry VIII, becoming Lord Deputy of Calais and accompanying the King to his famous meeting with King Louis of France at the Field of the Cloth of Gold in 1520. As a prominent courtier, Sir John required a country retreat close to the court, which was located only a day's ride away at Greenwich, and which would be suitable for entertaining monarchy.

The splendid gatehouse was built in 1497, one of the earliest brick gatehouses in England and an imposing statement of the owner's pre-eminence. Sir John's coat-of-arms is emblazoned above the gates. To the west of this was a full-sized tiltyard, to cater for the passion for jousting which Sir John shared with Henry VIII. The surrounding park was enclosed and stocked with deer, again to cater for the monarch's passion for hunting. The ability to entertain the king close to his capital was part of the popularity of Lullingstone, and stood Sir John in good favour.

Upon Sir John's death the manor passed to his nephew Sir Percyvall Hart, who held court offices under Henry VIII, Edward VI, Mary and Elizabeth until his death in 1580. The Hart

The Tudor gateway of Lullingstone Castle.

family continued in the service of the Crown throughout the Stuart era, until the death of the last male Hart, also called Percival, in 1738. This Percival was a good friend of Queen Anne, another frequent royal visitor to Lullingstone. It was he who built the Queen Anne façade onto the castle and also made additions to the Tudor interior of the building. The adjoining Church of St Bodolph, open occasionally to the public, contains memorials to 600 years of the Peche, Hart and succeeding Dyke families.

Lullingstone Castle is open to the public weekends and bank holidays, April to September. The garden and church are open Wednesday–Friday afternoons, April to September. There is an admission charge.

● Walk for half a mile along this drive to Lullingstone Roman Villa.

At the time of the Roman Conquest in AD43 there was an Iron Age farmstead on the present site. About AD80 it was replaced by a small villa built by the first Romanised Britons in the area, a farming family who gradually extended the villa over the next 40 years and who remained in occupation for over a century. Just behind the villa was a small circular temple, devoted to the worship of the local woodland deity.

With Watling Street, the main Roman road from the coast to London passing only 20 miles to the north, the Darenth Valley became a desirable residence for government officials looking for a country retreat. Around AD180 a new owner took over the villa, not a British farmer but possibly a wealthy Roman of Mediterranean origin. This owner is believed to have been a civil servant, whose work often took him into Londinium for long periods of time, but who chose to live in the countryside rather than in the bustle of the city. The simple villa was now converted into a luxury residence: the thatch roof was replaced by one of red tiles, a bathing suite was added to the south end, the northern wing was extended and extensive redecoration in the Mediterranean style was undertaken.

The villa was suddenly abandoned around AD200, possibly as a result of the political unrest prevalent in Britain at that time, and remained unoccupied for most of the next century. About AD280 it was reoccupied, this time by wealthy Romano-Britons, who used the villa as a base for an extensive farm and built a temple mausoleum behind the house. It was these owners who laid the striking mosaics still to be seen in the dining room and reception room and among the best to be found in Britain today. Around AD390 the owners of the villa converted to Christianity, and built a chapel in the villa.

The villa was finally abandoned around AD420, and over the years the gradual movement of soil down the hillside buried and thus preserved the walls and floors.

Lullingstone Villa is open daily from 1 April to 30 September 10am–6pm and October to March 10am–4pm. There is an admission charge, but it is free to English Heritage members.

● Passing the villa on your left, proceed down the quiet country lane, with the Darenth away to your left. After half a mile, the magnificent railway viaduct comes into view.

Wonderfully preserved mosaic floor in the roman villa at Lullingstone.

Built of red brick in 1847 to carry the main Swanley to Sevenoaks line across the Darenth Valley, the construction of the viaduct played a major part in opening the valley to commuters. It was necessary for the line, which came from the North East, to cross from the western side of the valley in order to continue its southern course on the eastern side of the valley, where it avoided the privately-owned land of the large estates of the Darenth Valley.

- Pass under the viaduct and continue along the lane. In quarter of a mile, pass Meadow View on your left, and follow your outward path back to the car park.
- It is worth detouring to see Eynsford Castle, a quarter of a mile's pleasant walk away. Pass in front of the Plough and cross the Darenth by the old hump-backed bridge, with the ford to your right. At the main road turn left. The Norman church opposite stands in a quiet country churchyard.
- Walk down the main road of Eynsford, still with reminders of its Tudor origin visible in such buildings as the Elizabeth Villas to your right.
- Turn left down what could be taken as a private driveway. Follow the drive around to the right to emerge at the ruins of Eynsford Castle.

Eynsford Castle was originally built by William De Eynsford in 1090. De Eynsford was a Norman, who had come to England after the conquest. William the Conqueror had given the biggest estates in the more politically sensitive areas to the barons who had accompanied him to England, as a reward but also so that they could subdue the country. De Eynsford came to England somewhat after the conquest, and was more of a courtier than a military baron. He thus was content to be given a smaller estate which was nevertheless in good agricultural land and conveniently close to the court in London. Consequently, Eynsford Castle was never built for any real military purpose, but was instead a fortified home. Nevertheless, it is one of the finest examples of a 'pre re-keep' castle in England, the original style of Norman castles.

The castle is built upon an artificial mound of earth called a motte, and surrounded by a moat and a D-shaped flint curtain wall, which was 30 feet high but was never crenellated. This is a sure sign that it was never expected to be used for any serious fighting, but rather to protect the owner's property from casual banditry. There is no sign that the bridge over the moat could ever be raised. Entry to the castle was via a magnificent fortified gatehouse, which was roofed with tiles taken from Lullingstone Villa. Eynsford Castle never had a keep, but within the defensive curtain wall there was originally a wooden tower built above a well, which was eventually replaced by a stone two-storey manor house, of domestic rather than military design.

In the reign of Henry II, a later De Eynsford was ex-communicated by Archbishop Thomas Becket for taking certain feudal financial benefits from a local priest, which Becket considered an attack on the church. It was this sturdy defence of the privileges of the church against any encroachment by the secular powers that led to Becket's murder in 1170. After the murder it is claimed that De Eynsford was so overcome by remorse that he vowed never to live in his castle again. The castle was gutted by fire in 1261 and abandoned.

Eynsford Castle is open March to October, weekdays 9.30am–5.30pm, Sundays 2–5.30pm and November to February, weekdays 9.30am–4.00pm, Sundays 2–4pm. Entrance is free.

WALK 7
Canterbury and the return of Christianity to Britain

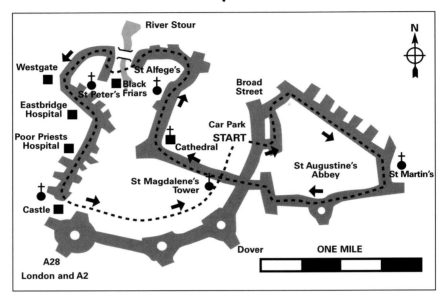

Distance: 3.5 miles

Map: OS sheet 179

Start and Parking: The walk starts at the Broad Street pay-and-display car park in Canterbury (grid ref: 153578). Broad Street is part of the inner ring road that circles the outside of Canterbury's mediaeval walls. It is the eastern sector midway between where the A2050 and the A28 join the ring road. The car park is against the town walls. There are several other car parks in Canterbury, but little street parking.

Refreshments: Public houses, shops, cafés and tearooms in Canterbury.

Historical Background

There has been a settlement at Canterbury since at least 300BC. It stands at a place where a ford over the River Stour allowed an easy crossing for the important trade route from the coast to the Thames valley, and where the river valley provided an easy route southwards through the North Downs. The Romans defeated the local Britons and built a camp that eventually grew into the city of Durovernum. After the Romans left, Canterbury emerged as the capital of the kingdom of Kent: its name means 'stronghold of the people of Kent'.

Canterbury is closely linked with the story of the re-emergence of Christianity in England. In AD597 Augustine landed near Richborough and journeyed to Canterbury, where he was aided by Queen Bertha, herself a Christian, in converting her husband King Ethelbert, and through him his subjects. An abbey and a cathedral were established and, although often in rivalry, helped the newly-returned religion to flourish.

With the Norman invasion the position of Canterbury as both a commercial and a religious centre was consolidated. The Normans gave the church a great deal of secular power, leading to a conflict which culminated in the murder of Archbishop Thomas Becket in his own cathedral at Canterbury. This event immediately made Canterbury into one of the leading places of pilgrimage in Europe, requiring the development of a massive infrastructure to accommodate pilgrims, and greatly increasing the town's wealth and prosperity. Additionally, Canterbury became a centre of healing, attracting Dominican and Franciscan monks to settle in the town and build several hospitals.

The secular power of the church in Canterbury declined finally during Henry VIII's reign. The abbey was dissolved in 1538, Becket declared a traitor and his shrine looted, and the priory was dissolved in 1540. Cathedral buildings and wealth were secularised. The following century the cathedral was damaged by puritan extremists during the Civil War. Although Canterbury shared in the prosperity created by the wool trade in Tudor times, it never returned to its former pre-eminence.

The Walk
This walk is entirely within the urban confines of old Canterbury, and its route follows the growth of Christianity in the city as well as passing sites that reflect its commercial and political power.

- Walk down the Broad Street car park, with the town wall on your right, until you reach a postern gate in the wall (the Quentin Gate). With your back to the postern, leave the car park and cross the ring road at the pedestrian lights. Go straight on up Lady Woottons Green, with its hedge-lined flower garden in the centre.
- At the top of Lady Woottons Green, turn left in front of the gate of Christchurch College and follow the road past modern bungalows.
- At a T-junction, turn right into Havelock Street.
- After 150 yards, turn right along North Holmes Road. Keep ahead, keeping the ragstone wall of Christchurch College on your right. Keep straight on when the wall becomes brick, soon passing the houses of St Martins Terrace on your right.
- At the end of the terrace keep straight on, now with the railings of a churchyard on your left, to reach the entrance to St Martin's Church.

St Martin's is England's oldest parish church. In AD562 Ethelbert, King of Kent, married Bertha of France, a Christian, who persuaded her new husband to build a church for her chaplain, Bishop Liudhard, in his capital Canterbury. This he duly did, and St Martin's Church was constructed sometime before AD570. As such, it pre-dated St Augustine's arrival

Canterbury Cathedral, where Thomas Becket was murdered in 1170.

in Britain on his mission of conversion by over 25 years. The church was built in part of red Roman brick, still visible in places, has blocked-up Saxon windows and a fine pre-Norman fort.

- Leave St Martin's via the lychgate and go straight ahead down the road, to meet the main road in 150 yards.
- Turn right along the main road for 300 yards, passing the entrance to Canterbury Prison, to reach St Augustine's Abbey.

St Augustine landed in Kent in AD597, at Ebbsfleet near Richborough (see walk 4). He had been sent by Pope Gregory to convert the Britons back into Christianity, the religion they had followed in the last century of the Roman Empire. He was welcomed by King Ethelbert, already sympathetic to Christianity, and founded the abbey here at Ethelbert's capital in AD598, to house the monks who had accompanied him to England. Augustine called it the Abbey of St Peter and St Paul, and it was consecrated in AD613; later it became known as St Augustine's Abbey. Ethelbert, his Queen Bertha, and Augustine are all buried in the Abbey, which also houses the tombs of all the earliest archbishops of Canterbury, as well as the kings of Kent. There was growing rivalry between the abbey and the nearby cathedral, and after AD758 archbishops were buried in the latter.

By the Middle Ages, the abbey had grown into one of the greatest and richest monasteries in Europe, until it was largely destroyed in 1538 during the Dissolution of the Monasteries. The gilded shrine containing the remains of St Augustine was secretly removed, and for a time rested in St Mary's Church, Chilham (see walk 18).

Open all year, April to the end of September, 10am–6pm, October to March, 10am–4pm. There is an admission charge, but it is free to English Heritage members.

- Continue along the road past the entrance to the Abbey. Turn right with the major road and then very shortly turn left down Church Street to St Pauls.
- At the end of Church Street cross the ring road at the pedestrian lights and pass through the city walls via Burgate.

Burgate is the site of one of the eight gates that pierced the mediaeval city walls of Canterbury.

- Pass the Cathedral Postern on your right and keep ahead up the cobbled street, passing the tower of St Mary Magdalene on your left.

The tower of St Magdalenes' survived German bombing raids during World War Two and is now used to display some old memorial stones.

- Ignore all turns to the left and follow the road to reach a square with a war memorial, in front of the Christ Church gate into the cathedral precinct.

In AD602 an existing church, part of the palace of King Ethelbert, was given to Augustine as a place of worship. This was the start of the complex that was to become Canterbury Cathedral. The church was added to over the next two centuries, but was burnt to the ground when the Danes sacked Canterbury in 1011 and kidnapped Archbishop Alfege. Lanfranc, the first of the Norman archbishops, was consecrated in the ruins of the church in 1070 and immediately set about building a suitable cathedral, work continued by his successor Anselm.

The power and independence of the church brought it into increasing disagreement with the Crown. In an attempt to stop these disputes Henry II appointed his trusted friend and Chancellor Thomas Becket as Archbishop of Canterbury in 1162. Far from solving the problem, this appointment exacerbated it, for the previously worldly and loyal Becket now threw his considerable energies and intelligence into the cause of the church and rapidly came into conflict with the king. The archbishop was exiled in 1163, but allowed to return in 1170, only to be murdered in the cathedral by four of the king's barons. Henry's infamous remark 'What cowards have I about me, that no one will deliver me from this lowborn priest!', was taken as the order for the murder, although whether it was intended to be such is uncertain.

Becket was immediately regarded as a saint, not so much for what he was or had done but for the fact that he had been martyred for his faith. The cathedral became a place of pilgrimage almost at once. When a fire destroyed much of the building four years later, the work of reconstruction started yet again, but this time funded by money pouring in from pilgrims. The present cathedral, known technically as the Church of Christ Canterbury, dates largely from the period 1275–1400, although some remains of the earlier building can still be found, most notably the early Norman crypt. The crowning glory of the cathedral, the magnificent Bell Harry Tower, was not completed until 1496.

A complex of other buildings grew up within the cathedral grounds: infirmaries for sick travellers, hostels and lodgings of graded comfort for pilgrims, cloisters to accommodate increasing numbers of visitors and schools. One of the finest of these buildings, Meister Omers, is now used as a boarding dormitory for the King's School, which was founded by Henry VIII during the Reformation, to divert education from the hands of the Catholic church. The wealth and buildings of the cathedral were used to subsidise this project.

As well as the shrine to Thomas Becket (which was looted during the Reformation), the cathedral contains a number of tombs, the most notable of which is probably that of the Black Prince. Interestingly, although the major cathedral in England, only one English king, Henry IV, is buried here.

The cathedral complex and the cathedral itself contain architectural splendours far too numerous to list individually here. The complex can be visited, and the main entrance is via the Christ Church Gate. Currently the cathedral precinct charges an entrance fee to visitors.

- Bear right past Christ Church Gate to reach a cross road, and turn right into Palace Street.
- Go down Palace Street, passing St Alfege's Church and Conquest House on the left.

The magnificent entrance to
Canterbury Cathedral.

St Alfege's is named after Canterbury's very own saint, Archbishop Alfege, who was carried off by the Danes in AD1012 for ransom and murdered by them at their camp in Greenwich after he refused to allow a ransom to be paid. It is Early English in style, and, although it is uncertain when it was actually built, it was described in 1166 as 'old'.

- At a T-junction, turn right into The Borough and pass the entrance of King's School on your right.
- Where the ragstone wall of the school ends on your right, and opposite the Jolly Sailor Ale House, turn left down St Radigunds Street.

This is the site of the north gate into Canterbury. You are following the course of the old city wall.

- After 30 yards bear left past a sunken garden and follow the road across a junction and past The Dolphin on your right.
- Fifty yards after The Dolphin and just before a bridge turn half-left at the top of Mill Lane and go through a gate and over a footbridge across a weir.
- Follow the footpath over another footbridge crossing sluice gates and turn left to follow the path through a quiet garden along the side of the River Stour.

The River Stour flows through the North Downs at Chilham (see walk 18) and has always been an important communications route leading into Canterbury. The old building on the river side in front of you is the remains of the Blackfriars, home to the Dominicans who came to Canterbury in 1237. Further up the river, not visible from here, is the Greyfriars, home to the Franciscans who had arrived 13 years before the Dominicans but did not have a permanent site for their friary until 1267. Both sets of friars were healing orders, who set up hospitals to tend the sick who were flocking into Canterbury in the hope of being cured at the shrine of St Thomas Becket.

- Leave the garden by metal gates and turn left for five yards to reach a road.
- Turn right along the road for 100 yards to a T-junction, where you turn left.
- Follow the road as it curves left *(following the course of the old city wall again)* to reach Westgate.

The Westgate is said to be the finest city gate in England. It was built in l380 by Archbishop Simon, part of the massive city wall defences and the only one of the eight city gates to survive. For a time it served as a city gaol. The Westgate was the entrance into the city for all travellers from London. Pilgrims' coming to pay homage at the shrine of Thomas Becket would have entered Canterbury through this gate.

- With your back to Westgate, go straight on down St Peter's Street.

St Peter's Street was the main thoroughfare into the city, and in the Middle Ages it would have been lined with taverns, boarding houses for travellers and pilgrims, shops and stalls selling not only provisions but also religious relics and all the other paraphernalia of a mediaeval tourist town. If you look above the modern shop façades to the first-floor level you can still see that many of the buildings in this street are of great age, and it is not hard to imagine what it would have looked like 600 years ago.

● Pass St Peter's Church on your left and, shortly after, the Weavers' House.

St Peter's Church is an interesting little church. It is Norman with re-used red Roman bricks included in its construction. It is worthy of a brief visit.

    The Weavers' House was built in 1561, although the mock half-timbering was added at a later stage. It was built as a refuge for Walloon and Huguenot weavers fleeing from the religious persecution that swept Flanders. Wool production and weaving was an important industry in Kent, and Canterbury was a major centre for the sale and despatch of woollen goods. The expertise that foreign refugees brought into the English woollen trade greatly enhanced Canterbury's position.

● Pass Eastbridge Hospital on your right.

Eastbridge Hospital was founded in 1190 as a hostel for poor pilgrims (the name 'hospital' has altered over the centuries and is today confusing as it is associated with the tending of the ill: 'hospice' would be a better translation of its meaning in the Middle Ages). It was built to accommodate pilgrims, many of them sick, who came to the shrine of St Thomas looking for a cure. They paid 4d (just over 1.5p) a night to stay there. It was also known as the Hospital of St Thomas the Martyr, and contains a Norman undercroft, some fine 12th and 13th-century frescoes and a chapel with a 13th-century roof. In the 16th century it became a charity school for poor boys, and later still it was turned into almshouses.

● Fifty yards past Eastbridge Hospital, turn right down Stour Street.
● Follow Stour Street past modern buildings and past the Canterbury Heritage Centre on the right.

The Heritage Centre is housed in the Poor Priests Hospital, built around 1200 by the Franciscan monks as a hospice for their members. It continued to be used until the reign of Elizabeth I, when it was given to the city for municipal use.

● Continue straight on, ignoring side turns, down the quiet road.
● Pass a car park on your left and keep straight on up Church Lane to St Mildred's Church.

St Mildred's was founded in the eighth century and is the oldest church within the city walls. The original church burnt down in 1246 and was replaced with the present building.

● Pass left around St Mildred's. Exit via gates and turn left through metal posts and up a brick paved road to reach Canterbury Castle.

All that remains of Canterbury Castle is the keep, the fifth largest in England. It was built partly of local flint, partly of recycled Roman bricks and stones, and faced in Kentish ragstone. It stands on a stepped plinth, 13 feet high and 6 feet wider than the keep itself and its high walls are reinforced with clasping buttresses. The keep was originally 80 feet high.

The first castle was a simple motte and bailey, a fort built upon an earthen mound and surrounded by a palisade. It was built by the Normans immediately after the Conquest in 1066 and was replaced in 1085 with a stone, three-storey castle. The castle had a permanent garrison of 15 knights and 40 foot sergeants, but with accommodation for many more in times of war.

Canterbury Castle never saw any fighting. It was captured without a struggle in 1216 by Louis, Dauphin of France, when he came to depose King John, but from then on was used as a prison. In 1277 Kentish Jews were held here before being deported. In 1380 the castle was attacked by Wat Tyler during the Peasants' Revolt against unfair royal taxation, when its inmates were released and the Sheriff forced to take the peasants' oath (see also walks 8 and 10). In 1539 the castle was involved in the religious disputes sweeping the country, when Archbishop Cranmer used the gaol to imprison two monks who objected to the dissolution of the monasteries. The castle ceased to be used in the 1590s, and by 1609 it was in ruins.

- Follow the brick-paved road to reach a tarmacked road. Cross the road and walk up the footpath to right of car park. Pass the toilets and go up the ramp on to the city walls.

Canterbury has been walled since Roman times. The present walls are mediaeval, totally encircled the city and were pierced by eight heavily fortified gates. In addition, there were 21 watch-towers at intervals. Todays walls have been restored and widened.

- Walk along walls, passing Dane John Mound on your left.

This mound was originally called the 'donjon' mound, the temporary site of a Norman keep-cum-prison tower (donjon being french for 'keep'). The name was anglicised to Dane John Mound, and it was surmounted by a monument in 1800 commemorating various civic reconstructions. The origin of the mound is far older, it being a burial mound used by the Romans but perhaps pre-dating even them.

- Follow the wall, crossing Watling Street by a bridge and continuing along the restored and widened walls.

The area of the city just to your left, that now contains the bus station, was devastated in June 1942 by German bombing raids, part of the so-called 'Baedeker' raids which specifically targeted sites of cultural or artistic interest, in retaliation for allied raids that had destroyed German historic cities. The cathedral itself, although a target, was missed.

- Descend and cross St George Street.
- Follow the walls back to Burgate.
- Turn right through the gate and then turn left back to the car park.

WALK 8
Rochester: the Norman Conquest takes hold

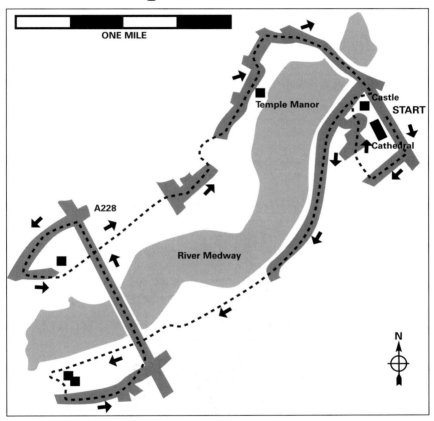

Distance: 7.5 miles

Map: OS sheet 178

Start and Parking: The walk starts from the War Memorial Garden in High Street, at the back of Rochester Cathedral (grid ref: 743685). The Northgate car park (pay and display) just off Corporation Street is the closest to the start, although there is plenty of other parking.

Refreshments: Public houses, shops, cafés and tearooms in Rochester. Public houses in Strood.

Historical Background

For the new Norman monarchy, the overwhelming need in the first decades after the Conquest was to impress upon their Saxon subjects the superiority of Norman culture, and so nip any thoughts of revolt in the bud. Huge new castles and cathedrals were an obvious outward sign of this superiority, the one displaying a vigorous defence of the realm, the other an equally vigorous defence of the faith. Nowhere can this be better seen than in Rochester.

William the Conqueror arrived with an army of only 6,000, many of them mercenaries who had been dismissed by 1070. The Conquest was not followed by a mass influx of settlers into England and was essentially the exchange of one aristocracy for a indifferent one. William won a personal kingdom for himself and then held it by rewarding his followers with lands captured from the defeated Saxons. These Norman landowners now had a vested interest in defending their new estates.

The Norman's brought with them the art of castle building to England. William himself saw to it that a castle was built in every county town, and at points of strategic importance. His nobles were allowed a free hand to build private castles to defend their lands. In the years immediately following the Conquest a rash of castles sprang up over England.

The Norman's were also a genuinely devout people. The church followed the Norman army into England, and although churchmen were often powerful landowners in their own right, they also set about building churches, monasteries and huge cathedrals as an outward sign of their faith. This Norman ecclesiastical architecture was on a far grander scale than anything achieved by the Saxons.

Even today, when the city has many high modern buildings, the cathedral and especially the castle are prominent. In 1080, when Rochester was a cluster of one and two-storey buildings, most built of wood and wattle, the psychological effect of these two massive buildings upon the defeated Saxons must have been overwhelming.

The Walk

This walk goes around the old city of Rochester, where it passes several sites that are a reminder of Charles Dickens's association with the city as well as the cathedral and castle. It then goes down the banks of the River Medway, past the site of the most significant battle of Roman times in Kent, and returns via a fortified manor house established by the Knights Templar.

● Standing in War Memorial Garden, with your back to the cathedral, turn right along the High Street.

Rochester was a stronghold of the Belgae, a tribe settled in Britain with connections on both sides of the channel and Rome's traditional enemies. It commands an important strategic position at the Medway's lowest crossing point. After the defeat of the Belgae in AD43, the Romans built a huge fortified camp here, with walls enclosing 23 acres. Soon the city of Durobrivae grew up, astride Watling Street, the major Roman road in the province, which ran from Richborough and Dover to London. High Street is part of Watling Street.

- In a few yards you will pass Watts Charity on your left.

Watts Charity featured in Dickens's short story The Seven Poor Travellers. *It is an Elizabethan boarding house, set up in 1579 by Richard Watt, MP for Rochester, to provide free board and lodging for six poor travellers. It continued to do so until 1939.*

- Pass Eagle Close on your right, with the old city wall visible on your right. (It is worth detouring down Eagle Court to have a closer view of the wall.)

The mediaeval town walls followed the course of earlier Roman ones. This part has survived to its full height, complete with battlements.

- Opposite the Dickens centre, turn right up Crow Lane.

Charles Dickens came to Rochester in 1817, at the age of five, when his father moved from Portsmouth to work in Chatham Dockyard, and he lived here much of his life. In 1856 Dickens bought Gads Hill Place, in nearby Higham, which became his home for most of his latter years and is where he died in 1870. Dickens loved Rochester and nearby Chatham, and the Medway towns feature in many of his novels, in particular Great Expectations *and* The Pickwick Papers. *It was Dickens's wish to be buried in Rochester Cathedral, but Queen Victoria decreed he should instead be buried in Westminster Cathedral.*

The Charles Dickens centre contains a wealth of memorabilia, including his 'Swiss Chalet', a garden house from Gads Hill where he did much of his later work.

Open daily 10am–6pm. Admission fee.

- Fifty yards past the entrance to King's School on the right, turn right into a park.

On the opposite side of the road is Restoration House, where Charles II stayed in 1661 on his return to England, en route for London and his Coronation. It features in Dickens's Great Expectations *as the home of Miss Havisham.*

- Bear right with the path and exit into a road. Turn right down the road, passing Oriel House on the right.

Look for the two firemarks on Oriel House: these were 18th-century metal plates that identified the companies who had insured the house against fire. Insurance companies provided their own fire service and would only fight the blaze in properties that could be identified as being insured with them!

- At the bottom of the road turn left, walking down Minor Canon Row.

The Norman cathedral at Rochester
was started in 1077.

Minor Canon Row was built in 1723 as homes for minor clergy. It features in Dickens's The Mystery of Edwin Drood.

- In 50 yards turn right at a T-junction and follow the road to the entrance of the cathedral.

The original cathedral in Rochester was founded in 604 by Ethelbert, King of Kent, for Justus, the first Bishop of Rochester, after the diocese had been founded by St Augustine. It was finally laid to waste by the Vikings. The foundations of the Saxon cathedral are visible outside the north door of the present cathedral.

In 1077 Gundulph, a monk from Bec in Normandy, was made Bishop of Rochester. This appointment was as much political as religious and Gundulph was a major landowner, with many holdings in Kent, including Rochester, Canterbury and Malling (see walk 9). In 1082 Gundulph, at the order of his patron Lanfranc Archbishop of Canterbury, set about building a new cathedral that would be a visible symbol of Norman wealth, piety and power. Gundulph was associated with a number of major building works in the first years after the Conquest: as well as Rochester Cathedral he supervised the building of Rochester Castle and the hub of the Tower of London, the White Tower. Gundulph was not an architect, but appears to have been a knowledgeable administrator who knew how to get good work done. Rochester Cathedral is England's second oldest cathedral, after Canterbury, and part of the crypt, the nave and the magnificent West Portal are original Norman.

- Facing the castle with your back to the cathedral entrance, turn left and walk around the castle, keeping the curtain wall on your right.
- Enter the castle via a gate in the curtain wall and walk forward to the wooden steps giving access to the keep.

Such was the strategic importance of Rochester that the Normans erected their first castle in the year following the Conquest. It was built by Odo, Bishop of Bayeaux, William's troublesome half-brother. In 1082 Odo rebelled against William and was briefly imprisoned. He recovered from this disgrace but in 1087, on William's death, supported William's son Robert against King William Rufus, the Conqueror's younger son and designated successor to the English throne. Rochester became a headquarters for the unsuccessful rebellion and was besieged and rapidly captured by the king. Odo was exiled, later to die on the first crusade.

After the siege, the king demanded that Bishop Gundulph supervise and pay for a much stronger castle at Rochester, in return for being confirmed as owner of the manor of Haddenham in Buckinghamshire. Gundulph duly greatly strengthened the curtain walls, towers and gatehouse.

Rochester was a royal, not a private, castle, but Henry I, William Rufus's successor, granted custody of Rochester Castle to the Archbishopric of Canterbury. It was during this period, in 1126, that the keep was constructed. It is the tallest Norman keep in England, standing over 100 feet high, with walls 12 feet thick and measuring 160 yards by 130 yards. However, a royal castle under the custody of some other lord is a potentially dangerous state of affairs, for

Rochester Castle, built by the Normans to impose their rule in England.

in 1215 Archbishop Langton, ever an enemy to King John, allowed the castle to be held against the king during the barons' rebellion. John recaptured the castle after a three-month siege. John's successor, Henry III, rebuilt and further strengthened the castle and took it back into royal hands, and it was thereafter controlled by a constable responsible solely to the king.

In 1264 Rochester Castle was besieged for a third time, by Simon de Montfort, during the Barons' rebellion against King Henry III. Although the attackers broke through the curtain wall into the bailey, the defenders successfully held the keep against all attack.

The defences of the castle and the town were further strengthened during the 14th century, for Rochester defended both the Medway and the land approaches to London against French raids during the Hundred Years War. In 1381 the castle was attacked for a fourth time, this time by Wat Tyler's forces during the Peasants' Revolt, when the townspeople of Rochester aided the rebels in the capture of the castle (for the Peasants' Revolt, see also walks 7 and 10).

By the end of the 14th century Rochester's fortifications were at their strongest, but the strategic importance of the castle was passing and Rochester Castle did not see action again.

Rochester Castle is open April to September, 10am–6pm, October to March, 10am–4pm. There is an admission charge, but it is free to members of English Heritage.

- Leave the keep and walk half-right down a broad gravel path to a bastion with a cannon, overlooking the road bridge.
- Leave the castle by descending a broad flight of steps onto the junction of Esplanade and Castle Hill.
- Cross the road to the river front and turn left. After 80 yards turn right into some riverside gardens. Turn left and walk alongside the Medway, passing the marina.

- Continue ahead through an open area to reach a road, keeping roughly parallel with the river front.
- On reaching the road turn right. Follow the road until it reaches the river again and continue ahead along the riverside walk.
- Follow the road for half a mile. Where the road turns left, just after passing warehouses on the left, keep straight on to a footpath into Batys Marsh Nature Reserve.
- Follow the path, with fences on the left and the river off to the right. Ignore a left turn at a barrier but keep straight ahead down a clear path.
- Follow the footpath out to a road. Keep ahead, descending with the road and passing the gates to Beacon Boat Yard.
- At the entrance to the Medway Bridge Marina, go ahead up the footpath to the left of the gates.
- Keep ahead along an enclosed footpath for 200 yards, keeping the fence to the marina on your right and ignoring a waymarked path off to the left.
- Where the marina fence turns right, cross a stile and turn right down to the river bank. Turn left along the foreshore.
- Pass a jetty on the right and keep straight on to cross a stile and enter an enclosed footpath.
- Follow the footpath under the Medway Bridge and keep straight on along the riverbank.
- Follow the path out to a track. Keep ahead and pass through a metal kissing gate beside a field gate. Keep ahead along the track.
- Where the track ends keep ahead along a narrow footpath for 30 yards and climb onto the embankment.
- Do not follow the clear path along the top of the embankment, but descend and bear left on a grassy path through shrubland.
- Follow the path as it swings left towards a row of houses.
- Go through a gate to the houses. At a fork in 10 yards, go left to pass along the front of the houses.
- Opposite the last house, go through a gap in the wall on the right and down some steps to enter a field.
- Go half-right across the field to reach a drive.
- Turn left up the drive for five yards to a road, and then turn left along the road for a third of a mile.
- Just after passing Nashenden Farm Lane on the right, and 30 yards before the bridge, turn left up a track to reach the walkway alongside the road over the bridge.
- Cross the Medway bridge but pause halfway across and look down at the river.

This is the site of the only major battle fought in Kent against the Romans when they invaded Britain in AD43. The Medway has not altered a great deal since that battle and it is possible to look out and down and picture the scene.

Following Caesar's two expeditions a century before, the Emperor Claudius launched a full-blown invasion of Britain. Four full legions and auxiliaries, nearly 50,000 men in total, landed at Richborough (see walk 4). Although the Britons had intelligence of their arrival, the Romans landed later in the campaigning season than expected and the British army, mainly tribal irregulars, had dispersed to bring in the harvest. In consequence the Roman landing was unopposed and the legions thrust northwards through Kent, while the Britons hastily re-assembled their army.

A British army of 60–80,000 men drew up on the western bank of the Medway (to your right as you look down), just downstream of where you are standing, confident that the river would provide a defensive barrier to the Roman legions drawn up on the east (left) bank. However, the Roman army included auxiliary troops from the Batavi tribe in Holland, experienced at swimming fully armed. These swam the river just in front of you and attacked the Britons on their flank. While the Britons turned to face this attack, a Roman legion was able to flounder its way across the shingle banks and mudflats further downstream and establish a bridgehead. Although strongly counter-attacked, the Romans poured their remaining legions across the river to reinforce their comrades, and after two days of fighting routed the British forces.

This battle was the most decisive action in the whole Roman invasion. Never again would the Romans be opposed in Kent, which soon settled down to become the most affluent and Romanised part of the new province of Britannia.

- At the far end of the bridge follow the footpath up to the A228.
- Turn left and walk down the left-hand side of the A228 for half a mile, crossing a railway bridge and passing the entrance to a recycling centre.
- One hundred yards past the recycling centre, turn left down a tarmacked lane.
- Descend the lane and pass between houses. Where the tarmacked lane ends, turn right down a drive and just before the railway, turn left to pass to the right of a house.
- Follow an enclosed footpath for 15 yards, and then keep straight on along the bottom edge of the field, with the railway on your immediate right.
- Cross the stile at the field end and keep straight on along the next field, passing under the Medway bridge to a stile. Pass through a narrow band of trees and bear half-right up to the field.
- Maintain the same line direction along the next field, now with the field boundary on the right, and follow out onto a road.
- Cross the road and keep ahead down Norman Close.
- At the end of Norman Close keep ahead up a footpath to the left of metal factory gates. Follow the footpath around to the left, keeping iron railings on your right, as it passes between industrial units.
- At the end of the units climb and turn right, now with a railway on your left.
- Do not cross the railway bridge but keep straight on down an enclosed footpath, with the railway on your left.
- Turn right and follow the path, now concrete and gently stepped, down between fences and out to a road.
- Turn left along the road, ignoring side turnings. In 350 yards, pass a pillar box on the left at a road junction. Thirty yards later, pass Temple Manor on the right.

Temple Manor is a 13th-century hall built to provide lodgings for the Knights Templar as they journeyed to or from the Holy Land. The Templars were a military religious order founded around AD1118, when Hughes de Payen and eight other knights banded together to protect pilgrims en route to Jerusalem. Their original headquarters were on top of the Temple mound in Jerusalem, hence 'Templars'.

The order soon gained papal approval and rapidly grew in numbers and wealth. The loss of the Latin Kingdoms, modern-day Palestine, forced the order to relocate to the West, where they established themselves as bankers to the various monarchs. Their independence and wealth made them arrogant and they eventually became hated by both clergy and secular authorities. In 1307 the order was attacked by Philip IV of France, who seized Templar land and property and accused the order of heresy. Pope Clement V was bullied into issuing a papal edict dissolving the order. Although the Templars continued to exist in England, Germany and Spain for some years after their expulsion from France, they never regained their former influence and power, and, as the Holy Land ceased to be a major issue in European politics, the order gradually withered away. (Another Templar property can be seen at West Peckham, walk 17.)

- Continue along the road for another 350 yards, ignoring side turnings. The road, called Knights Road in memory of the Templars, turns sharp left and 30 yards later reaches a more major road at a give way sign.
- Turn right down the major road. At a T-junction, turn right down Commercial Road and follow the road under a railway bridge.
- Keep ahead along the right-hand pavement. Pass a subway entrance and keep ahead. Do not go onto the bridge but keep forward to the riverfront for a fine view of the castle and part of the town wall across the river.
- Climb steps onto the bridge and cross the river.

This bridge was built in 1857, but the Medway has been bridged at this point since Roman times. The present bridge replaced a mediaeval one, built between 1383 and 1393. It had crenellated towers at each end as part of the defences of Rochester, and a drawbridge between its piers to allow tall ships access to the sheltered and protected Medway. This mediaeval bridge was so well built that 400 years later gunpowder was needed to demolish it.

- At the end of the bridge cross The Esplanade and keep ahead. Cross Gundolph Street on the right.

The corner of Gundolph Street marks the position of Rochester's old North Gate and is the site of the Crown Inn, the first and one of the most affluent inns travellers would encounter on entering the city. Anne of Cleves stayed there en route for her Coronation.

- Keep ahead up High Street to return to War Memorial Gardens on your right.

Look out for the Guildhall on your left as you enter High Street, built in 1687 and one of the finest 17th-century civic buildings in Kent.

WALK 9
West Malling: Norman feudalism in action

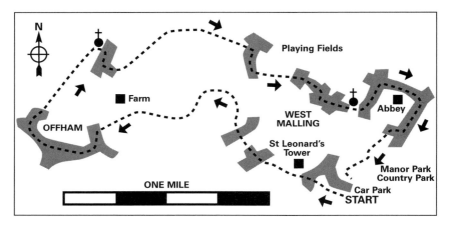

Distance: 5 miles

Map: OS sheet 178 or 188

Start and Parking: The walk starts from Manor Park Country Park (grid ref: 679571) at the southern end of West Malling, which is itself just south of the junction of the A20 and the A228, 10 miles east of Sevenoaks and six miles west of Maidstone. The country park is signposted from both A roads.

Refreshments: Public houses, tearooms and shops in West Malling, public house in Offham.

Historical Background

The area of West Malling and Offham were once largely part of the estates of Gundulph, Bishop of Rochester. They were given to Gundulph shortly after the Norman Conquest by King William, an extensive area of rich agricultural land which was soon to be organised in accordance with Norman feudalism.

When William the Conqueror seized the English Crown he brought with him a concept new to English thought, the theory that all land was the king's by right, and that land was held by others only by the king's gift, and in return for specified services. This service was initially military, since the king needed to ensure that his new subjects were properly subdued and that his new realm could be protected without the Crown bearing the cost of a standing army. The king held all the privileges of monarchy in return for swearing to defend his subjects against attack and granted land to his barons and to the clergy, who in turn were expected to provide arms and men to fight when required. These great landowners granted land to their knights in return for military service when required, and so on down through all strata of society.

Gundulph organised his estates along these lines, with holdings of land being granted to lesser landlords in return for military service. He also set about developing his holdings, in a display of Norman power and wealth designed to overawe his Saxon vassals. An abbey was established at East Malling, the Saxon church was redeveloped and extended, and a fortified keep built to protect and impress the manor.

The Walk
This walk passes the ruins of Gundulph's keep and the abbey he established, and goes through woods and farmland to visit Offham, whose village green and quintain give a strong reminder of its feudal past.

- Standing facing the access road to the car park, take the waymarked footpath to the left of the road. Follow the path alongside the road.
- Descend to the access road and go forward for a few yards. Just before the bridge turn left down a waymarked path to reach a lane.
- Follow the lane past cottages to the main road. Cross the road to the track opposite, and go up past the tower.

St Leonard's Tower was built around 1100 as a fortified keep by Gundulph, Bishop of Rochester from 1077–1108, who was also responsible for the building of Rochester Cathedral and Castle (see walk 8). Gundulph had extensive holdings of land across Kent (see also walk 1) and the area around West Malling was especially important to him. This tower is the keep of a small fortified manor house, built by the Archbishop partly as an occasional residence but also as a base from which to protect his lands. It would normally have been manned by a very small garrison, but provided the facilities to act as a base for a much larger force in times of troubles. The base of the tower is made from tufa, a volcanic stone favoured by the Normans in their fortifications, and the outline of the walls of a small chapel can still just be distinguished adjoining the tower.

- Continue along a fenced track. Pass through a gate and continue along the track to join a tarmacked farm drive. Follow the drive to a road.
- Turn half-left across the road and go down a track between buildings. The track soon becomes a footpath. Follow this out to a lane.
- Cross the lane and cross a stile opposite, then 'turn right and walk down the field edge, alongside the lane. Cross a drive and keep ahead along the side of the field, still with a hedge and field on the right.
- Swing left with the path. At a junction of tracks keep ahead. Do not enter the wood along a waymarked path but instead take the path to the left, passing the wood on your right.

- Keep ahead along the edge of the field, with trees on your right. Where the trees swing away to the right, keep straight on, keeping the field on your left.
- At the field end, turn left and follow the field boundary, still with the field on your left and now with a hedge on your right.
- At a farm track, turn right through a gap and then immediately turn left. Go ahead down the next field, maintaining the same direction but now with the hedge on your left.
- Follow the hedge right and then left. Where the hedge ends, turn right at a waymarked post and follow the path across the middle of a field, aiming at a red roof seen ahead.
- At a T-junction with a track, in the middle of the field and 100 yards short of the red roof, turn left.
- In another 100 yards, at another T-junction of tracks, keep straight on along a footpath across the field, aiming for trees seen ahead.
- At the field edge cross a stile and keep straight on down an enclosed footpath to reach a road by an ex-public house.
- Keep ahead down the road (Church Road) for a few yards, to a T-junction with Teston Road. Turn right up Teston Road, soon to reach the village green of Offham with its quintain.

'Tilting' was a popular sport from Roman times, and came to prominence in England with the arrival of the Normans. The quintain is a two-armed post which pivots around a central pole. It would have a target fixed on one arm and a heavy sandbag on the other. A horseman would ride at the quintain, aiming to strike the target, thus causing the quintain to spin, and then avoid being struck by the sandbag.

Quintains were used in the Middle Ages for 'tilting'. This one, on the village green at Offham, is the only one left in England.

Although a sport enjoyed at festive times, the origin of the quintain has a serious military purpose, being to teach the art of fighting on horseback. Knights were the most wealthy and powerful men in a manor, and were required to provide their lord with military service for a specified number of days each year, 40 days a year in times of peace and 60 days in times of war. They were also required to undergo a number of days training per year. The quintain was a popular training tool, although they would have been located in the castles where the knights lived and worked, not on village greens.

The quintain at Offham is the only one in England. It is not original, but is periodically replaced.

As an aside, the less affluent populace were required to do their military service as foot soldiers, armed with a pike and, by the 14th century, the deadly English longbow. These people too were required to train, in their case with the bow for an hour every Sunday after the church service had finished. Their training ground was the archery butts, and many older English towns and villages still have a street named 'The Butts' in consequence.

- Continue to follow the road, passing the Kings Head public house. Fifty yards past the pub turn right down Pepingstraw Close.
- Where the road bends right, keep straight on up a footpath, at a concrete footpath sign and passing a horse barrier.
- Follow the footpath into woods. At a fork, keep right on the path following the edge of woods.
- When the path reaches a field keep straight on down a tree-lined path, with a field on your right.
- Emerge from the trees and keep ahead to farm buildings.
- Pass a barn on your right. At a T-junction turn right and follow the drive out to the road beside Offham Church.
- Turn right down the road, 50 yards past the church, opposite Church Farm, turn left up a drive.
- Where the hedge on the left ends and the drive emerges into an open field, turn half-left and follow the footpath across the field, aiming for woods seen ahead.
- At trees (an outlier of the wood) and a marker post, cross farm tracks and continue along the same line into the woods ahead.
- Enter the woods and follow a broad footpath through trees.
- At the end of the woods emerge into field at a junction of tracks. Do not cross a stile but keep ahead down the field, with a fence on the left and West Malling seen ahead.
- Follow the path to a stile at a junction of roads. Do not go down Norman Road, but turn sharp right up the lane.
- Follow the lane for 250 yards and around a left bend. Pass steps descending the bank on the right and immediately turn left onto a footpath along the side of a field.
- Go along the right-hand side of the field and keep ahead down an enclosed footpath, now with a recreation field on the left.
- At the end of the recreation field, follow a tarmacked path between garden fences and out to a road.

- Cross the road and continue down the path between garden fences to reach another road
- Keep ahead along this road (Epsom Close), ignoring a footpath on the left in a few yards, and crossing Sandown Road in 60 yards.
- At a T-junction turn right, passing between garages, and 50 yards later turn left along the road.
- At a crossroads in 50 yards time, keep ahead down Churchfields.
- Where the road bends, keep straight on up a footpath, with the road behind the hedge on the left, aiming for the church spire seen ahead.
- At the end of the footpath keep ahead and follow an alley into the churchyard.
- Follow the path past the church and out to the road.

The church of St Mary the Virgin is Norman in origin, with a 19th-century spire, and an Early English chancel with fine Jacobean alabaster tombs. It has a James II coat of arms, possibly carved by Grinling Gibbons, a famous carver of wood and stone who collaborated with Sir Christopher Wren. Some of Gibbons's work can be seen in Hampton Court.

- Turn left up the main road and pass through the Market Square.

West Malling has been an affluent market town for many centuries, and its wide market square is flanked by houses from Elizabethan, Jacobean and Georgian times.

- At a white-painted outfitters shop, turn right down Swan Street. In 200 yards pass St Mary's Abbey on your right.

The original Abbey of East Malling was part of the holdings of Gundulph, Bishop of Rochester, and protected by his nearby keep, St Leonard's Tower. This abbey was destroyed in 1190, along with most of the old village, and rebuilt as a nunnery. Part of the original Norman building still remains, now incorporated into the later building. It is still used as such today, being shared between the Benedictine nuns and the Cistercian order.

- Proceed for a further 200 yards past the Abbey gate, looking our for Sluice exit in the wall on the right. Turn right down Lavenders Road, following the wall of the Abbey.
- In 300 yards turn right into Water Lane, and 50 yards later turn left through a kissing gate into Manor Park Country Park.
- Keep straight on along a broad grassy track. At a fork in 60 yards, drop down right to the lakeside.
- Turn left and walk with the lake on your right.

The Manor House seen across the lake is Douce House, once home of Thomas Douce, whose 18th-century estate included all the land that is now Manor Park. The house is now owned by Commercial Union as a training centre.

- At the end of the lake, turn left up the access drive back to the car park.

WALK 10
Appledore: raiders and traders in the Middle Ages

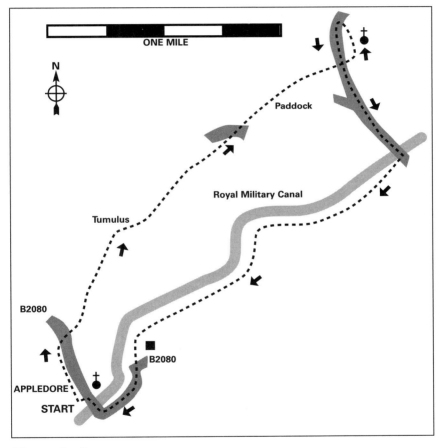

Distance: 5 miles
Map: OS sheet 189
Start and Parking: The walk commences from Appledore Church (grid ref: 958292). Appledore is on the B2080, six miles south-east of Tenterden. There is road-side parking in the middle of Appledore village.
Refreshments: Public houses, tearoom and shop in Appledore.

Historical Background

Today Appledore is nine miles from the sea, but until the end of the 14th century it was a busy port. The area that is now Romney Marsh was then all sea, and the low coastline behind it a maze of creeks and estuaries winding through sandbanks and reedbeds. These estuaries provided sheltered anchorages facing the channel and the lucrative continental trade. Appledore was at the head of a tidal creek formed by the River Rother winding its way to the sea at Romney.

The period of Appledore's affluence was from about AD1100 to about AD1400. It was the home port for a flotilla of vessels that carried English wool and linen to France and returned with wines, silk, lace and all manner of other luxury goods. It also had a busy ship-building industry. The town flourished for 300 years, before the silting up of the Rother estuary cut the port off from the sea and Appledore gradually faded into obscurity.

Proximity to the channel and to Europe was a source of danger as well as prosperity. The remote coastline with its many secluded inlets and poor land communications was vulnerable to attack by England's enemies, and the wealth of the town brought it problems during the periods of social unrest in the Middle Ages. Even before there was a town at Appledore the Vikings had realised the strategic importance of the location and used it as a base for a year-long raid, in AD893–94. In 1380, during the Hundred Years War, the French raided this coast, sacking Appledore and burning the town. The following year, the ordinary people of Appledore were swept along in the Peasants' Revolt against the inequalities of society and attacked their wealthy neighbours before marching on London. The following century, governmental corruption was blamed for the decline in fortunes in the area, and the people of Appledore joined the campaign for better government led by Jack Cade (see walk 14).

In the 19th century the threat posed by Napoleon Bonaparte brought Romney Marsh and Appledore back into the front line, and the Royal Military Canal was built to provide a defence against invasion.

The Walk

This walk follows the line of the coast during Appledore's mediaeval heyday. It passes various sites that reflect the town's history as a port and the raids made upon it over the centuries. It returns along the Royal Military Canal.

● Walk up the main street of Appledore away from the canal and in the direction of Tenterden, passing the Swan Hotel on your right.

Appledore has many fine old buildings, some dating back to the 14th century, homes of local merchants and ship-owners. The splendour of these houses speaks of the affluence of this tiny town in the past.

● Eventually you will reach some playing fields on your right, opposite the entrance to Magpie Farm.

- Enter the playing fields beside the toilet block at a footpath sign.
- Cross the sports field diagonally, aiming for a gate in the top left-hand corner.
- Go through the gate and turn left along the field edge, with houses and a field beyond.
- In 200 yards, turn half-right across the field, aiming for a prominent oak tree in the far right corner.
- In the corner, cross a stile and footbridge. Go half-left across the next field, aiming for a stile ahead.
- Cross the stile and continue half-left across the next field, continuing the same line of advance and aiming at a tumulus seen on the skyline ahead.

The tumulus is a round barrow dating from the Bronze Age, and was used to bury the cremated ashes of one man or at most one family, presumably a person or persons of importance. The barrow is a small round stone chamber, buried beneath a mound of earth. At the time it was constructed, all the flat lands to your right would have been beneath the sea, the gentle slopes ahead and to the left would have probably been densely wooded, with an area of marshy reeds and sandbanks up which you are walking. The tumulus would have stood, lonely and prominent, on this desolate shoreline.

- Cross the top of the tumulus.

Ahead and to the left are the chimneys of Hornes Place. The original house was destroyed during the Peasants' Revolt. In 1381 the government of King Richard II, desperate for revenue, levied the third poll tax in four years. This one was quite the harshest, and well beyond the means of most peasants to pay. Tax collectors were assaulted, attempts to enforce the law provoked resistance, and the countryside of Kent and Essex erupted into mutiny. In Kent this Peasants' Revolt was led by Wat Tyler, whose force marched through the county, ever increasing in numbers as it swept towards London. The peasants of Appledore rose up, attacked the local squire, William Horne, and burnt his home, Hornes Place, to the ground, before joining the revolt (see also walks 7 and 8 for the Peasants' Revolt in Kent).

As a footnote, the rebels reached the capital where they were joined by the London mob. King Richard in person met with the leaders and made them promises in return for their laying down their arms. These promises were rapidly broken, the leaders executed, and throughout the county, Appledore included, there was massive and savage retribution upon all those involved in the revolt.

- Continuing the same line of advance, descend to a stile ahead on the field edge. Do not cross the stile but turn half-right to go down the field, with a line of trees on your left.
- At the end of the line of trees, continue half-left across the next large field. As you cross the summit of the field a gate will come into sight in line ahead of you.
- Go through this gate, at a waymark, and continue the same line of advance across the next field, aiming between two trees standing like goalposts on the far side.
- Cross a plank footbridge between these two trees and continue the same line of advance across a third field, to reach a stile beside a footpath sign, leading onto a road.

- Cross the road and enter the field opposite, beside a concrete footpath sign. Go half-right across this field, keeping well to the left of a clump of trees seen standing in the field ahead, and aiming just to the right of a telegraph pole. Soon a stile comes into sight in the trees ahead.
- Cross the stile and descend some steps to a second stile. Ignore a cross track, go over a second stile and climb the bank to a third stile, leading into a small paddock.
- Keep ahead along the right-hand edge of the paddock to cross a stile into a large field.
- Effectively you want to go more or less straight across this field. Initially, keep straight on along the edge of the field, keeping the field boundary to your right. Where the hedge ends, go quarter-right to the corner of the hedge seen ahead. Follow this hedge on your right hand for 250 yards. Where the hedge goes sharp right at a waymarker, aim half-left to a stile seen opposite.
- Cross the stile and turn left for 10 yards to cross a stile on the right.
- Go ahead, following the left-hand edge of the field around corners to reach a church.

In the ninth century this spot was a headland overlooking a creek, a main channel of the River Rother. The Vikings sailed across the North Sea and up the English Channel from Denmark, up the creek from Romney to this easily-defended headland. Here they built a fortified encampment in AD893 from which to raid the surrounding countryside. The Vikings were persuaded to leave by King Alfred, rather than face a pitched battle, but not before they had spent a year on this coast, raiding with a fleet of 250 longships.

A church was built upon this spot to commemorate Alfred's victory, enlarged in 1170 when the tower was built. In 1380 the French raided this coastline during the Hundred Years War and burnt the church at the same time as sacking Appledore. The church was rebuilt, but the tower was struck by lightning in 1559, and the subsequent fire burnt the rest of the church again. The building was rebuilt but is now only used on occasions.

- Follow the left-hand edge of the churchyard to cross a drive at a parking area to a stile ahead.
- Cross the stile and keep straight on across the field to a second stile.
- Cross this stile and the corner of a field to another stile 10 yards ahead. Cross this stile and descend some steps to a lane.
- Turn left up the lane.

If you look to your left you will see the rocky outcrop which formed the promontory upon which the church was built.

- After half a mile, turn left at a T-junction.
- Go down the lane for a quarter of a mile to cross the Royal Military Canal via a road bridge. Immediately on the other side of the bridge turn right into a parking area.
- Go through the parking area to a stile leading onto the canal bank. Keep along the bank, with the canal on your right, for nearly two miles.

In 1803 this coastline was again threatened by the French; however, not a mere raid this time but a full invasion by the armies of Napoleon. The first line of defence was to be a line of forts, called Martello Towers (see walk 22), along the coast itself. Inland of this was to be a canal, running for 23 miles along the inland edge of Romney Marsh, to provide a fall-back line of defence. The ability to combine infantry, cavalry and artillery into one devastating combined attack was what had given the French mastery on battlefields across Europe. The canal was built to disrupt this ability, by forcing any advance to be made piecemeal. Artillery and cavalry would be unable to cross, and infantry would be unlikely to get across without swimming, which would render their muskets useless.

As you will clearly see as you walk along, the canal was built in a series of zigzags, and every quarter of a mile, on each corner and at intervals between, a gun emplacement was built. These would provide interlocking fields of fire which would devastate any enemy trying to cross. In addition, a service road was built along the far side, which would enable troops to be moved quickly to any spot where the enemy did manage to cross.

As a further defence, sluice gates were built at intervals into the canal, to allow the low-lying Romney Marsh on your left to be flooded if necessary, thereby further disrupting an enemy invader. Some of these can still be spotted as you walk along, since many were refurbished in 1940, to be used to counter any German invasion.

The canal was finished in 1809, but by that time the threat of invasion had receded and it was never used.

- Eventually pass a pumping station on your left and follow the concrete track out to a road.
- Turn right along the road for a quarter of a mile to reach Appledore Bridge. Turn right across the bridge.

The Royal Military Canal, built as a defence against Napoleonic invasion.

To the left across the bridge you will see a pillbox, dating from World War Two. In 1940–41 there was the threat of invasion by Nazi Germany, when again this region of Kent was seen as a likely landing spot. The 19th-century gun emplacements were replaced by the 20th-century equivalent.

● Continue up main street back to your car, passing the church on your right.

The original church in Appledore was Saxon, enlarged by the Normans. In 1380 the French raided up Rother Creek and devastated the land around. Appledore was sacked and burnt, and the church was destroyed. It was rebuilt after the raid, with a view to also providing a secure refuge in case of further attacks. The walls were built to almost fortress proportions, the tower enlarged, and the nave and north aisle built as a single unit, thereby providing a large open space for people seeking sanctuary. (Other examples of this style of fortress church can be seen in Sandwich: see walk 4.) The grandeur of the church, disproportionate to the size of Appledore today, speaks of the towns former wealth. In front of the church was the wide marketplace, in use until the last century.

WALK 11

Old Soar: mediaeval manors and Civil War churches

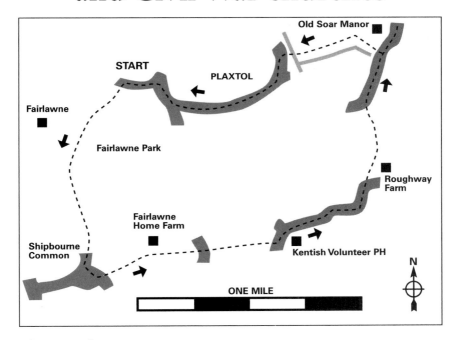

Distance: 5 miles

Map: OS sheet 188

Start and parking: The walk commences from the church at Plaxtol (grid ref: 602537). Plaxtol is on a minor road, one mile to the east of the A227 Tonbridge to Ightham road, five miles north of Tonbridge. There is on-street parking in Plaxtol, down side roads leading off the main street.

Refreshments: Shops and public houses in Plaxtol. Public house at Shipbourne. Public house at Dunks Green.

Historical Background

In the Middle Ages the majority of Kent, Surrey and Sussex was covered by the huge Wealdan forest, a vast expanse of woodland with only scattered communities living in its clearings and with few roads winding through the dark trees. A livelihood was scratched out based on agriculture. Fields were cleared for growing wheat and grazing cattle and the all-prevailing forest offered timber, firewood, charcoal and summer acorns for pigs, the main livestock. Living in the forest was a hazardous business. The forest provided a refuge for outlaws and bandits as well as a hunting ground for common thieves, who preyed upon the small isolated communities as well as the few travellers along the often empty roads.

Law enforcement was often a local matter, with the lord of the manor responsible for adjudicating the less serious disputes among the local peasants and the Manor House often serving as a manorial court house. The lord also had to look to his own resources to defend himself, his family and his property against outlaws and robbers who roamed the forest, looking for easy pickings.

Old Soar Manor House was built in 1290 as a defensive home for the local lord of the manor and is one of the best examples of a mediaeval fortified manor house in England.

The Walk
The walk starts in Plaxtol and passes one of the very few churches to be built in England during the Commonwealth, as well as the home of a leading parliamentarian of that period. It then passes through orchards to visit Old Soar Manor House.

- With the war memorial at your back and the church on your right, walk up Plaxtol Lane, passing a row of weatherboarded cottages on your right.

Plaxtol church is very unusual in that it was built in 1649, during the Commonwealth. The king had been executed, Parliament ruled England, and Puritanism in its many forms set the style for religious observance. As a consequence of the puritan beliefs, Plaxtol church is not dedicated to any saint. In the south transept there is a Cromwellian carved screen, portraying the Crossing of the Red Sea, with both Israelites and Egyptians in 17th-century costume. The churchyard contains gravestones of a style unique to the Kent–Sussex border, with head-shaped humps carved with skulls. The church has a magnificent hammerbeam roof.

- Continue along the road, now with the wall of Fairlawne Estate on your left. After 250 yards turn left across a stile into the estate.
- NB. There is no visible path across the estate grounds. However, there is a public right of way which is easy to keep to if the instructions are followed.
- With your back to the stile go straight across the park for 100 yards, aiming for a marker post in front of some ornate gates.

These gates, seemingly standing in the middle open parkland, are the back entrance to Fairlawne Manor. A drive leads from the park to the house and provided access to it for riding. The gateway is magnificent, and offers an imposing façade to the house when seen from across the park.

- From the marker post, head half-right around the gateway and then aim for a clump of four mature trees standing 50 yards ahead.

- From these trees, another marker post can now be seen down the slope, 200 yards away along your same line of advance. Pass to the left of a clump of six mature trees, to the right of an enclosure of new trees, to reach the marker post.
- From this post, keep straight on to a stile 75 yards ahead.
- Cross the stile and continue on the same line to a third marker post, seen ahead.

Looking back and right you get your best view of Fairlawne. The Manor was built mainly in the 17th century, with later additions, and was the home of the Vane family. Sir Henry Vane, one-time governor of Massachusetts, was a close friend of Oliver Cromwell and a prominent parliamentarian during the years leading up to the Civil War. During the Commonwealth he was a radical reformer and became an outspoken critic of Cromwell, whom he viewed as having betrayed the revolution. With the Restoration of the monarchy, Sir Henry was tried for treason and was executed on Tower Hill, London, in June 1662. His headless corpse is buried in Plaxtol church, and his ghost is claimed to walk the grounds in the company of his wife, on the anniversary of his death!

- At the third marker post, head half-left from your previous line of advance. Soon a fourth marker post becomes visible ahead, leading you down to a gate in the park corner, heading into trees.
- Pass through this gate and descend to a drive.

There is an excellent view of the largest of the ornate pools landscaped into the grounds of Fairlawne, a product of the 18th-century fashion for reshaping natural features into more aesthetically-pleasing designs.

- Turn left along the drive, and almost immediately take a right fork, passing a bridge and buildings on your right. Keep straight on past the buildings where the drive ends, to a small wooden gate standing beside a field gate.
- Go through the gate and straight on along a path, passing occasional prominent trees just to the right of you. Pass between immature trees to reach a footbridge over a river.
- Cross the bridge and proceed half-right up the field, aiming for the corner of a protruding hedge seen ahead.
- Go through a stile in the field corner and along an enclosed footpath.
- On reaching a drive, keep straight on to Shipbourne village green, in front of the Village Hall and on the edge of an expanse of common.
- Bear left down the side of the green, keeping houses on your left, to converge with the main road in 100 yards.
- Turn left along the main road, but in 10 yards turn left down a footpath at a concrete marker, to the right of a white house and just to the left of No.1 New Cottage.
- Pass between a hedge and a garage to enter a field.
- Keep straight on down the right-hand edge of the field.
- Where the hedge on the right swings away, keep straight on across the field, aiming for an obvious track going up the slope ahead.

- Ascend the track, passing the buildings of Fairlawne Home Farm on your left.
- Keep straight on past the farm buildings on your left and keeping a large field to your right, to go onto a farm access road.
- Follow the access road down to a lane.
- Cross the lane to a stile immediately opposite and go straight on across the field, aiming for a stile visible in the middle of the wood directly ahead.
- Cross the stile into the wood and take the left fork of the path. Follow the path through woods to a field.
- Go half-right across the shoulder of the field, aiming for the roof of a building that soon comes into sight. Continue to a stile that is soon seen ahead.
- Cross the stile and keep on down the right-hand side of a small paddock, to a kissing gate leading onto a lane.
- Turn left along the lane for 100 yards to reach the Kentish Volunteer public house.
- Follow Roughouse Lane in front of the Kentish Volunteer for a quarter of a mile, to cross a small stream at a road bridge.
- Continue along the lane as it climbs uphill, swinging left and then right.
- Nearly at the summit of the hill, and immediately before the prominent Roughway Farm, turn left onto a footpath leading into some orchards.
- Keep the buildings of the farm on your right and pass around the right-hand edge of two small orchards.
- Cross a cross track and continue straight on, with orchards to your left and a high hedge to your right. Continue along the track, ignoring side turnings, for nearly a quarter of a mile, until a metal field gate is reached.
- Go through the gate and onto an enclosed track. Turn left and follow the track down to a country lane.
- Turn right along Old Soar Lane for a third of a mile to reach Old Soar Manor.

Old Soar Manor House was built in 1290 and is one of the finest examples of a fortified knights house in England. It was built by the Culpepper family, who were the lords of the manor of Plaxtol and lived there until 1600.

There was no village at Plaxtol in 1290. The manor consisted of scattered farms built along the only two proper roads through the forest and isolated peasants dwellings, little more than hovels, in the forest. The nearest settlement of any size was Wrotham, five miles away along narrow and isolated roads through the forest. Although Wrotham was a sizeable settlement, with an Archbishop's court, it was a two or three-hour hazardous journey away.

Old Soar Manor House is stoutly built of Kentish ragstone and easily defensible against banditry. Access was by only one small and solid door leading into the undercroft, a large room into which livestock and movable possessions could be gathered quickly in an emergency. The slit windows had cross-loops from which the defender could easily train a cross bow to cover all approaches to the house.

The main living quarters were on the first floor, with a great hall for the communal living of the time and a chapel. The only access to the first floor was up one narrow spiral staircase. Should intruders manage to gain access to the ground floor, they would still have to fight their way up the staircase. This is of the standard mediaeval design, spiralling in a clockwise direction and therefore giving the advantage to a defender retreating up the stairs while wielding a sword in his right hand. Finally, there was a door of solid local oak at the top of the stairway, the final defence against intruders.

Old Soar could not have withstood a serious assault or a siege, but was ideal for withstanding the hit and run raids of casual bandits.

Old Soar Manor is open from April to September, 10am–6pm daily and entry is free.

- After looking at Old Soar Manor, retrace your steps down Old Soar Lane for 150 yards, passing cottages on your left, to reach a dip in the road at a stream. Here turn right onto a signposted footpath.
- Follow the right bank of a small stream, at first along a broad track. Where this track swings away to the right, keep straight on along a narrow and vague footpath, keeping the stream to your left.
- Continue to follow the stream around to the left, on a path which soon becomes clearer, until a field is reached.
- Keep straight on along the left-hand edge of the field. At the bottom of the field, ignore a stile on the left, but five yards further on cross a wooden footbridge.
- Keep straight on up the path to reach a lane. Turn left and follow the lane into the outskirts of Plaxtol.
- Bear right with the road, walking up The Street. Keep going up the bill, passing residential side turnings and eventually passing the Papermakers Arms.
- Continue up the road to a T-junction, where you turn right back to the church.

A Georgian extension onto the Old Soar Manor House.

WALK 12

Leeds Castle: fortresses and prisons in the Middle Ages

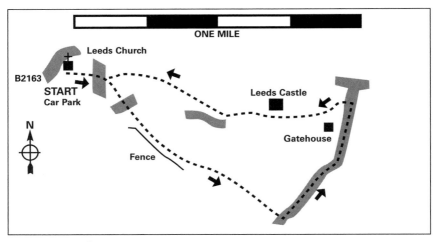

Distance: 2.5 miles

Map: OS sheet 188

Start and Parking: The walk commences at Leeds Church (grid ref: 826533), at the north end of Leeds village. Leeds is on the B2163, one mile south of the A20, and three miles east of Maidstone. There is a car park at the church itself.

Refreshments: Public house in Leeds. Tearoom in Leeds Castle.

Historical Background

The original castle at Leeds was Saxon, built in 857 by Ledian, chief minister to King Ethelbert. After the Norman Conquest it was given to the Crevecour family, who enlarged the castle substantially. During the Barons' rebellion of 1258–65, Robert Crevecour originally supported the King, but changed allegiances just in time to be on the losing side and so was dispossessed by Henry III. Leeds Castle officially became a royal castle during the reign of Edward I.

Edward II appointed Lord Badle mere as 'castellan', a royal officer who held a castle on behalf of his sovereign. It was during this period that Leeds saw its only military activity. In 1321 Edward's wife, Queen Isabella, on pilgrimage to Canterbury, decided to stay at Leeds. Lady Badlemere, in charge of the castle during her husband's absence and fiercely hostile towards the Queen, barred the gates and refused Isabella entry. In the ensuing argument her men killed six of the Queen's retinue. In the heated climate of factional in-fighting that surrounded Edward's court at this time, insults were heaped onto injury until the king himself led a small army, predominantly of Londoners, to besiege Leeds Castle. The castle fell after a few days fierce fighting, its 'seneschal' (chief military officer) Walter Colepepper was hung and Lady Badlemere was confined to the Tower of London.

Leeds Castle was a royal possession for a further two centuries, during which time it saw service mainly as a prison. Richard II was briefly imprisoned here after his deposition by Henry IV. Henry IV imprisoned his queen, Mary de Bohun, here for supporting her sons in their dispute with their father in his later years. Eleanor of Gloucester was tried for witchcraft in Leeds in 1431 in an attempt to discredit her husband, the powerful Lord Protector Duke Humphrey, and spent the rest of her life imprisoned here. During the 17th century, French and Dutch prisoners of war were confined in Leeds Castle.

Henry VIII gave the castle to Sir Anthony St Leger as a reward for services rendered, and thereafter the castle passed into the hands of various private landowners, including the Colepepper family, whose ancestor had been executed for doing his duty defending the castle.

The Walk
This short walk crosses the parkland around Leeds Castle and the quiet lanes and fields nearby, as well as passing under the walls of the castle itself.

● Leave the car park and turn right to enter the churchyard.

The Church of St Nicholas is Saxon in origin, with the typical high narrow nave of Saxon churches and two Anglo-Saxon windows on the north wall. The tower is a Norman addition and there is a fine rood screen from the slightly later Perpendicular period of architecture.

● Pass through the churchyard, passing the church on your left and keeping to the right-hand fence, to exit via a kissing gate at the bottom of the churchyard.
● Cross the field, aiming for the left side of a hedge seen opposite. Follow the hedge on your right hand to a gate into a lane.
● Cross the lane and go through a kissing gate into a field.
● Go half-right aiming for a stile on the far side of the field, between two tall trees.
● Cross the stile and keep ahead, crossing a drive and passing to the left of a clump of mature trees 50 yards ahead, aiming for the corner of a fence beyond.
● At the corner of the fence, keep ahead, with the fence close on your right.
● Once the field corner is reached, pass through a field gate and bear half-right to pick up a path through trees. Continue along the same line of advance along a path.
● Leave the plantation and keep straight on along an enclosed footpath.
● When the path meets a cross track, turn left down the track and follow it out to a lane.

- Turn left down the lane. Pass a post box and then some cottages on your right and follow the lane to cross a stream.

This stream is the River Len, whose waters were diverted to provide the artificial lake now surrounding Leeds Castle.

- Go along the lane for nearly another half mile, climbing steadily up a hill and then descending the other side.
- Pass the private entrance to Leeds Castle on your left, and after a further 50 yards turn left through a gate and descend some steps to a golf course.
- At the bottom of the steps leave the path and turn left, following the field boundary around to reach a drive.
- Turn right along the drive. Ignore a turn to the left in 200 yards but keep straight on towards the castle.

The original Saxon castle was reasonably large by the standards of the ninth century, but nowhere near the size seen today. It originally stood on dry ground, without the lake we see now. The first enlargements were made by the original Norman owners, the Crevecour family, who initially constructed a motte and bailey, an earthen mound surrounded by a simple wooden palisade. The Crevecours soon replaced the wooden stockade with a stone curtain wall, and then substantially enlarged the keep in 1119 (seen today on the innermost of the islands upon which the castle stands).

Two hundred years later, during the reign of Edward I, the de Leybourne family strengthened the fortifications in line with the new military technology imported into

Leeds Castle, dating from Norman times, has been considerably altered and extended over the centuries.

Britain by the king and built the stone curtain wall, turrets and gatehouse we see today. They also surrounded the castle with a dry moat, crossed by a drawbridge, and protected this by increasing the strength of the gatehouse and building a Barbican or gatehouse at the outer end of the drawbridge.

In the 17th century the castle was under the charge of Sir John Evelyn, who flooded the dry moat by diverting the River Len, built a new drawbridge between the two mounds, now islands, brought fresh spring water into the castle, and created the artificial lake seen today.

In the 19th century Leeds Castle passed to the Wykeham–Martin family, who built a range of mock-tudor buildings on the central island. Much of the 'mediaeval' building seen today is in fact a 19th-century folly, although some of the 13th-century fortifications can still be seen.

The castle is privately owned and often used as a conference centre. It is open to the public on occasions and contains an impressive collection of paintings and furnishings, and a pair of Anne Boleyn's shoes. There is an admission charge for the castle but with public rights of way across the grounds.

- Cross between the moat and the lake to the castle entrance. Turn right opposite the bridge.

On the right is a fortified mill. The mill was an important part of a mediaeval castle, producing flour for the lord and his retainers, and a channel from the River Len provided the motive power for the mill wheel. This fortified mill was built in 1300, connected by a covered way and fortified walls to the Barbican, with iron gates over the millstream to prevent access. It was constructed in order to provide a continued source of flour even during siege conditions.

- Follow the drive. Do not turn right at an exit sign but keep straight on, keeping the lake on your left and climbing the drive.
- Pass through a gate beside a cattle grid and bear right across the grassy slope, keeping the drive just to your left and aiming for a marker post just to the right of where the drive turns left.
- At the marker post, keep ahead up the grassy slope, maintaining the same line of advance and leaving the drive behind you. Aim just to the left of a stand of trees seen ahead. Two marker posts lead you to a kissing gate.

There are fine views back from this point across the parkland, formally landscaped in the 18th century by Capability Brown, to the castle.

- Keep straight on along the bottom of a field, with the field boundary on your right hand side, to reach a gate in the fence on the opposite side.
- Cross the next field, keeping to the right-hand edge, and pass into a lane.
- Cross the lane, enter the field and keep ahead with the field boundary on your left. Where the hedge bends left, keep straight on to a gate into the churchyard.
- Pass through the churchyard and back to the car park.

WALK 13

Ightham Mote: from Plantagenet stronghold to Tudor home

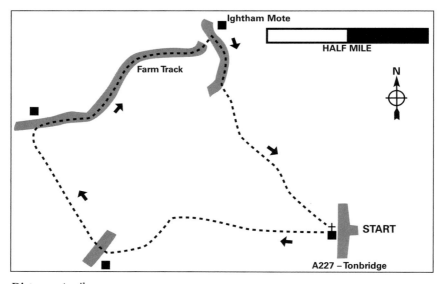

Distance: 4 miles
Map: OS sheet 188
Start and Parking: The walk starts from Shipbourne Church (grid ref: 591523). There is free parking on Shipbourne Common, opposite the church. Shipbourne itself is on the A227, three miles north on Tonbridge.
Refreshments: Public house at Shipbourne

Historical Background

Ightham Mote is two miles south of Ightham village, one of the oldest and prettiest villages in Kent. It dates from Saxon times and took its peculiar name from the Saxon king Ehta or Ohta and the Saxon word 'ham' or homestead. The house stands on the spot where the Saxon council, or Moot, used to meet, and the name of the house probably derives from this, rather than the fact that it is moated.

The house itself was built over a period of three centuries. It was started in 1340 as a fortified home by the Cawne family, loyal supporters of the Plantagenets who were rewarded for their services by grants of land in Kent. In the middle of the 14th century Kent was still heavily forested in many places, with poor communications and widely-spaced settlements, and the rich and wealthy had to look to their own protection. In consequence, Sir Thomas Cawne built his home with high strong walls and small, easily-protected windows, and surrounded it with a wide moat.

With time the countryside of Kent became less wild. More and more villages surrounded by rich agricultural land grew up, the forests receded, roads improved and the county became far less lawless. This was reflected by changes in Ightham Mote, where the emphasis shifted from construction for defence to building for comfort.

Although the moat remained and crenellations were added in Tudor times, their purpose was largely for decoration. From the 17th century onwards, Ightham was the family home for rich London merchants, whose property might be threatened by burglary but no longer needed the house's impressive defences.

The Walk
This walk starts at Shipbourne and goes through rolling arable land, still with a hint of the forests that used to cover the area. It then climbs along the Greensand Ridge to Ightham before returning through woods and fields to Shipbourne.

- Enter the churchyard via the lychgate and follow the path around the church, keeping the church to your left. At the rear of the church, leave the churchyard via a kissing gate.
- Ignore a stile immediately on the right, but instead keep straight on down the side of the field, with a fence on the right.
- Leave the field through a large gap in the hedge. Bear quarter-right across the large field in front. Aim for the right-hand corner of the wood seen ahead, protruding into the field.
- At the corner of the wood, cross a stile and enter the trees. Follow the footpath straight on as it winds through the trees, with the boundary of the field parallel to the path on the right.
- Where the field on the right ends, climb with the path to join a crossing track. Turn right for 10 yards, then turn left onto a footpath, climbing through trees.
- After 100 yards, where the path levels out, ignore a path to the right but instead keep straight on along a broad grassy track.
- Follow the track, soon with a fence on your left, as it winds gently downhill through trees, ignoring all turnings to the right and left.
- The track becomes fenced on both sides and drops towards a cottage seen ahead. Upon reaching the cottage (Budds Oast), turn right to reach a road.
- Turn right along the road for 15 yards, then turn left across a stile by a field gate.
- Once over the stile, immediately turn right through a gap in the hedge, then immediately turn left again. Walk down the side of the field, with your back to the road and the hedge on your left.
- Where the hedge turns left at a prominent tree, continue half-right across the field, making for the edge of a wood ahead.

- At the edge of the wood, go through a gap in the hedge and cross a footbridge.
- Continue straight on across the field, aiming for the edge of some trees seen 100 yards ahead.
- On reaching the trees continue straight on up the field edge, with the field on your right and trees on your left.
- At the top of the field cross a stile. Continue straight up the field, aiming for a stile just to the left of a house seen ahead.
- Cross the stile and turn right into a metalled drive.
- Follow the track for a mile, crossing over a cross track after half a mile.
- The track eventually reaches Mote Farm. Pass through the farm outbuildings to a road and turn right past the entrance to Ightham Mote.

Ightham Mote is a late mediaeval building, extensively remodelled in Tudor times and lived in for the past 600 years. Built of oak and local ragstone, Ightham Mote contains architectural gems from many periods.

The earliest part of the house was built in the middle of the 14th century by Sir Thomas Cawne, who fought in France with the Black Prince at the start of the Hundred Years War and who lived in Ightham from 1340 until his death in 1374. Of his building, the moat, the Great Hall, the Chapel and Solar all still remain as fine examples of the Decorated Period of architecture.

On Sir Thomas's death, the house passed to the Haute family, the most famous member of which, Sir Edward Haute, was a cousin of Elizabeth Woodville, Edward IV's queen, and who was appointed High Sheriff of Kent in 1478. He built the Gate Tower and squared off the west and south wings. Haute was party to the attempts by the Woodvilles to keep Richard of Gloucester, later Richard III, from power. When Edward IV died in April 1483 it was his

The moated Tudor manor house of Ightham Mote.

wish that his brother, Richard of Gloucester, should be Lord Protector of England, to avoid the factional in-fighting that seemed likely. Haute was part of the group that tried to hurry the young Prince Edward (later Edward V) to London and crown him before his fathers wish could be carried out. This was frustrated by the prompt action of Richard. Vaughan, Rivers and Grey, leaders of the Woodville clan, were executed for this act. Haute escaped this fate but later that same year he joined the Duke of Buckingham in his revolt against Richard, for which he was condemned and his lands confiscated. Haute was later pardoned by Henry VII.

In 1521 a minor Tudor courtier, Sir Richard Clement, bought the house and extensively remodelled it. The Tudor Chapel dates from 1521 and contains a magnificent painted ceiling and glass with coats of arms, including the Tudor Rose and the pomegranate, symbol of Katherine of Aragon, as signs of the family's loyal support for the ruling house. Clement also added the Oriel Room, remodelled the courtyard, and crenellated the outer walls, more for artistic fancy than for any need for defence. A later Clement married Lady Dorothy Selby, a lady-in-waiting to Queen Elizabeth I.

In 1637 the house passed from the Clement family to Dorothy Selby and her family, affluent London merchants and powerful figures in the local politics of Kent rather than players on the national political scene. The Selbys continued to add to and remodel the house: the Oriel room contains a fine Jacobean fireplace, while the drawing room has a Palladian window from the 18th century.

The Mote is owned by the National Trust and is open from mid-March to the end of October, 10.30am–5.30pm daily, apart from Tuesdays and Saturdays.

- One hundred yards past the entrance to Ightham Mote, cross a stile on the left and follow the right-hand edge of the field to a stile.
- Cross the stile and bear left across a small field to cross a stile into woods.
- Follow the track with a fence on your left through conifers. Ignore a cross track and follow the track to reach a stile into a field.
- Go straight across the field. At the far side, turn left and follow the hedge down and around to the right, to the bottom of the field.
- At the bottom of the field, cross a track to a stile opposite.
- Cross the stile and head half-right across the field, aiming just to the right of a plantation of trees seen ahead.
- Keep the plantation on your left side and continue up the field to a stile.
- Cross the stile and continue to a second stile five yards ahead, leading into the corner of a field.
- Go up the left side of the field, aiming towards the church. Cross a tarmacked drive and keep straight on towards a stile seen ahead, recrossing the drive in the process.
- Turn left to the kissing gate back into Shipbourne churchyard.

Shipbourne Church was rebuilt in 1723 on the site of an older mediaeval church. It contains a fine monument to local landlord Lord Barnard.

WALK 14
Knole House and Jack Cade's revolt 1450

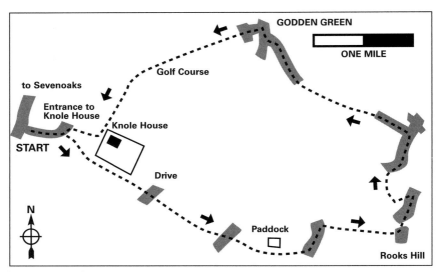

Distance: 6 miles

Map: OS sheet 188

Start and Parking: The walk starts at the main gates to Knole Park (grid ref: 534543), located at the southern end of Sevenoaks High Street and clearly signposted from the town. There is ample parking in Sevenoaks itself, both in car parks and on the road.

Refreshments: Shops, pubs and tearooms in Sevenoaks; tearoom at Knole House when open; pub at Godden Green.

Historical Background

By the 15th century Kent was enjoying a period of major economic prosperity. Its proximity to Europe meant that its ports and its inland market towns benefitted from the increasing trade with the Continent. The growing population in nearby London meant ever-bigger markets for its rich agricultural lands. It had a buoyant textile trade based on wool, with both London and the Continent.

However, by the middle of the century the people of Kent perceived their prosperity to be threatened. The loss of France at the end of the Hundred Years War and the resulting closure of continental markets was blamed on the incompetence of royal advisers during Henry VI's minority. Londoners were perceived to have received licence to poach on the preserves of

Kentish merchants. The textile trade was threatened by the influx of Flemish refugees who offered cheap and efficient competition. On top of all this, there was widespread corruption by royal and county officials, who controlled the courts and parliament and thus stifled any legitimate route of protest. One of the chief offenders was Lord Saye & Sale, Lord Lieutenant of Kent and owner of Knole House and Hever Castle (see walk 15).

This deepening sense of grievance erupted in 1450. A series of spontaneous revolts broke out among the people of Kent, not among the peasantry but among people of substance who were protesting about their loss of prosperity and influence. These protests were soon pulled together into one movement, led by Jack Cade, a gentleman soldier of fortune with ambiguous political ambitions. Cade imposed a reasonable military discipline on his followers, assembled a vast following in Ashford and marched on London. At Sevenoaks he defeated a royal army sent to oppose him. He was welcomed into London by its populace, and there the rebels executed Lord Saye & Sale. Henry VI acceded to the rebels demands, then went back on his word, and the rebellion foundered. Cade died while fleeing for safety.

The Walk
This walk goes through Knole Park, near the site of one of Jack Cade's victories. It then crosses the attractive Greensand landscape to Godden Green before returning through woodland to Knole House.

- Enter Knole Park via the main gates and proceed up the drive. After 100 yards, bear right off the main drive up a tarmacked footpath.
- Where the footpath forks, bear right and continue uphill.
- As Knole House comes into sight ahead, bear off half-right from the tarmacked path, at a 'Greensand Link Path' sign, and proceed around and up the hillside, aiming for the right-hand corner of the wall that surrounds the grounds of the house.

Just off to the right of the path is a brick dome. This is the roof of an Ice House. Before modern day refrigeration techniques, the storage of meats all year around was extremely difficult. Up until the early Middle Ages, meat could either be eaten almost as soon as it was killed, or heavily preserved with salt. This made the diet increasingly unpalatable as the winter months progressed. An ingenious solution was the ice house, a deep brick-lined cylinder dug into the earth and roofed. In the winter months, blocks of ice would be cut and placed in the cylinder, which was straw lined to keep the temperature stable. If the ice house was correctly designed, a supply of slowly melting ice would remain available until the following winter, enabling meat to be preserved fresh throughout the year.

- Turn around the corner of the wall.

Pause just after turning the corner and look to your right across the valley, to the church seen through the trees on the opposite side. That point, just outside the boundary of Knole Park, was where Jack Cade's rebels defeated the royal army. The king's military advisers were

guilty of complacence and arrogance in dealing with the rebellion. They assumed that because they were soldiers and gentlemen and their opponents commoners and rebels, that it would be an easy task to crush the rebel force. In this, they totally underestimated the military skill of Cade, himself a professional soldier who had, in remarkably short time, forged his men into an efficient and disciplined fighting force. They also totally overestimated their own abilities as soldiers. The royal army was routed in a battle lasting less than an hour, and Cade's men marched on towards London, where they lured a second royal force into ambush and defeat at Eltham.

- Continue with the wall on your left for one complete side of the walled grounds.

The walls were built for both privacy and defence. They would not withstand determined assault but, with the memory of Jack Cade's rebellion still fresh in the builder's mind, are high enough to keep out casual bandits or marauders.

- Where the wall turns a corner, keep straight on across the park, following a rough track.
- One hundred and fifty yards after leaving the wall, turn right with the track into trees and bracken. Pass around a fallen tree (blown down in the hurricane of 1987) and 40 yards later cross a track and continue straight on down a tarmacked path.
- After 800 yards cross over a driveway and continue straight on, now on a grassy path. Walk alongside a deer fence to a gate leading onto the road.

The Tudor mansion of Knole House, standing in 1,000 acres of parkland.

- Cross the road and follow a footpath into the woods. Follow the footpath as it winds through trees to a stile leading into a paddock.
- Cross the stile and turn right, following the right-hand edge of the paddock around two sides of the field, to exit in the bottom right-hand corner over a somewhat concealed stile.
- Descend and cross over a track to a stile opposite.
- Cross the stile and follow an enclosed footpath for 500 yards along the top of a field, past a tennis court and fenced grounds. Eventually reach the road at the entrance to a house.
- Turn left up the road. After 100 yards turn right up a footpath, signposted Greensand Way.
- Climb steadily up through trees, staying to the main path and ignoring side turnings. After 400 yards cross an open area with a bench to your left and continue straight on into trees again.
- Two hundred yards later, turn right at a T-junction of paths.
- At a fork in 50 yards, stay to the right, and 30 yards later turn right with the path and descend to enter a wood.
- Follow the path as it winds down through trees, with steep drops and intermittent wide views to the right. Eventually descend with the path down some steps to the driveway of a house at Rooks Hill.
- Turn left at the bottom of the steps and go steeply up a track through trees.

- At the top of the slope, bear right along a tarmacked drive, passing houses on your left. 150 yards past the last house, turn sharp left onto a bridleway.
- At a T-junction of paths, turn left.
- Continue along the path for 150 yards, then turn right downhill for 20 yards to join another path at a T-junction. Here turn right again.
- Descend this wider path through trees and bracken. At a junction of paths in 300 yards turn right.
- Follow the path for a further 300 yards to reach a road. Turn right and follow the road as it climbs, passing houses on the left.
- Just before reaching a crossroads, turn left up a driveway, at a concrete footpath sign and with a post bearing a dozen house names.
- Go down the drive for 400 yards. You initially have houses to your left and a hedge to your right, then paddocks to the left and cottages to the right. Where the drive turns into the gates of a house called 'Cherry Trees', keep straight on down an enclosed footpath.
- Ignore a path off to the left apparently leading to a tennis court, but keep straight on to a stile.
- Cross the stile and keep straight on across a field, aiming for the end of a band of trees seen ahead. Continue uphill, keeping to the left-hand side of the field.
- Continue straight on through a band of trees. Where the trees end, keep straight on, aiming for a stile into woods on the opposite side of the field. You will need to curve slightly right around a clump of trees ahead in order to maintain your forward direction.

The gatehouse of Knole house.

- Cross the stile and continue up into the woods. Keep straight on, crossing over two cross tracks.
- The path eventually emerges onto an unmade drive. Keep straight on up the drive. You soon join a tarmacked lane at the gates of Godden Clink, where you continue straight on to reach a road.
- Turn right up the road. 30 yards past the Bucks Head public house, turn left at a concrete footpath marker.
- Keep straight on along an unmade track for 100 yards to reach a lane. Cross the lane to a footpath opposite leading to a swing gate into woods.
- Follow the path into the woods. After 100 yards, bear left at a T-junction, onto a sandy track.
- Follow the track to a gate and kissing gate. Pass through the kissing gate into Knole Park.

Knole House is visible off to your left, and Sevenoaks soon becomes visible to the right. Sevenoaks is now largely a dormitory for London. It was named in AD1100 from the seven oak trees that stood nearby, and traditionally seven oaks have been maintained in the town ever since. Six of the seven oaks that were ceremoniously planted to commemorate the coronation of Edward VII in 1901 were blown down in the great storm of 1987, and six new ones were replanted the following year.

The park itself covers 1,000 acres, and is six miles in circumference. There is an extensive deer herd roaming the park, access to which is free to walkers. Deer had once freely grazed the forests of Kent, but by the end of the 15th century increasing agricultural use and the heavy demand for wood to provide charcoal had resulted in the forest shrinking dramatically. Increasingly, great landowners would enclose large swathes of land and stock them with their own deer herds, especially bred and managed to provide hunting for the landowner and his guests.

- Follow the track, now metalled, as it descends into the park and crosses a golf course, before climbing to reach Knole House.
- On reaching the house, turn right to reach the main entrance.

Knole House was originally a small manor house until it and its surrounding parkland were bought by Lord Saye & Sale, who extended it to create a country home suitable for a leading courtier. The death of Lord Saye & Sale during Jack Cade's rebellion put Knole Park and manor house on the market, in a climate where property prices in Kent were depressed. Thomas Bouchier, Archbishop of Canterbury, bought Knole in 1455 for the knockdown price of £256, and he set about redesigning the house to transform it into a palace fit for a prince of the church. It remained an ecclesiastical palace until the 1530s, when Henry VIII dropped heavy hints to Archbishop Cramner that he would like Knole as a royal palace (the same tactic Henry had previously used upon Cardinal Wolsey to acquire Hampton Court).

It remained in the hands of the Crown until 1566, when Elizabeth I gave Knole to her cousin Thomas Sackville, first Earl of Dorset. Sackville considerably extended the house to basically its current shape. Sackville was both a poet and a diplomat and the house has stayed in the family ever since. A descendant of the first Earl was the poet Vita Sackville-West, whose friend Virginia Woolf describes Knole in her novel Orlando.

Knole is one of the largest private houses in England. Architecturally it is one of the finest and certainly one of the largest Tudor houses in England. Its roofs cover four acres. An intriguing feature is the link of its design to the calendar: it contains 365 rooms, one for each day of the year, 52 staircases, one for each week, seven courtyards, one for each day of the week, and 12 entrances, one for each month.

Although the basic outline of the house remains as it was laid down in the time of Henry VIII, it has been added to and altered over the centuries by the Sackvilles and today contains a fascinating mixture of architectural developments: its two gatehouses are largely unchanged since Archbishop Bouchier's day, the Great Hall is Tudor and has a magnificent carved-oak screen, the great staircase and associated galleries date from the Stuart era, while many of the bedrooms leading off the galleries remain as they were redeveloped in Georgian times, with four-poster beds in all the major bedrooms.

The family still live in part of the house, while the rest is administered by the National Trust. It contains a fine collection of paintings, tapestries and furnishings, combining a history of the Sackville family with a history of English furniture and textile design.

It is open from Easter to the end of October, Wednesday to Saturday, 12 noon–4pm. There is an admission charge, but it is free to National Trust members.

● On leaving the house, go directly away from the front door down the driveway opposite. At a T-junction take the footpath opposite and follow it downhill to reach the drive back to the main gates.

WALK 15
Hever Castle and two Tudor queens

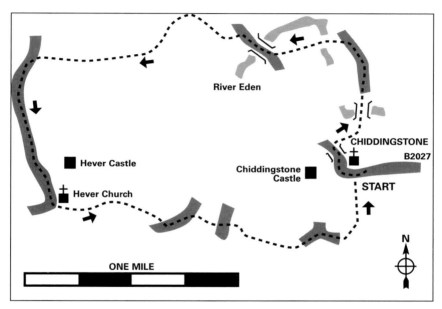

Distance: 5 miles

Map: OS sheet 188

Start and Parking: The walk starts from the church at Chiddingstone (grid ref: 501452). Chiddingstone is on a minor road one mile south of Bough Beech, which is itself on the B2027 between Limpfield and Tonbridge. There is limited parking in the village of Chiddingstone. As an alternative, the walk could be started from Hever.

Refreshments: Public house and tearooms in Chiddingstone and a public house in Hever.

Historical Background

Hever Castle has close connections with two of the wives of Henry VIII. In 1527 England was facing a dynastic crisis. For nearly a century the smooth succession of the Crown had been disputed, by Civil War, rebellion and factional in-fighting. The major obsession of Henry VIII was to ensure that the Crown would pass without dispute to his heir. This meant a son, for it was feared that any woman would see her claim contested and Civil War would be unleashed again.

But Henry's happy marriage to Katherine of Aragon for 20 years had produced only a daughter, Mary, and a string of still-births. Dynastic demands, and maybe his own deeply-held religious beliefs as well, led Henry to put aside Katherine in favour of the vivacious and intelligent Anne, daughter of Sir Thomas Bullen of Hever.

Forcing through a divorce from Queen Katherine required Henry to take the extreme step of breaking with the Church of Rome and being excommunicated, and his second marriage to Anne raised disquiet among many of his nobles due to her perceived lowly origins. To cap it all, Henry's dynastic plans were thwarted when Anne only succeeded in giving birth to another daughter, Elizabeth. A second divorce was seen as impossible, and trumped-up charges of adultery and incest were needed to dispose of Anne, who was beheaded in 1536. Sir Thomas Bullen left court under a cloud and died at Hever in 1538. His estates passed to the Crown.

Henry's third wife Jane Seymour gave him the son he needed so desperately, but Jane died during childbirth. In 1540 Henry married for a fourth time, this time for purely diplomatic reasons.

In order to cement an alliance with Protestant northern Europe, he married Anne, daughter of the Duke of Cleves. The marriage was never consummated and divorce followed shortly after. Anne co-operated fully with Henry's decisions and was rewarded with a generous pension and several properties, including the Hever estates of her predecessor.

The Walk
This walk starts in the Tudor village of Chiddingstone, with its mock-mediaeval castle, and goes through the peaceful Eden Valley to Hever. Here it passes Hever Castle and Hever Church, burial place of Sir Thomas Bullen, before returning through Greensand landscape.

● Standing in the main street of Chiddingstone, with the houses and shops on your left and the church on your right, walk down the road, bearing right around the church.

Chiddingstone is a perfectly preserved mediaeval and Tudor village. The house that is now the village post office and shop dates from 1453. Other houses bear such dates as 1638 and 1643, presumably the dates of subsequent alterations since the deeds of the houses show them to be much older, and their half-timbered construction and overhanging first floors argue for an earlier construction. The houses were mainly built by local farmers and tradesmen and reflect the affluence of the village. At the end of the street are wrought-iron gates leading into Chiddingstone Castle. Originally, the main street of the village passed through these gates and ran through the castle grounds, but the road was diverted in the late 18th century by the castle owners, to give themselves more privacy

The village takes its name from Chiding Stone, an ancient sarsen stone that was used in mediaeval times as a pulpit at which those who had offended against the code of conduct of the village would have their misdemeanours listed and would be punished by their neighbours. The original chiding stone is in the garden of the houses opposite the church.

The Church of St Mary was largely rebuilt after a fire in 1624, although the tower and its rude gargoyles are 15th century and the lower part of the nave arcades and some of the windows are from the 14th century. Inside the church are grave slabs made of iron, a reminder of the former Wealdan iron industry upon which much of the wealth of the area is based. The earliest grave slab dates from 1601, for Richard Streatfield, ironmaster. In the churchyard is the mausoleum of the Streatfield family, owners of Chiddingstone Castle. It contains over 60 coffins and is ventilated via a false altar tomb nearby.

- One hundred yards past the church, the road crosses a bridge. There are views of Chiddingstone Castle across the lake to the left.

Richard Streatfeild made his fortune out of the local iron industry during the first Industrial Revolution (see also walk 17) and settled in a Tudor manor house where Chiddingstone Castle now stands. A later Streatfeild replaced the Tudor building with a fashionable brick house called High Street House, around 1680. At the beginning of the 19th century Henry Streatfeild fancied himself as a feudal lord of the manor and turned the house into a mock-mediaeval castle by adding battlements and turrets and digging an artificial lake. He then high-handedly diverted the village street away from his property and demolished a few cottages that spoilt his view. The building was completed by Henry's son in 1835 and stayed in the family until the last Streatfeild died in 1938.

Chiddingstone Castle contains Tudor panelling and 16th-century stained glass, as well as Jacobite relics and a collection of Oriental Objects D'art.

- Immediately after crossing the bridge, turn right through a metal swing gate and walk down the right-hand side of a field.
- At the bottom of the field turn right through a gap in the hedge and follow the path half-left across the field, aiming at a stile at the left corner of the wood seen ahead.
- Cross the stile onto a metalled footpath and turn left. Follow the footpath between fields to a footbridge over a river.
- Cross the footbridge and continue straight on along an enclosed footpath to reach a gate onto a driveway.
- Keep straight on along the driveway, passing cottages on the right. Bear left with the drive, passing Rectory Cottage on the left and, 250 yards later, North Cottage on the right.
- Twenty yards past North Cottage, cross a stile on the left. Walk straight across the field (the path may not always be in evidence) and down to a metal-railed footbridge across the River Eden.

On the left is a brick pillbox built during World War Two to command the River Eden. In 1940–41 there was a real threat of a German invasion, and successive lines of defence were built along all natural features, from the channel coast right up to London. These were designed to contest an enemy's advance at every stage.

- Cross the bridge and continue straight on across the next big field. Again, the path may not be evident, but aim for a gate visible on the far side and almost directly in front of you.
- Cross a stile by the gate and turn right along the road, again crossing the Eden.

Another of the pillboxes defending the Eden crossing is seen on the left.

- Continue along the road for 150 yards, then turn left across a stile by a gate.
- Continue straight on up the left-hand edge of the field for 100 yards, then turn left through a gap in the hedge. Immediately turn right and, continuing the line of advance, go on up the right-hand edge of the field.
- After 300 yards, at the top of the slope, bear right through a field gate. Still continue the former line of advance, now on the left-hand side of a field.
- Just past a barn and field gate, turn left down an enclosed path to cross a stile onto a track.
- Turn right along the track for 10 yards, then cross a second track to a stile into a field.
- Turn left along the left-hand edge of the field.
- At the bottom of the field cross a stile into the golf course.
- Turn left for 20 yards to reach a wooden shelter, then continue straight on down the track to cross the fairway.
- Follow the track across a bridge, and 20 yards later go straight on across a cross track. Go through a large gap in the hedge and up a broad tree-lined track, with a hedge on the right and trees and fairway on the left.
- Continue straight along the track for half a mile, in between fairways and with a half-timbered building visible off to the right. Ignore all cross tracks and side turns.
- Where the track turns right to the clubhouse, keep straight on across a stile and along an enclosed footpath. Follow the path for 200 yards to reach the road.
- Turn left along the road. After a quarter of a mile Hever Castle can be glimpsed across the fence to your left.
- Cross the bridge with the road and continue for a further 100 yards to reach Hever Castle.

Hever Castle started as a fortified manor house, with moat, drawbridge and portcullis (it contains the only working wooden portcullis left in England) and was built by Walter de Hevere around 1340. The manor was rarely used as a home, but passed through a number of distinguished owners in the next hundred years, including Sir John Fastolf (immortalised as Falstaff by Shakespeare) and Lord Saye & Sale, the unpopular Lord Lieutenant of Kent who also owned Knole House and was beheaded by Jack Code's rebels (see walk 14).

In 1462 it was bought by Sir Geoffrey Bullen, a Norfolk yeoman and businessman who rose to become Lord Mayor of London. Sir Geoffrey married into society, one of the very few means of advancement for families of non-noble birth. Geoffrey's son William improved the family fortunes still further by marrying a daughter of the Earl of Osmonde. William's son Thomas cemented the family's place by marrying the daughter of the powerful Thomas Howard, Duke of Norfolk. Thomas's daughter Anne married the king.

Hever Castle, home to both Anne Boleyn and Anne of Cleaves.

After the fall of Anne Boleyn (she changed the spelling of her name to a more fashionable version), Hever passed to Anne of Cleves. Anne was not the 'Flemish Mare' of legend, but was certainly plainer than her portraits had suggested and was also dull and straight-laced by the standards of the English court. She failed to attract Henry, who almost instantly decided upon another divorce. Anne shrewdly appealed to the romantic in Henry by asking for his help and guidance and was rewarded with a generous financial settlement, several palaces and the continued trappings of royalty. Anne lived for a further 17 years in happy retirement, much of it spent at Hever. On her death she was buried in Westminster Abbey, the only one of Henry's wives to achieve that honour.

After the death of Anne of Cleves, Hever eventually passed into private hands. During the 17th and 18th centuries it was used as a 'safe house' for smugglers bringing contraband up from Deal (see also walk 21) to meet wealthy customers who came down from London, with a percentage going to the owners of Hever. In 1903 it was bought by William Waldour Astor, an American millionaire who became the first Lord Astor and who renovated the house in a mock Tudor style. He also added the lake and a row of 'Tudor' cottages for effect.

The castle is now privately owned. It is open from March to November, 11am–5pm. There is an admission charge.

- Pass the front entrance of Hever Castle to reach Hever Church.

St Peter's Church was built in the 13th century in the Perpendicular style. It has an unusual shingle spire and a Jacobean pulpit. It also contains a fine 15th-century brass of Margaret Cheyne. Its main claim to fame is the side chapel to the Bullen Family, which contains a Tudor fireplace and chest, as well as a magnificent brass of Sir Thomas Bullen in the robes of the Order of the Garter. Thomas Bullen was a successful Diplomat in Henry VIII's foreign service, became treasurer to the Royal household in 1522 and was elevated to the peerage as Viscount Rochford in 1525. He introduced both his daughters, Mary and Anne, to court and both caught the attention of the king. Bullen was rewarded by becoming Earl of Wiltshire and Earl of Ormonde, before falling from favour after Anne's execution.

- Enter the churchyard via the lychgate and take the footpath to the right of the church. Do not circle the church but keep straight on, to reach an enclosed footpath at the bottom of the churchyard.
- Descend the footpath, cross a footbridge and ascend between gardens and a field.
- Follow the enclosed footpath with the drive to Hever Castle on your left.

Mock-mediaeval jousting takes palace in the meadow on the other side of the drive.

- Follow the path as it leaves the drive and enters woodland.
- Cross the drive via a footbridge and continue until the path joins a drive.
- Continue along the grass verge until the drive is barred by a gate. Go through a smaller gate to the left, cross the drive and follow the path to the left of the cottage.
- Follow the path through a band of trees, with garden fences on the right, and down through scrubland, now with the hedge on the right.
- Cross a track, with houses close by on the left, and keep straight on along a footpath for 30 yards to reach a road.
- Cross the road and continue along an enclosed footpath. Follow the footpath to the right over a stile and along the left-hand edge of the field.

Across the field to the right can be seen both round and square oast houses. The oast house is used for drying hops, part of the brewing industry which was for many years a stable part of the Kentish economy. Oast houses were originally square, but Kentish hop-growers decided that a round house would be more efficient, since it would not have any corners in which hops could collect and remain undried. Thus the round oast house, so associated with the image of Kent, came into being. With use, it was discovered that the round oast was no more efficient than the square one.

- After 50 yards cross a footbridge on the left.
- Climb with the path through a wood and continue straight on where the slope levels out, to reach a stile into a field.

- Cross the stile and follow the enclosed path between deer fences around the left-hand edge of the field and into woods.
- Pass through a gully carved out of the Greensand and down through trees to join a track by a gate.
- Go through the gate and along the drive for 50 yards, then turn right up a sloping metalled track.
- At Hill Hoath Farm at the top of the slope, fork left into farm buildings. Pass a barn on the right and keep straight on along a footpath for 20 yards with a field fence on your left, to reach a stile by a gate.
- Cross the stile and keep straight on along the left-hand edge of the field and through a belt of trees to reach a stile on your left.
- Cross the stile and turn left to follow a footpath across the field. Chiddingstone Church soon becomes visible ahead.
- Cross a stile into an enclosed path and keep straight on for 175 yards, crossing a further stile en route, to reach a road at a kissing gate.
- Turn left back into Chiddingstone village.

WALK 16
Penshurst: the growth of a Tudor palace

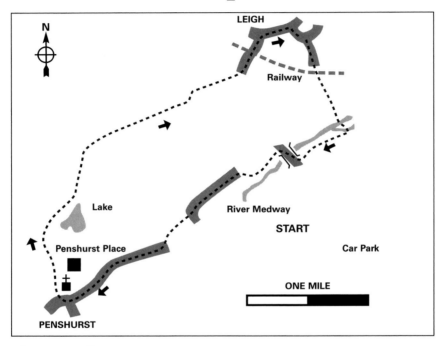

Distance: 5.5 miles
Map: OS sheet 188
Start and Parking: The walk starts from the village green at Leigh, on the B2027, four miles west of Tonbridge (grid ref: 550465). There is ample on-street parking in Leigh.
Refreshments: Public houses and shops in Leigh. Public house, shop and tearooms at Penshurst.

Historical Background
Penshurst Place, like Knole House (walk 14), is more like a village than a single house, with wings added to existing buildings by successive generations of owners. Although of mediaeval origin, it flowered into one of the greatest privately-owned palaces of the Elizabethan age and is forever associated with one of the men whose life encapsulates that age: Sir Philip Sidney.

The Sidneys came to prominence under the Tudors. Sir William Sidney served Henry VIII as a soldier and a diplomat. His son Henry served both Edward VI and Mary as an able civil servant and wore himself out, physically and financially, in the service of Elizabeth. But it is for Henry's son Philip that the family is remembered.

Born in 1554 and named after his godfather Philip II of Spain (then the husband of Queen Mary), Philip was the quintessential renaissance man, brilliant, charming and heroic, who died young before court intrigue had chance to pull him down. Philip was a fine poet, whose major work, *Arcadia,* was inspired by the countryside around Penshurst. He was a witty and sparkling conversationalist and an excellent dancer, a sparkling courtier who soon became the favourite of Queen Elizabeth, and whose charm and smooth tongue enabled him to survive periodic falls from the monarch's grace. Philip died at the age of 32 from a wound received fighting the Spanish at the siege of Zutphen, an heroic if unnecessary end, which cemented his legend.

Philip lived much of his life at Penshurst, and even when he was a prominent courtier he would periodically retire to its tranquillity. It was here that he wrote most of his poetry and entertained friends, most famously his cousin Robert Dudley, Earl of Leicester, who unsuccessfully wooed Queen Elizabeth here.

The Walk
This walk starts from the village of Leigh and passes through the Medway Valley that so inspired Philip Sidney's poetry, before reaching the Sidney home at Penshurst Place and returning across Penshurst Park.

- On the opposite side of the village green and cricket pitch from the main road is the club house of the local cricket team. Facing this clubhouse, take the road, signed as no through road, to the right of the clubhouse.
- Go up this short road, soon passing Lealands Avenue on your left.
- At the end of the road, go through a kissing gate and along a broad footpath, descending to cross under the railway.
- Continue along the footpath, now enclosed, for 60 yards, to a field gate. Go through the kissing gate beside the field gate and continue straight on along the field, keeping the fence to your right.
- Where the fence ends, proceed half-left across the field, towards a metal footbridge seen ahead.
- Cross the bridge over the River Medway and bear left for 50 yards with the path, to cross a footbridge on the right.

The Medway traditionally divides Kentish Men from Men of Kent: the former are born to the west of the river, the latter to the east.

- Ignore a left turn but go straight on for 30 yards to a squeeze stile into a field.
- Bear half right and follow the field edge for 20 yards to cross another stile.

- Keep straight on along the bottom of a very large field, keeping the hedge on the right, for nearly quarter of a mile, to eventually cross a stile onto a road.
- Turn right along the road and cross the Medway again. Immediately after crossing the bridge, turn left through a squeeze stile onto the river bank.
- Follow the river bank for quarter of a mile, keeping the river close on your left.
- Thirty yards after passing through a line of hawthorns, turn right at a waymark and cross the meadow to a footbridge visible in the hedge opposite.
- Cross the footbridge and bear half-left up the bank.
- Follow marker posts across the field to a stile, with a cluster of houses on your left.
- Cross the stile, turn right for 10 yards, then turn left at a T-junction onto a concrete drive.
- Follow the concrete drive for quarter of a mile through fields. When the drive turns sharp left, keep straight on down a grassy track.
- After 80 yards, pass through a squeeze stile into a field.
- Bear half-left across the field, crossing the brow of the hill (Penshurst Place now becomes visible ahead) and aiming for a stile in the bottom left corner of the field.
- Go through a squeeze stile, down the left-hand side of a field, and through a second stile onto a road.
- Turn right along the road. After a quarter of a mile, do not turn into the car park, but continue straight on, passing the walls of Penshurst Place on your right.
- Pass through the archway of the old gatehouse onto the road.
- Turn right along the road for 25 yards, then turn right up the steps and into the forecourt of Leicester Square.

Penshurst village, just slightly further up the road, is a fine cluster of old houses and a inn, many dating from Tudor times. The best of the buildings are the half-timbered cottages that form a huge inhabited lychgate to the church and are known as Leicester Square, named after the Earl of Leicester. (Exactly which Earl it commemorates is debatable: it is probably Robert Sidney, who built the final major extensions to Penshurst Place, although some sources romantically believe it is Robert Dudley, cousin to the Sidneys and Queen Elizabeth's favourite, who spent much time here with the Queen.)

The ending 'hurst' is a common one for villages in Kent and means 'wooded hill', a reminder that the great Wealdan Forest covered most of the county at one time. Many settlements grew up in the forest, as men moved ever further into the trees in search of timber, charcoal and grazing. place names ending in 'ton', 'ing', 'ley' and 'ham' reflect this.

- Pass though the archway ahead and into the churchyard, and bear left to the porch door.

The Church of St John the Baptist is 13th century in origin, built out of sandstone with vast pinnacles on the Perpendicular tower. The nave has 13th and 14th-century arcades of the style known as Early English, with Victorian additions. Inside the church is the Chapel to the Sidney Family, built in 1820 and containing a history of the family. The tomb of Sir William Sidney is in the church, but the most famous of the Sidneys, Philip, is not here: he is buried in St Pauls Cathedral. There is a collection of 13th-century coffin lids.

- Bear left around the church and follow a box hedge to a stile in the far corner of the churchyard.
- Cross the stile and bear half-right across the park, keeping a fence on your right. When the fence ends, keep the moat and wall on your right.
- Where the moat and wall swing away to the right, keep straight on to a gate seen in the fence ahead.

Penshurst Place started life as a mediaeval manor house, built about 1340 by a London wool merchant Sir John de Pulteney, a mediaeval magnate who was four times Lord Mayor of London and who died in 1349 as a result of the Black Death. This stone house still forms the south front of the present building and contains Pulteney's Great Hall, 60 feet high with beams that are of chestnut rather than the usual oak and are supported by grotesque carvings of human figures. In 1430 it was bought by John Duke of Bedford, brother of Henry V, who

Penshurst Place, country retreat of soldier, poet and courtier Sir Phillip Sidney.

enlarged the building by adding the south-eastern wing known as the Buckingham Building. The house later passed to John's brother Humphrey, Duke of Gloucester.

In 1527 it was given by Edward VI to Sir William Sidney, a distinguished soldier and diplomat. He had fought at Flodden Field against the Scots and attended Henry VIII at the Field of the Cloth of Gold, the resplendent meeting in 1520 where the English and French kings sought a lasting peace. (Also present was Sir John Peche, owner of nearby Lullingstone Castle, see walk 6.) William's son Henry Sidney was a boyhood companion of the king's young son, Prince Edward. Henry Sidney really established Penshurst as the family seat, adding the north and west fronts and building the State Dining Room onto the older mediaeval hall. The house was enlarged into a magnificent renaissance palace by Henry Sidney's younger son Robert, who extended the house southwards with the Long and Nether galleries.

Both Robert and his son, also Robert, continued the family tradition of royal service for both James I and Charles I. But of the next generation, two sons fought against the king in the Civil War, while a third helped depose James II.

As well as its architectural interests, the house contains a collection of tapestries, furniture and paintings, and also an armoury with a collection of mediaeval and Elizabethan arms, including the helmet of Sir Philip Sidney There is also a toy museum.

Penshurst Place is privately owned and is open from April to September, 1–5.30pm daily, except Mondays. There is an admission charge.

● Pass through a squeeze stile onto the drive. Cross the drive and exit through a second squeeze stile.

Hunting was a passion of the aristocracy. Deer and wild boar had once freely roamed the abundant forests of England, and although under the Norman Laws of the Forest they were the sole property of the king his nobles were allowed to enter the forest to hunt. By the end of the 15th century increasing demand for living space and for wood had resulted in drastic deforestation. Consequently, in order to continue hunting great landowners needed to enclose large swathes of land and stock them with their own deer herds. Penshurst Park is one of a number of parks that still contain deer descended from those Elizabethan herds.

● Keep straight on down an avenue of trees, passing the cricket pitch to your right.
● On reaching a brick pillbox on your left, leave the avenue and drop half-right down to a stile in the fence ahead.

Much of this area of Kent is studded with pillboxes dating from World War Two. Fears of invasion were high in 1940 and 1941, and pillboxes were built to command any wide open spaces that could provide a landing ground for German parachutists. The park was criss-crossed with wooden spiked fences to obstruct gliders, and covered by strategically placed pillboxes which could act as fire points.

● Cross the stile and turn right. Curve around the lake to a stile.

- Cross the stile and bear half-left through an avenue of trees to reach a fence on the far side of the field.
- Turn left and follow the fence uphill to a stile.
- Go through the stile and keep straight on uphill for quarter of a mile, through an avenue of trees.
- At the top of the slope, turn right and follow a broad grassy track along the ridge for 600 yards to a stile.
- Cross the stile and continue down the avenue of trees for a further 600 yards to reach the end of the wood.
- Where the wood ends, you need to continue straight on across the field, aiming for a gate in the top left corner (the right of way actually follows the left-hand fence around).
- Cross a stile beside a gate and continue straight on down a clear track, descending to a road.
- Turn left along the road. In 250 yards pass the entrance to Leigh station.
- Continue for a further 200 yards to a T-junction. Turn right to follow the road back to the village green.

It is worth staying to the right-hand side of the main road and observing the old dovecote preserved in the garden of a cottage just before you reach the post office, and also the old almshouses just beyond the post office.

WALK 17
Peckham: the first industrial revolution in the 16th century

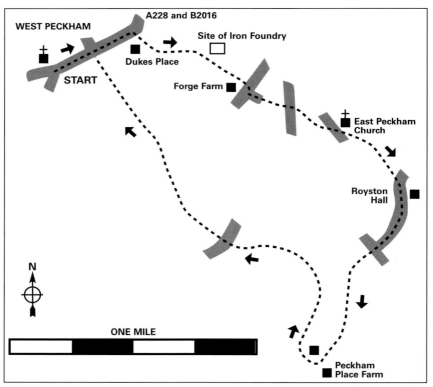

Distance: 4 miles

Map: OS sheet 188

Start and Parking: The walk starts from West Peckham Church (grid ref: 645526). West Peckham is five miles north-east of Tonbridge, on a minor road signposted just off the junction of the A26 and the B2016. There is limited parking in West Peckham near the church.

Refreshments: Public house in West Peckham.

Historical Background

Travelling around Kent today it is hard to realise that in Tudor times the county was the industrial heart of England. This process had started in the 14th century, when Edward III settled Flemish weavers in Kent to start a cloth industry. The small towns and villages in the centre of Kent soon grew in prosperity, both through manufacturing cloth and raising sheep.

But the real take-off of Kentish industry came in the 16th century. Iron had been mined in the Weald since Roman times, but smelting had used foot-pumps and the resulting metal had been of poor quality. During the Tudor period the use of water-powered smelting was perfected, and the production of iron of a much higher quality began. The demand for Kentish iron exploded, driven at least in part by the need to service the new Royal Navy dockyards that Henry VIII founded around the Kentish coast in 1515. Ore was extracted, often using open-cast mining or shallow mines, and smelting plants sprang up on streams all over the Weald. Trees were cut down at an alarming rate to feed the charcoal-fired engines. As the supply of trees in an area was exhausted, the iron mills simply moved further into the forest, thereby accelerating the process of deforestation.

This can truly be called England's first Industrial Revolution, and Kent remained the industrial heart of England until the mid-18th century, when the invention of coal-powered machinery moved the focus to the coalfields of the Midlands and North.

The main centres of Tudor industrialisation were in the Weald, but the woods and streams of the Greensand Ridge also attracted their share of industry. The transient nature of the industry and subsequent redevelopment of the land have left little trace now on the ground. A few remains of the foundries can still be discovered, and memorials in some churches and the names of some of the farms and houses still bear witness to this forgotten chapter of the county's past.

The Walk

This walk starts in the interesting old village of West Peckham, passes the 'ghost-town' around East Peckham, and sees hints and traces of the first Industrial Revolution, while going through quiet and little-walked countryside.

West Peckham has an extensive village green, somewhat unusual in that it is not enclosed by buildings but remains open on one-and-a-half sides. St Dunstan's Church is Saxon in origin, with a Saxon tower containing a double-splayed Saxon window. The rest of the church dates mainly from Norman times. Inside the church there is a Squires Pew, built above the chancel, with its own separate entrance from the churchyard. It is panelled and comfortably furnished, and so high sided that it gives total privacy from the vicar as well as from the congregation.

- With the church on your left, walk down the road, passing the village hall on your right.
- At a road junction, keep straight on down Mereworth Road.

St Dunstan's Church, West Peckham, dates from Saxon times.

- Follow the road, with houses on the right and a field on the left. The last house, shielded by high hedges, is Dukes Place.

Dukes Place was believed to be a presbytery of the Knights Templar, who were granted land in West Peckham in the 1330s. The Templars were founded in AD1118 to protect travellers journeying through the Holy Land. Their name comes from the fact that their original headquarters was on top of the Temple Mound in Jerusalem.

The order grew in numbers and wealth, and when the loss of the Holy Land forced them to relocate to the West, they established themselves as bankers to the various monarchs. They grew in independence, wealth and arrogance and they eventually became hated by both clergy and secular authorities. The order were expelled from much of Europe in 1307 by the combined might of the Pope and King Philip IV of France, and moved their centre of operations into England and Germany instead. They never regained their former influence and power and gradually withered away as the Holy Land ceased to be an issue for European monarchs.

- Immediately after Dukes Place, turn right down a concrete drive, at a footpath sign and waymark post.
- Where the concrete drive bends sharp right, keep straight on for 20 yards down a track and cross a stile on the left into a field.
- Cross the field half-left, aiming for a gate in the middle of the hedge on the opposite side.
- Do not go through the gate but turn right and follow the field boundary, keeping alongside the hedge on the left.

- Fifty yards before reaching the corner of the field, cross a stile on the left, and then continue along the same line down the edge of the field, now in an enclosed track.
- Cross over a footbridge and climb to a stile beyond.

To the left just past the footbridge is an earthen bank, once the retaining wall of a small dam. Iron was mined at many locations throughout the county and worked in forges that relied on local waterpower and burnt charcoal that was available in abundance in the Wealdan Forest. This dam would have driven a water wheel which in turn would have powered either a forge hammer or the bellows for a charcoal furnace.

Iron was in increasing demand in the 16th and 17th centuries, to meet the ever-increasing needs of England's fleet. It was the cutting of oaks for warships and the burning of lesser trees for charcoal that led to the virtual deforestation of south-east England by the end of the 18th century.

- Keep ahead towards a gate in the far-right corner of the field, beside a farm.
- Cross two stiles, the second next to the gate, and keep ahead up the track to pass to the left of the oast houses of Forge Farm and out to the main road.

The name Forge Farm is another echo of the area's industrial past.

- Turn right along the road for 50 yards and then turn left into a narrow lane, concreted initially but after 20 yards overgrown and grassy.
- Follow the lane for 300 yards and then cross a stile onto a road. Cross the road to the lane opposite and climb with the lane, winding uphill for 500 yards to reach a road junction with Old Church Lane.
- Cross the lane and go up a flight of steps to enter the churchyard by a stile, and pass around the church keeping it to your left.

The village of Peckham was originally around what is now the Church of East Peckham. The area was abandoned when the settlement moved two miles west to what is now West Peckham, in order to be near the river which was the source of waterpower and hence employment in the 16th century. The church was abandoned but restored in the 19th century.

- Ignore a path leading down to the lychgate but keep around the side of the church for a further 10 yards, and then turn right down a narrow path through the gravestones to a narrow gateway in the churchyard wall.
- Go through the gate and bear left, keeping the wall on your left, to cross a stile into a field.
- Go half-left down the field the opposite side. Turn right, keeping the field boundary on your left, to reach a stile.
- Cross two stiles in quick succession. Follow an enclosed path downhill, skirting a conifer plantation, and reach a stile in front of Royston Hall.

Royston Hall was built in 1535 but little of the original building remains. The west front that can be seen through the gate is original in parts, although even here later alterations have blurred its lines.

- Turn right down the road, passing the rear entrance to the hall, and follow the lane until you reach a T-junction.
- Cross the road and go through a gate opposite at a footpath sign. Go straight on across the field to a stile in the opposite fence.
- Cross the stile and go ahead for 15 yards through scrub to reach a field edge.
- Turn left and walk with a conifer hedge on your left.
- When the hedge ends, maintain the same line of advance across the field, passing an isolated tree on your left, and then soon picking up a line of trees on your left.
- Descend the field to the corner. Ignore a gap on the left but keep ahead through a gap in the hedge in front to reach a fence and a stile crossing into the field on your right.
- Cross the stile and go half-left across the field to a gap in the hedge in the bottom corner, aiming at the buildings seen in the trees beyond.
- Go through the hedge and cross a narrow stone footbridge.
- Follow a clear grassy track to the corner of a drive.
- Keep straight on up the drive, passing outbuildings on your right and leaving the farm and ponds away on your left.
- Go through the gates (labelled Peckham Place Farm) and immediately turn right onto a track.
- After 100 yards, at a junction of tracks where the fence on the right ends, turn right onto a track.
- Follow the track through a band of trees and across a large field.
- Eighty yards short of the far side of the field, turn left at a waymark post (Weald Way) and follow the footpath across the field.
- Cross a stile and go half-left across the next field. At the far side cross over a farm track and climb a stile onto the road.
- Cross the road half-right to a stile at a footpath sign.
- Cross a brick bridge to a stile beyond. Go over a cross track with a gate on the left and keep ahead, to enter a fenced track.
- Follow the track, with a ditch on the left, and keep straight on, soon to enter a field.
- Keep straight on along the edge of the field, with a ditch on the left.
- On the far side of the field cross a stile and then bear half-right across the field, aiming for a stile in a clump of trees seen on the far side.
- Maintain the same line of advance across the next field, aiming for a stile in the top right corner of the field.
- Maintain the same line of advance across the next field, then cross a stile and continue up the left-hand edge of another field, to enter an enclosed footpath.
- Follow the footpath to a gate at a road junction. Turn left and follow the lane back to West Peckham Church.

WALK 18
Chilham: the evolution of a village from pre-historic times to the 17th century

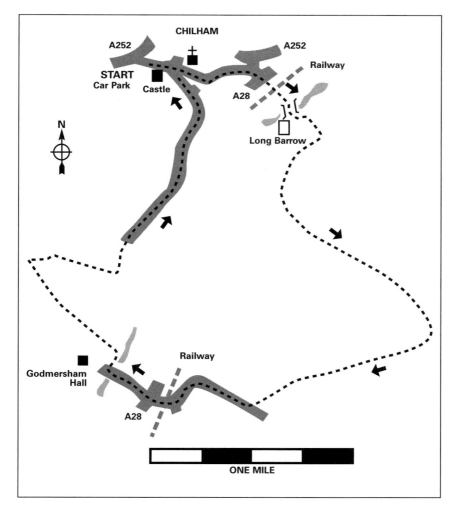

Distance: 5 miles

Map: OS sheet 189

Start and Parking: The walk starts from the free car park on the north side of Chilham village (grid ref: 066537). Chilham is just off the A252, seven miles south of Canterbury. Drive west along the A252 and take the second turn to Chilham, and the car park is immediately off the main road.

Refreshments: Public houses and tearooms and a shop in Chilham.

Historical Background

Chilham was built in a commanding position on a hilltop, easily defensible, and near one of the main routes connecting Canterbury to London. The hill had been used by the Romans as an army camp during Julius Caesar's second invasion in 54BC, offering as it did a defensible site on high ground above the marshy River Stour valley, on the line of Caesar's advance from the channel coast towards the Thames valley. After the Conquest, the Romans settled in the area.

Chilham later became a Saxon stronghold, possibly of a local lord named Cille (in Saxon Chilham means the 'ham' or settlement of Cille). Although most of the area was covered by the great Wealdan Forest, itself a source of wealth for those communities able to exploit it, Chilham stood on the banks the River Stour with its rich and fertile agricultural land.

Chilham was a settled community from at least Saxon times, and its layout is a splendid example of Saxon society recorded in buildings. The houses of the village clustered around a central square on the top of the hill with roads leading off from each corner. On one side of the square was the castle, originally a wood and earth fortification of the local Saxon lord, but later a more substantial stone-built structure for the village's Norman landlords. On the other side of the square stood the church. The twin powers of church and lord dominate the village and the landscape.

The prosperity of Chilham grew over time, and its wood and earth Saxon dwellings were replaced by more substantial stone and later brick buildings. The market square and the four lanes leading off it, one in each corner, are today lined with buildings from the Tudor and Jacobean era and is little altered since that time.

The Walk

This walk starts in the perfectly-preserved village of Chilham and then crosses the River Stour to ramble through the hills opposite, with fine views over Chilham. It returns via Godmersham Park, with its associations with Jane Austin.

● From the car park turn right into the lane and walk up to the village street. Continue to the main village square, with tearooms on the left and the castle gates on the right.

The site of Chilham Castle was originally a Roman and then a Saxon stronghold, a fortified earthworks with wooden palisades. After the Norman Conquest, the land was granted by William the Conqueror to his half brother Odo, Bishop of Bayeaux, who also held estates at

The market square at Chilham is surrounded by fine Tudor and Jacobean buildings.

Chevening (see walk 19) and at Rochester (see walk 8). Odo started by building a simple motte and bailey castle here, an earthen mound with a wooden palisade around it. In the 12th century the land passed to a Norman knight, Fulbert de Lacy, whose daughter married a bastard son of King John. De Lacy extended the castle, building one of the only two octagonal keeps in England. The castle became Crown property during the Wars of the Roses, when the then owner Lord Rees was convicted of treason.

The castle fell into disrepair, and in 1616 the Norman ruins were largely pulled down and replaced with a new castle by the then owner Sir Dudley Digges, Master of Roles to James I. Built to designs by Inigo Jones, and constructed largely of brick on the unusual ground plan of five sides of a hexagon, this is one of the finest examples of a Jacobean castle and gardens in England. The garden designs were modified by the famous landscape gardener Capability Brown and contained the first wisteria in Britain.

The gardens used to be open to the public. At the time of writing this is no longer so, although this may change in the future.

● With your back to the castle gates, walk down the square to the entrance to the church, beside the White Horse public house.

Although St Mary's Church originated in Saxon times, the present building dates from the 14th century and it was much rebuilt in the Victorian era. It has a flint Perpendicular tower.

Chilham was on the Pilgrims' route and the church was used by worshippers en route to Canterbury. In 1538, when St Augustine's Abbey in Canterbury was dissolved, the gilded shrine containing St Augustine's bones was brought to Chilham but disappeared a few years later. Today the church houses many monuments to the former residents of Chilham castle, the Digges Family, and some fine stained-glass windows.

- Facing the entrance to the churchyard and the White Horse, turn right and walk down The Street, with the church off to your left and passing between Clements Cottage and Chantry House. Descend The Street.

It is worth strolling slowly down The Street and taking the time to look at the fine Tudor and Jacobean buildings you pass. The other streets leading off the square are worth exploration either now or on your return to Chilham at the end of the walk.

- Pass The Woolpack on your right and bear left with The Street. Ignore all side roads and follow The Street out of the village, to reach the A252 in a quarter of a mile.
- Pass a spur onto the A252 on your left and follow The Street as it bears around to the right and in 100 yards reaches a T-junction with the A28, opposite a garage.
- Cross the A28 and continue straight on down a no through road, passing the garage on your right. In 50 yards cross the railway.
- Follow the road across a bridge over the River Stour and bear right up a fenced drive, passing Mill House on the left.
- Cross a second bridge and turn left into a track.
- At the gates to a cottage, turn left and follow a footpath along the river bank, soon climbing through trees to reach a cross track.

In the field behind the cottage is a Neolithic long barrow or burial mound. The mound was reopened in the third century AD and the bodies of a Roman adult and two children were buried in it, possibly affluent Romano-British settlers who lived in the vicinity. The site is now called Julliberrie Down, named after Julius Laverius, a Roman officer who was part of Caesar's second expeditionary force and who died in a skirmish with British guerrillas near the same spot in 54BC. Despite a local legend, neither Laverius nor any other Roman soldiers are buried in the mound.

- Cross over the cross track and continue ahead up a grassy track, which soon narrows to become a path and leads into a field.
- Keep forward along the left-hand edge of the field. Follow the field edge around two sides to cross a stile on the edge of the wood.
- Turn right along a track, which is initially tree-lined, then with a field to the right, then tree-lined again. Reach a cross track, with a concrete footpath sign on the left.
- Turn left and climb up the cross track for 15 yards to a field gate.
- Go through the field gate and follow a broad path half-right across the field towards woods.
- On reaching the woods, turn left with the track and proceed with trees on your right. After 25 yards, turn right into trees, still on the broad track.
- Pass through a band of woodland to emerge into a field. Turn left and follow the left-hand edge of the field uphill.

- At the top of the field keep straight on through a band of trees into another field.
- Turn right and follow the right-hand edge of the field, walking along the bottom of the field with a hedge on your right, for 100 yards, to reach a waymark post on the right.
- With your back to the post, walk half-right across the field, contouring around the slope and avoiding climbing towards the trees on your left. Soon you reach a stile in the hedge ahead.
- Cross the stile and descend along a clear path through scrubland. The path is soon enclosed by hedges and in 50 yards reaches a stile.
- Cross the stile and keep straight on along the hedged footpath between fields.
- At a cross track, where the path starts climbing deeper into the trees, turn right onto a narrower waymarked footpath through trees, with a field over the fence on the right.
- Cross a stile and keep straight on along the bottom of a field, with the field boundary on the right. At the end of the field, cross over a track to a stile.
- Cross the stile and keep ahead along a narrow footpath through trees.
- In 150 yards, turn right at a waymarked post and gently descend with the path into a field.
- Keep straight on down the right-hand edge of the field. At the bottom of slope, cross a ladder stile and immediately turn right to cross two metal gates in quick succession. After the second gate go half-left across the field to a stile in the left-hand fence.
- Cross the stile to go up an enclosed footpath for 50 yards to reach a track.
- Turn right and follow the track, soon passing between buildings. When the track becomes metalled, and just after exiting through gates, turn left over a stile into a field.
- Go half-right up the field, aiming for a stile visible on the horizon in the top-right corner of the field.
- Cross the stile, with a buried reservoir to the right, and go straight ahead into a field.
- Follow the right edge of the field for 130 yards, then turn right through the hedge and then immediately turn left, to continue the former line of advance, now with the hedge on your left.

There are fine views of Chilham over to your right, clearly demonstrating its commanding hilltop position. In mediaeval times, when most of the land would have been forested, occasional glimpses of Chilham would have been visible through the trees, in particular views of those two symbols of feudal authority which still dominate the view of the village, namely the church and the castle.

- At a waymark post in 120 yards, turn half-right and descend across a large field, following a vague path, to descend steeply through a gap in the hedge.
- Continue the same line of advance across the next large field to reach a stile in the bottom corner onto a lane.
- Turn right along the lane for half a mile. At a T-junction of lanes, turn right under a railway bridge and go up the lane for 300 yards to reach the main road.

- Cross the main road and continue down the road opposite, signposted to Godmersham Church.
- Cross a bridge and go ahead to the right-hand set of gates beside the lodge opposite. Pass through a pedestrian gate and immediately turn right through a wooden gate.
- Keep ahead across the park for 170 yards, initially with a fence on the left, then continue straight ahead where the fence ends, aiming for another fence ahead. Follow this fence for a few yards, then turn left through a gate and up an enclosed drive.

To the left is the house of Godmersham Park, built in 1732 by Thomas Brodnax and later home of his cousin Edward Knight, Jane Austin's brother (who had to change his name to Knight in order to inherit Godmersham). Jane was a frequent visitor to Godmersham but, as her letters reveal, she considered the people she met during her visits neither her cultural nor her intellectual equals. She used the house and the society she encountered there as models for many scenes in Mansfield Park *and* Pride and Prejudice.

- After 200 yards, at a junction of tracks, keep straight on, passing the entrance to Deer Lodge on your right.
- Climb with the track, cross a stile and bear right.
- After 30 yards, stop following the track but bear half-right across the hill, aiming first for a marker post in the field and then to a stile beyond.
- Cross the stile and maintain the same line of advance across the field beyond, aiming for a marker post at the edge of the woods ahead.
- Cross the stile into the woods. Immediately turn right and follow a track along the edge of the woods.
- Go through a kissing gate beside a field gate and turn right along a cross track, still following the edge of the woods, now downhill.
- Leave the wood and follow an enclosed track downhill.
- Follow the track, now tree-lined, as it bends left around a corner. Follow the track, ignoring all turns to the left, to reach a lane.
- Keep ahead down the lane. Follow it for three quarters of a mile, until you reach School Lane on the left.
- Go up School Lane into Chilham Square. Pass the castle gates on the left and turn left down the hill back to the car park.

WALK 19
Chevening: landscapes and landowners in Georgian times

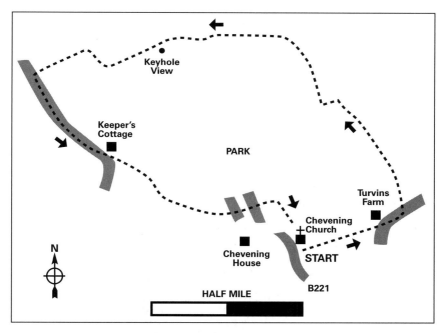

Distance: 4.5 miles

Map: OS sheet 188

Start and parking: The walk starts from St Botolph's Church, Chevening (grid ref: 489577). To reach Chevening, leave the A25 at Sunbridge and go north along the B221 signed Chevening. After two miles turn left (north) off the B road up a minor road signed Chevening. There is limited parking in the village outside the church.

Refreshments: None

Historical Background

Very often the physical landscape as we now see it has been moulded by the wishes of great landowners of the past. In our towns and cities the evidence of this is often now obscured by modern development of the land, but in rural areas clear examples are still to be found.

While Chevening Park has never been one of the great estates of England, it contains some good illustrations of how generations of landowners have left their mark on the countryside.

The village of Chevening itself was built by the then lord of the manor to house his retainers, and to this day it remains the property of the Chevening Estate. The Church of St Botolph's, at the end of the carriageway from Chevening House, was greatly extended by later landowners to provide a chapel for their tombs. Ancient roadways were diverted to remove them from the lord's grounds. The park was extensively re-landscaped to meet the recreational requirements of the owners.

Chevening House itself, built between 1616 and 1630, is a good example of a country seat, conveniently close to London and used by generations of administrators as somewhere to relax after toiling in the capital.

The Walk

This walk passes Chevening House, a superb example of the classical design, and climbs along the North Downs escarpment for some exhilarating views over the park and surrounding countryside, before descending through woods and back into Chevening Park.

● Enter St Botoph's churchyard via the lychgate. Pass through the churchyard with the church on your left. Where the path divides, keep straight on to exit the churchyard via a gate.

There has been a church on this site since at least 1122, when the parish was still known by its Saxon name of Civilinga. The oldest part of the present St Botoph's Church dates from the 13th century, when the nave and chancel were enlarged. The tower and typically Kentish turret were built in 1518. A chapel was added in 1585 by John Lennard of Chevening Place and ever since has housed the monumental tombs of the Lennard and Stanhope families.

● Keep straight on along an enclosed track to cross a stile into a field.
● Continue along the left-hand edge of the field to enter a second enclosed track. Keep straight on to reach a road.
● Turn left along the road to pass Turvins farm.
● Follow the road, 100 yards past Turvins farm, turn left over a stile and walk along an enclosed path.
● Leave the enclosed path over a stile. Continue straight on up the right-hand edge of the field. At the top of the field, turn left with the hedge for 20 yards, then turn right up some steps to a stile.
● Cross the stile and follow the hedge up the right side of the field. At the top of the field, turn left and continue straight on along the top of three fields, keeping the woods to your right and views to your left. There are 'North Downs Way' signs at intervals along your route.

St Botolph's Church at Chevening.

- Near the end of the third field, turn uphill, following the right-hand edge of the field, still with woods on your right, to reach a stile on the right, beside a gate.
- Cross the stile and walk forward and quarter left, aiming for the corner of a wood 100 yards ahead.
- Turn left around the corner of the wood and follow the field edge, keeping the woods on your left, for a quarter of a mile.
- Where the field boundary swings slightly right, ignore a kissing gate in the corner but swing right with the hedge for 10 yards, to cross a stile on the left.
- Follow the path for 200 yards through a wood. At the end bear left with the path and enter a field
- Turn right along the right-hand edge of the field. Cross it, keeping the hedge to your right, to a gate.
- Pass through the gate, turn right for 10 yards, then turn left into a large field.
- Keep straight on, following the left-hand edge of the large field to enter a second field.
- Proceed for 100 yards along the left-hand edge of the field, to the famous 'keyhole view' of Chevening on your left.

In 1769 Lord Chatham borrowed Chevening as a residence from its owner, his cousin, the 2nd Earl Stanhope, and built a carriageway through the park, to provide easy recreational riding. As part of this scheme, he had a 'keyhole' cut through the woods above Chevening to provide a view down over the house when resting from his exertions.

- Continue along the left-hand edge of the large field, going around nearly two sides of it, to reach a stile on the left into woodland.
- Cross the stile and follow the path for quarter of a mile through the edge of the woodland, to reach a field.
- Turn left and follow the edge of the field for 200 yards to reach a road.
- Turn left into the road, and walk down it for half a mile, until Keepers Cottage is reached on your left.
- Pass the cottage, and immediately turn left through the yard and proceed straight ahead along a broad and intermittently-metalled track into the woods.
- Follow the track for quarter of a mile. When the track reaches a gate and the metalling ends, turn right with the track, now grassy.
- Follow this grassy track for 150 yards to reach a field.
- Continue down the left-hand edge of the field to cross a stile, and then continue through a narrow strip of woodland.

There is an excellent view from this point down across Chevening Park to Chevening Place and beyond it, to St Botolph's Church. The original route of the Pilgrims' Way crossed the park directly in front of the house but was diverted by the 3rd Earl Stanhope to the top of the North Downs ridge. Another ancient right of way, the Fish Route, used for transporting fish from Rye to London, ran parallel to the drive that now leads to the house. This too was diverted out of the park, to the east.

- Enter the field and descend the left-hand edge of the field to reach a kissing gate.
- Pass through the gate and turn left onto a track.
- Follow the track downhill with woods on the left and Chevening House on the right. Immediately before reaching a farm track ahead, turn right over a stile.
- Continue down the left-hand edge of the field, keeping the farm track to your left to reach the main drive to Chevening House. Cross the drive using stiles.

You are now crossing the carriageway laid down by Lord Chatham, which is still known as Chatham Drive. The original course of the Pilgrims' Way was along the foot of the slope you have just descended.

Chevening Place was the country estate of Bishop Odo of Bayeaux, half-brother of William the Conqueror, who accompanied the invading Normans in 1066 as father confessor to the army. Odo, who commissioned the Bayeaux Tapestry to commemorate the successful Norman invasion of Britain, acted as Regent of Britain whenever William had to return to Normandy, and also had considerable ecclesiastical duties in the newly-conquered territories. Odo lived and ruled from his palace in Greenwich, conveniently close to the capital, but used his estates in Chevening as a place to relax from the affairs of state. Odo also built the castle at Chilham (see walk 18) and the first castle at Rochester (see walk 8).

From Odo the estate passed to Adam de Chevening, a Norman baron who built the original village on his land for his retainers. It then passed through the hands of four families before being bought by the Lennards in 1551. It was the 13th Baron Lennard who commissioned the famous Stuart architect Inigo Jones to rebuild the house in its present form.

In 1715 the house passed to the Stanhope family, who were industrious public servants for much of the later Stuart and early Hanoverian period. General James Stanhope was a soldier, diplomat and parliamentarian and was rewarded with the title Earl Stanhope. Charles, 3rd Earl Stanhope, was a notable patron of science and technology and a brilliant scientist himself. He invented a calculating machine which was to be the forerunner of Babbage's famous calculator, from which modern computers are descended. Charles also closed down the two ancient trackways, the Fish Route and the Pilgrims' Way, and diverted them outside the boundaries of the estate, where they would be less inconvenient to him.

In 1959 Chevening House was bequested to the nation by the 7th Earl Stanhope, to be used as a residence either for Cabinet ministers or for descendants of King George I. Between 1974 and 1980 Prince Charles lived in Chevening.

- Keep straight on, keeping the fence to your right, until a wood is reached ahead. Turn left along the front of the wood and follow the edge of the wood to a stile on to a private drive.
- Cross the drive by stiles to enter a field. Keep straight on along the right-hand edge of the field to reach a stile.
- Cross the stile and turn right into an enclosed footpath. Follow the footpath between fields and through a horse barrier until it emerges on to a drive opposite the gate into St Botolph's churchyard.
- Enter the churchyard and follow the path, keeping the church on your right, back to the lychgate.

WALK 20
Upnor: coastal defences during the 17th century

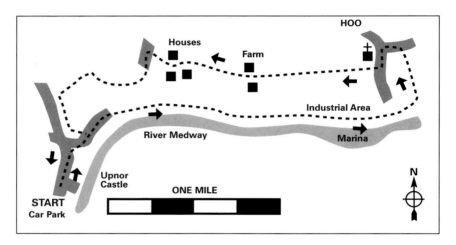

Distance: 5.5 miles
Map: OS sheet 178
Start and Parking: The walk starts from the car park in Upnor Village (grid ref: 757706). Upnor is two miles north-east of Strood, on a minor road clearly signposted off the A228 Strood–Grain road. Follow signs for the village and Castle, and the car park is on your right as you approach the town.
Refreshments: Public houses in Upnor.

Historical Background
The River Medway has been associated with the Royal Navy ever since the latter was created by Henry VIII in 1515. Initially the river was used to provide secure and sheltered anchorage for vessels that were 'laid up', that is, not in active service. Provisioning facilities were available, and very soon ship-building and boat-repair yards were developed. By the start of Elizabeth I's reign, Chatham was the foremost Royal Naval yard in England. Vessels that were laid up were without masts and rigging, and so were highly vulnerable, and in 1559 Queen Elizabeth ordered the building of a fort at Upnor to protect Chatham and the Medway anchorage from attack. The original castle was completed by 1564, and reinforced in 1585, when open war with Spain was declared.

The castle never saw active service during Elizabeth's reign but remained central to the defences of the Medway throughout the Stuart era. It saw its only action in 1667, during the Second Dutch War. Lulled into a false sense of security after defeating the Dutch at sea, the English fleet were laid up in Chatham as an economy measure. Against expectations, the Dutch, under Admiral de Ruyter, sailed up the Medway, burned the unfinished fort at Sheerness and threatened Chatham itself. Upnor Castle put up a spirited defence but was unable to prevent part of the English fleet being burned and the flagship, the *Royal Sovereign*, being carried off by the Dutch.

The Medway defences were drastically overhauled after this disaster. New forts and gun platforms were built further downstream, and Upnor became redundant. In 1668 the fort was converted into a gunpowder magazine. It was used both as this and as a barracks until 1827, servicing the English fleet throughout the wars of the 18th century and the Napoleonic wars.

The Walk

Although this walk is probably the least scenic in this series, it does contain much of historical interest. It starts at Upnor castle and goes along the Medway, passing various stages of the river's defences and going through the marinas and boatyards for which the banks of the Medway are used today. It returns through pleasant agricultural land and across the high ground above Upnor.

- Leave the car park by the pedestrian exit, signposted 'Castle and Village', at the opposite end of the car park to the car access. Go out onto the road.
- Before starting the walk proper, make a small detour to Upnor castle. Go straight ahead down the old High Street, past old weatherboarded houses and pubs.

The village of Upnor is little more than one street. It is actually only 400 years old as a settlement, which grew up outside the walls of the Tudor castle to provide taverns for the garrison and married quarters for the troops.

- At the end of the High Street is a bench with a fine view over Chatham Dockyard and the Medway Anchorage. The entrance to Upnor Castle is immediately on your left.

The buildings you can see around the present gateway into the castle are a brick-built three-storey barracks. They were built in 1718 to replace the former accommodation in the castle, when this was taken over to provide storage for gunpowder. Parliament had been wary about constructing permanent bases for a standing army ever since military power had been abused by the Stuarts, and these were among the first purpose-built barracks to be constructed in England. Beside the barracks is the 18th-century guardroom.

The castle itself is hidden from sight. It has evolved over time and was originally, in Tudor times, a small rectangular building designed to provide a simple gun platform. Looking out across the river to the site of the Tudor dockyards on the opposite bank, you can appreciate how these guns would have commanded the entrance into the anchorage. The defences were increased by building a strong gatehouse and curtain wall on the landward side, with a dry ditch around the outside. When the castle was converted into a gunpowder magazine in 1667, the frontage onto the river was drastically modified, the courtyard redesigned and the interior extensively altered.

Upnor Castle is open from April to October, 10am–4pm. There is an admission fee but it is free to members of English Heritage.

- To start the walk proper, retrace your steps up the High Street to the car park pedestrian entrance. Do not enter the car park but turn right, away from the Kings Arms, and follow the road.
- At a road junction in 80 yards, keep straight on, immediately passing the gates to Upper Castle House, and bear off right on a footpath, with the walls of the house on your right.

The house to the right was the official residence of the storekeeper of the Upnor Magazine. Once the castle ceased to be the front line of defence, there was no need for a full strength garrison or for a commanding officer to live in the fort itself. The garrison was now from the ordnance corps, and the commander was officially a 'storekeeper', for whom a separate and quite luxurious residence was built.

- Eventually descend some steps with the footpath onto a road. Turn right and follow the road around past the gates to the dockyard and past a boatyard.
- Pass The Ship public house, and immediately opposite at The Pier public house bear right away from the road onto a footpath that stays to the riverside.
- Pass an obelisk on the left and pass between metal posts onto a drive. Keep straight on along the drive, and go through the first set of gates marked 'Medway Yacht Club', but at the next set of gates bear right and follow the footpath between the river and a fence.
- At the end of the fence the path descends to the shoreline for a few yards and then climbs steeply up the bank into the trees.
- At the top of the bank, keep the same direction across an open area for 10 yards, and then go through a gap in the fence onto a footpath through the woods.
- Follow a clear track that winds through the trees, keeping the shoreline between five yards and 30 yards away to your right. Follow the woodland path for a mile.
- The path leaves the trees, where there is a sign announcing 'gas mains under river' on your left, and a white jetty marks the boundary of permanent moorings.

Where you are now standing was the site of the Cockham Wood Fort, and the low flat island seen behind the marina is Hoo Ness. Even prior to 1667 there had been a chain stretched between Hoo Ness and the opposite (eastern) bank of the Medway. This was immensely thick, capable of being lowered and raised, and designed to block one of the two channels up the Medway and force all ships to enter by the western channel, under the guns of Upnor.

The gatehouse to Upnor Castle, built in 1718 to replace the original Tudor building.

After the humiliation of 1667, new defences were built to strengthen the Medway. Two new gun batteries were built, one here at Cockham Wood and one on the opposite bank, at Gillingham. In addition, a smaller battery was built on Hoo Ness itself. Between them, these three batteries could command the entrance to the upper Medway, and enemy vessels would have been under constant fire as they manoeuvred slowly through the shoals and mud flats of the river.

- Continue ahead along the footpath, with grass lawns edged with telegraph poles on your left and permanent houseboat moorings on your right.
- Pass through gates and continue along the drive towards the marina. Where the drive swings left through some gates, continue straight on along the footpath at a concrete footpath marker. The footpath soon becomes enclosed with a hedge on the left and a fence on the right.
- Do not enter the marina but keep ahead with the fence intermittently on your right and prefabs on your left.
- Ignore a drive to your left but keep ahead, passing to the right of a yellow-brick and corrugated-iron building.
- Pass garages on your right and keep ahead up the track, with the link fence of a boatyard on your immediate right. Bear left with the fence to cross the entrance of Hoo Marina. Ignore a drive to the left and keep ahead, still parallel with the river, to pass through small industrial units.
- The path soon becomes enclosed again, with a concrete fence on the left, and then emerges into a tarmacked parking and turning area. Ahead is a fence surrounding a boatyard, while to your right an open field is visible 50 yards away.
- Turn left and walk up a tarmacked drive for 50 yards. Where the drive turns left, keep ahead following the signposted footpath across a field.

Pause on this path and look over your right shoulder, towards the power station downstream. In the estuary beyond was Fort Darnet, a gun battery built in 1668 on a mud flat in midstream. Another battery stood on the mudflats beyond the power station, and these two, in combination with the batteries at Cockham Wood and Hoo Ness, would have laid down a deadly fire upon any enemy ship trying to force its way up river. In addition, huge sharpened poles were sunk into the mud at low water, designed to rip the bottom out of any vessel trying to go close to the shore to avoid the barrage from the batteries.

- Opposite the church, you should ignore a footpath to the left (it is not a right of way) but keep straight on until the houses ahead are reached.
- Turn left in front of the houses and follow the road for 100 yards to a T-junction.
- Turn left in the main road for 60 yards, and then turn right onto a footpath into the churchyard.
- Follow the footpath through the churchyard, keeping the church on your left, to exit at the end of the churchyard. Do not turn left into a new housing estate, but turn right down an enclosed footpath for 30 yards to reach an open field.

- Turn left in the field and follow the boundary for 20 yards to reach a metalled track.
- Turn right along the track. After half a mile pass through a gate and keep straight on past a barn on the right, to come to a junction of tracks in front of a farmhouse. Do not turn down towards the farmhouse but keep ahead, passing a large chicken house on your left, walking with a line of trees on your right.
- A quarter of a mile past the farm, ignore a footpath going off to your right but keep ahead along the track. The track soon passes between trees on the right and the wall of a house on the left.
- At the house gates do not turn right down the drive but keep straight on along a footpath beside a wall. Follow the footpath, soon enclosed, out to a road.
- Turn left along the road. In 100 yards, at a turning point at the road end, keep straight on down a track, which soon becomes a footpath. Follow the footpath downhill and curve right.
- Just around the bend, do not go down shallow steps on your right, but follow the path as it curves rightwards and descends, soon passing a seat with a magnificent view over the Medway.

On the opposite bank of the river you can see the old Royal Naval Dockyard at Chatham, currently being restored to its 18th-century state, and open to the public. The red-brick building on the waterfront that you can see was the gatehouse to the Royal Naval Yard, built in 1726 by Sir John Vanbrugh. Behind the gatehouse you can see the sheds which housed the sailmaking shops, while the long, low building housed the ropemaking shop. The harbour front would have been alive with derricks for replacing masts and replenishing supplies, while behind were dry docks for more drastic repairs.

Upnor Castle can be seen on the waterfront down to your right, and its strategic position, commanding the entrance to the dockyards in Tudor times, can be appreciated. After 1668 it became a gunpowder magazine. The powder was stored on the opposite side of the river to the warships and dockyards, in case of an accidental explosion. Small boats or 'lighters' would have been rowed across the river from the warships at anchor off Chatham and collected supplies of gunpowder.

To your left and just around the bend in the river were the batteries of Cockham Wood and Hoo Ness, the Medway's defences after 1668. In addition, two further batteries were located in the woods, along the ridge you are now standing on, to provide yet another field of fire to be poured into any attacker. The Admiralty was determined that any repetition of the humiliation of 1667 would be avoided at all costs!

- Follow the path as it gently descends. At a T-junction, with a path on the left and steps and a path on the right, turn right and climb, keeping to the left-hand boundary of an open grassy area.
- In 60 yards cross a stile ahead and climb through trees. Follow the path through trees until it crosses a footbridge, and five yards later a stile.
- Cross the stile and turn right along an enclosed footpath. In 200 yards cross the top of a drive and continue straight on through a gate.

The cannon at Upnor commanded the entrance to Chatham and the Medway.

- Descend the path, still enclosed, with an iron fence on the left and the boundary of archery club land on your right. Follow the path as it climbs, turns and drops again, eventually reaching a stile.
- Cross the stile and turn left for 20 yards. Just before a road, turn left and follow the path, with the road on the right through the trees. The path eventually becomes enclosed and drops to the road.
- Turn left down the road for 50 yards, then turn right at a footpath sign, up steps. Retrace your outward journey for 250 yards, keeping the wall on your left, to reach the Kings Arms and the car park entrance again.

WALK 21

Deal: Tudor castles and 18th-century port

Distance: 8 miles
Map: OS sheet 179
Start and Parking: The walk starts from the entrance to Deal pier (grid ref: 378528). There is plentiful parking along the seafront, north of the pier, and some street parking near the castle. There are also pay and display car parks in the town itself.
Refreshments: Public houses, shops and cafés in Deal.

Historical Background

From the 17th until the middle of the 19th century, Deal was one of England's major seaports, despite having neither harbour nor docks. Three miles out to sea are the notorious Goodwin Sands, a vast sandbank lying for most of the time just below the surface of the water, responsible for wrecking countless vessels and claiming more than 50,000 lives in the past three centuries. The water between the Goodwin Sands and the shore, called the Downs, is sheltered by the sandbank and is one of the largest safe anchorages around Britain's coastline. In times of war merchant ships would creep down the coasts to congregate in the Downs, waiting to form up into huge convoys, often of many hundreds of ships, before setting sail across the world. Royal Navy fleets of warships and transports would also wait in the Downs for departure. Deal grew to preeminence as a town for supplying the needs of these convoys and fleets, and as a terminus for travellers and mail joining the ships.

Smuggling began in earnest all along the south coast in the 17th century. Proximity to France and wide open beaches made Deal a smugglers' paradise, and smuggling was a major part of the local economy. Spirits, tobacco, tea, silk and fancy goods crossed the channel at night in the famous 'Deal Galleys', boats with false keels and hollow masts for the hiding of contraband. Much of the town was involved in, or turned a blind eye to, smuggling, and many members of the aristocracy or the wealthy classes would travel to Deal to openly buy smuggled merchandise. Consequently, it was extremely difficult for customs officers to gain sufficient public support to suppress this activity. After 1816, stern measures were taken to suppress smuggling: the Coastal Blockade was started, and after many violent confrontations the trade was finally stamped out by the middle of the 1850s.

However, as well as being a major point of departure from Britain, the flat beaches and safe anchorage around Deal made the area a major danger spot at times when invasion by a continental enemy threatened. To counter one such threat, Henry VIII built three massive castles – Walmer, Deal and Sandown – to defend the beaches. These castles

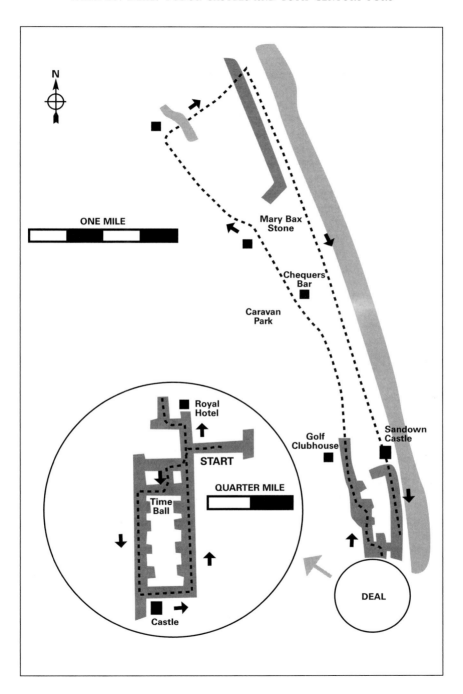

again saw service during the Napoleonic Wars, when the Downs were used as a springboard from which the English fleet and expeditionary forces could attack the French.

The Walk
This walk goes through historic Deal and passes many sites from its heyday in the Napoleonic era, and then rambles through links and dunes before returning along the coast. The walk also encompasses two of Henry VIII's great fortifications, and the landing site of Caesar's second expedition in 54BC.

- With your back to the pier entrance, cross the road and turn left.
- Cross Broad Street and turn down it for 20 yards, and then turn left into Middle Street.
- At the end of Middle Street, turn right down the broad South Street.

South Street was always the terminus for public transport coming into Deal. During the 18th and 19th centuries horse-drawn coaches used to arrive and depart from South Street, connecting Deal with destinations across all of England. Passengers sailing from England would travel to Deal and stay in one of its numerous inns until their fleet was ready to sail. Navy captains would also often join their ships here rather than sailing down the coast with their vessel, travelling overland and staying in comfort onshore until it was time to depart.

The entrance to Deal Castle, one of the finest examples of military building from the reign of Henry VIII.

- At the bottom of South Street, turn left. Shortly cross Sondes Road and keep straight on.
- Keep to the left-hand side of the road and cross over four side roads to reach Deal Castle.

Henry VIII's foreign and domestic policies culminated in the break from the Church of Rome in 1534. This resulted in war and made invasion by the leading Catholic powers, headed by France, seem likely. The coastline around Deal was fortified by three huge castles. These were state-of-the-art military architecture. For mediaeval castles, assault had been by foot soldiers backed by primitive siege weapons, and therefore high thick walls were all important. But by the 16th century gunpowder had revolutionised siege warfare, and assault would now be backed by efficient cannon. Castles had to be redesigned to cope with this new threat.

Deal is a classic example of Henrician military architecture, comparatively low and squat but with thick rounded walls to deflect cannon ball, flat gun platforms which would give visibility over as great an arc as possible and which could provide fields of interlocking cannon fire, and a dry moat which could be riddled by musket fire from commanding windows and turned into an effective killing field.

Deal Castle has six huge semi-circular bastions, surmounted by a further six smaller bastions, providing a 360 degree field of fire. It had an oven for heating cannon balls, and cunningly placed sally ports which enabled the defender to launch an attack on any assailants from the rear. Deal would normally have had a defence force of a captain and 24 men (although in times of trouble many more could be accommodated), and the captain of Deal Castle also had responsibility for the nearby garrisons in Walmer and Sandown Castles.

The only time Deal Castle saw any fighting was during the Civil War, when the castles were held for the king and besieged in 1648 by parliamentary forces. Major-General Gibson held Deal for some weeks against an attacking force of 2,000 men before finally surrendering.

Deal Castle is open from 1 April to 30 September daily, 10am–6pm. There is an admission charge, but it is free to English Heritage members.

- Walk past the castle onto the seafront. Turn left along the sea front towards the pier. In 200 yards pass the time ball on your left.

The tower, which is now crowned by a time ball, stood at the main entrance to the Naval Yard in Deal. The Naval Yard was built in the late 18th century to provide Royal Navy vessels anchored in the Downs with a governmental victualling yard rather than relying on the free enterprise of the town.

The tower was built in 1795–96 as a signalling tower, as one of a series, each one within sight of the next in line, stretching from Deal to London, with the purpose of alerting the government to any impending invasion by the French. The tower originally housed a shutter semaphore, which passed signals by means of huge wooden shutters in front of a lamp to the next tower along the line. A signal could be transmitted from Deal to the Admiralty in London in under two minutes. In 1816 the semaphore was replaced by two huge arms on a pole as a more effective means of communication, but this fell into disuse in 1842.

In 1853 the present time ball was installed, as the tower was put to the new use of receiving a time signal from Greenwich Observatory transmitted down the line of towers to ports around the coast. At 12.55 the ball was raised to the top of the mast, and at 1pm precisely the ball dropped, providing an accurate visual time signal against which all the ships anchored in the Downs could set their timepieces. The time ball was used until 1927, when the invention of radio rendered it obsolete.

The Tower now houses a small museum and is open May to September, 10am–5pm, except Mondays.

● Pass the pier and continue along the seafront for another 100 yards, as far as the Royal Hotel.

The Royal Hotel was the most prestigious hotel in Deal, used by many famous personages awaiting the arrival of the fleet or waiting for their ship to be ready for departure. Horatio Nelson often stayed in the Royal, accompanied in later years by his mistress Emma Hamilton.

● Cross the road in front of the Royal Hotel and turn left down King Street. Take the first road on the right, Middle Street, and follow it as it winds parallel to the seafront, ignoring all side turns.

Middle Street is the oldest part of Deal and was once the main road in the town. It grew to prosperity in the 1600s, with the influx of many Flemish refugees. It contains buildings from many eras, and some of its present buildings date from the early 18th century.

Deal had a reputation for being a very rough town, combining all the worst excesses of a port with the lawlessness associated with being a smugglers haunt. In 1710 it was described as being 'an impious and remorseless town: fraud, oppression, theft and rapine reign'. Middle Street and the maze of courts and narrow alleys running of it was at the insalubrious heart of Deal, teaming with smugglers, press gangs, brothels and inns.

During the Napoleonic Wars, the smugglers were tolerated as they provided a valuable source of information about what was happening on the Continent as well as bringing goods to England through the French blockade.

● Eventually reach Alfred Square.

The Prince Albert public house, on the corner of Middle Street, was built in 1717. At one time its landlord, William Riley, was strongly suspected of being the leader of the Deal smuggling community, although this was never proven and he was never brought to justice.

- Turn left down Alfred Square, and at the bottom turn right (College Road).

The road you are turning into is called College Road. Its continuation southwards is called High Street. Up until around 1600, this road marked the old shoreline: gradually a shingle beach was laid down by the sea, where the current shoreline now is, and a brackish marsh formed between beach and shore. Over the next century this marsh was reclaimed and the land used for the expanding town of Deal. High Street is so-called not because it was the main street of the town but because it once marked the limit of the high tides.

- Follow College Road for nearly half a mile, passing from the old town into newer housing. Cross Harold Road and keep straight on, now up King Edward Road.
- At a T-junction turn left into Godwyn Road.
- At the bottom of Godwyn Road, turn right into Golf Road.
- Follow Golf Road, ignoring side turns as it becomes a no through road and passes a Southern Water Treatment Plant on the right.
- Keep straight on up the road, with a golf course on the right, soon passing the golf club house on the left.
- At the end of the tarmacked road do not turn into the entrance of Leisurescope Caravan Park but keep straight on along a sandy trackway, with golf links to your right.
- After half a mile pass a pillbox on your right and keep ahead along the track.

This World War Two pillbox is a reminder that the threat of invasion onto this flat and accessible coast was not confined to Tudor or Napoleonic times. This whole coastline was heavily fortified with mines and barbed wire backed by fortified gun emplacements.

- The track ends at the Chequers Bar. Join the road and maintain the same direction, passing the entrance to the caravan park on your left.

You are following an ancient trackway that threaded its way through the dunes just above what used to be the high-water mark before the sea wall was built. It was used by smugglers to move their wares between Deal and Sandwich while avoiding the main road, which was likely to be patrolled by excise men.

- Turn left with the road, avoiding a track straight ahead marked with a 'Private Property' sign. The right of way now no longer follows the road but runs along the top of a bank about 30 yards to the left. This is at first overgrown, but soon becomes a clear pathway, with good views over the fens to the left.
- Just before a cottage, pass the Mary Bax Stone, set on the right of the bank.

This stone marks the spot where Mary Bax, a local woman, was murdered in 1782 by a foreign seaman.

- Cross the drive to the cottage and cross a stile opposite to continue along the top of the bank.
- In 100 yards, where the bank turns away to the right, keep straight on to a stile by a field gate.
- Go over the stile and maintain the same line of advance, with the fence on your left.
- At the end of the field, go through the gate and continue ahead, still with the fence on the left.
- Cross the stile and maintain the same line of advance through a third field, still following the fence on your left.
- Pass a pumping station off to your right, and then cross into the next field. At the time of writing there was no stile at this point, but keep straight on, still with the fence on your left.
- At the end of the field, cross a stile into a farm drive and turn right. Follow the drive, passing the farm on your left, and continue to the road.
- Cross the road and cross a stile opposite and enter a field.
- Cross the field to a stile on the opposite side. Cross the stile to enter rough pasture.
- Keep straight on, following a series of concrete marker posts, to a stile onto the golf course.
- Continue across the golf course, following concrete markers, and soon bear right with the now wider path, and then curve left again.
- Cross a stile onto the coast road and turn right.
- Pass in front of houses and continue along the coast road.

Somewhere along this stretch of coastline, between Sandwich and Sandown Castle (no one knows exactly where), is the site of Julius Caesar's second landing in Britain, in 54BC. Caesar had made a brief reconnaissance the previous year, landing four miles south of here, near modern Walmer, but the expedition had been pinned to its beachhead and forced to evacuate. In 54BC Caesar returned, this time earlier in the year and with a far larger force. He conducted a vigorous campaign, thrusting up through Kent and across the Thames, fighting a series of skirmishes against British guerrillas before defeating his main opponent Cassivellaunus at Wheathampstead in Hertfordshire. The Romans then withdrew from Britain for nearly a century, until returning to launch a full-blown invasion, landing five miles north of here, at Richborough, in AD43 (see walk 4).

- Where the houses end and the road turns right, keep straight on along the sea wall at the top of pebble beach.
- Follow the sea wall for one and three quarter miles. The footpath is now officially below the sea wall on the right, along the edge of the golf course. This is softer walking but loses the view of the sea. It is suggested you take either the sea wall or the footpath, or alternate between the two, whichever you prefer.
- Eventually reach houses and a road. Turn left onto the promenade.

The circular bastion at the end of the promenade marks the site of Sandown Castle.

Built in 1539–40 as the third of Henry VIII's 'Castles of the Downs', Sandown was smaller than Deal or Walmer, having only four semi-circular batteries rather than six. It was under the command of the captain of Deal Castle.

Sandown Castle never saw action in Henry's day, but during the Civil War was held by royalist troops for three months. After the end of the Civil War, it was used as a prison for Colonel Hutchinson, one of the signatories to Charles I's death warrant, who languished in its damp vaults for a year before dying of pneumonia.

During the 18th century the castle was abandoned and much damaged by the encroaching sea. It was regarrisoned during the invasion scare of 1803–07, but was finally abandoned in 1815 and allowed to crumble away.

● Keep along the promenade until you reach the pier.

The road along the promenade is Beach Street. As Deal had no harbour, in the 18th and 19th centuries this was the boatman's area of Deal, with boats running straight on and off the beach. Not only did fishing boats land here, but ferries carried passengers from the inns of the town and victuals from the port out to the waiting ships. All of the trades that supported a fleet getting ready for sea – rope and sail making, boat building, bakeries, breweries etc – were clustered along Beach Street, as well as provisioners for meat, fruit and vegetables.

WALK 22
Hythe and the Napoleonic Wars

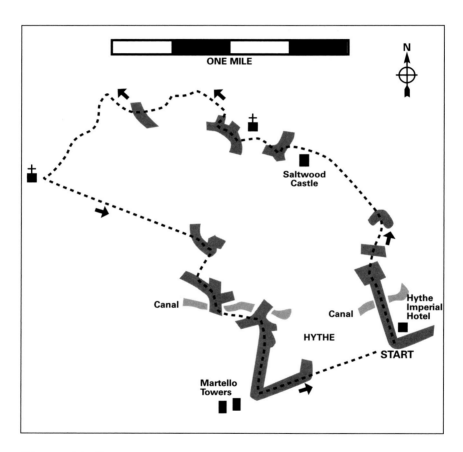

Distance: 5.5 miles

Map: OS sheet 179 or 189

Start and Parking: The walk starts from the Hythe Imperial Hotel, on Princes Parade, which is part of Hythe seafront (grid ref:168344). There is a car park opposite the hotel, or street parking along Princes Parade.

Refreshments. Public houses, shops and tearooms in Hythe.

Historical Background

In 1802 the Peace Treaty of Amiens ended nine years of war between Britain and revolutionary France. This was only a temporary respite, for 14 months later the war resumed. This time France was led by a far more formidable enemy, Napoleon Bonaparte, whose primary war aim for the next two years was the invasion of England.

Napoleon's obvious invasion route was the short sea crossing from the Pas de Calais to the beaches of Kent, in particular the coast between the cliffs of Hastings in the west and Folkestone in the east. Here wide beaches were backed by the flat fields of the Romney marshes, ideal countryside for the highly-manoeuvrable French army. Although the first line of defence was the English Navy, there was always the danger that the French fleet would manage to secure the channel for 24 hours, all the time that would be necessary for an invasion armada to hand Napoleon's Grande Armee on England's shores. Protection for many miles of exposed beaches became of paramount importance, with only limited funds available for the task.

The solution was the Martello Tower, a string of brick-built gun-platform-cum-watch towers built in close proximity to each other all along the coast, providing mutual reinforcement and interlocking fields of fire. No single tower was strong enough to withstand prolonged naval bombardment, but they could repel assault by infantry, and their sheer numbers would ensure devastating firepower against any landing force.

However, if an invasion force did manage to suppress the beach defences and get ashore, a fallback line of defence was required to stop the French spilling rapidly across the Romney Marshes. This was provided by the Royal Military Canal, effectively a moat running along the inland edge of the marsh. The great strength of the Napoleonic army was its ability to combine the three wings of infantry, cavalry and artillery into one devastating combined attack. The canal was built to combat this strength, by providing a barrier which would break up any combined attack trying to cross under fire. It would stop cavalry and artillery from crossing and any infantry who swam the canal would not arrive on the far side with dry powder, and thus fall easy prey to the waiting British.

The Walk

This walk goes through the hilly countryside above Hythe and passes mediaeval Saltwood Castle. It returns through Hythe, going along part of the Royal Military Canal, and visiting two Martello Towers.

- From the car park, and facing the Hythe Imperial Hotel, walk directly away from the sea, down the road to the left of the hotel, signed Town Centre. Cross over South Street and Fisher Close, and quarter of a mile from the seafront, cross over the Royal Military Canal.
- Continue on to the main road. Cross the road and keep straight ahead, to the left of the Bell public house.

This main road was the shoreline in the Middle Ages, when Hythe was an important port. The name Hythe is old english for harbour, which crops up in other ports e.g. along the Thames as part of Greenhithe.

Hythe was one of the original Cinque Ports, a group of ports along the English Channel which were granted special privileges by the Crown in return for supplying ships to them in time of war. (Before the time of Henry VIII there was no Royal Navy: when ships were needed to fight at sea or for transport duties private vessels were hired by the king.) The importance of Hythe is reflected in the fact that the town sent 11 ships to fight against the Spanish Armada in 1588, an unusually large contingent.

- After 50 yards cross a quiet back lane and go straight on up Mill Lane, soon a footpath, passing an old converted mill on your left.
- At the top of the footpath climb some steps up to a road. Cross the road and continue straight on down an enclosed footpath.
- After 350 yards turn right with the footpath and climb some concrete steps to emerge onto a drive.
- Turn left past the gate to Saltwood Lodge and walk down the track. After 40 yards do not turn left with the track but cross the stile ahead.
- Continue ahead along the top of a field, with fence, trees and disused railway embankment on your right.

The railway line was built at the end of the era of 19th-century railway mania, when branch lines were being constructed to any conceivable destinations. This line connected Sandling on the main line to Sandgate on the coast, to bring holidaymakers onto the coast. The plan was to extend the line to Folkestone, but it had proved economically unviable before the work was completed. The Sandling–Sandgate link was closed as a result of the Beeching cuts of the 1960s.

- Follow the fenced embankment down to a gate and stile.
- Cross the stile and keep straight on along a track, still following the embankment. The track is soon fenced and leads to a metal gate.
- Pass through the gate and keep ahead along the track, soon passing the walls of Saltwood Castle on your left.

Saltwood has been fortified since the time of the Romans. In those days Saltwood was on the coast and a fortified port, standing just off Stane Street, the Roman arterial road running from Lympne and linking a series of minor channel coast ports to Canterbury. In AD488 Aesc, son of the legendary Saxon warlord Hengist, built a fort here to protect the harbour, one of a string of fortifications along the so-called Saxon Shore.

The present castle was built in the 12th century by Henry de Essex, standard-bearer to Henry II and Warden of the Cinque Ports, of which Hythe was one. It was jointly owned by de Essex and the Archbishop of Canterbury, Thomas Becket. When de Essex was disgraced for cowardice, his share of the castle reverted to the Crown. Becket demanded that total control of the castle be given to him, but Henry II appointed the Sheriff of Kent, Randolph de Broc, as constable. De Broc was later excommunicated by Becket for seizing church land, and became the Archbishop's bitter enemy. In December 1170 de Broc offered shelter to four knights newly arrived from France and en route to Canterbury to carry out King Henry's instructions to murder Becket (see walk 7). Afterwards they stayed at Saltwood again before departing to France to report the success of their mission to the king.

The castle remained jointly owned by the Archbishopric of Canterbury and the Crown until 1540, when Archbishop Cranmer gave it to Henry VIII. In 1580 an earthquake rendered the castle uninhabitable, until it was restored in the 19th century by the Deedes family. Later the castle was owned by the historian Sir Kenneth Clarke and then his son, Alan Clark MP.

- Follow the track, soon broad and tree lined, around the moat and curtain wall of the castle and out to a road.
- Turn left along the road and follow it around a bend. Ignore a side turn. At the end of the farm yard on the right, and opposite some houses, turn right into a footpath along the farm boundary.
- At the end of the enclosed footpath go through a kissing gate and turn half-left across a field to a gate into the churchyard.
- Follow the path through the churchyard and exit via a lychgate. Follow the path to a road.
- Turn right along the road. In 30 yards ignore a footpath on the right, but in another 30 yards turn right down a no through road.
- Where the road bends right, keep ahead up a bridleway that initially runs alongside the road but soon climbs away, passing orchards on the left.
- Descend with the path to cross the top of a track coming in from the right. Keep ahead up the bridleway and in 100 yards turn left over a stile.
- Immediately over the stile, fork right and follow a path uphill.
- After 100 yards, at a cross track, turn left downhill, keeping the fence on the right, to eventually cross a stile.
- Continue ahead on a clear path through open scrubland. The path soon becomes enclosed and descends to cross a footbridge onto a road.
- Turn half-left across the road to a kissing gate. Follow the footpath (Saxon Shore Way) along the right-hand edge of a field and through a gate into woods.

In Roman and Saxon times the shoreline was considerably further inland than at present. Over the centuries the coastline has receded, leaving former ports such as Saltwood and Lympne stranded inland, and leading to the development of new ports such as Hythe on the new coastline. Now the port of Hythe has itself been cut off from the sea by the shingle beach that is followed by the present promenade. The Saxon Shore Way is a long-distance path following the course of the coastline as it was in the Dark Ages.

- Descend through the woods, but in 100 yards, just before a gate, turn left and descend through trees to cross a footbridge.
- Continue along the footpath through the woods. In a quarter of a mile ignore a turning to the right but keep straight on up a grassy track. Soon swing left up a slope into trees and to a gate to enter a field.
- To cross this field you must use two rights of way which are not, however, the most direct line. From the gate, cross half-right, aiming at the church and house seen opposite.
- Cross a stile, turn left for 15 yards past the rear of the church, then turn left through a gate back into the field you have just left.
- Follow the fence on the right. Ignore a stile on the right after 100 yards and continue down the fence to gates at the bottom right corner. Pass through the pedestrian gate beside the metal field gate.
- Continue ahead with a fence on your right. At the end of the fence, go half-left across the field to a gate seen in the distance.
- Go through the gate and along a fenced footpath down the edge of a wood. Follow the path as it drops, soon with a field on the left.
- Ignore two stiles on the left, but descend and swing right to cross a footbridge.
- Continue along the path, bearing left to continue ahead with a fence on the right.
- Ignore a kissing gate on the left and keep straight on, soon ignoring a turning on the right.
- At a T-junction, turn right and follow the track as it swings around to the left and eventually comes out at the head of a tarmacked road.
- Cross over the end of the road and turn right down a footpath, passing between garden fences to reach a road.
- Turn left down the road. In 150 yards cross Barrack Hill and bend right with the road to reach traffic lights.
- Cross Military Road at the lights. Keep straight on to cross a bridge over the canal, with the entrance to the Hythe and Dymchurch Light Railway on the opposite side of the road.
- Immediately over the bridge, turn left onto a path along the edge of the canal.

The Royal Military Canal was constructed on the orders of Prime Minister Pitt the Younger in 1803, when the fears of invasion by Napoleon were at their height. This was a deep channel running for 23 miles along the inland edge of Romney Marsh, to provide a fall-back line of defence should the French manage to gain a beachhead.

The canal was built to break up any combined assault by Napoleon's Grande Armee, by providing a deep ditch running in a series of zigzags, thus allowing a deadly cross-fire from the gun emplacements built every quarter of a mile along the far side. As a further defence, sluice gates were built into the canal to allow the low-lying Romney Marsh to be flooded if necessary, thereby further disrupting an invaders advance. The canal was finished in 1809, but by that time the threat of invasion had receded and it was never used.

- Follow the canal bank. Ignore a footbridge and keep ahead, until the path swings to join the road and the canal passes under a road bridge.
- Cross half-left over the road and resume the walk along the canal bank, still with the canal on your left.
- Two hundred yards past the road bridge, turn up the first road on the right, St Leonard's Road, passing Waterside Court and a school on your left.
- At a road junction keep ahead up St Leonard's Road to reach the seafront.
- The Martello Towers are along the beach to your right. To view them more closely, descend onto the pebble beach and turn right. Walk past fishing boats and fishermen's sheds to the Martello Towers.

In 1804–05 a line of towers were built along the shoreline of England, most of them along the coast from Portsmouth to Folkestone. These were called Martello Towers, named after a

Martello Towers on the beach at Hythe, built to withstand the threat of invasion by Napoleon.

stone-built tower at Mortella on Corsica. Circular fortified towers had fallen out of fashion by the 16th century, when the invention of gunpowder made them vulnerable to bombardment, but when Mortella Tower had been occupied by pirates and held out for two days against the Royal Navy, this wisdom was reassessed.

Each Martello Tower had the same design. They were 33 feet tall, with walls between 13 feet wide at the base to 6 feet wide at parapet level, and slightly elliptical in shape, with the thickest part of the walls seaward. They were built of brick and strengthened with lime mortar to withstand bombardment. Entrance was at first-floor level, on the landward side, and there was room for a garrison of 24 men and one officer to be rapidly posted into each tower when required, with slit windows to enable the beach to be raked with musket fire. On the flat roof of each tower was a gun capable of traversing 360 degrees. This could fire either a 24-pound cannon ball 1,000 yards, which would have caused immense damage to lightly-built landing craft approaching the beaches, or it could fire grape-shot, a canister which would spray between 84 and 232 musket balls up to 350 yards, with devastating effect upon infantry. Where the threat was greatest, as here at Hythe, the towers were built to be 700 yards apart, so that they could command the whole beach with interlocking cannon fire.

The towers were cheap and quick to build, and in total 103 were built at the instruction of Prime Minister Pitt the Younger. The destruction of the French and Spanish navies at Trafalgar in 1805 removed the threat of invasion and the towers never saw active service. Many were allowed to fall into disrepair during the 19th century, and some were used for naval target practice and destroyed. In 1940 the surviving towers were repaired and put on a war footing again in the face of threatened German invasion.

The towers at Hythe are good examples of Martello Towers and clearly show how their interlocking fields of fire would have operated. Six miles down the coast, at Dymchurch, there is a fully-restored tower which is well worth visiting. Open weekends March to July 12–4pm, daily during August 12–4pm. There is an admission charge, but it is free to English Heritage Members.

● Retrace your steps to the promenade and keep ahead along it for three quarters of a mile to return to the car park.

The fifth house you pass, 100 yards along the promenade, is a converted Martello Tower.

WALK 23
Westerham:
Wolfe and Churchill

Distance: 5 miles
Map: OS sheet 187 and OS sheet 188
Start and Parking: The walk starts from the centre of Westerham (grid ref: 447541). Westerham is situated on the A25, five miles west of Sevenoaks. Although there are several car parks and limited street parking in Westerham, it is recommended that you park in the pay and display car park, on the north side of the A25, just on the eastern edge of Westerham.
Refreshments: Public houses and tearooms in Westerham.

Historical Background

Westerham is the most westerly village in Kent (its name comes from the Anglo-Saxon for western 'Ham' or settlement), and there has been a settlement here or nearby since the Iron Age. Although very picturesque in its own right, its main claim to fame is its association with two of Britain's most famous heroes, General James Wolfe and Sir Winston Churchill.

James Wolfe was born in Westerham in 1727 into a military family. He gained his commission in the army at the age of 14 (not especially young for the 18th century), fought with distinction at the Battle of Culloden, and rose to be England's youngest-ever Major General at the age of 30. In 1759 he was given command of the expeditionary force sent to dislodge the French from Canada. After an inconclusive winter campaign up and down the St Lawrence River, Wolfe retrieved the situation by a brilliant but risky assault upon Quebec in March 1759. Through a combination of an audacious night time ascent of the Heights of Abraham and poor French generalship, Wolfe won the battle which made Canada British, but he lost his life in the process.

Winston Churchill's early career was brilliant if also chequered. A soldier and a war correspondent, Churchill entered parliament as a Conservative in 1900 but swapped to the Liberal party in 1904 He held a succession of cabinet offices until 1921 and was involved in a number of controversial political decisions. With the fall of Lloyd George in 1922, Churchill lost both office and seat. He returned to parliament in 1924, this time as a Conservative again, but he was not trusted by party or public, and in 1929 he went into a political wilderness, from which he emerged in 1940 to become one of Britain's greatest-ever wartime leaders. Although rejected by the electorate in 1945, Churchill became Prime Minister again in 1951, before finally retiring four years later.

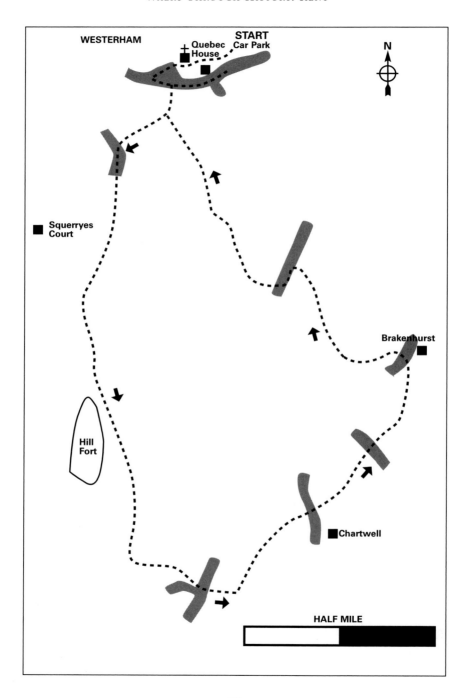

The period of Churchill's political exile in the 20s and 30s, and most of his post-war years were spent at his home at Chartwell near Westerham, where he did much of his writing and painting.

The Walk
This walk goes through rolling and wooded countryside on the Greensand Ridge, passing the original Iron Age settlement in the area and going past both Chartwell and Wolfe's childhood home, Quebec House.

● From the car park, follow the clearly-marked footpath that runs parallel with the main A25 back into the village. Pass through the churchyard and onto the village green.

The Church of St Mary the Virgin is partly 13th century, with the low tower and short spire common to many churches in Kent, and with 19th-century restorations. It has a 14th-century spiral staircase leading to the tower and the coat of arms of Edward VI, the only examples of either found in a Kentish church. There is also a memorial stone to General Wolfe. His body lies in St Alfege's Church in Greenwich.

On the green are statues of Westerham's two famous heroes: a modern bronze statue of Sir Winston Churchill, by sculptor Oscar Nemon, and an older statue of an earlier hero, General James Wolfe.

The village green at Westerham.

- Standing on the green, with your back to the statue of Churchill, cross the main A25 to a footpath, signposted up a short flight of steps and called Water Lane.
- Descend the enclosed footpath, crossing two small streams, to reach a swing gate leading into a meadow.
- Pass through the swing gate and turn right, following a path with a hedge and stream on your right and a slope initially on your left.
- Follow the path to a swing gate beside a footbridge. Go through the gate onto a lane and turn left to cross the bridge.
- Follow the rough track to reach a half-timbered house. Proceed to the left corner of the house, where there are two stiles. Cross the rightmost stile (marked Greensand Way Link Path) onto an enclosed track.
- Follow the enclosed path up the slope to a stile.

Looking back and to the left there is a view of Squerryes Court nestling in the trees below. This is a fine William & Mary mansion built in 1681 and it was the home of the Warde family from 1731, who built up the fine collection of Dutch Old Masters on view today. The young James Wolfe, who lived nearby in what is now called Quebec House, was a friend of the family and often visited Squerryes Court.

Squerryes Court is privately occupied but open to the public on occasions.

- Cross the stile and continue along the enclosed path across Squerryes Park.
- At the end of the enclosed path, continue straight on, aiming for a stile in the middle of a band of trees seen ahead.
- Cross this stile, pass through trees and continue straight on to another stile heading onto a farm track.
- Turn left onto this track and follow it as it descends into the valley bottom.
- At a T-junction in the valley bottom, keep straight on for 100 yards to reach a stile at the corner of a wood.

In the woods is an old Iron Age hillfort. The ramparts of its northern perimeter can just be seen if you look carefully to the right, just beyond the fence. This fort was quite small, only 400 yards long by 100 yards at its widest, with a single rampart and ditch.

- Cross the stile and continue straight on, with the wood and fort on your right and the valley dropping away to the left.
- Cross a stile and continue straight on, soon on a clear track across more level ground, leaving the wood and a distinctive white house away to your right. Continue straight on to a stile seen ahead, leading into woods.
- Cross the stile and take the middle of three tracks, the most straight one of the three, climbing steeply up through woods and rhododendrons.
- Pass over a cross track and continue straight on. The path soon levels out, and then climbs again, more gently this time, to reach a T-junction.

- Turn left onto an initially broader path.
- After 250 yards, at a fork, take the left fork and descend steeply.
- Join another path and continue to descend.
- At the bottom of the slope, turn briefly right to reach a drive to a house. Do not turn into the drive gates but turn left and follow the drive up to a road.
- Cross the road onto a bridle path and climb steeply.
- At the top of the slope, where a path joins from the right, keep straight on with a fence on your right, for 50 yards to a fork. Here turn left, following the Greensand Way.
- In 250 yards, at a fork, take the right fork, maintaining a generally forward direction The path is still signed Greensand Way.
- Descend through coppiced woodland, ignoring all side turns. The path descends ever more steeply, until finally steps are reached down onto a road.
- Cross the road to a footpath opposite, labelled 'French Street', just to left of gates to Chartwell.

There has been a building on the site of Chartwell since 1350, although only a modest farmhouse for many centuries. It was enlarged as a Victorian country mansion in the middle of the 19th century, and is surrounded by 800 acres of grounds. It was bought by Churchill in 1922 and was his home for the next 40 years. Its park and setting appealed immediately to Churchill the painter, and he saw in its grounds and gardens the tranquillity necessary for writing. He extensively redesigned the house and had much of it rebuilt, and in the grounds he indulged in another hobby, bricklaying: many of the walls in the gardens were built by Churchill for recreation.

The purchase of Chartwell followed Churchill's loss of government office and a parliamentary seat in 1922. He returned to parliament in 1924 and also returned to the government under Stanley Baldwin for the next five years. But in 1929 Churchill lost office and was in the political wilderness until 1939. During that time Churchill called Chartwell an 'oasis in his political desert' and devoted himself to personal interests – writing, painting, bricklaying and his family. It was here that he wrote his History of the English Speaking Peoples.

Chartwell was closed for the war: it was too close to the channel coast and the threatened invasion of Kent to be a safe residence for the Prime Minister, which he had become in 1940, and its lakes made it an easily-identifiable target from the air. When Churchill fell from office in 1945 he again retired to Chartwell, which remained his home for the rest of his life.

The house is a fascinating museum to Churchill the private man rather than the public figure. The museum room contains gifts given to him by international figures during a career spanning half a century, a collection of his more exotic clothes and memorabilia of his life, including the Boer War 'Wanted Dead or Alive' poster of Churchill. The rest of the house reflects the many facets of his life, and includes his study, his writing desk and his easels.

Chartwell is open from March to the end of October, Wednesday to Sunday, 11am–5.00pm. There is an admission charge, but it is free to National Trust members.

Winston Churchill, whose statue stands on Westerham village green, made Chartwell his home from 1922 onwards.

- Climb the enclosed footpath for a quarter of a mile to reach a road at the top of the slope. Cross the road and go through a gate opposite.
- Keep straight on down a bridle path, soon descending.
- After 250 yards, keep right at a fork (still signed Greensand Way).

Across the valley to the right is a view of distinctive Kentish oasthouses. Oasthouses were designed to store and dry hops. This one, at Outridge farm, is square, which was the original shape for them throughout the country. Hop farmers in Kent decided that oasthouses would be more efficient if they were round, thereby avoiding corners in which undried hops could accumulate. In fact, round was no more efficient than square as a shape, and the design was discontinued, but not before the round oasthouse had become the fixed image of what one should look like.

- Four hundred yards later, bear left at a fork and 50 yards further on emerge onto a tarmacked drive.
- Turn right up the drive for 50 yards, then turn left onto a footpath, just before the gates to Brackenhurst.
- Keep straight on along the path through the woods.
- At a T-junction, turn left up a waymarked path. Keep straight on for 300 yards, ignoring tracks to left and right and crossing a cross track.
- When a deeply rutted tractor track is reached, turn left for 30 yards and then turn right again to continue the same line of advance along a waymarked footpath. The path soon widens.
- Follow the footpath to eventually emerge at a car park.
- Follow the left-hand edge of the car park to the road. Cross the road and turn left for 40 yards, before turning half-right onto a footpath. This path is initially narrow and overgrown and starts off parallel to the road, but soon veers away from it.
- At a T-junction with a broader track, turn right and descend for 200 yards to reach wooden posts.
- Pass through the wooden posts, turn right and descend the track.
- After 300 yards, turn right at a T-junction. Continue to descend, with woods on your left and soon with a fenced driveway on your right, to reach a stile.
- Cross the stile and turn right sharply uphill.
- At the top of the slope, keep straight on. Soon the spire of Westerham Church is seen directly ahead. Keep straight on until the slope starts to descend, and then bear half-left on a clear path to a stile.
- Cross the stile and continue to descend, aiming to the right of tennis courts seen ahead to reach a swing gate.
- Pass through the swing gate and climb the enclosed path (Water Lane again) to reach Westerham village green.
- Cross the road to the green but instead of crossing the green back to the churchyard, turn right down the A25. In 300 yards you reach Quebec House on your left.

In 1726 the Wolfe family moved into The Spires, as it was then called, and the following year James was born in the nearby Westerham Vicarage. James's father was an officer in the Marines and there was a long tradition of military service in the Wolfe family, which it was always assumed James would follow. Young James lived here for the first 12 years of his life until in 1739 his family moved to Greenwich, in order for James to attend the prestigious Westons Military College there.

The house is a Tudor brick building with a fine collection of gables, and was renamed Quebec House after Wolfe's death to commemorate his famous victory Although somewhat

James Wolfe, hero of Quebec, lived at
Quebec House in Westerham.

altered in the intervening years, the basic house is still as it was when Wolfe lived there and today contains much memorabilia, especially paintings, statues and uniforms. The stable block has a display devoted to the Battle of Quebec.

The rather fine street wall of Quebec House was the inspiration for some of Winston Churchill's wall-building efforts in the gardens of Chartwell.

Quebec House is open from 1 April to the end of October, Wednesday to Sunday, 1–4.30pm. There is an admission charge, but it is free to National Trust members.

● Continue for 100 yards along the A25 to reach the car park on your left.

WALK 24
Dover: White Cliffs and two World Wars

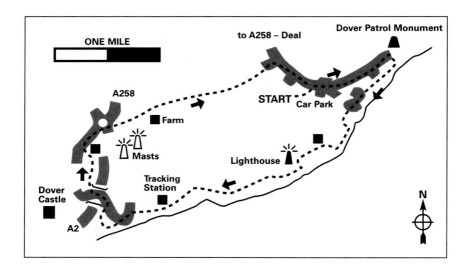

Distance: 8.5 miles
Map: OS sheet 179
Start and Parking: The walk starts from St Margaret's at Cliffe (grid ref: 359446). St Margaret's at Cliffe is four miles north of Dover and six miles south of Deal, at the end of a minor road signposted off the A258 Dover–Deal road. There is a free car park in the middle of the village.
Refreshments: Public houses, shops and a café at St Margaret's at Cliffe, café at the Dover Patrol monument.

Historical Background
Dover, standing at the narrowest crossing point to the Continent, has always been the gateway into England for merchant, traveller and conqueror. It was the first point Julius Caesar made for in his reconnaissance raid of 55BC and William the Conqueror made it his target after defeating the English at Hastings. The massive fortifications built by the Normans have been added to over the centuries and the castle has remained garrisoned for 1,000 years, testimony to the castle's enduring importance to the nation's defences.

Dover saw its greatest wartime action during the two world wars of this century. Dover was the nerve-centre for the Royal Navy's Channel Command, and from here the Dover Patrol operated in 1914–18, keeping open the vital cross-channel link with the British forces fighting on the Western Front. In 1940, with the fall of France, the British Expeditionary Force of nearly a quarter of a million men, virtually the whole of Britain's fighting force, was left trapped in Belgium. The evacuation of this force from the beaches of Dunkirk was masterminded from operations rooms buried in the cliffs below Dover Castle.

Dover played a vital part in the defence of Britain during its time of greatest danger, the early years of World War Two. In the summer of 1940 Hitler decided upon Operation Sealion, the seaborne invasion of Britain. The prerequisite for this was the destruction of the RAF, in order that the invasion fleet could cross the channel unopposed. To achieve this, Reichmarshall Hermann Goring organised the Luftwaffe, the German airforce, for a sharp and decisive onslaught aimed at destroying Britain's aircraft and air fields. Radar defences installed along the clifftops provided the early warning system vital for the RAF to defend itself and the country.

The Walk
This walk starts in St Margaret's at Cliffe and passes the Dover Patrol memorial. It then goes along the spectacular cliffs to Dover, passing many reminders of the action seen by this area in two world wars, and returns across rich agricultural land.

- Leave the car park at St Margaret's at Cliffe via the access road. Return to the main road through the village and turn right.
- Pass the Hope Inn on the left and descend the main road. Follow the road as it curves left and ascends a hill.
- At the top of the rise, pass Lighthouse Road on the right and The Driveway on the left. Ten yards later, at a village green with a memorial, turn left into Granville Road.
- Follow Granville Road for half a mile. At a junction with Hotel Road on the right, and just after an unsuitable for long vehicles sign, keep straight on up Victoria Avenue.
- Keep straight on for 300 yards to reach the Dover Patrol monument.

This monument was put up to commemorate the men who lost their lives in the Dover Patrol, a force of small ships that kept the channel open during World War One. A similar monument stands on the cliffs of Cap Blanc Nez on the opposite side of the English Channel, which are clearly visible on a fine day.

During the first decade of the 20th century, Britain had been involved in an arms race with Germany for naval supremacy. Resources had been poured into building battleships, cruisers and destroyers, and by the outbreak of World War One the Royal Navy had an immensely powerful surface fleet. However, the immediate problem in 1914 was to keep the vital supply route to France open, and to keep the English Channel clear of enemy mines. No provision had been made in pre-war planning for this essential task, and it was left to Admiral Hood, commander-in-chief at Dover, to improvise a defence force.

Monument to the men who lost their lives on the Dover Patrol during World War One.

Hood scratched together a hotchpotch of fishing boats and redundant naval vessels, unarmed apart from the occasional rife, manned mainly by local fishermen. In 1914 the Dover Patrol consisted of one yacht and four drifters; by the end of 1918 256 vessels had served in the patrol. This fragile flotilla served throughout the whole war, mainly clearing the mines that the Germans regularly scattered into the channel, occasionally having to protect shipping against German E-Boats (lightly armed fast motor boats) and submarines. On average each vessel swept 250 miles of sea each day for four years. In total 1,507 mines were destroyed. Over 2,000 men lost their lives doing this arduous and dangerous work. Thanks to the efforts of the Dover Patrol, the British Expeditionary Force was convoyed to France without mishap, and thereafter the supply route across the channel was kept open for four years with only very occasional interruptions.

- After hooking at the monument, and perhaps visiting the café, retrace your steps back along the road for just a few yards. Just behind a National Trust sign, 'The Leas' on the left, turn left onto a vague footpath and descend through bushes.
- Follow the path to the cliff edge and turn right along the cliff. Eventually descend through trees. Nearly at the bottom of the slope, ignore steps on the left but follow the main path, soon with a fence on the left, out to a road.
- Turn left in the road and follow the road downhill.
- Immediately before the road bends sharply left and downhill, at a letter box, turn right up an unadopted drive, signposted 'Pine gardens and Museum'.

Downhill this road leads to St Margaret's Bay, a peaceful little pebble-beached cove which is the traditional starting point for cross-channel swimmers.

- In 30 yards fork left down Beach Road.
- Where the road ceases to be tarmacked, keep ahead up a rough track, passing houses on the left.
- At a cross track, turn left up a rough flinty track to reach a disused lighthouse on top of Lighthouse Down.
- Pass the lighthouse on your left to reach a footpath along the cliff top, and turn right along the cliffs.
- Walk along the cliffs. When a small wood bars your way, turn right and walk up to a track beside a cottage. Turn left along the track, now with the wood between you and the cliff edge.
- The track eventually bends right. Just after the bend, at a junction of tracks, turn left and follow the track to the gates of a lighthouse.

These 400-foot high cliffs stand at the narrowest part of the English Channel. Three miles out to sea are the Goodwin Sands, a vast sandbank, most of the time just submerged and therefore an invisible but lethal danger to passing ships. Over the last 300 years over 50,000 lives have been lost by vessels being wrecked. To counter this hazard there has been a light on St Margaret's Cliffs since at least the Middle Ages, to warn sailors of the location of the sands.

Initially it was a beacon fire, manned intermittently by monks. Charles I granted permission for a permanent lighthouse to be built.

- Turn left on a track, with the lighthouse on your right. Do not enter the gates of the keepers cottage, but keep ahead down an enclosed footpath between the cottage and the lighthouse.
- Follow the path to the cliff edge and turn right.

Dover harbour is now in sight ahead.

- Follow the path along the cliffs for one and a half miles. Keep to the upper path where there is a choice.

You are walking along the famous White Cliffs of Dover, immortalised as an evocative image of peace in Vera Lynn's famous wartime song, and now green and tranquil. During World War Two this stretch of cliff was very different. Heavy guns were mounted on these cliffs, not only to command the Straits of Dover and deny passage to enemy shipping, but also heavy enough and with a long enough range to bombard enemy occupied France, 22 miles away. Although the guns have long since been removed, the concrete platforms upon which these huge guns stood can still be seen among the grass at intervals along the cliffs between here and Dover.

- After a mile and a half, with Dover harbour now close in front and below, you will get the choice a bearing left along a broad shoulder around the cliff, or going ahead up fenced steps. Go up the steps.
- Follow the fence to reach a kissing gate in 100 yards. Do not go through the gate but pass above it, keeping the fence on your left, with a radar tracking station just up the slope to the right.
- Pass through a kissing gate, with the fence of the tracking station just on your right. The harbour is plainly in sight below you.
- Follow the path as it leads into a National Trust car park. Walk through the car park, passing toilets on your right, to the entrance drive, and follow the drive out to a road.
- Keep straight on. In a few yards, where the road bends sharp right downhill, keep straight on onto a footpath. Dover Castle is clearly seen in front of you.

Dover Castle has been continuously occupied since the Iron Age. It is of vital strategic importance, commanding the port of Dover and the shortest sea crossing to Europe, and as such has been occupied and reinforced by successive invaders. The Romans occupied the old British hillfort here as early as 55BC, and after the invasion of AD43 soon built a massive fort here. They also built a lighthouse, to warn sailors of the presence of the cliff and the Goodwin Sands offshore. The bottom 20 feet of the Roman lighthouse can still clearly be seen beside the Saxon church within the castle walls. The Saxons built a fortified township on the site.

The present castle dates from Norman times and is one of the greatest examples of Norman military architecture in Britain. The castle was ordered by William the Conqueror immediately after the Conquest. It has a massive outer wall with 27 towers and a dry ditch cutting off the landward approaches, and a motte and bailey keep. The castle seen today is largely from the time of Henry II, who added an inner wall in 1180 with a further 14 towers. He also built the massive three-storey central keep and improved and strengthened the outer wall.

The castle has seen action several times: in 1216 it was defended for King John against Louis, Dauphin of France, it was captured by rebel barons during de Montefort's rebellion in 1265, and it was captured by parliament during the Civil War. But perhaps the greatest moment of the castle came in 1940. Beneath the castle there are a labyrinth of tunnels, started in 1797 as a bombardment-proof headquarters in the event of French invasion. They were greatly enlarged in the years leading up to 1939 and continuing up until 1943. These tunnels housed the headquarters of Coastal Command, containing telephone exchange, coding and cipher centre, operations rooms, a hospital and accommodation for headquarters staff and garrison. It was from here that Admiral Ramsay, commander of the Straits of Dover, organised the evacuation of 338,000 British and French soldiers from the beaches of Dunkirk in May 1940.

The castle, including the World War Two tunnels, Roman lighthouse and Saxon church, is open to the public from April to October, 10am–6pm, November to March, 10am–4pm. There is an admission charge, but it is free to members of English Heritage.

- Descend steeply with the path, and soon go down some steps, passing to the left of a terrace of red-brick houses.
- At the foot of the steps, and at the end of the handrail on your left, do not follow a tarmacked path ahead but turn right onto an initially vague grassy path, with the hedges of gardens on your immediate right.
- Follow the path, keeping the A2 in its cutting close on your left hand and ignoring first a turn to the right and then one to the left.
- Follow the path through trees, now on a level with the A2.
- Bear right with the path and climb, finally up wooden sleeper steps, to a road.
- Turn left along the road and cross the A2 on a road bridge. Immediately over the bridge, turn right down some steps, following a footpath sign.
- Cross a stile and keep straight on up the right-hand edge of a field, with the A2 now on your right.
- At the end of the field exit via a gate. Do not turn right under the A2, but instead turn left through a gate and up a track.
- Follow the track through the farm to a road.
- Turn right along the road for a third of a mile to reach a roundabout.
- Go anticlockwise around the roundabout. Cross the A2 signed as 'Jubilee Way Dover' and continue to the next exit, the A258 Deal road.
- Go down the Deal road for 200 yards. Where the road bends, and just after a bend sign, turn right over a stile.
- Follow the left-hand field edge for 200 yards.

The vast keep of Dover Castle was largely
built during the reign of Henry II.

Radio masts have stood on this cliff since World War Two, when they provided a vital part of the nation's defences during the Battle of Britain. In August 1940 the RAF could put 749 aircraft into the skies, to oppose 2,550 German aircraft, and those aircraft had an endurance of little more than one hour. In that time they had to take off and gain sufficient height to intercept incoming enemy bombers and their escorts. To do this effectively, it was vital the fighters did not take off too early, or be put into the air to oppose a raid that was only a diversion. Radar stations such as the one here on Dover Cliffs played a vital part in supplying early and accurate information regarding the enemy's numbers and direction. The importance of these stations was recognised by the Germans, who on 12 August 1940 aimed huge raids specifically against radar installations, followed in the next four weeks by massive and near-continuous raids against RAF bases every day. On 15 September, in a desperate bid to break British resistance, the Luftwaffe turned its attentions to the terror bombing of London rather than concentrating upon defeating the RAF. This decision was the turning point in the Battle of Britain, for the switch to bombing the cities rather than airfields gave the RAF a vital respite. Had the Germans but known it, RAF losses in aircraft and especially in trained pilots were rapidly approaching crisis point. Although the Blitz of London and other cities continued until May 1941, the survival of the RAF was never again threatened, and with it the threat of invasion defeated.

Such was the ferocity of the aerial dogfights that took place in the skies above Dover Cliffs, as RAF Spitfires and Hurricanes battled to stop the German attack, that this area became known as 'Hellfire Corner'. By the time that the Battle of Britain ended in May 1941 England had lost 915 aircraft but had destroyed 1,733 enemy planes and forever blunted the Germans' capability of controlling the skies over Britain and with it the capacity to invade these shores.

- After 200 yards, cross a stile on the left and go along the right-hand edge of a field, passing between pillboxes.

The pillboxes are an eloquent reminder of the very real threat of invasion in 1940 and 1941. Designed as cheap gun-emplacements, thousands upon thousands of concrete pillboxes were pre-fabricated and erected very rapidly at all points where enemy forces could land, either by sea or from the air. The pillboxes had good all-round fields of fire from which the surrounding countryside could be commanded, and were sited to provide mutual support for each other. Each pillbox could be manned by only a very small handful of men. They were especially congregated in Kent, providing line after line of defensible positions from the coast to the outskirts of London, which would enable a fighting retreat, hugely costly to an invader, to be fought if necessary.

- At the end of the field cross a stile and pass through a patch of scrub to cross a second stile onto a T-junction of farm drives.
- Keep straight on up the drive opposite, passing the backs of barns on your right.
- Go through a gate and keep straight on up a grassy track for 10 yards to enter a field.
- Bear half-right across the field, making for the middle of woods seen ahead.

- On reaching the edge of the woods, bear half-left to continue along the right-hand edge of the field, now with a hedge and woods on your right.
- Where the woods turn away right, go quarter right across the next large field to reach a stile.
- Cross the stile and go half-right across the next field, aiming for a stile in the fence.
- Cross this stile and bear quarter-left, to follow the bottom edge of the field, with a fence on your left.
- Follow the fence to a stile in the far corner of the field. Cross the stile and continue straight on along an enclosed track.
- At the end of the track, cross a stile and descend to the road. Turn right along the road to reach a T-junction.
- Turn right and follow the road into the village of St Margaret's at Cliffe. Ignore side turns, pass a garage on the left, and the Village Stores on your right. Fifty yards past the Village Stores, turn right up some steps into the churchyard.

The Church of St Margaret of Antioch was built in the 12th century and remains virtually unaltered since then. It has a fine carved west door leading into an archaded nave which in turn leads through a splendid pointed arch into a wide chancel.

The church was twice hit during World War Two by shells, fired from France.

In 1696 a local farmer fell over the cliff and was mortally injured but survived long enough to bequeath money for a bell to be rung every evening during the winter months, to keep travellers away from the cliff edge. The tradition survives to this day.

The church has a Book of Remembrance for the sailors who died serving in the Dover Patrol. More recently, a window was installed in 1987 in remembrance of three local men who died on the Herald of Free Enterprise *in Zeebrugge.*

- Pass through the churchyard, keeping the church on your left and passing an interesting late-Victorian family tomb behind the church. Follow the path out of the churchyard and back into the car park.